Epica Book 25
Europe's
Best Advertising

DIRECTOR
Andrew Rawlins

EDITOR
Richard Högqvist

ART DIRECTORS
Richard Högqvist
Patrick Taschler

SYNOPSES
Mark Tungate

EDITORIAL ASSISTANT
Francelina Pacarić

COVER IMAGE
Andreas Franke
(Braun Precision Trimmer,
courtesy of Impact BBDO, Dubai)

PUBLISHER
AVA Publishing S.A.

DISTRIBUTION
North America
Ingram Publisher Services
All other countries
Thames & Hudson Ltd.

PRODUCTION
AVA Book Production Pte Ltd.

Printed in Singapore

EPICA
65 rue J.J. Rousseau,
92150 Suresnes, France
Tel: 33 (0) 1 42 04 04 32
www.epica-awards.com
info@epica-awards.com

Contents

I never want ***to work in advertising*** *is great.*

"I never want to work in advertising", is a statement we unfortunately hear only too often from just the sort of people who actually possess the right skills for a successful career in our industry - respect for individuals.

Great advertising has a lot to do with respect. Respect for taste, intelligence, culture, habits and the creative process itself. Respect is also demonstrated by one's attitude towards the environment and, last but not least, towards one's self. Every year outstanding advertising campaigns are honoured and celebrated at national and international award shows, yet the sector is still not perceived as desirable by many of those with the most appropriate talents.

The reason for this can be found in the advertising we encounter day-by-day that neither respects its viewers nor itself. Respect is not a given that we can just assume, it's something that's only acquired over time and by hard work.

This kind of respect cannot only be achieved by work that does well in award shows and demonstrate how witty, funny, interesting and involving advertising can be, but by the sort of advertising that confronts people day-by-day across all media channels.

Our goal should be to produce "everyday" advertising that consistently matches the high standard of work that is honoured in award shows. Advertising that one loves to see again, to share and to talk about.

Advertising that deserves respect is advertising that succeeds in showing a brand in an intelligent, involving or humorous way; making people think differently about it and encouraging a change of behaviour.

But respect is not something that a brand possesses automatically, it's something that must be earned and built upon on a daily basis.

What does this brand stand for in society? How relevant are its benefits? What is its story and how does this differ from those of its competitors?

Good stories only deserve respect if they are based on a truth that is intimately connected to a brand, because the consumer understands very quickly if a story is exaggerated, but true, or just a lie. They know whether the narrative matches the brand in question - or not.

But nowadays a brand does not acquire respect simply by telling great stories, but by involving people, stimulating their minds and encouraging them to re-evaluate their own relationships with the it and with what it represents. Even greater respect can be earned by doing something that benefits society as a whole, changing the world for the better - even in a very modest way.

If all of us in advertising agencies, along with our clients, put people and their needs at the very heart of our campaigns then our industry will certainly win respect - and become a sector in which everyone with talent will aspire to work. Then maybe the popular refrain will become, "to work in advertising is great!"

Martin Spillmann
Founder & Executive Creative Director
Spillmann/Felser/Leo Burnett
Zurich

Epica d'Or (Film)

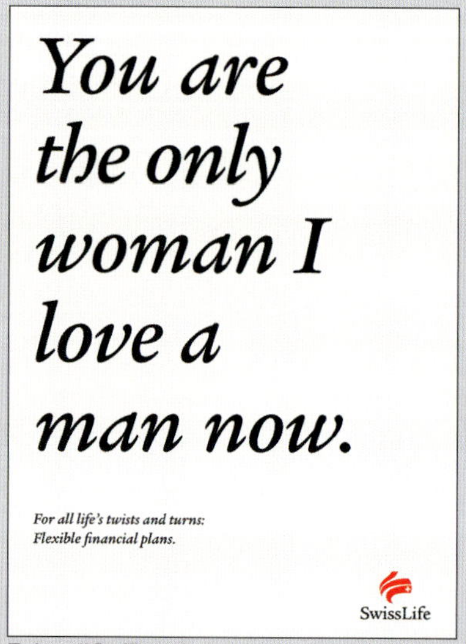
You are
the only
woman I
love a
man now.
For all life's twists and turns:
Flexible financial plans.
SwissLife

Epica d'Or (Press)

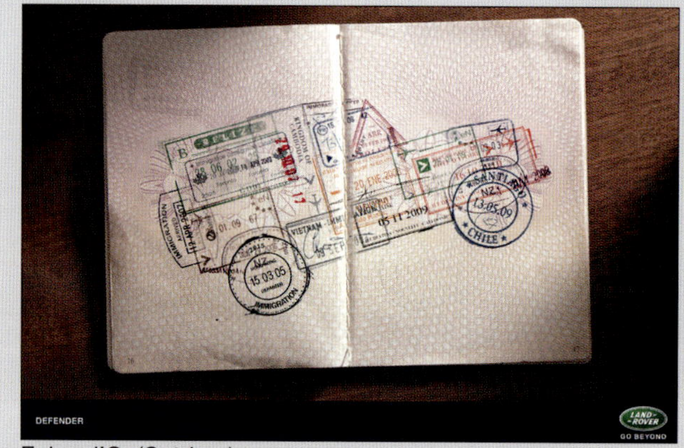
DEFENDER

Epica d'Or (Outdoor)

MINI
Stockholm

Epica d'Or (Interactive)

GRAND PRIX		
EPICA D'OR (FILM)	WIEDEN+KENNEDY AMSTERDAM	HEINEKEN, "OPEN YOUR WORLD" CAMPAIGN
EPICA D'OR (PRESS)	SPILLMANN/FELSER/LEO BURNETT, ZURICH	SWISS LIFE, "LIFE'S TURNS IN A SENTENCE" CAMPAIGN
EPICA D'OR (OUTDOOR)	RAINEY KELLY CAMPBELL ROALFE/Y&R, LONDON	LAND ROVER DEFENDER, "PASSPORT STAMPS"
EPICA D'OR (INTERACTIVE)	JUNG VON MATT STOCKHOLM	MINI, "MINI GETAWAY"
FILM WINNERS		
FOOD	SAATCHI & SAATCHI, LONDON	WALL'S SAUSAGES, "KITCHEN" & "GARAGE"
CONFECTIONERY & SNACKS	ABBOTT MEAD VICKERS BBDO, LONDON	DORITOS CHIPS, "DIPS DESPERADO"
DAIRY PRODUCTS	STINK, LONDON (FOR W+K, LONDON)	LURPAK BUTTER, "KITCHEN ODYSSEY"
ALCOHOLIC DRINKS	WIEDEN+KENNEDY AMSTERDAM	HEINEKEN, "OPEN YOUR WORLD" CAMPAIGN
NON-ALCOHOLIC DRINKS	MARCEL, PARIS	CONTREX MINERAL WATER, "CONTREXPERIENCE"
COMMUNICATION SERVICES	SAATCHI & SAATCHI, LONDON	T-MOBILE, "WELCOME BACK"
TRANSPORT & TOURISM	LOS&CO, OSLO	NETTBUSS, "WHOEVER YOU ARE"
RETAIL SERVICES	McCANN MANCHESTER	ALDI SUPERMARKETS, "LIKE BRANDS" CAMPAIGN
FINANCIAL SERVICES	TRY ADVERTISING AGENCY, OSLO	DNB NOR SAVING SERVICES, "FINALLY MARRIED"
PUBLIC INTEREST	OGILVY & MATHER DUBLIN	ISPCC, "I CAN'T WAIT"
HOME ELECTRONICS & AV EQUIPMENT	GREY LONDON	SONY 3D TVS, "TWO WORLDS"
HOMES, FURNISHINGS & APPLIANCES	SERVICEPLAN GRUPPE, GERMANY	SANTEC VIDEO SURVEILLANCE, "SANTEC PRISON"
HOUSEHOLD MAINTENANCE	EURO RSCG ISRAEL, TEL AVIV	COLON 101, "101 STAINS"
BEAUTY PRODUCTS & SERVICES	TBWA\PARIS	DIOR, "J'ADORE"
TOILETRIES & HEALTH CARE	FORSMAN & BODENFORS, GOTHENBURG	APOTEKET, "STOMACH TEST" CAMPAIGN
CLOTHING & FABRICS	FRED & FARID PARIS	QUECHUA, "WE ALL NEED WARMTH"
FOOTWEAR & PERSONAL ACCESSORIES	WIEDEN+KENNEDY AMSTERDAM	NIKE, "WRITE THE FUTURE"
AUTOMOBILES	RUF LANZ WERBEAGENTUR, ZURICH	HYUNDAI, "APPROVED BY VW CHAIRMAN"
AUTOMOTIVE & ACCESSORIES	SERVICEPLAN GRUPPE, GERMANY	BMW LANE DEPARTURE WARNING, "HEADS"
MEDIA	ADVICO Y&R (Y&R SWITZERLAND), ZURICH	SONNTAGSZEITUNG, "PEACE TALKS"
RECREATION & LEISURE	OGILVY FRANCE, PARIS	SCRABBLE, "BLOCK PROJECT"
PROFESSIONAL SERVICES	NEXT ADVERTISING, BUCHAREST	IQADS.RO, "JEALOUSY"
CORPORATE IMAGE	LOS&CO, OSLO	NETTBUSS, "WHOEVER YOU ARE"
PRINT WINNERS		
FOOD	DEMNER, MERLICEK & BERGMANN, VIENNA	JA! NATÜRLICH, "DESIGN CLASSICS"
CONFECTIONERY & SNACKS	CLM BBDO, PARIS	CELEBRATIONS, "YOUR OWN CELEBRATION" CAMPAIGN
DAIRY PRODUCTS	LOLA, MADRID	MAGNUM ICE CREAM, "MAGNUM ART" CAMPAIGN
NON-ALCOHOLIC DRINKS	FRED & FARID PARIS	SCHWEPPES, "UMA" CAMPAIGN
COMMUNICATION SERVICES	TBWA\ISTANBUL	TIVIBU IPTV, "PAUSE LIVE TV"
TRANSPORT & TOURISM	KING, STOCKHOLM	SWEDISH RAIL, "A SMARTER WAY TO TRAVEL" CAMPAIGN
RETAIL SERVICES	DDB, LONDON	HARVEY NICHOLS, "WINDOW SHOPPING" CAMPAIGN
FINANCIAL SERVICES	SPILLMANN/FELSER/LEO BURNETT, ZURICH	SWISS LIFE, "LIFE'S TURNS IN A SENTENCE" CAMPAIGN
PUBLIC INTEREST	180 AMSTERDAM	SIRE, "MARKED FOR LIFE" CAMPAIGN
HOME ELECTRONICS & AV EQUIPMENT	DEMNER, MERLICEK & BERGMANN, VIENNA	LEICA SHOP, "FACE RECOGNITION" CAMPAIGN
HOMES, FURNISHINGS & APPLIANCES	DDB&CO, ISTANBUL	DANK, "HISTORY IS FREE" CAMPAIGN
HOUSEHOLD MAINTENANCE	SERVICEPLAN GRUPPE, GERMANY	FABER CASTELL, "TRUE COLOURS" CAMPAIGN
BEAUTY PRODUCTS & SERVICES	CONCEPT, ISTANBUL	PILATES WITH GERDA, "BAGS" CAMPAIGN
TOILETRIES & HEALTH CARE	JWT / FABRIKANT, ZURICH	HAKLE TOILET PAPER, "SEE YOU LATER"
CLOTHING & FABRICS	FRED & FARID PARIS	WRANGLER, "STUNT" CAMPAIGN
FOOTWEAR & PERSONAL ACCESSORIES	CLM BBDO, PARIS	TAG HEUER, "PRECISION" CAMPAIGN
AUTOMOBILES	RAINEY KELLY CAMPBELL ROALFE/Y&R, LONDON	LAND ROVER DEFENDER, "PASSPORT STAMPS"
AUTOMOTIVE & ACCESSORIES	DDB TRIBAL GROUP, MUNICH	VW SIDE ASSIST, "EARLY WARNING" CAMPAIGN
MEDIA	BETC EURO RSCG, PARIS	CANAL+, "MOVIE FLOWCHARTS" CAMPAIGN
RECREATION & LEISURE	RUF LANZ WERBEAGENTUR, ZURICH	LUCERNE MUSIC FESTIVAL, "EMERGENCY EXITS"
PROFESSIONAL PRODUCTS	SCHOLZ & FRIENDS BERLIN	STIHL CHAIN SAWS, "WARRIORS" CAMPAIGN
PROFESSIONAL SERVICES	ABBY NORM, STOCKHOLM	KVÄLLSPRESSEN IMPACT, "UNALTERNATIVE MEDIA"
CORPORATE IMAGE	HEIMAT, BERLIN	CNN INTERNATIONAL, "THE CNN MIRROR LAKES"
PRESCRIPTION PRODUCTS & SERVICES	WUNDERMAN (Y&R SWITZERLAND), ZURICH	PHONAK HEARING AIDS, "SPICE" CAMPAIGN
RADIO		
RADIO ADVERTISING	McCANN NORWAY, OSLO	MAARUD POPCORN, "MICROPOP" CAMPAIGN
DIRECT MARKETING		
CONSUMER DIRECT	JUNG VON MATT STOCKHOLM	MINI, "MINI GETAWAY"
BUSINESS TO BUSINESS DIRECT	SCHOLZ & FRIENDS HAMBURG	SCHOLZ & FRIENDS RECRUITING, "PIZZA DIGITALE"
MEDIA USAGE		
MEDIA INNOVATION - TRADITIONAL MEDIA	KEMPERTRAUTMANN, HAMBURG	EDDING, "EDDING DIGITAL HIGHLIGHTER"
MEDIA INNOVATION - ALTERNATIVE MEDIA	PROXIMITY BBDO, DÜSSELDORF	WRIGLEY'S EXTRA, "MINT PARKING TICKET"
BRANDED CONTENT		
SOCIAL NETWORKS	FORSMAN & BODENFORS, GOTHENBURG	REEBOK, "THE PROMISE KEEPER"
MOBILE COMMUNICATIONS	ESTER, STOCKHOLM	LAFA, AIDS PREVENTION PROGRAMME, "SEX PROFILES"
BRANDED ENTERTAINMENT	GREY LONDON	BRITISH HEART FOUNDATION, "ANGINA MONOLOGUES"
PR & PROMOTIONS		
PUBLIC RELATIONS	SERVICEPLAN GRUPPE, GERMANY	SKY TV, "SKY FOOTBALL OPERA"
PROMOTIONS & ACTIVATION	SPILLMANN/FELSER/LEO BURNETT, ZURICH	MICASA FURNITURE STORE, "NAMES" PROMOTION
CRAFT & IMAGERY		
FILM CRAFT	CHI & PARTNERS, LONDON	TALKTALK, "HOMES WITHIN HOMES"
PRINT CRAFT	FP7/DXB, DUBAI	BATELCO, "BATELCO DIRECTORY" CAMPAIGN
ADVERTISING PHOTOGRAPHY	FRED & FARID PARIS	WRANGLER, "STUNT" CAMPAIGN
ILLUSTRATION	KNSK WERBEAGENTUR, HAMBURG	WMF, "WMF PEELERS" CAMPAIGN
DESIGN		
GRAPHIC DESIGN (2 WINNERS)	HAVAS 04, PARIS	MONOPRIX, "NOT YOUR EVERYDAY EVERYDAY"
	KEMPERTRAUTMANN, HAMBURG	PHILHARMONIKER HAMBURG, "SOUND LOGO"
PUBLICATION DESIGN	OGILVY & MATHER, DÜSSELDORF	ABTEI GINKGO PLUS, "THE RED-THREAD-BOOK"
PACKAGING DESIGN	SCHOLZ & FRIENDS BERLIN	FESTINA PROFUNDO WATCH, "WATER PACKAGING"
WEB		
CONSUMER INTERNET SITES - DURABLES	OGILVY & MATHER, FRANKFURT	MOTO WAGANARI, "DIRECTING SHADOWS"
CONSUMER INTERNET SITES - NON-DURABLES	LOWE BRINDFORS, STOCKHOLM	MAGNUM ICE CREAM, "PLEASURE HUNT"
BUSINESS TO BUSINESS INTERNET SITES	RAINEY KELLY CAMPBELL ROALFE/Y&R, LONDON	AWARD CALENDAR COUNTDOWN WEBSITE, "T-MINUS"
ONLINE ADS	MEDIAMONKS, HILVERSUM, (FOR DCS, PARIS)	DESPERADOS BEER, "THE DESPERADOS EXPERIENCE"
ONLINE FILMS	WIEDEN+KENNEDY AMSTERDAM	HEINEKEN, "THE ENTRANCE INTERACTIVE FILM"
INTEGRATED		
INTEGRATED CAMPAIGNS	McCANN ERICKSON, BUCHAREST	ROM, "AMERICAN ROM"

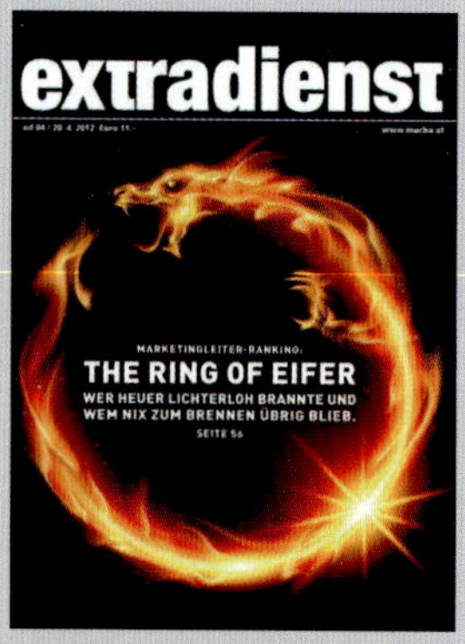
extradienst
THE RING OF EIFER
WER HEUER LICHTERLOH BRANNTE UND WEM NIX ZUM BRENNEN ÜBRIG BLIEB.
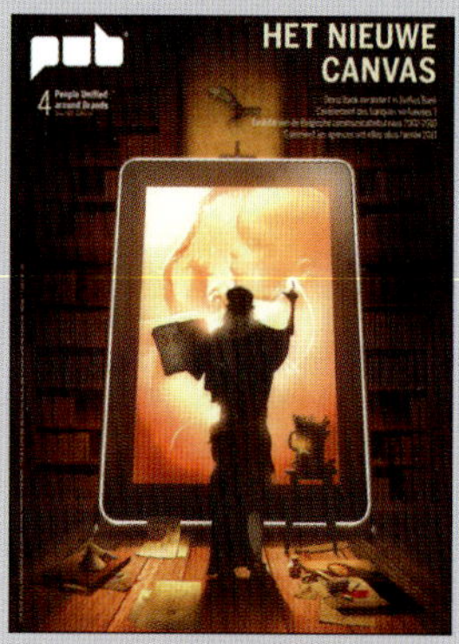
pub
HET NIEUWE CANVAS

STRATEGIE
ROZUMĚT MÉDIÍM

Markedsføring
KVINDER
Dinosaurerne uddøde ikke.
De flyttede ind i bestyrelserne.

signcare
6 years
POWERFUL
ideas
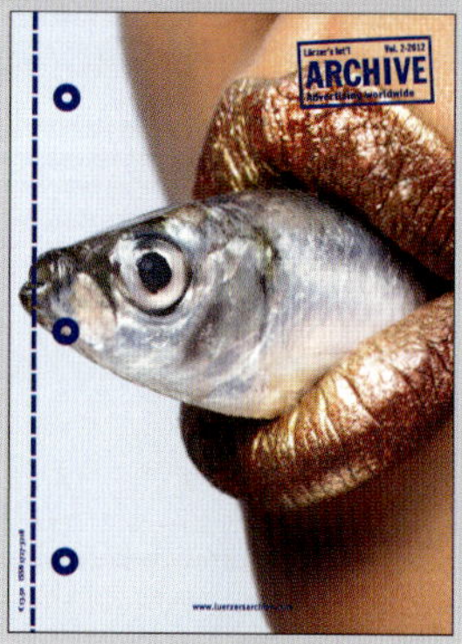
ARCHIVE

W&V
DIE DIGITAL-PLÄNE VON PROSIEBENSAT.1

MarketingWeek
Trust me, I'm a marketer

THE DRUM
OLYMPIC PRETEND

kreatív
ELMÚLÓ VILÁG

IMJ
DIRECT MARKETING
THE FUTURE'S BRIGHT

nc
Cover Story
White, Red & Green
L'etica dell'eccellenza dinamica

Pubblicità ITALIA
ARCHIVE
Madonna

PUBBLICO
P
APPREN
STREGO

KAMPANJE
REVOLUSJONEN
MOBIL

Exclusive: Grand Press 2011
Press
Poczobut
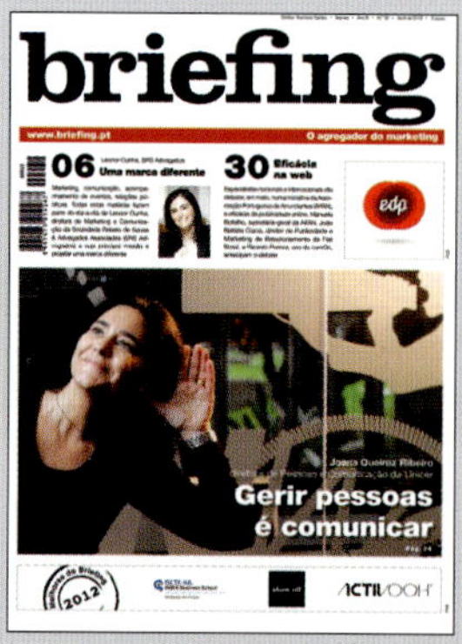
briefing
Gerir pessoas é comunicar
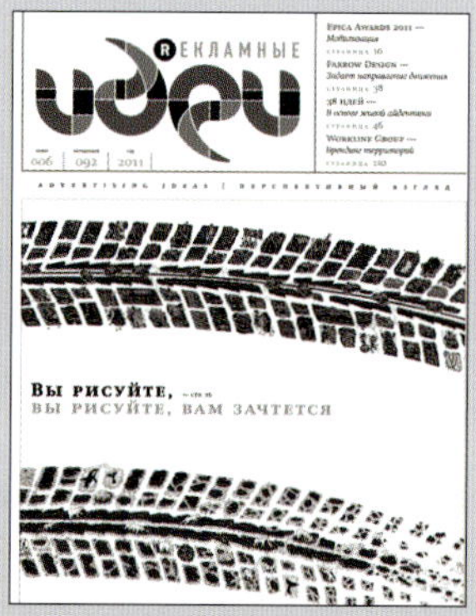
ВЫ РИСУЙТЕ,
ВЫ РИСУЙТЕ, ВАМ ЗАЧТЕТСЯ

Straté
DOBRÁ BANKA „PRIMITÍVNE" JE
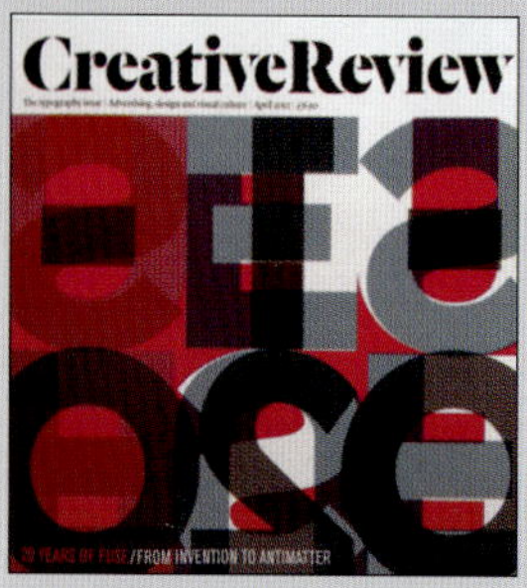
CreativeReview

NEW MOMENT
A HISTORY OF AVANT-GARDE IN EASTERN EUROPE

el publicista

Resumé
SÅ SPRACK SCHERMANS DRÖMAFFÄR

perso

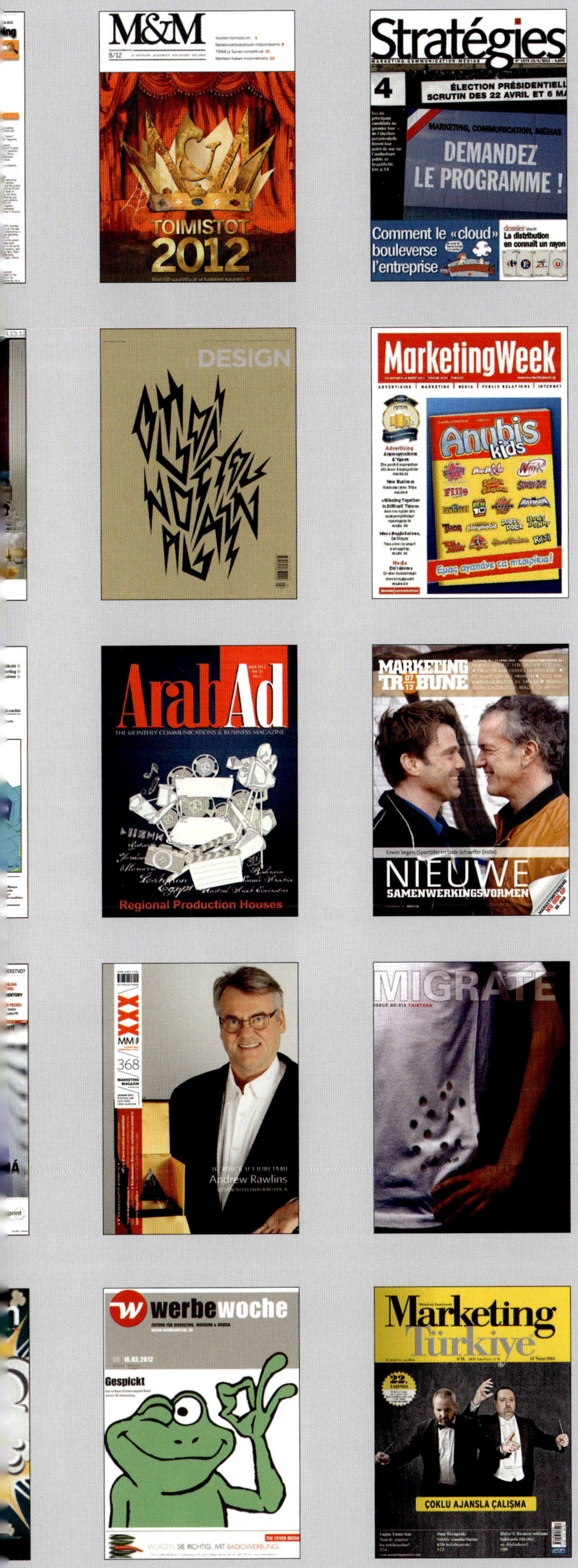
M&M
TOIMISTOT 2012
Stratégies
ÉLECTION PRÉSIDENTIELLE
DEMANDEZ LE PROGRAMME !
Comment le «cloud» bouleverse l'entreprise
DESIGN
MarketingWeek
Anubis kids
ArabAd
THE MONTHLY COMMUNICATIONS & BUSINESS MAGAZINE
Regional Production Houses
MARKETING TRIBUNE
NIEUWE SAMENWERKINGSVORMEN
MIGRATE
Andrew Rawlins
werbewoche
Gespickt
Marketing Türkiye
ÇOKLU AJANSLA ÇALIŞMA

The jury

The Epica jury is made up of journalists from leading advertising magazines in Europe and the EMEA region. A total of 35 publications from 28 countries were represented on the jury in 2011.

AUSTRIA
Extra Dienst

BELGIUM
Pub

BULGARIA
Sign Cafe

CZECH REPUBLIC
Strategie

DENMARK
Markedsføring

ESTONIA
Best Marketing

FINLAND
Markkinointi & Mainonta

FRANCE
Stratégies

GERMANY
Lürzer's International Archive
Werben und Verkaufen

GREAT BRITAIN
Creative Review
Marketing Week
The Drum

GREECE
+ Design
Marketing Week

HUNGARY
Kreatív

IRELAND
IMJ

ITALY
NC Nuova Comunicazione
Pubblicitá Italia
Pubblico

LEBANON
ArabAd

THE NETHERLANDS
Marketing Tribune

NORWAY
Kampanje

POLAND
Press

PORTUGAL
Briefing

RUSSIA
Advertising Ideas

SERBIA
New Moment

SLOVAKIA
Stratégie

SLOVENIA
MM

SOUTH AFRICA
Migrate

SPAIN
El Publicista

SWEDEN
Resumé

SWITZERLAND
Persönlich
Werbe Woche

TURKEY
Marketing Türkiye

EPICA AWARDS
2011

Photos: MM Slovenia/Epica

Annual report

The awards ceremony took place in the Kino Šiška Centre for Urban Culture in Ljubljana on January 20th, 2012. It was combined with a full-day's conference featuring presentations by local Slovenian agency Pristop and 2011 Epica winners from Kempertrautmann, Demner Merlicek & Bergmann, Wieden+Kennedy, Fred & Farid, Los&Co and Spillmann/Felster/Leo Burnett. Entertainment was provided by the Serbian rock band Sevdahbaby. The event was hosted by the Slovenian magazine MM.

Epica celebrated its 25th anniversary in 2011 with 19% entry growth and 11% more entrants than the previous year.

The film Epica d'Or was won by Wieden+Kennedy Amsterdam for the new Heineken "Open your World" campaign, "The Entrance" and "The Date", produced by Sonny London and directed by Fredrik Bond.

The press Epica d'Or went to Spillmann/Felser/Leo Burnett, Zurich for the Swiss Life campaign, "Life's Turns in a Sentence".

The outdoor Epica d'Or was won by Rainey Kelly Campbell Roalfe/Y&R, London for the Land Rover Defender "Passport Stamps" poster.

The Epica d'Or for interactive advertising went to Jung von Matt, Stockholm for their "Mini Getaway" operation.

The "American Rom" operation took top honours in the integrated campaigns category for McCann Erickson, Bucharest.

In the country rankings Germany moved up from 4th to 1st, thereby regaining the position it's occupied 7 times over the last 10 years. France, Sweden and the UK each lost position as a result of Germany's return to form.

Forsman & Bodenfors, Gothenburg was the most successful entrant for the second year in a row with Ogilvy Germany just behind. Germany's Serviceplan Gruppe, Fred & Farid Paris and Wieden+Kennedy Amsterdam were the only agencies to win 4 top awards.

All the gold, silver and bronze winners feature in this 25th edition of the Epica book, together with a selection of other high-scoring entries.

	Entrants	Entries	Gold	Silver	Bronze
Austria	18	43	2	–	1
Azerbaijan	1	2	–	–	–
Belarus	2	4	–	–	–
Belgium	4	30	–	2	1
Bulgaria	6	25	–	1	–
Croatia	6	8	–	–	–
Czech Republic	17	76	–	2	–
Denmark	8	26	–	–	1
Faroe Islands	1	1	–	–	–
Finland	21	70	–	–	3
France	33	478	11	31	24
Germany	86	803	15	45	29
Greece	10	31	–	–	1
Hungary	8	25	–	–	–
Iceland	2	10	–	–	–
Ireland	7	29	1	–	1
Israel	6	34	1	1	3
Italy	28	104	–	3	3
Jordan	1	4	–	–	–
Kazakhstan	1	2	–	–	–
Latvia	1	1	–	–	–
Lebanon	2	12	–	–	1
Lithuania	4	14	–	–	1
Luxembourg	1	1	–	–	–
Macedonia	2	7	–	–	–
Namibia	1	3			–
Netherlands	26	136	6	8	9
Norway	15	79	4	6	5
Oman	1	5	–	–	–
Poland	9	19	–	–	1
Portugal	8	22	–	–	–
Qatar	1	6	–	–	–
Romania	11	33	2	1	–
Russian Federation	34	191	–	2	6
Saudi Arabia	2	13	–	–	–
Serbia	5	18	–	–	–
Slovakia	8	42	–	–	2
Slovenia	5	7	–	–	1
South Africa	4	10	–	–	–
Spain	13	69	1	2	3
Sweden	55	375	8	19	31
Switzerland	14	335	8	8	5
Tunisia	1	3	–	–	–
Turkey	21	111	3	2	3
Ukraine	14	38	–	3	1
United Arab Emirates	10	102	1	6	5
United Kingdom	52	277	12	9	20
United States	3	5	–	–	1
Total	589	3739	75	151	162

Opening a new world

by Mark Tungate

How Wieden+Kennedy Amsterdam wove magic from awkward moments, eccentric characters and vanishing beer.

It sounds like the beginning of a joke: "A man walks into a party." But while *The Entrance* isn't devoid of humour, the spot's hero is no laughing stock. In fact he's a self-assured man of the world.

Most of us might be daunted by the prospect of strolling alone into a glamorous embassy soirée, but our hero looks perfectly at home, greeting a diverse range of international types as if they're old pals. He returns an eye-patched general's glass eye, enjoys a mock shoot-out with a Texan oilman and saves a mysterious beauty from potential embarrassment. And with the help of Heineken, he wins over a martial arts expert whose attentions are far from amicable.

To top it all, he ends up jamming – on the flute, no less – with the fabulous Mette from Danish pop combo Asteroids Galaxy Tour. Quite an entrance, indeed.

"The idea was to play on young men's anxieties and aspirations," says Eric Quennoy of Wieden+Kennedy Amsterdam, who devised the spot with his fellow executive creative director Mark Bernath. "So we thought about the moment you walk into a party and you want to make an impression."

Previous Heineken spots had focused on the beer, but the new campaign, "Open Your World", flips the camera around to focus on the drinker. "It's an homage to the men of the world: the kind of witty, open-minded, culturally aware guy who drinks our beer. The question then was how we could best showcase this character."

The Legend was born: a man who breezes through situations that make normal folk feel apprehensive. It's no coincidence that the second film in the series is called *The Date*. Entering a Chinese cabaret through the back entrance, the central character shows his lovely companion skills such as speed cooking, close-up magic and eel taming. Never has a first date gone so smoothly.

Both *The Entrance* and *The Date* have an exotic feel about them. The first was filmed in Barcelona, the second at a Victorian ball-room in Lewisham, England. But on screen they appear to be lo-

cated in a mythical realm inhabited by suave guys, beautiful girls and globetrotting raconteurs.

Actually, it's possible that the films could only have been made by Wieden+Kennedy Amsterdam, which is exactly that kind of place. "You have people from about 25 different nationalities working here," confirms Eric – who is Franco-Australian. "In fact the original script of *The Entrance* showed our hero greeting people from many different parts of the world in the appropriate manner."

The story evolved with the help of director Fredrik Bond, something of a legend himself. "It's been a wonderfully collaborative process. We were coming up with ideas literally the day before the shoot. So a film that began life as a series of greetings – bowing, rubbing noses with an Eskimo and so on – exploded into so much more."

Watching *The Entrance*, one can't help wondering about the colourful cast of characters the hero meets. Quennoy, Bernath and Bond help out with a series of vignettes providing the back story of each persona. They were accessible via an interactive version hosted on Heineken's Facebook fan page and also on YouTube.

"We wanted to imply that there were deeper relationships behind the moments you see in the spot," says Mark Bernath. "Where did the eyeball come from? Is the karate black belt his nemesis from years of martial arts grappling? We wanted to show that this guy has a past."

One of the highlights of *The Entrance* is, of course, the music. Eric explains: "We knew he'd end up on stage with the band, so they had to look spectacular as well as sound great. We work with a music research company called Agoraphone, who introduced us to Asteroids Galaxy Tour. They had the perfect spirit – and Mette looks fantastic."

The presence of the band led to an amusing incident during the shoot. The beer you see on screen is prepared by a sort of "beer wrangler" named Ray. Eric says: "The beer has to look perfect, so Ray prepares each glass: the colour, the beads of moisture, the head – it's almost a science. The trouble was, when he turned his back the band drank the beer. It was watered down, so they must have had a somewhat negative view of our client's product."

The experience certainly doesn't seem to have affected their energetic performance, which incorporates our hero's flute solo. Although he catches the eye of more than one woman at the party, it speaks volumes that he ends up with the rock star.

"It's also interesting that he plays a flute." Mark adds. "He's a sort of pied piper character. Plus I think that adds to his slight edge of eccentricity. The flute is unexpected, but he makes it look cool."

You may have noted that the heroes of the two spots are different. "That was quite deliberate," says Eric. "We wanted our audience to feel they could somehow become these very confident guys, so we decided to use different actors, rather than stick with one character."

But their shared trait is likeability. If they took themselves too seriously, or pushed coolness to a superhuman level, they'd be irritating. The heroes of the films are skilled but not "slick".

Eric observes: "They even look a bit vulnerable at times. It's clear that the hero of *The Entrance* knows nothing about martial arts – his karate moves are ridiculous. And the guy in *The Date* is a gangly dancer. We try to work that into every spot. We call it 'the moment of awkwardness'."

Cool but approachable, talented but not smug. They are the men we'd all like to be. Even though we probably can't play the flute or tame eels, at least we can treat ourselves to an occasional Heineken.

She's my everything went wrong.

For all life's twists and turns:
Flexible financial plans.

SwissLife

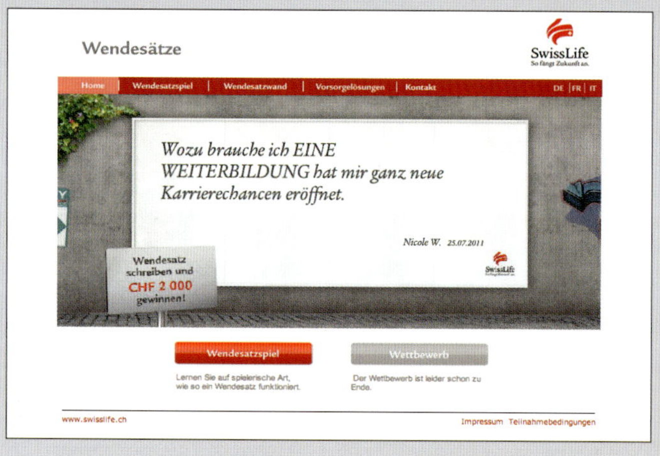
Wendesätze
SwissLife
So fängt Zukunft an.
Home | Wendesatzspiel | Wendesatzwand | Vorsorgelösungen | Kontakt
DE | FR | IT
Wozu brauche ich EINE WEITERBILDUNG hat mir ganz neue Karrierechancen eröffnet.
Nicole W. 25.07.2011
Wendesatz schreiben und CHF 2 000 gewinnen!
Wendesatzspiel
Lernen Sie auf spielerische Art, wie so ein Wendesatz funktioniert.
Wettbewerb
Der Wettbewerb ist leider schon zu Ende.
www.swisslife.ch
Impressum Teilnahmebedingungen

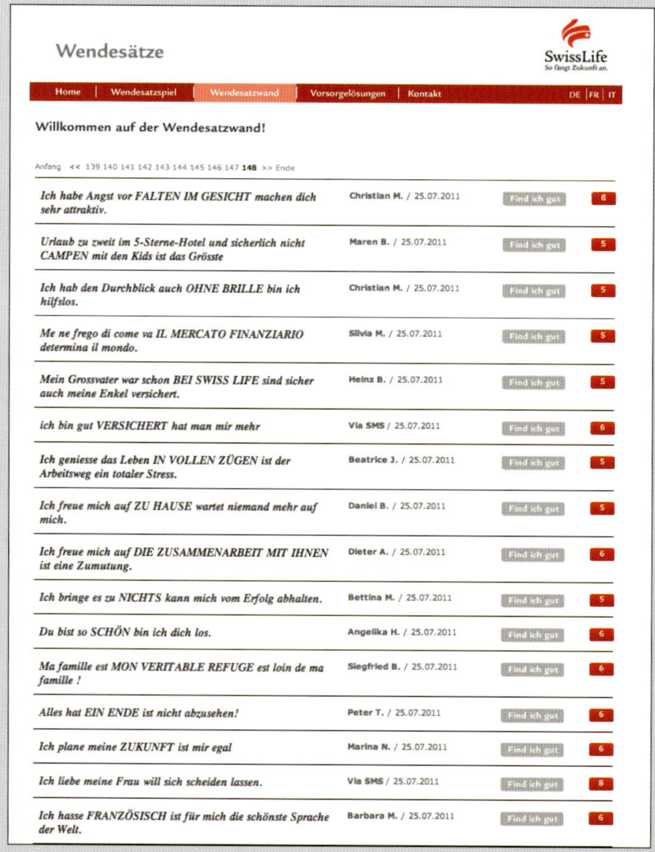
Wendesätze
SwissLife
So fängt Zukunft an.
Home | Wendesatzspiel | Wendesatzwand | Vorsorgelösungen | Kontakt
DE | FR | IT
Willkommen auf der Wendesatzwand!
Anfang << 139 140 141 142 143 144 145 146 147 148 >> Ende
Ich habe Angst vor FALTEN IM GESICHT machen dich sehr attraktiv.
Christian M. / 25.07.2011
Find ich gut
8
Urlaub zu zweit im 5-Sterne-Hotel und sicherlich nicht CAMPEN mit den Kids ist das Grösste
Maren B. / 25.07.2011
Find ich gut
5
Ich hab den Durchblick auch OHNE BRILLE bin ich hilfslos.
Christian M. / 25.07.2011
Find ich gut
5
Me ne frego di come va IL MERCATO FINANZIARIO determina il mondo.
Silvia M. / 25.07.2011
Find ich gut
5
Mein Grossvater war schon BEI SWISS LIFE sind sicher auch meine Enkel versichert.
Heinz B. / 25.07.2011
Find ich gut
5
ich bin gut VERSICHERT hat man mir mehr
Via SMS / 25.07.2011
Find ich gut
6
Ich geniesse das Leben IN VOLLEN ZÜGEN ist der Arbeitsweg ein totaler Stress.
Beatrice J. / 25.07.2011
Find ich gut
5
Ich freue mich auf ZU HAUSE wartet niemand mehr auf mich.
Daniel B. / 25.07.2011
Find ich gut
5
Ich freue mich auf DIE ZUSAMMENARBEIT MIT IHNEN ist eine Zumutung.
Dieter A. / 25.07.2011
Find ich gut
6
Ich bringe es zu NICHTS kann mich vom Erfolg abhalten.
Bettina M. / 25.07.2011
Find ich gut
5
Du bist so SCHÖN bin ich dich los.
Angelika H. / 25.07.2011
Find ich gut
6
Ma famille est MON VERITABLE REFUGE est loin de ma famille !
Siegfried B. / 25.07.2011
Find ich gut
6
Alles hat EIN ENDE ist nicht abzusehen!
Peter T. / 25.07.2011
Find ich gut
6
Ich plane meine ZUKUNFT ist mir egal
Marina N. / 25.07.2011
Find ich gut
6
Ich liebe meine Frau will sich scheiden lassen.
Via SMS / 25.07.2011
Find ich gut
8
Ich hasse FRANZÖSISCH ist für mich die schönste Sprache der Welt.
Barbara M. / 25.07.2011
Find ich gut
6

Life sentence

by Lewis Blackwell

It's an old saying that 'simple is best'. But with the expansion of interactive media, and the complexity of integrated media, it is easy to lose sight of how advertising does not always need big execution. Instead Big Ideas, which lead to the most powerful stand-out advertising, usually thrive on brevity. This year's winner of the Press Epica d'Or makes that abundantly clear.

With the economy of just a few words and without images, Spillmann/Felser/Leo Burnett of Zurich produced a campaign for Swiss Life that had the awards' judges excited and also fired up mass-participation from viewers.

The 'Life's turns in a sentence' campaign managed to encapsulate the case for the client's insurance products with witty and poignant short statements that show how our lives can so often turn out extremely differently to the plans we set out with. "Once we got the idea, the lines just flowed," says Peter Brönnimann, who was the creative director on the project with Martin Spillmann. "We had previously had this idea of doing real stories about how people's lives change unexpectedly but that was long copy and we needed something more immediate. We arrived at the most condensed way of telling – and everybody responded.

"I was then a bit doubtful when it was suggested we could also invite people to post in their own ideas at the website, creating their own extension of our ads. I thought 'why would people want to do that?' But it was incredible how they engaged, with more than 8,000 responses being filed quickly and even hundreds a day being added after we stopped running the campaign. And some of them very good! It seemed to touch a really strong nerve about how we see our lives."

Page after page of quick-witted lines are filed in multiple languages on the Swiss Life site (http://tinyurl.com/7bkz8f3), demonstrating that an idea that begins in print can successfully leap across media.

Suddenly the apparently dry subject of selling life insurance had become a rich, emotional playground where people could reveal

Tout va bien dans mon entreprise est au bord de la faillite.
La vie est pleine d'imprévus.
Nos solutions de prévoyance s'y adaptent.
SwissLife

Ich werde dich niemals verlassen Sie sich auf unsere Anwälte.
Das Leben ist voller Wendungen.
Unsere Vorsorge passt sich an.
SwissLife

Prendo la pillola, quel giorno l'ho dimenticata.
Sono tante le svolte della vita.
La nostra previdenza si adegua.
SwissLife

insights about how life works... and perhaps doesn't work. In short – how life is unpredictable and full of black humour.

"You think the campaign is a little dark in its taste?" says Brönnimann. "It's funny, no – but real, too. For example, so many men say 'I don't want to get married' but then before they know it they are planning the wedding day. Or they say they don't want children but then, when the children inevitably arrive, of course they love them and it's great. Life is full of strange and sometimes wonderful twists."

That insight of the 'strange twist' served to inspire a technique of writing the ads that opens out an almost infinite range of possibilities. It all hangs on starting a sentence as if saying one thing and then using a middle word in the phrase to veer sharply into a direction that is 180 degrees around from where the meaning seemed to be headed. At their best, the lines are poetic, quite balletic as the writing pirouettes around to surprise us with its statement. The best sentences are more than just a joke – they are really sharp insights into how we deceive ourselves and then change our mind, or how new circumstances can mean we are prepared to give up what we love, and so on.

For Brönnimann it is a surprise to find the campaign quite so awarded: "We were amazed at the response. With life insurance as a subject, you don't tend to expect fans and followers."

To look at the English-language version that was submitted for awards entries is to only get a hint of the creative challenge. That version came later, whereas the campaign started with having to speak in the three languages of the Swiss population. The original treatment, by copywriters Thomas Schöb and Simon Smit working with art directors Reto Clement and Daniele Barbiero, was in German but then the campaign was reworked to versions for the French and Italian speakers. The agency used translator-copywriters to come up with variations on the original German of the creative team, often having to greatly change the basic message in order for it to work in the other languages. "It was a fresh challenge each time to get it to work across each language," says Brönnimann. "What you can say in German is not necessarily possible as a way of communicating in the other languages, so you have to approach it fresh and really think how the words and speech work in those languages." What stayed the same was the understated art direction, with Legacy Medium Italic being the typeface used for the principal line across the campaign.

Previously Spillmann/Felser/Leo Burnett had built a platform of campaigning over several years for Swiss Life largely using TV commercials for the greatest effect. This narrative and visual medium had proved powerful in its ability to deliver compelling stories. However, now the impact of the 'Life's turns in a sentence' posters, with its haiku-like sentences out of which many stories can flower in the reader's head, has prompted the client and the agency to think again. It looks likely the campaign idea will be developed and the print medium will once again be key, working in tandem with web-based interaction. The old and young media seem made for partnering – if the ideas are big enough.

There's an old joke: 'If you want to make God laugh, tell him your plans.' The genius of the Swiss Life campaign is that it turns that joke on its head as we see and embrace the absurdity of how life's twists can up-end us all. The campaign invites us to chill a bit and accept that fate dishes out weird tricks and that is how things are. And, without hammering the point, the sign-off in the bottom left of the Swiss Life logo invites us to think that perhaps a little insurance might be a good idea...

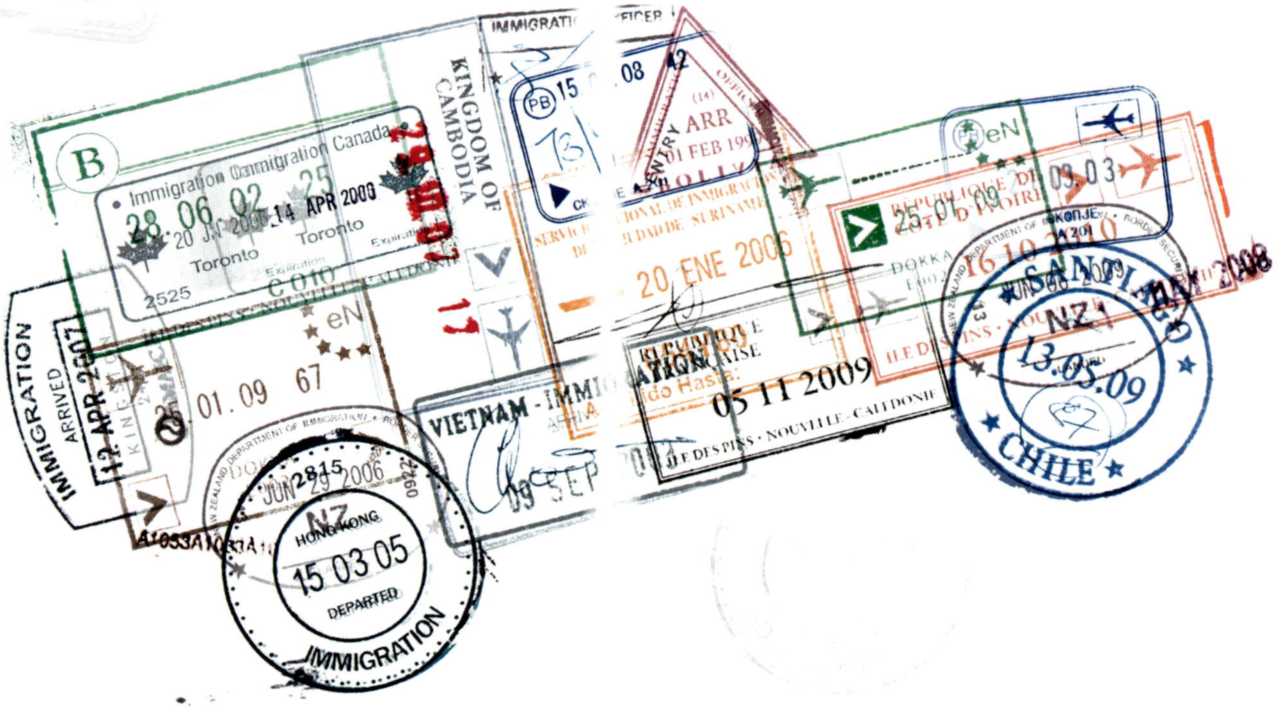
KINGDOM OF CAMBODIA
IMMIGRATION
ARRIVED
12 APR 2007
Immigration Canada
VIETNAM - IMMIGRATION
20 ENE 2006
05 11 2009
15 03 05
DEPARTED
IMMIGRATION
SANTIAGO
13.05.09
CHILE

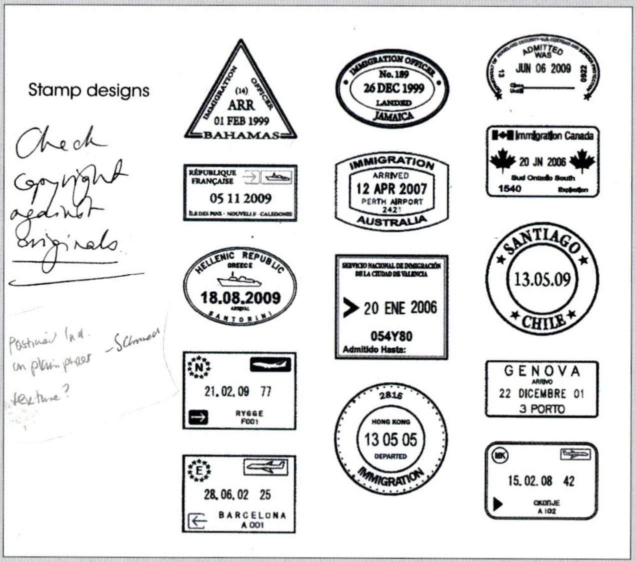
Stamp designs
Check copyright against originals
ARR
01 FEB 1999
BAHAMAS
26 DEC 1999
JAMAICA
JUN 06 2009
05 11 2009
12 APR 2007
AUSTRALIA
20 JN 2006
18.08.2009
20 ENE 2006
SANTIAGO
13.05.09
CHILE
21.02.09 77
GENOVA
22 DICEMBRE 01
3 PORTO
13 05 05
IMMIGRATION
28.06.02 25
BARCELONA
15.02.08 42

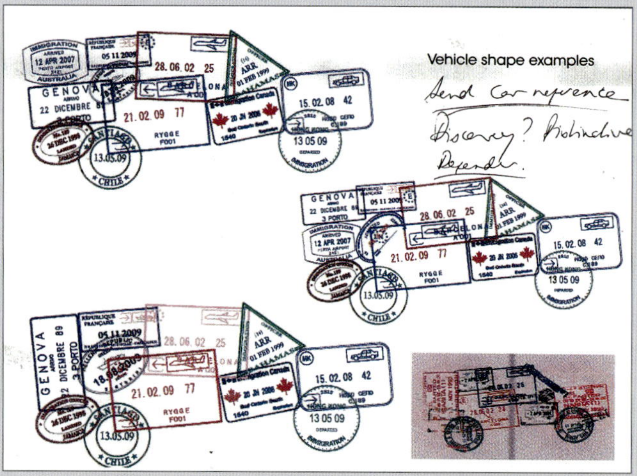
Vehicle shape examples

Stamps of approval

by Lewis Blackwell

Ever suffered from passport envy? It's the description we give to seeing that somebody else's passport has a lot more stamps in it than our own, and from more exotic places, and from which we conclude that perhaps the holder has had a more rich and interesting life than our own.

Nonsense, of course, but nevertheless devastating to the ego to contrast a colourfully-illustrated document to your own scarcely soiled one. In that stamp-envy lay a germ of an idea that caught fire in the imaginations of creatives at Rainey Kelly Campbell Roalfe/Y&R, London. The result was an outstandingly crafted piece of work that went on to win the Outdoor Epica d'Or.

"Originally we had this brief to pitch the Land Rover Defender to diplomats with a money-off deal," explains copywriter Phil Forster. "It was a pretty small-scale job." Apparently the Defender, which is the all-terrain vehicle closest to the original Land Rover, is much favoured by diplomats, certainly the British ones: it combines a fine sense of tradition with also a sense that you might get some protection from the rocks on the road and any other dangers coming your way in strange territories.

"As we thought about it, inquired into the vehicle story and also what we knew about diplomats, the idea emerged to celebrate how the Defender is so internationally embraced," says Forster. "There are also few vehicles you could do this graphic pun with as it has such an iconic shape and others typically do not... in fact, most vehicles look pretty similar if not almost identical in profile whereas the Defender has very distinctive features that have been with us a long time."

Forster and art director Tim Brookes researched stamps and countries on the internet and sketched out ways of working the idea. They knew it was always going to have to be about

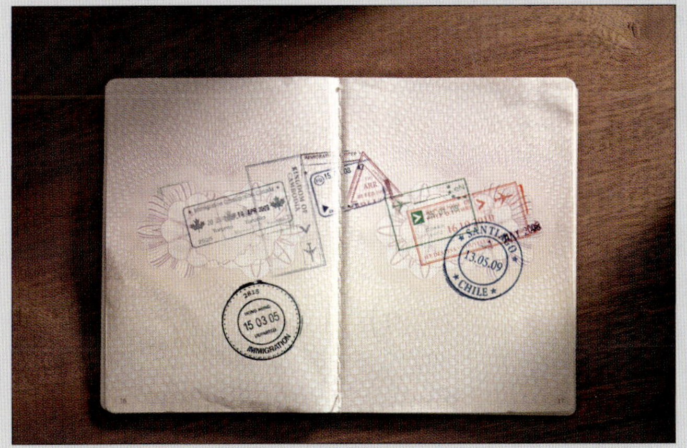
CHILE
13.05.09
15 03 05
IMMIGRATION

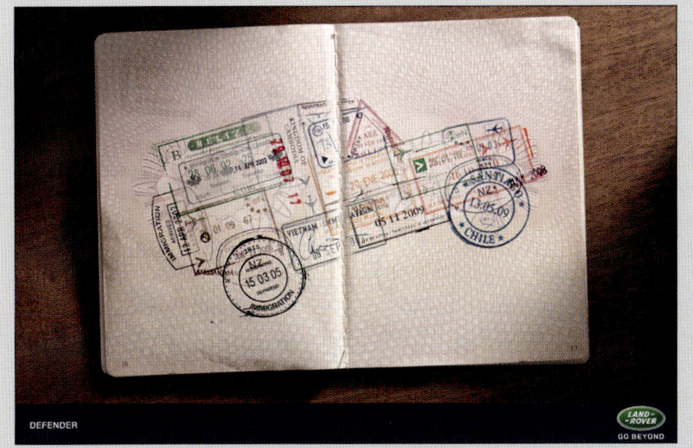
CHILE
13.05.09
15 03 05
IMMIGRATION
DEFENDER
GO BEYOND

creating a very convincing illusion – there was no way you could do it 'for real' with actual passport stamps. Not only do the stamps not exist precisely in the forms needed, but many countries would be inappropriate. On top of that, there would be the small matter of fraud to deal with if you actually attempted to include real stamps.

"You know that the stamps could never happen like this but the whole trick is to do it well enough that people suspend disbelief and both get the idea and love the execution," says Forster. "Lots of different stamps and combinations were tried and eliminated. The final result was a long way from the first go."

While just about all viewers would realise that there is not a world of rubber stamping officials out there in immigration officer-land willing to shape this picture of a car, at the same time the craft of making it look like it could have happened is very important. It is the joy in craft that creates the willing suspension of disbelief in the viewer. To achieve this, Brookes worked closely with typographer Lee Aldridge to study different stamps and then model out how they could combine to both create the memorable shape and yet also still be convincing passport stamps. The whole thing was finally assembled with a blank British passport page, photographed by Carl Warner.

"We had an extra challenge in that the countries had to be both varied but also not politically-sensitive," says Forster. "The client understandably did not want war-torn territories to feature."

Visual anthropologists can perhaps one day learn both a fair bit about advertising and British political sensitivities by decoding which countries did make it into the final cut. Chile, for example, is a name that stands prominently on one of the wheels – Britain has strategically managed to retain decent relationships with Chile through dictatorship and democracy (if you want to fly to the Falkland Islands you have to do it from Chile, not Argentina). The Cote d'Ivoire (Ivory Coast) is also in there, one of the safer African nations to associate with, as is the tiny nation of Belize (a British protectorate and sometime tax haven).

But for all that we can have fun speculating on the diplomat politics that might have been in the original thinking, the fact is that the ad was so compelling that the client quickly decided to adopt it for a much wider push and use it nationwide.

So the irony is that while the tightest of briefs - sell a deal on the Defender to a few hundred diplomats – inspired the original idea, the result was an image of such wide appeal that the resulting communication became something quite different. The ad could and probably did sell Land Rover Defenders to yummy mummies in Chelsea instead.

There is a lesson in that, a profound conclusion to be drawn perhaps... but I am not sure I know it. Perhaps it is that old saying, that you need rules, you need restrictions, in order to be able to play a game and win. What is clear is that small but essential creative craft details are often the making of great ads and that was certainly crucial in this case.

Lewis Blackwell is an author, publisher and creative director. His many books include Photowisdom and the bestselling Life & Love of Trees, as well as the recently republished classic The End of Print. He is former editor-in-chief of Creative Review and was worldwide creative head of Getty Images.

BURGER KIN

DO THE IMPOSSIBLE
IN STOCKHOLM
NEXT WEEK.
KEEP 50 METRES
AWAY FROM ALL
STOCKHOLMERS.
GETAWAY
STOCKHOLM
2010
WIN THE NEW MINI COUNTRYMAN.
READ MORE OR DOWNLOAD THE APP AT MINIGETAWAYSTOCKHOLM.COM
MINI

BECOME HUNTED
BY 11.413 PERSONS
AROUND THE CLOCK
UNTIL SUNDAY.
WIN THE NEW
MINI COUNTRYMAN.
DOWNLOAD THE APP AT APP STORE: SEARCH FOR "MINI GETAWAY STOCKHOLM".
OR GO TO MINIGETAWAYSTOCKHOLM.COM.
GETAWAY
STOCKHOLM
2010.
MINI

The Swedish job

by Mark Tungate

How to take a Mini in the middle of Stockholm when there are 11,000 people chasing you.

The agency knew things had got out of hand when the helicopter arrived. The pilot's strategy was simple: hover over the Mini, grab it, and fly away before anyone else could get their hands on it.

Now you're thinking: how is it possible for a helicopter to grab a Mini? Using some kind of giant magnet, perhaps? The answer is far more straightforward. The car wasn't real, but virtual. In fact, it may have been the most sought-after virtual car in history.

Flashback to the autumn of 2010. BMW approached Jung von Matt, Stockholm, to handle the launch in Sweden of its new Mini Countryman, a crossover sport utility version of the beloved runabout. The global concept was already in place: "Getaway". The Mini Countryman helped young urban dwellers escape.

"We also felt that the launch should reflect the playful element of the Mini brand," says Jung von Matt copywriter and founding partner Magnus Andersson. "Our research showed us that Mini fans, while not exclusively young, were 'mentally young'. They all had a youthful, exuberant mindset."

A decision was made: the campaign would be fully integrated, but at its heart would be a GPS reality game: "Mini Getaway".

So how did it work? Users downloaded an app that enabled them to hunt for a virtual Mini hidden somewhere within Stockholm. When they got within 50 metres of the vehicle, they could "take" it with their iPhone. Then the real fun began, because other players could track the Mini down and grab it for themselves. The app showed not only the location of the car, but all the players.

Whoever still had the virtual Mini at the end of the week-long game would win a real Mini Countryman.

The physical aspect of the game, plus the speed and agility needed to play it, was perfectly aligned with Mini's brand

TELIA 3G
11:02
D. H. M. S.
06 12 56 04
Hide
GPS
Kungliga biblioteket
Birger Jarlsgatan
Sturegatan
YOU
MINI
Regeringsgatan
Norrlandsgatan
Kungsgatan
Lästmakargatan
Jakobsbergsgatan
Klaratunneln
YOU CAN TAKE THE MINI WITHIN 50 METRES.
Game
Rules
MINI Countryman

values. Plus, it reversed the idea of a conventional video game by bringing gamers outdoors. And the Countryman is all about experiencing the great outdoors.

First, the build-up. Alongside press and TV advertising, "Mini Getaway" was launched with a trailer on YouTube. A PR strategy was also devised to get the media talking about it.

The game "board" was strictly limited to the centre of Stockholm. Andersson explains: "We wanted to keep it within a narrow space, where it would be very difficult to stay 50 metres from anyone else, because that would make it much more fun to play. It also gave the impression that you had a better chance of taking control of the car and winning."

To make sure the entire country could take part, national rock radio station Bandit ran a competition with the prize of a trip to Stockholm. Meanwhile, gamers began downloading the app and plotting their strategies. Andersson says: "Before the game began, there was a great deal of chatter on the internet about the best way to win the car."

Soaring levels of interest created a problem when the game kicked off: the server crashed almost immediately. Luckily, extra capacity was quickly put in place and the players dashed off in search of the phantom Mini Countryman.

"The small gaming area and the ease with which you could take or lose the car meant it was an extremely exciting chase," says Jung von Matt art director Daniel Wahlgren. "That's why people played it for so long: an average of five hours per player."

By the end of the week, the game had attracted 11,000 players. "Our goal was 5,000," Wahlgren points out.

In order to take part, players had to register through Facebook. But just before the final day the social network changed its login procedures, effectively locking new players out. An urgent phone call to Facebook in the US resolved the problem.

When the last day dawned, Andersson recalls: "The centre of Stockholm was packed with players. We brought the city to a virtual standstill. The police showed up but they didn't close us down – in fact they had a good sense of humour about it."

And that's when the three guys in the helicopter appeared. "They thought that by grabbing the car from above, they could hold on to it more easily. They didn't succeed."

Gamers who couldn't afford a helicopter were often on rollerblades or mopeds. In the end, the car was won by a 22-year-old photographer who played with his dad. They had a strategy too: one of them would take the car, race away from the rival players and then allow the other to take it. In other words, a relay system that kept the virtual car bouncing between the same two people.

"Mini Getaway" became a worldwide talking point, attracting online followers in more than 90 countries. Sales of Mini in Sweden increased by 108% after the game.

And the concept did not stay in Sweden. It quickly moved on to Tokyo, where it attracted 20,000 players. Other agencies have "borrowed" the mechanic for campaigns for different brands, with varying levels of success. One thing is certain: "Mini Getaway" showed gamers all over the world that the best games are not necessarily played indoors.

Mark Tungate is the author of several books about branding and communications, among them Adland: A Global History of Advertising, Luxury World: The Past, Present and Future of Luxury Brands and the recent Branded Beauty: How Marketing Changed the Way We Look.

Wall's
WHAT
WE
WANT

Wall's
SAUSAGE ROLL
WHAT
WE
WANT

Agency Saatchi & Saatchi, London
Executive CDs Paul Silburn, Kate Stanners
Creative Directors Andy Jex, Rob Potts
Copywriter Dan Warner
Art Director Andy Vasey
Production Rattling Stick, London
Film Director Andy McLeod
Producers Kirsty Dye, Anne O'Neill
Editor Andy McGraw
Post Production Big Buoy, London
Sound Design Wave
Business Leader Charles Pym
Account Executive Camden Hague
D.O.P. Stuart Graham
Advertiser Wall's Sausages, "Kitchen" & "Garage"

A woman brings a plate full of sizzling Wall's sausages to her husband. Overcome with emotion, he places a small jewellery box on the table in front of her. When she opens it, she sees a tiny bull terrier with a Casio keyboard. In a Cockney accent, the dog sings: "Thank you, for all the meaty sausages. Thank you, for all the Wall's. You're the best wife in the world, mummy bear. But he can't tell you that because he's just a bloke really." Wall's. That's what men want.

A man buys a Wall's sausage roll at his local garage. Taking a bite, he's clearly in heaven. He passes the astonished cashier a jewellery box. When she opens it, the small bull terrier with the synthesizer sings: "Thank you, for selling Wall's…you're the loveliest garage lady in the land. But obviously he can't express himself because he's just a bloke really." Wall's. What we want.

ja!
Natürlich.
Our masterpieces.

Agency	Demner, Merlicek & Bergmann, Vienna
Creative Directors	Franz Merlicek Rosa Haider
Copywriter	Arno Reisenbuechler
Art Director	Roman Steiner
Photographer	Bernhard Angerer
Graphic Design	Stefan Oehner
Acct. Supervisor	Katharina Schmid
Art Buying	Ilona Urikow
Final Artwork	Mario Goldsteiner
Advertiser	Ja! Natürlich Organic Food, "Design Classics"

1,000,001

WE CARE BECAUSE
OUR NAME'S ON IT.
Warburtons

Agency Rainey Kelly Campbell Roalfe/Y&R, London
Creative Director Mark Roalfe
Copywriter Mark Waldron
Art Director David Godfree
Production Gorgeous Enterprises, London
Director Vince Squibb
Producer Jody Allison
Advertiser Warbutons Toastie Farmhouse Loaves, "Celebration"

Inside the Warburtons factory, the one millionth loaf of bread is about to complete its journey along the conveyor belt. Everyone stops to stare as the golden loaf emerges from the oven and the boss holds it triumphantly aloft. A spontaneous party breaks out with hugs, dancing and streamers. Then it's back to work as usual – until the million and first loaf appears. We realise that every single loaf is a cause for celebration at Warburtons. "We care because our name's on it."

It would be a shame to lose our carnivore side

CHARAL

CHARAL

Agency Leo Burnett, Paris
Creative Director Guillaume-Ulrich Chifflot
Copywriter Hadi Hassan Hélou
Art Director Jérôme Gonfond
Production Gang Films, Paris
Director Tim Hamilton
Advertiser Charal Meat, "The Wolves" & "The Ostriches"

In the dark of night, three wolves gather on a mountaintop to howl at the moon. Except one of them – who bleats like a sheep instead. His friends look at him disdainfully and turn to go. It would be a shame to lose our carnivore side. Nourish it.

A cheetah slinks across the African savannah. Suddenly, he spots three ostriches. In their usual response to danger, they stick their heads in the ground. The cheetah does the same thing. The ostriches look up, bemused. Then they wander off, leaving the cheetah stuck. It would be a shame to lose our carnivore side. Nourish it – with Charal meat.

I
LOVE NAPPING ON THE COUCH ALMOST AS MUCH AS
my cat
whiskas

I
HAD A FAVORITE SWEATER BUT NOW IT BELONGS TO
my cat
whiskas

I
PLAY THE PIANO ALMOST AS WELL AS
my cat
whiskas

JOHN WEST
WITH OMEGA 3.
BECAUSE SOMETIMES THEIR BRAINS NEED A LITTLE EXTRA HELP.

Agency	TBWA\Berlin
Executive CDs	Kurt Georg Dieckert Stefan Schmidt
Creative Directors	Philip Borchardt Dirk Henkelmann
Copywriters	Stefan Schmidt Felicitas Olschewski Nadine Nedreboe
Art Directors	Leila El-Kayem Heribert Wilmerdinger
Illustrators	Chehad Abdallah Benedikt Gansczyk
Advertiser	Whiskas, "I Love my Cat"

Agency	Boys and Girls, Dublin
Creative Director	Rory Hamilton
Copywriters	Rory Hamilton Roger McGrath
Art Director	Bairbre McGlade
Photography	Adrian Stewart
Typographer	Jonathon Cullen
Digital Artwork	Anthony Gold
Advertiser	John West, "Railings"

PROSCIUTTO DI PARMA
CUT INTO FINEST SLICES
CITTERIO

Agency	Advico Young & Rubicam, Zurich
Creative Director	Thomas Schöb
Art Director	Isabelle Hauser
Photography	Lorenz Cugini
Typographer	Annik Weber
Account Manager	Carmela Dias
Advertiser	Citterio Ham, "Cut into Finest Slices"

i'm lovin' it

IT HAS TO BE
HEINZ
Tomato soup
100th BIRTHDAY

Agency	Leo Burnett, London
Creative Director	Justin Tindall
Copywriter	Jon Fox
Art Director	Rik Brown
Production	Blink, London
Director	Simon Willows
Producers	James Stevenson Bretton Kirsten Kates
Advertiser	McDonald's, "Go With the Flow"

Three decorators work so well together than their movements seem perfectly synchronised. As they toss brushes, paint tins and tools to one another, their fluid movements form a veritable dance of DIY. The apartment gets decorated in no time. As a reward, they settle down to an appropriate meal: a McDonald's BCO. Delicious bacon, succulent chicken and crispy onions. The perfect combination of three ingredients.

Agency	Abbott Mead Vickers BBDO, London
Executive CD	Paul Brazier
CDs	Steve Jones Martin Loraine
Creatives	Matt Welch Simon Welch
Production	Rattling Stick, London
Director	Andy McLeod
Producers	Kirsty Dye Lindsay Hughes
Editor	Richard Orrick
Advertiser	Heinz, "Happy Birthday"

This spot captures a very important moment in the ritual of soup drinking. We see clips of many different people blowing on their warm spoonful of soup before taking the first mouthful. As the scenes continue, we realise that the different tones of blowing are forming a tune: "Happy Birthday to You." Heinz Cream of Tomato Soup is 100 years old.

HEINZ
קטשופ
חריף ומתובל

DAMN, IT'S HOT
Chili

Agency Shalmor Avnon Amichay/Y&R Interactive, Tel Aviv
Creative Director Yariv Twig
Copywriter Lior Shoham
Art Directors Alejandro Feldman, Carmel AbuZelf
Photography Menachem Reiss
Client Director Adam Polachek
Acct. Supervisor Revital Levy
Acct. Manager Mor Elyashiv
Advertiser Heinz Ketchup, “Spaghetti”

Agency Publicis, Sofia
Advertiser Olineza Chili Sauce, “Damn it’s Hot”

Considering the quality of our ingredients, this picture is quite the disappointment.
We use the same ingredients as you would do at home. Our food is just cooked in a bigger kitchen. You still beat us on the look though. Hopefully.
Findus

TASTE THE GOOD OLD DAYS

TASTE THE GOOD OLD DAYS
MENIER

Agency	Forsman & Bodenfors, Gothenburg
Copywriter	Johan Holmström
Art Director	Samuel Åkesson
Photography	Emil Larsson
Acct. Supervisor	Stefan Rudels
Client	Elisabeth Yllfors
Acct. Manager	Joachim Levin
Advertiser	Findus, "Bad Picture"

Agency	Publicis Conseil, Paris
Creative Directors	Olivier Altmann Fabrice Delacourt Olivier Desmettre
Copywriter	Patrice Lucet
Art Directors	Philippe Boucheron Antoine Dezes-Richard
Photography	Herve Plumet
Art Buying	Soone Riboud
Acct. Supervisor	Celine Colin
Clients	Bernd Homann Florence Audoyer
Advertiser	Menier, "Old Days"

Any plans for tonight?
ISN'T THAT
YOUR EX?
Wanker
She still fancies you.
WHAT YOUR
MOUTH'S
MADE FOR

SHOPPING
SHOPPING
SHOP
Puis-je
SORRY,
WE DON'T SPEAK
FRENCH.
Hola Chica
WHAT YOUR
MOUTH'S
MADE FOR
Weirdo.

Agency	Openhere, Antwerp
Creative Directors	Stijn Gansemans Koen van Deun Johan Roelandt
Copywriter	Koen van Deun
Art Director	Johan Roelandt
Production	Caviar, Brussels
Director	Keith English
Producers	Werner de Coninck Bo de Groot
Advertiser	Bicky, "Talking Ears"

Welcome to the odd world of people who are forced to talk by waggling their ears – because their mouths are too busy enjoying Bicky burgers. In the first spot, three blokes are "chatting" when a pretty blonde walks in. "Isn't that your ex?" waggles one. "Yes, but keep it down." After joining her own friends, the girl casts a look at the boys. "Wankers," her ears signal. "She still fancies you," interprets the guy's pal. Bicky: what your mouth's made for.

In the second spot, we're still at the café. The girls are complaining about the "nerds" in the corner when one of them spots a handsome guy strolling down the aisle. "Helloooo sexy," she signals with her ears. Unfortunately, the message is received by an oily Don Juan type across the room. "Hola chica," he waggles, to her disgust. Ear talking has its disadvantages.

Now it's the boys' turn to complain about the girls, whose ears flap the single word "shopping" over and over. They are interrupted when a guy comes to their table and talks not with his ears – but with his nose. "Sorry, we don't speak French," replies one of our heroes. When the Frenchman has wandered off, the taller of the three friends adds: "Weirdo." Bicky: what your mouth's made for.

Cheeseburger. Only 1 €.
i'm lovin' it

shawarma republic shawarmarepublic.com
IMPROVE
SHAWARMA
REPUBLIC
United we sandwich

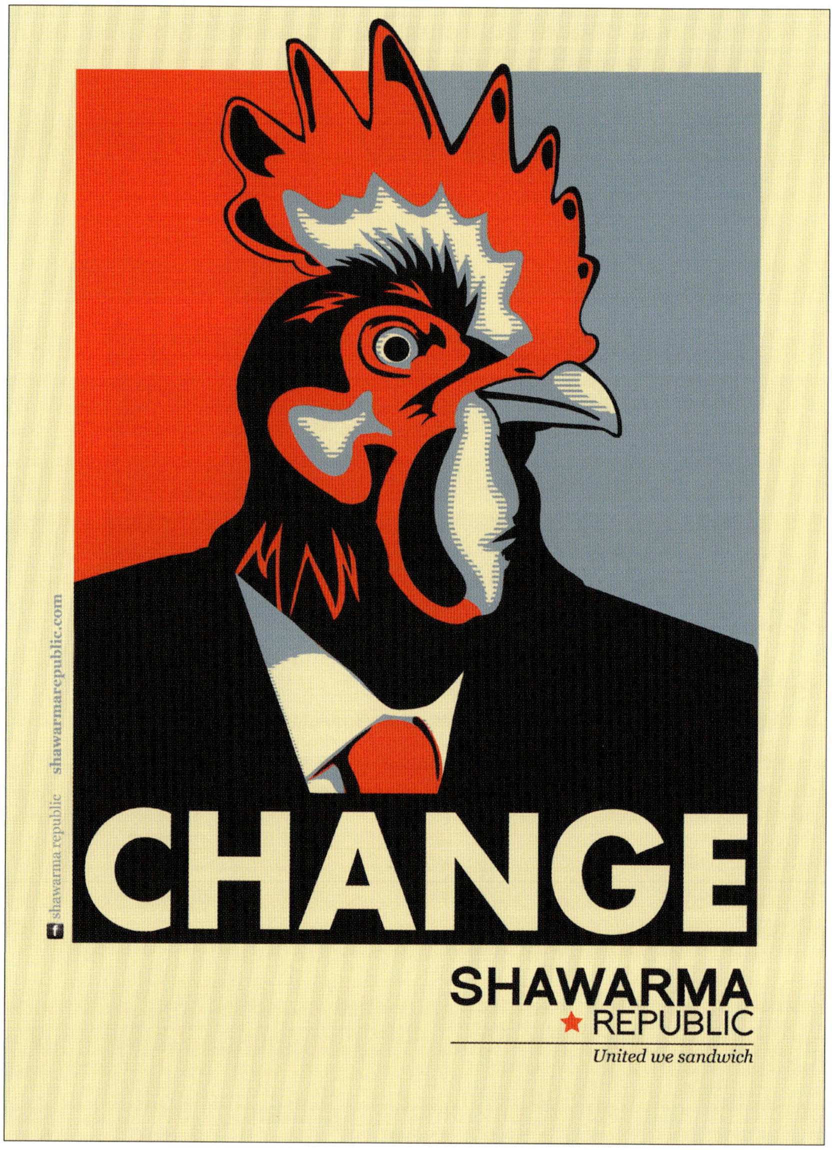
shawarma republic shawarmarepublic.com
CHANGE
SHAWARMA
REPUBLIC
United we sandwich

Agency DDB Helsinki
Creative Director Vesa Tujunen
Art Director Jukka Mannio
Illustrator Fake Graphics, Helsinki
Graphic Design Antti Salminen
Account Team Jarno Lindblom, Pia Eiro
Planner Teppo Juuvinmaa
Clients Tomi Wirtanen, Christoffer Rönnblad, Olli Tiainen
Advertiser McDonald´s, "One Euro Cheeseburger"

Agency Nineteen84, Beirut
Creative Director Said Francis
Associate CD Omar Kabbani
Copywriter Said Francis
Art Directors Omar Kabbani, Cathy Frangie
Illustrator Omar Kabbani
Managing Partner Adib Basbous
Brand Manager Rhea Kurban
Advertiser Shawarma Republic, "United we Sandwich"

GIVE IN TO
GÜ
JCDecaux

Agency	BBDO, Moscow
Creative Director	Adrian Ely
Copywriter	Dmitry Nikolaev
Art Directors	Elena Dozhdikova Nikita Voblikov
Typographer	Sergei Dementyev
Advertiser	Pedigree Jumbone, "Longer Lasting Bone"

Agency	DDB London
Creative Director	Grant Parker
Copywriters	Oli Rimoldi Sigrid Egedal
Art Directors	Sigrid Egedal Oli Rimoldi
Advertiser	Gü Puds, "Drums"

EL FLICKO
1969

THE DIP DESPERADO

Confectionery & Snacks

Agency	Abbott Mead Vickers BBDO, London
Executive CD	Paul Brazier
Creative Director	Mark Fairbanks
Copywriters	Paul Knott Prabs Wignarajah
Art Directors	Tim Vance Jeremy Tribe
Digital Producers	Suzanne Melia Steve Bond
Production	Independent Films, London
Director	Glue Society: Gary Freedman
Editors	Adam Jenkins Jeff Stevens
Producers	Jason Kemp Suzy MacGregor
Post Production	The Mill, London
Music	Human
Sound Design	Human 750mph, London
Digital Production	Acne Stockholm
Advertiser	Doritos, "Dips Desperado"

Esteban discovers that he's a crack shot with tortilla chips. He begins with a man's hat, progresses to beer bottles, and pretty soon he's winning trophies and being fêted as a celebrity. But there's a certain sadness within Esteban: he turns to drink and his wife leaves him. A down-and-out Esteban seeks redemption when a local desperado challenges him to a chip-flicking duel. But we're left in suspense with his Doritos chip frozen in mid-air above its target, a jar of salsa. Instead, we're encouraged to try our own hand at chip-flicking by visiting the Doritos site and downloading the game.

WHEN
YOU
WANT TO
CELEBRATE

WHEN
YOU
WANT TO
CELEBRATE

SCHOOL BUS
Celebrations
WHEN
YOU
WANT TO
CELEBRATE

Agency CLM BBDO, Paris
Creative Directors Jean-Francois Sacco, Gilles Fichteberg
Copywriter Julien Perrard
Art Director Lucie Vallotton
Photography Clive Stewart
Art Buying Sylvie Etchemaite
Advertiser Celebrations, "Your Own Celebration"

Mars
get back on track

MIKADO EVEN IF YOU SHOULDN'T

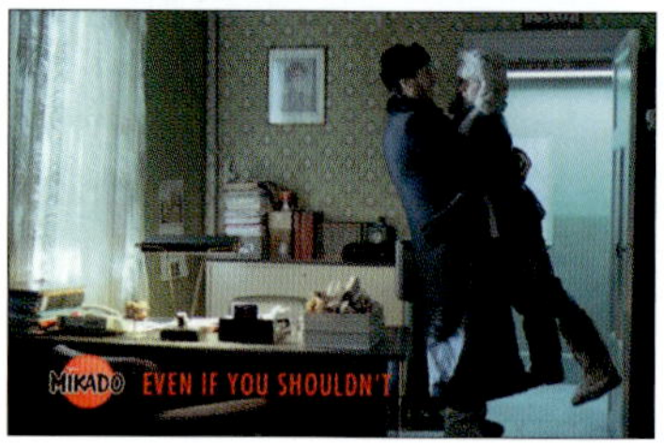
MIKADO EVEN IF YOU SHOULDN'T

Agency CLM BBDO, Paris
Creative Directors Jean-Francois Sacco, Gilles Fichteberg
Copywriter Julien Perrard
Art Director Lucie Vallotton
Photography Thomas Czarnecki
Art Buying Sylvie Etchemaite, Dominique Mornet, Corinne Tozy
Advertiser Mars Bar, "Get Back on Track"

Agency BETC Euro RSCG, Paris
Creative Directors Stéphane Xiberras, Marie-Laure Billette
Copywriter Valérie Chidlovsky
Art Director Agnès Cavard
Production Quad, Paris, Wizz, Paris
Director Niel Harris
Producer David Green
Advertiser Mikado, "Even if You Shouldn't"

We're at an auction house, where for some reason the auctioneer is asking for bids for a "magnificent musk ox." An uninterested spectator takes out his packet of Mikados and selects one, looking at it with relish. The auctioneer spots the gesture and says: "Sold to the gentleman in tweed!" The man's wife is furious, but he shrugs. Then they have to get the ox home. It's a bit of a squeeze in the car. Mikado: even though you shouldn't.

A business meeting draws to an end. "Just one more thing," says the boss, "who's up for the new position in Siberia?" A distracted employee selects a Mikado and gazes at it happily. His boss spots the slender stick. "Tom! Excellent! Get him something furry!" A furry hat and boots appear in front of Tom. Next we see him being embraced by a strapping Siberian. Occasionally, try to resist Mikado.

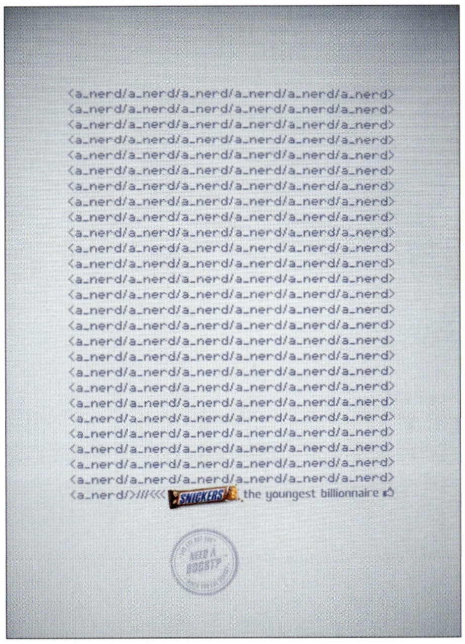
<a_nerd/a_nerd/a_nerd/a_nerd/a_nerd/a_nerd>
<a_nerd/>///<<< SNICKERS the youngest billionaire
NEED A BOOST?

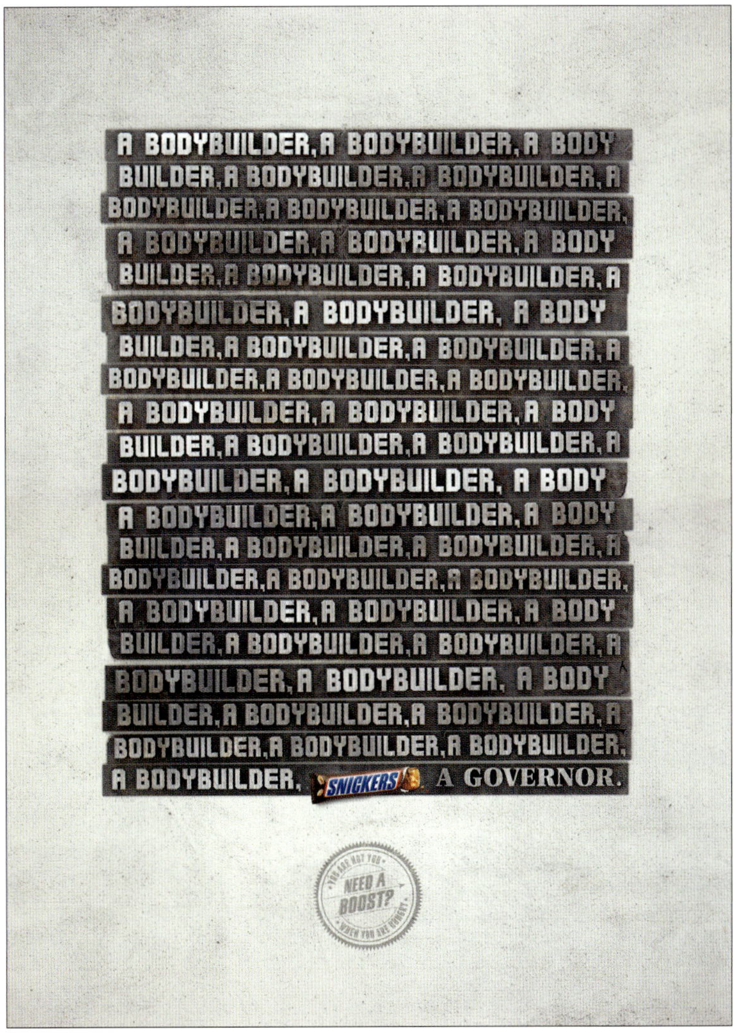
A BODYBUILDER, A BODYBUILDER, A BODY
BUILDER, A BODYBUILDER, A BODYBUILDER, A
BODYBUILDER, A BODYBUILDER, A BODYBUILDER,
A BODYBUILDER, SNICKERS A GOVERNOR.
YOU ARE NOT YOU
NEED A BOOST?
WHEN YOU ARE HUNGRY

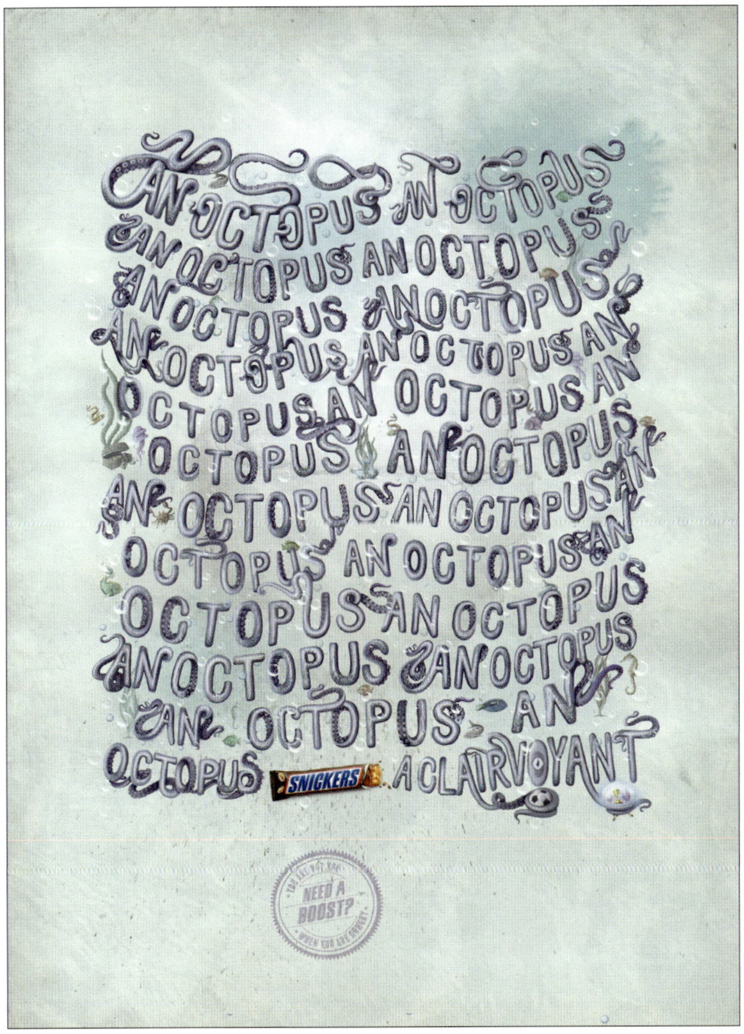
AN OCTOPUS AN OCTOPUS
OCTOPUS SNICKERS A CLAIRVOYANT
NEED A BOOST?

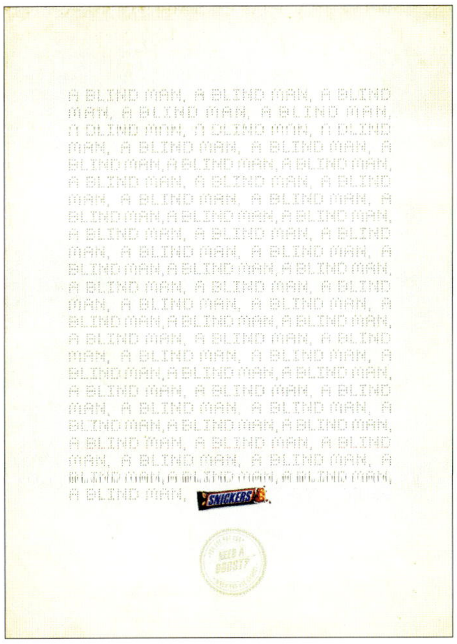
A BLIND MAN, A BLIND MAN, A BLIND
A BLIND MAN, SNICKERS

Agency	CLM BBDO, Paris
Creative Directors	Jean-Francois Sacco Gilles Fichteberg
Copywriter	Vincent Cusenier
Art Director	Victor Mutel
Illustrator	Am I Collective
Typographer	Am I Collective
Art Buying	Sylvie Etchemaite Isabelle Darmendrail
Advertiser	Snickers, "Metamorphosis"

WAY OUT

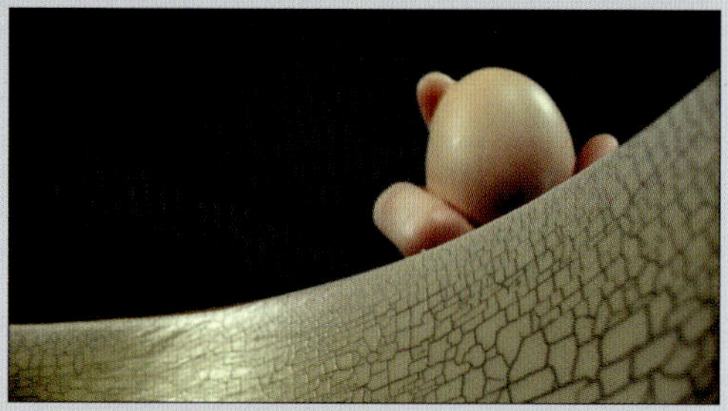

LURPAK
BUTTER
GOOD FOOD DESERVES LURPAK

Dairy Products

Agency	Wieden+Kennedy, London
Creative Directors	Tony Davidson Kim Papworth
Production	Stink, London
Director	Martin Krejci
Producers	Louise Gagen Anna Smith
Advertiser	Lurpak, "Kitchen Odyssey"

"Post-work," says narrator Rutger Hauer, as a man gazes at the contents of a fridge: a couple of eggs and a ready meal. "Tis the hungry man's witching hour, and a dinner in a box is calling. Think: what would the French do?" Suddenly inspired, the man grabs the eggs, cracks them into a bowl and whips up the perfect omelette, with a knob of Lurpak butter and some grated cheese. All this is captured in dramatic close-ups. The man sits down to his meal, pleased with himself. "Bon appétit, intrepid fridge forager." Good food deserves Lurpak.

Insanely overfilled with stuff
The New Magnum Temptation Chocolate

Preposterously overfilled with stuff
The New Magnum Temptation Orange

Ridiculously overfilled with stuff
The New Magnum Temptation Fruit

Agency	Lola, Madrid
Creative Director	Pablo Monzón
Copywriters	Pablo Monzón Martín Feijóo
Art Directors	Gustavo Marioni Esteban Franco
Photography	Mike Diver Pedro Aguilar
Advertiser	Magnum Ice Cream, “Magnum Art”

Пуск
You will lick your fingers!

DO NOT RUN
REAL!
ICECREAM

REAL!
ICECREAM
Mars

Agency	TBWA\Central Asia & Caucasus, Almaty
Creative Director	Juan Pablo Valencia
Copywriter	Juan Pablo Valencia
Art Director	Juan Pablo Valencia
Photography	Bside
Digital Artwork	Bside
Advertiser	Pusk Cheese Spread, "Wrinkled Finger"

Agency	CLM BBDO, Paris
Creative Directors	Jean-Francois Sacco Gilles Fichteberg
Copywriter	Jamie Standen
Art Director	Mark Forgan
Photography	Achim Lippoth
Art Buying	Sylvie Etchemaite
Advertiser	Mars Ice Creams, "Snickers" & "Mars"

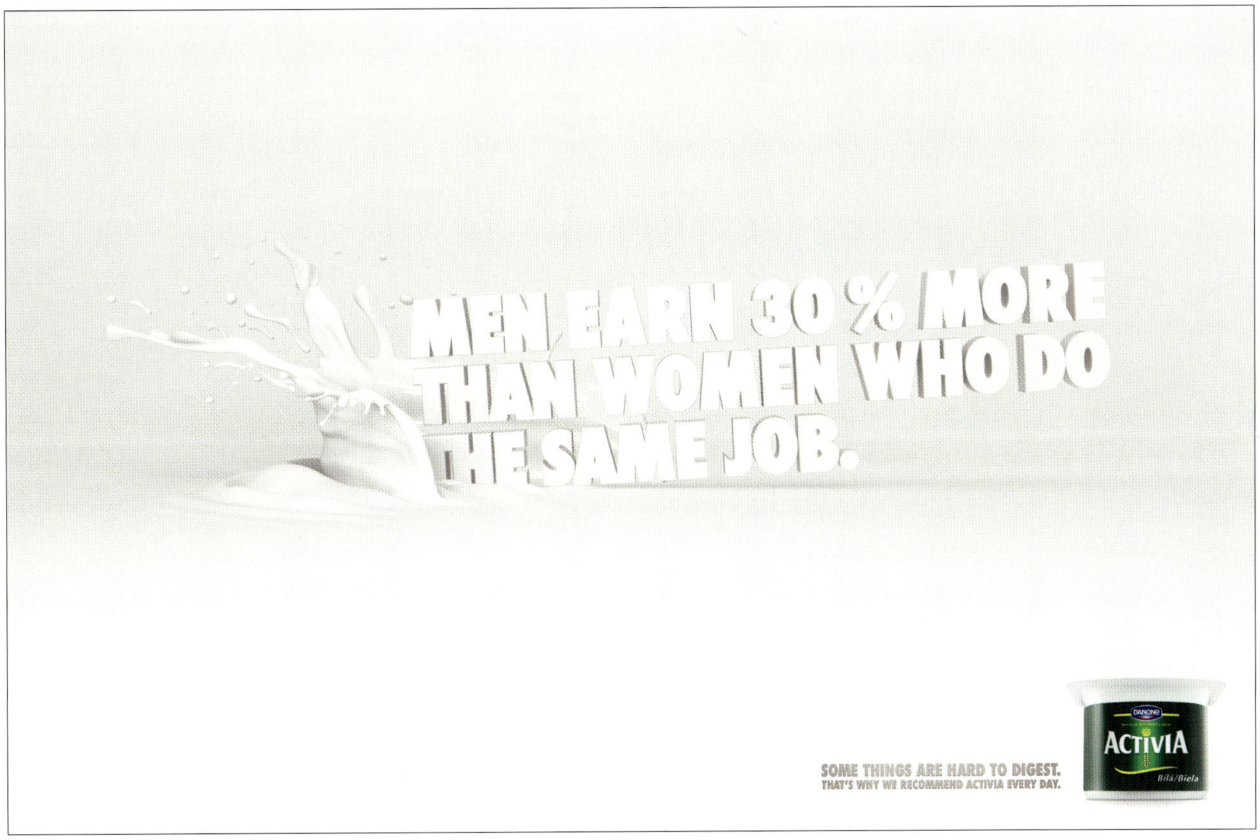
MEN EARN 30 % MORE THAN WOMEN WHO DO THE SAME JOB.
SOME THINGS ARE HARD TO DIGEST.
THAT'S WHY WE RECOMMEND ACTIVIA EVERY DAY.
DANONE
ACTIVIA
Bílá/Biela

WOMEN LEAD 65 % OF ALL FAMILIES, BUT ONLY 3 % OF COMPANIES.
SOME THINGS ARE HARD TO DIGEST.
THAT'S WHY WE RECOMMEND ACTIVIA EVERY DAY.
DANONE
ACTIVIA
Bílá/Biela

Agency	Young & Rubicam, Prague
Executive CD	Jaime Mandelbaum
Creative Director	Jitka Bret Srbova
Copywriter	Jitka Bret Srbova
Art Directors	Jaime Mandelbaum Marco Antonio do Nascimento
Post Production	Furia, Barcelona
3D	Marek Motalik
Advertiser	Activia, "Hard to Digest Facts"

TRADE MARK
Heineken®
open your world
facebook.com/heineken

Alcoholic Drinks

Agency Wieden+Kennedy, Amsterdam
Executive CDs Mark Bernath, Eric Quennoy
Creative Directors Mark Bernath, Eric Quennoy
Copywriters Roger Hoard, Carlo Cavallone
Art Directors Alvaro Sotomayor
Production Sonny, London
Head of Production Erik Verheijen
Director Fredrik Bond
Producer Tony Stearns
Account Team Clay Mills, Jasmina Krnjetin
Planning Director Martin Weigel
Post Production The Mill, London
Global Brand Director Cyril Charzat
Global Comm. Mgr. Sandrine Huijgen
Advertiser Heineken, Open Your World Campaign, "The Entrance"

A bearded young man arrives at an embassy party, where his popularity prevents him from impolitely grabbing the first bottle of Heineken that comes to hand. He first returns a general's missing glass eye, hinting at previous adventures. Then he charms a host of guests, including the gorgeous wife of an ambassador, a gun-slinging Texan who turns out to be a pal, and a kung fu champ. He winds up on stage playing flute with the cool band, The Asteroids Galaxy Tour. And then, finally, he can take a sip of Heineken.

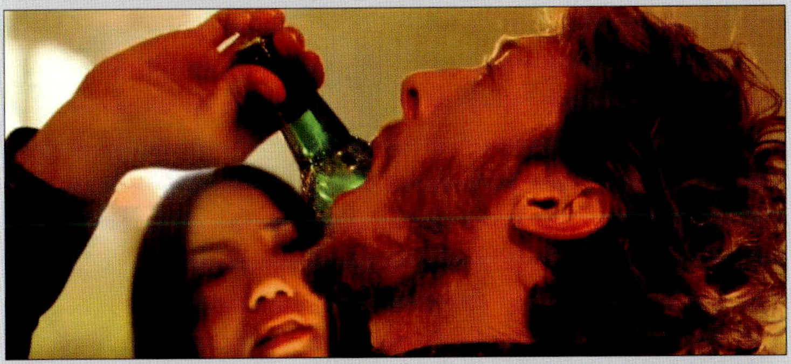

TRADE MARK
Heineken®
open your world
facebook.com/heineken

Agency	Wieden+Kennedy, Amsterdam
Executive CD	Mark Bernath Eric Quennoy
Creative Directors	Mark Bernath Eric Quennoy
Copywriter	Roger Hoard
Art Director	Alvaro Sotomayor
Production	Sonny, London
Director	Fredrik Bond
Head of Production	Erik Verheijen
Producers	Helen Kenny Alicia Bernard
Agency Producer	Tony Stearns
Associate Producer	Niko Koot
Account Team	Clay Mills Jasmina Krnjetin Dan Colgan
Post Production	The Mill, London
Global Brand Director	Cyril Charzat
Global Comm. Mgr.	Sandrine Huijgen
Advertiser	Heineken, Open Your World Campaign, "The Date"

Our cooler-than-cool Heineken hero takes a girl on…not just any date. First he whisks her into the kitchen, where he helps create their meal. Next he encourages eels in a tank to leap in the air for her. The date takes on a surreal tinge as the couple meet a magician, are mobbed by showgirls and chased by a Chinese dragon. Finally, they arrive on the dance floor and shimmy to the exotic music before taking their seats. A clink of Heineken bottles sets the seal on a memorable evening that's only just begun.

GUINNESS

SOME ARE MADE OF MORE
drinkaware.co.uk for the facts

SOME ARE MADE OF MORE
drinkaware.co.uk for the facts

Alcoholic Drinks

Agency	Abbott Mead Vickers BBDO, London
Executive CD	Paul Brazier
Creative Director	Paul Brazier
Production	Infinity, London
Director	Tom Hooper
Producers	Molly Pope Yvonne Chalkley
Editors	Paul Watts Bruce Townsend
D.O.P.	Ben Smithard
Advertiser	Guinness, "Made of More"

An army arrives on a rain-lashed hillside, led by a bare-chested warrior holding a black flag. The opposing army carry red flags. They throw their shields and swords to the ground. Both sides meet in hand-to-hand combat, scrabbling in the mud and the downpour. The black flag keeps changing hands. Finally, the hero wrenches the flag from an enemy, uses it to vault over his opponents, and plants it in the ground on their territory. We realise that this whole epic is a metaphor for international rugby, as sponsored by Guinness. Only one nation will be "made of more".

Agency	Abbott Mead Vickers BBDO, London
Executive CD	Paul Brazier
Creatives	Paul Brazier Thiago de Moraes
Illustrator	Thiago de Moraes
Head of Design	Hugh Tarpey
Designer	Thiago de Moraes
Final Artwork	Mark Deamer
Advertiser	Guinness, "Made of More"

AMUNDSEN
Six times distilled.

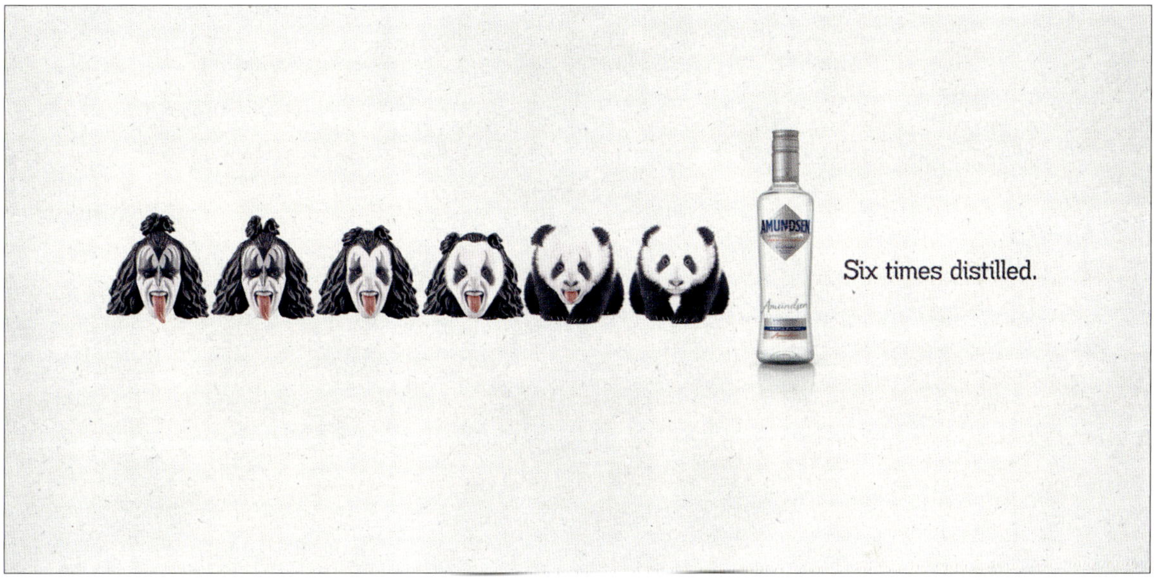
AMUNDSEN
Six times distilled.

Agency Ogilvy, Prague
Creative Directors Tomáš Belko, Will Rust
Copywriter Martin Demartini
Art Director Dmitri Lebedev
Advertiser Amundsen Vodka, “Stalinclaus” & “Kisspanda”

Agency Wieden+Kennedy, Amsterdam
Executive CDs Eric Quennoy, Mark Bernath
Copywriter Zach Watkins
Art Director Craig Williams
Production Stink, London
Director Martin Krejci
Producer Richard Fenton
Agency Producer Jaime Tan
Head of Production Erik Verheijen
Advertiser Heineken, “UCL Opera House”

What if some soccer matches are so dramatic that, to fans, they’re like an opera? That’s the thinking behind this scene, in which Clarence Seedorf prepares to boot a ball towards goalkeeper Gianluigi Buffon in the setting of a magnificent opera house. A host of angels watch the scene. Angels also offer bottles of Heineken to the smartly dressed spectators: Rene Adler, Patrick Vieira and Ruud Van Nistelroy. The ball sails towards its goal, the angelic voices soar…but we’re left in suspense.

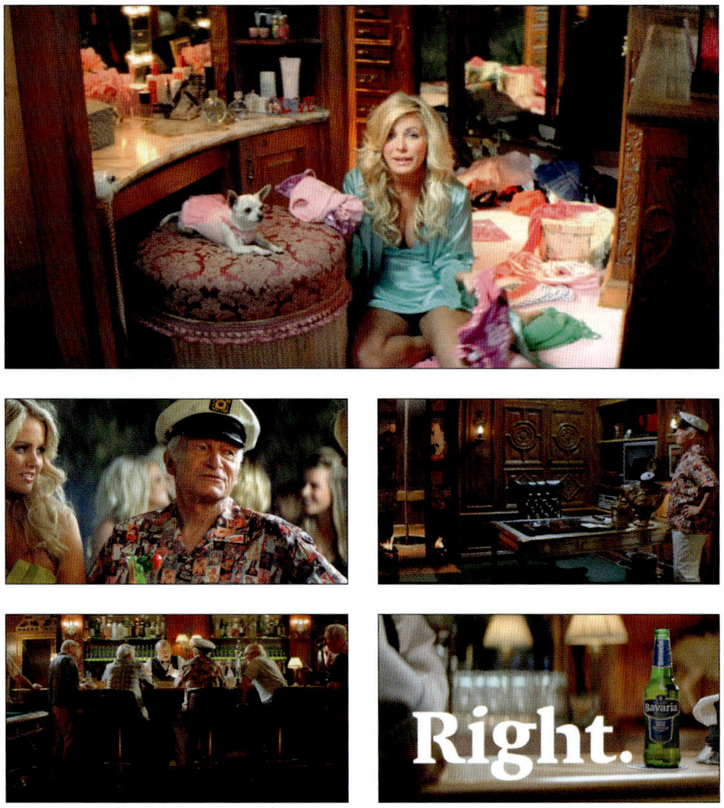
Right.
Bavaria

Agency	Selmore, Amsterdam
Creative Directors	Poppe Van Pelt Diederick Hillenius
Copywriter	Ard Brunnekreef
Art Director	Tibor Van Ginkel
Production	Bonkers, Amsterdam
Director	Jonathan Herman
Producers	Saskia Kok Jan Jinek Marga Bierema Richard H. Coll
Acct. Supervisor	Olivier Koning
Clients	Peer Swinkels Frenkel Denie Niels Oudega Mathieu Veldhuijzen
Account Team	Vincent Breedveld Marieke Foppen
Post Production	Hectic Electric, Amsterdam
Editor	Martin Heijgelaar
D.O.P.	Glynn Speeckeart
Advertiser	Bavaria Premium Beer, "Hugh Hefner"

At the Playboy Mansion, Hugh Hefner reads the newspaper in bed as two "bunnies" pillow fight. He looks bored. Also by a half-naked blonde's complaint that her tiny dog doesn't "know what to wear". A bouncy blonde tennis match leaves him unmoved. And he looks with disdain at a cocktail handed to him during a pool party. Finally, he opens an escape hatch in his study and slides down a pole into a refreshingly masculine bar, where he's greeted by the old-time barman and handed a bottle of straightforward Bavaria beer. It's just "right".

EVEREST 1953
Carlsberg
Carlsberg

THE SOCIAL NETWORK OF BULGARIA SINCE 1882

Agency	Fold7, London
Creative Director	Ryan Newey
Copywriters	Ryan Newey John Yorke
Art Directors	John Yorke Ryan Newey
Production	Rattling Stick, London
Director	Daniel Kleinman
Producer	Sam Balderstone
Advertiser	Carlsberg, "Everest"

Mount Everest, 1953. After a gruelling ascent, a man finally makes it to the peak. Back at base camp, his colleagues wait anxiously. The man hurries to return, charging down the slopes with a long cord trailing behind him and even completing part of the journey by sliding on a tray. When he finally arrives, we see that he's not planted a flag at the top of the mountain, but a TV aerial, so they can all watch the big match. That calls for a Carlsberg! Unfortunately, a gust of wind knocks over the aerial. The guys look at the climber apologetically…

Agency	Noble Graphics, Sofia
Creative Directors	Chavdar Kenarov Marsel Levi
Copywriter	Victor Vidas
Art Directors	Miroslav Krustev Mihail Naydenov
Director	Stoyan Radev
Producers	Eddie Schwartz Vera Svarc
Advertiser	Shumensko Beer, "The Bulgarian Social Network"

This silent movie shows us what "social networking" was like in Bulgaria in the good old days. Outside a bar, four people join the group "I love Shumensko" by raising glasses of the beer. A woman gives her handkerchief to a man to "friend" him. 14 people "comment" on Miss Mimi's new dress. 7 people "change their profiles" during a punch-up. And two men "write on a wall" – by peeing on it. 5 people join the cause "Unification of Bulgaria". Millions "like" that, giving it a thumbs up. Shumensko: the social network of Bulgaria since 1882.

Corvus
Corvus
BORNOVA
MİSKET
2,02€

Corvus
Corvus
CORPUS
2006
11,86€

Corvus
VINEYARDS
PASSITO
3,06€

Agency	Big, Istanbul
Creative Directors	Kagan Kucuk Kemal Hayit
Copywriter	Cahit Turan
Art Director	Kemal Hayit
Photography	Nihal Gunduz
Final Artwork	Bugra Atici
Advertiser	Corvus Wine

2000
CALORIES
2000 calories
Contrex
My slimming partner

Agency	Marcel, Paris
Creative Director	Anne de Maupeou
Copywriter	Martin Rocaboy
Art Director	Souen Le Van
Production	Wanda Productions, Paris
Director	Xavier Mairesse
Producers	Claude Fayolle WAM, Paris: Timothe Rosenberg Cleo Ferenczi
Account Team	Michel Kowalski Audrey Tato Anne Dimier-Vallet Guillaume Le Gorrec
Planning	Anne Dimier-Vallet Guillaume Le Gorrec
Clients	Emmanuel Manichon Marie-Cecile Pelle Lancien Stephanie Perrin
Editor	Sam Danesi
Cameraman	Nicolas Karakatsanis
Sound Prod.	Clemens Hourriere Boris Nicou Mathieu Sibony
Post Production	Sandra Haize Olivier Glandais
Advertiser	Contrex, "Contrexperience"

Evening strollers – mostly women – are drawn to a line of pink exercise bikes in front of a large building. As they start to pedal, they see that the bikes trigger an array of pink fairy lights. As if by magic, the lights turn into an animated male stripper on the façade of the building: the harder they pedal, the more clothes he removes. Finally, having removed his last item of clothing, he appears with an illuminated sign that congratulates them for burning 2000 calories. With Contrex mineral water, slimming doesn't have to be boring.

Schweppes
Fruits...well kind of.

Schweppes
Fruits...well kind of.

TAXI
Schweppes
Lemon
Fruits...well kind of.

Agency	Fred & Farid, Paris
CDs & Copywriters	Fred Raillard Farid Mokart
Art Directors	Fred Raillard Farid Mokart Feng Huang
Photography	David LaChapelle
Clients	Hugues Pietrini Stanislas de Parcevaux
Account Manager	Nathalie Chopra
Art Buying	Carmela Guiragossian
Advertiser	Schweppes, “Uma”

Drink Different

Agency	ACW Grey, Tel Aviv
CCO	Tal Riven
Creative Director	Ida Markovits
Copywriter	Shani Gershi
Art Director	Itay Belfer
Production	Rabel, Tel Aviv
Director	Keren Hochma
Producers	Rony Rotman Meital Tzoref
Post Production	JCS, Tel Aviv
Advertiser	Schweppes, "Cannibals"

A cartoon explorer meets two cannibals. He tries to converse with them, but they reply only with the phrase: "Mooga booga." Finally he decides that they want to trade their fruit for his Schweppes. But when he takes a bite of the fruit, he keels over. Cut to a real-life recording studio, where the "cannibals" are rather posh black actors providing voice-overs. "Well that was nonsense," says one with an impeccable English accent. His pal replies: "Preposterous, if you ask me – who speaks like that?" After a refreshing Schweppes, they leave. Schweppes: drink different.

burn

12939

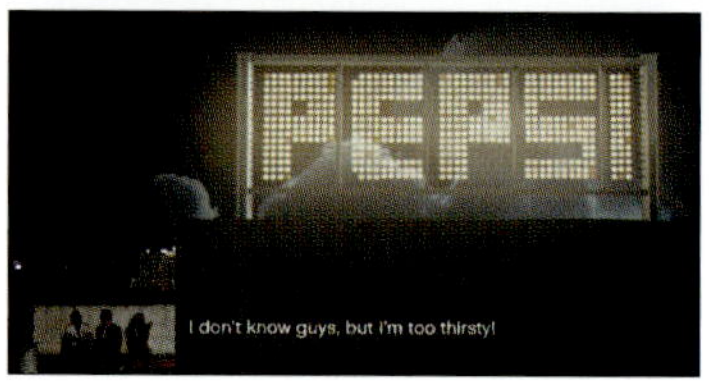
PEPSI
I don't know guys, but I'm too thirsty!

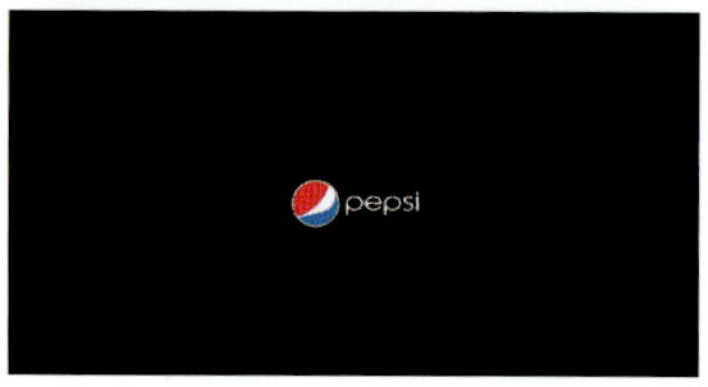
pepsi

Agency	Publicis, Milan
Creative Directors	Bruno Bertelli Cristiana Boccassini
Associate CD	Costanza Rossi
Copywriter	Michele Picci
Art Director	Marco Viganò
Production	Curios Film, Sidney
Director	Ash Bolland
Producer	Mariella Maiorano
CSD	Bela Ziemann
Client	Francesco Cibò
Editor	Fabrizio Squeo
Advertiser	Burn Energy Drink

In Buenos Aires, an apocalyptic storm is brewing. But that doesn't deter pro skateboarder Rune Glifberg and his crew. They ride the storm, accepting the savage weather and the urban landscape as a challenge to their boarding skills. Each time they perform a trick, sparks appear, their creativity blazing a trail of flame. Finally, Glifberg hurls his board into a massive twister, which catches alight. "No matter what gets thrown at you," he says, "create, inspire, stop at nothing." Burn energy drink: fuel your fire.

Agency	M&V, Valencia
Creative Directors	Víctor Suñer Marcs Pitarch
Copywriters	Víctor Suñer Marcs Pitarch
Art Director	Inma Sales
Production	Vessmedia, Valencia
Director	Víctor Suñer
Producers	Marcs Pitarch Miguel De Juan
Advertiser	Pepsi, "Numbers"

Three not-so-bright friends are hanging out on a rooftop behind a large illuminated sign. One of them says: "12939. What does that number mean?" "No idea – and what's it doing there?" says the girl. The camera pulls back and we see the number, glowing in neon. "Maybe it's a date?" says the third friend. "What are you, a historian?" mocks the girl. They agree that it doesn't make any sense. As the camera pulls back to show the other side of the sign, we see that it actually says "PEPSI". "I don't know guys," says the first friend. "But I'm too thirsty."

The world's
fastest coffee
capsule system.
DELIZIO

ON AIR
Perrier

Agency	Ruf Lanz, Zurich
Creative Directors	Danielle Lanz Markus Ruf
Copywriter	Maren Beck
Art Director	Isabelle Hauser
Photography	Chris Tribelhorn
Account Manager	Heike Rindfleisch
Client	Aurel Keller
Advertiser	Delizio Coffee System

Agency	Ogilvy France, Paris
Creative Directors	Chris Garbutt Thierry Chiumino
Copywriter	Benjamin Bregeault
Art Director	Eve Roussou
Photography	Jean-Yves Lemoigne
Final Artwork	Adrien Bénard
3D	Mathematic Studio, Paris
Art Buying	Laurence Nahmias
Acct. Supervisor	Thomas Christiaen
Advertiser	Perrier, “Studio”

evian

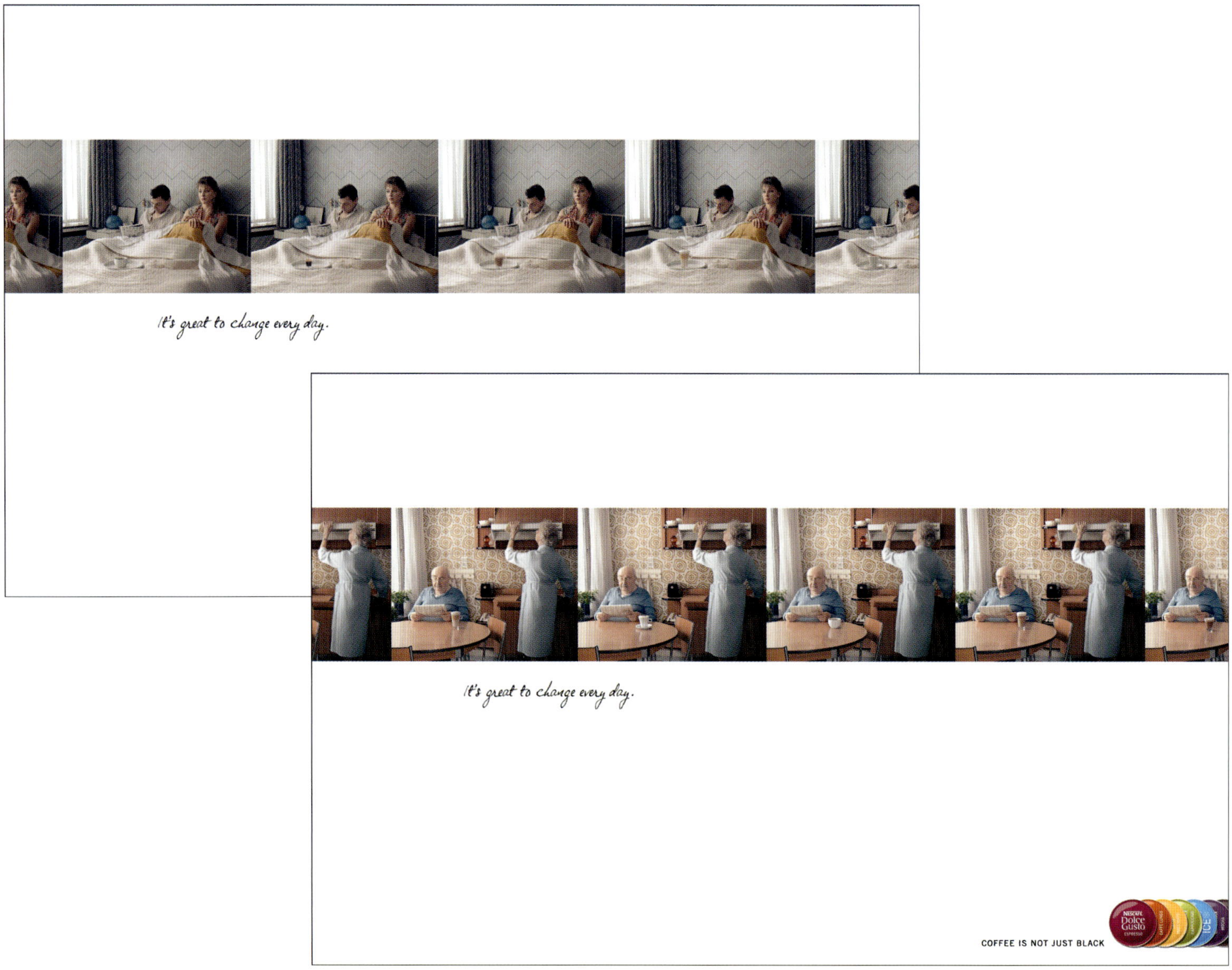
It's great to change every day.
It's great to change every day.
COFFEE IS NOT JUST BLACK

Agency BETC Euro RSCG, Paris
Creative Director Rémi Babinet
Copywriter Valérie Chidlovsky
Art Director Agnès Cavard
Production Wanda Productions, Paris
Legs, New York
Directors Geremy Jasper
Georgie Greville
Producers Fabrice Brovelli
Coumba Fall
Advertiser Evian, "Baby Inside"

The Evian babies are famous the world over as symbols of the water's purity and "youth-giving" properties. In the latest take on the idea, baby torsos printed on the t-shirts of adults come to life and dance thanks to brilliant stop-motion photography. Drink Evian and "live young".

Agency Publicis Conseil, Paris
Creative Directors Olivier Altmann
Frederic Royer
Copywriter Marie Lorgeron
Art Director Benoit Blumberger
Photography Marc Paeps
Art Buying Jean-Luc Chirio
Soone Riboud
Account Team Celine Colin
Sophie Duverne
Nathalie Bousquet
Advertiser Nescafé Dolce Gusto, "Bed" & "Kitchen"

VOLUPTUOUS ORANGE FLAVOR

VOLUPTUOUS ORANGE FLAVOR

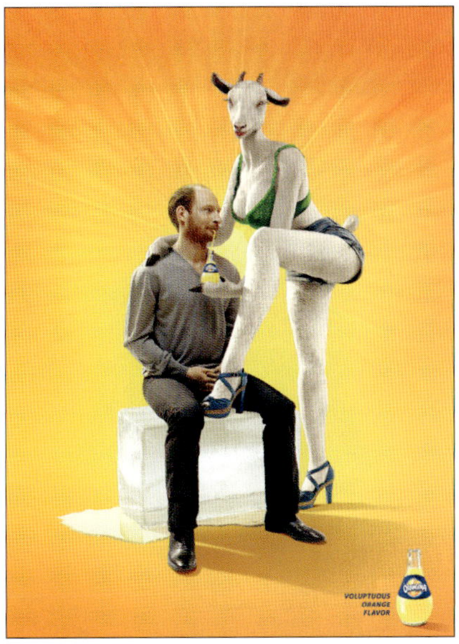
VOLUPTUOUS ORANGE FLAVOR

ENERGIE
NATURELLE
Tropicana

Agency	Fred & Farid, Paris
Creative Directors	Fred Raillard Farid Mokart
Copywriters & ADs	Fred Raillard Farid Mokart Eric Landowski
Photography	Romain Laurent
Account Team	Hugues Pietrini Stanislas de Parcevaux Florence Burtin
Advertiser	Orangina, "Couples"

Agency	DDB Paris
Executive CD	Alexandre Hervé
Creative Directors	Alexander Kalchev Siavosh Zabeti
Copywriters	Alexander Kalchev Siavosh Zabeti
Art Directors	Alexander Kalchev Siavosh Zabeti
Photography	Clemens Ascher
Advertiser	Tropicana, "Powered by Oranges"

Heathrow
International Arrivals
Heathrow
Heathrow Terminal 5
27th October 2010
Life's for Sharing
T··Mobile
youtube.com/lifesforsharing

Communication Services

Agency Saatchi & Saatchi, London
Executive CDs Paul Silburn, Kate Stanners
Copywriter Stephen Howell
Art Director Rick Dodds
Production Smuggler, London
Director Henry-Alex Rubin
Producers Ray Leakey, James Faupel
Sound Design Grand Central, London, Ben Leeves
Editors Marshall St Editors, London, Spencer Ferzst, Patric Ryan
Post Production The Mill, London
Account Team Sarah Galea, Laura Mills, Anna Mills
Business Leader Charles Pym
Music Director Shai Fishman
D.O.P. Brett Turnbull
Advertiser T-Mobile, "Welcome Back"

This ad continues T-Mobile's series of "flash mob" events. Here, an unsuspecting passenger is welcomed back to Heathrow Airport's Terminal 5 by a professional singer and an a capella accompaniment. As more passengers come through the gate, they're greeted by various singers performing appropriate hits for each arrival. Although no "real" instruments are used, the vocal imitators and singers swell into a giant chorus. Some of the arrivals turn out to be singers too – it's a great party and proof once again that advertising can be truly uplifting.

KING
DING
DONG
KONG
DON'T LET THE DOORBELL INTERRUPT YOUR MOVIE.
PAUSE AND RESTART IT FROM WHERE YOU LET OFF. TiViBU IPTV.
tivibu®

Agency	TBWA\Istanbul
Creative Directors	Ilkay Gurpinar Volkan Karakasoglu
Copywriter	Ercin Sadikoglu
Art Director	Levent Yalgin
Advertiser	Tivibu IPTV, "King Kong"

Guillaume...

Orange
Cineday
BUY ONE TICKET = GET ONE FREE

Agency	Publicis Conseil, Paris
Creative Directors	Olivier Altmann Fabrice Delacourt Olivier Desmettre
Copywriter	Patrice Lucet
Art Directors	Philippe Boucheron Antoine Dezes-Richard
Production	Partizan, Paris
Director	Antoine Bardou Jacquet
Producers	Georges Bermann Frederic Genest Pierre Marcus
Advertiser	Orange Cineday, "Hussars"

It looks exactly like a trailer for a historical action movie. Two brothers find themselves divided by the Napoleonic wars. In a cruel twist of fate, they are both in love with the same woman. The conflict drives them towards a final confrontation. Suddenly, one of them voices the question we've all been asking ourselves: who's the guy in modern dress following the hero around? "Oh, it's my buddy Fred. On Tuesday you can invite anyone to the movies, with Orange." Orange Cineday – buy one ticket, get one free.

-Hi darling

Forward your mail when you move

ADRESSÄNDRING
Swedish postal services

Agency	TBWA\Stockholm
Copywriter	Kalle Widgren
Art Director	Alexander Fredlund
Production	Adamsky, Stockholm
Director	Jesper Ganslandt
Producers	Lars Nilsson Erika Hellström
Account Team	Robert Scherin Ulrika Sörensen Marika Hedström
Post Production	Chimney Pot
Advertiser	Swedish Post, "Love Swing"

A pretty young woman answers a phone call from her mother. The mother says: "The swing you ordered arrived in the post today. Are we going to be grandparents?" For some reason, the girl goes pale at this news. "But…you can't open my mail!" she cries. "Sorry, we were so excited. Dad has already mounted it in the garden," mother continues. We see that it's actually a Love Swing sex toy. "Did it come with diapers? Big ones?" the mother asks innocently. To get your mail forwarded when you move, contact Swedish Postal Services.

Hairdresser?

1888
Welcome!
The fast telephone directory

Agency	Kitchen Leo Burnett, Oslo
Copywriter	Thomas Askim
Art Director	Eirik Stensrud
Production	Social Club, Stockholm
Director	Lukas Hammar
Producer	Caroline Werring Otnes
Acct. Director	Bjørn Polmar
Advertiser	1888 Telephone Directory, "The Brat - Hair"

A small boy glues blonde hair to a side table. As the camera pulls back, we see that not only is the hair human, but it belongs to a woman who is napping on the sofa, possibly the boy's mother. The boy leaves the room and returns with a pair of cymbals. He pauses – then clashes them together. We don't see what happens, but we hear the scream. Need a hairdresser? Get the number by sending an SMS to 1888 Welcome, the fast telephone directory.

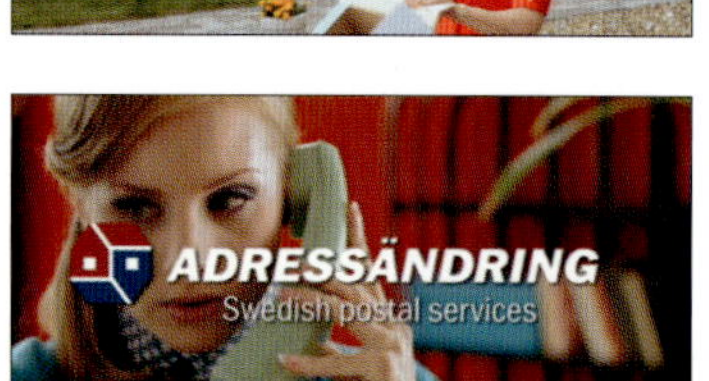

Don't keep it to yourself
Spread your knowledge to millions on Wikipedia. Become an author at wikipedia.org
Wikipedia
10
years of contributions by people like you

Hotel La Famille
The best location for a family holiday. Quiet, peaceful four-star hotel with plenty of attractions nearby to suit all members of the family. Whether you want to go shopping or take in a show, it's right on your doorstep. Our friendly staff are here to fulfill your every wish.
HOTEL LA FAMILLE
SeX
XXX GIRLS
Google maps
Know before you go

Agency	Jandl, Bratislava
Creative Director	Pavel Fuksa
Copywriter	Adam Rovný
Art Directors	Pavel Fuksa Matúš Nemčík
Photography	Miro Minarových
Advertiser	Wikipedia, "Don't Keep it to Yourself"

Agency	BBDO, Moscow
Creative Director	Adrian Ely
Copywriter	Daria Artamonova
Art Directors	Adrian Ely Victor Zerzele
Photography	Jonathan May
Final Artwork	James Lucas
Advertiser	Google Street View, "Sexshop"

Life's for Sharing
T · · Mobile
go in store or visit
t-mobile.co.uk/youfix

Agency	Saatchi & Saatchi, London	
Executive CDs	Paul Silburn Kate Stanners	
Copywriters	Stephen Howell Piers O'Kelly	
Art Directors	Rick Dodds Liam Scott	
Production	Smuggler, London	
Director	Jamie Rafn	
Producers	Ray Leakey James Faupel	
Editors	John Mayes Guy Savin	
Post Production	The Mill, London	
Sound Design	Ben Leeves	
Account Director	Laura Mills	
Planner	Tom Gibson	
Business Leader	Charles Pym	
D.O.P.	Brett Turnbull	
Advertiser	T-Mobile, "Parking Ticket"	

Traffic wardens are behaving even more sadistically than usual. They slap fines on cars everywhere, even when the driver has just left the vehicle for five seconds to buy a ticket. Or when the drivers arrive five minutes before the ticket expires. The drivers are outraged, but the wardens don't care. "If you've got an issue, have a tissue," says one. It's all a practical joke, of course. The "fines" are actually ten pound notes. The candid camera trick illustrates T-Mobile's flexible payment plan: because no-one likes nasty surprises.

20:37
Where are you?
At the movies.
What's on?

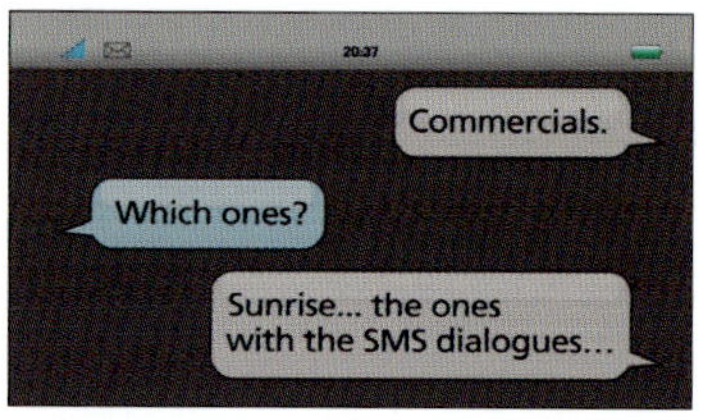
Commercials.
Which ones?
Sunrise... the ones with the SMS dialogues...

They're really funny...
Not this one...so far.
Wait... there'll be a funny punchline.

Not this one...so far.
Wait... there'll be a funny punchline.
Nope.

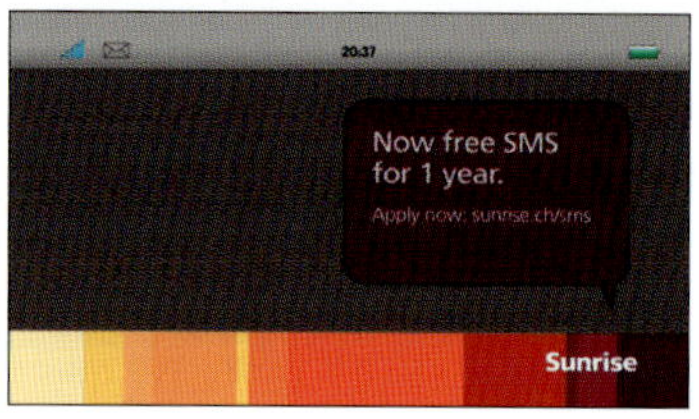
Now free SMS for 1 year.
Sunrise

JUDIT
JUDIT
She is a home loving meat farmer from Småland

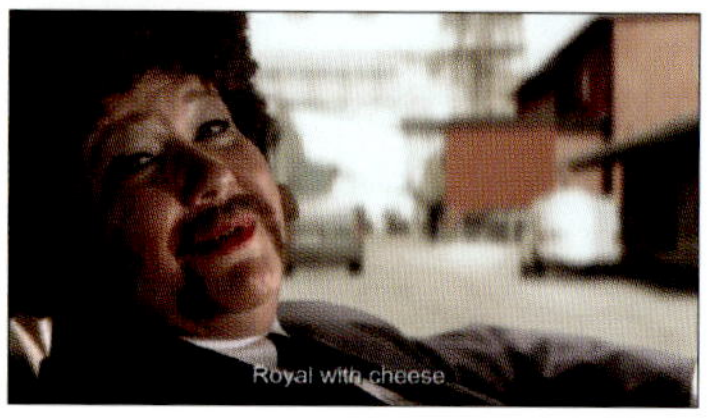
Royal with cheese

com hem

Communication Services

Agency	Spillmann/Felser/ Leo Burnett, Zurich
Creative Directors	Martin Spillmann Peter Brönnimann
Copywriters	Peter Brönnimann Diana Rossi
Art Directors	Martin Spillmann Friederike Coninx
Production	Ultra Images, Zurich
Producer	Suzana Kovacevic
Advertiser	Sunrise Telecommunication, "At the Movies"

Sunrise continues its series of ads featuring SMS dialogues with this exchange: "Where are you?" "At the movies." "What's on?" "Commercials." "Which ones?" "Sunrise… the ones with the SMS dialogues." "They're really funny." "Not this one…so far." "Wait… there'll be a funny punchline." (Long pause.) "Nope." But at least Sunrise is now offering free SMS for a year.

Agency	King, Stockholm
Creative Director	Frank Hollingworth
Copywriter	Hedvig Hagwall Bruckner
Art Directors	Lotta Ågerup Philip Åstmar
Production	Traktor The Producers
Directors	Mats Lindberg Erik Nilsson
Producer	Anders Gernandt
Advertiser	Com Hem, "On Demand"

Ads for Swedish pay TV provider Com Hem always feature two larger than life characters called Judit and Judit, who normally sit behind a reception desk gossiping. But here they appear in the kind of shows you can watch on demand via Com Hem: ballroom dancing, Disney cartoons, talent shows, an Ingmar Bergman film, sports, quiz shows, crime shows, science fiction and even a re-enacted scene from Pulp Fiction. Thousands of programs and movies, any time you want.

Now! Digital Television
right into your TV.
Do whatever you want with your
boxes, remotes and cords.
com hem

Batelco
DIRECTORY

Agency King, Stockholm
Creative Director Frank Hollingworth
Copywriter Hedvig Hagwall Bruckner
Art Director Lotta Ågerup
Photography Bsmart
Costume Designer Sahara Widoff
Advertiser Com Hem, "Digital TV Without Box"

Agency FP7/DXB, Dubai
Creative Director Fadi Yaish
Art Director Supparat Thepparat
Photography Illusion, Bangkok: Surachai Puthikulangkura
Illustrators Illusion, Bangkok: Surachai Puthikulangkura, Supachai U-Rairat
Producer Clarisse Mar Wai May
Advertiser Batelco, "Batelco Directory"

Transport & Tourism

Agency Los&Co, Oslo
Copywriter Ragnar Roksvåg
Art Director Jo Espen Johansen
Production Social Club, Stockholm
Directors Jesper Ericstam
Giulio Musi Wennergren
Advertiser Nettbuss,
"Whoever You Are"

This epic film celebrates the disparate lives of the people who take Nettbuss every day. Five main characters are revealed: a naughty schoolboy running from bullies, a Goth girl on her way to a family wedding, a married man who's carrying on a gay affair, and a young man and a kindergarten teacher who fall in lust when they accidentally bump heads across the aisle. Their interwoven stories are all told with sympathy and tenderness. Nettbuss – whoever you are, wherever you're going - we drive for you.

SJ
A smarter way to travel.

SJ
A smarter way to travel.

SJ
A smarter way to travel.

Agency	King, Stockholm
Creative Director	Frank Hollingworth
Copywriters	Hedvig Hagwall Bruckner Jens Englund
Art Director	Lotta Ågerup
Photography	Petrus Olsson
Advertiser	SJ (Swedish Rail), "A Smarter Way to Travel"

DB GERMAN RAIL
www.bahn.de

Agency	Ogilvy, Frankfurt
CCO	Stephan Vogel
Creative Director	Matthias Storath
Copywriter	Bent Kroggel
Art Directors	Bent Kroggel Catrin Farrenschon
Production	Jo!Schmid, Berlin
Director	Martin Schmid
Producers	Michael Schmid Jennifer Porst Michael Heinemeyer
Acct. Supervisor	Martina Huschka
Cinematographer	Peter Meyer
Sound Design	FunDeMental Studios
Clients	Ulrich Klenke Gabriele Handel-Jung Peter Kraemer
Advertiser	Deutsche Bahn (German Rail), "Back Seat Holiday"

A couple of kids are bored in the backseat of the car. The older boy has drawn a picture of the family, but the parents' faces are blank. That's because he can only see the back of their heads. "Tell me," he asks his younger brother. "Do you remember what they look like from the front?" "Don't ask me: you've known them longer than I have." Cut to the same journey on the train. This time, the boys are facing their parents – there is interaction and fun. A car holiday is no holiday. Take German Rail.

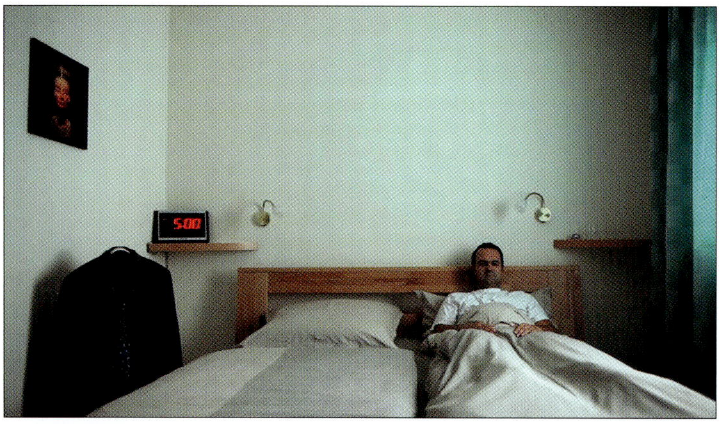

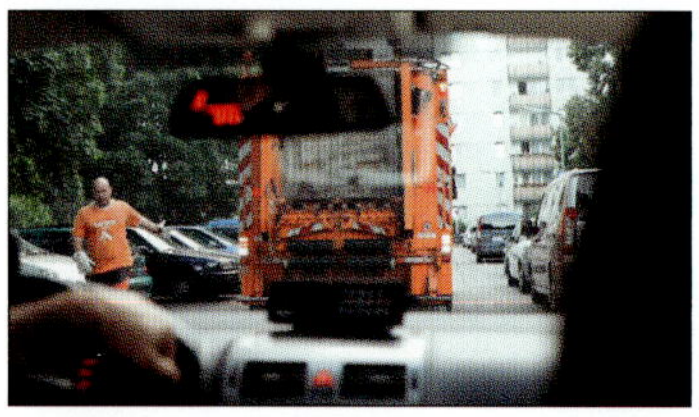

DB GERMAN RAIL

Guys, our Boss is coming!

Agency	Ogilvy, Frankfurt
CCO	Stephan Vogel
Copywriters	Bent Kroggel Daniel de Leuw
Art Directors	Bent Kroggel Catrin Farrenschon
Production	Doity Produktion, Berlin
Director	Martin Schmid
Producers	Sascha Pollack Michael Heinemeyer Julia Staerkel
Advertiser	Deutsche Bahn, "Travel Symphony"

5am. A business traveller in a bland hotel room. His alarm clock goes off. Then a car alarm. Now he's in a taxi. Beeps and crackly voices from the radio. The beep of the car reversing. The louder beep of a refuse truck reversing. The whine of a security scan at the airport. Beeping telephones on the plane. His beeping rental car. A beeping, squeaking car-park barrier. The man's stress is mounting to bursting point. But suddenly – silence. He's on the train. Every day there are more reasons to take German Rail.

Agency	Ogilvy, Frankfurt
CCO	Stephan Vogel
Copywriters	Bent Kroggel Daniel de Leuw
Art Directors	Bent Kroggel Catrin Farrenschon
Production	Doity Produktion, Berlin
Director	Martin Schmid
Producers	Sascha Pollack Michael Heinemeyer Julia Staerkel
Advertiser	Deutsche Bahn, "The Boss is Coming"

We see an office in debauched chaos. There's partying, drinking, flirting, even a cock fight. One of the guys glances out of the window. He exclaims: "Our boss is coming!" "So early?" says another. A cry of "He's in the elevator!!!" is the cue for them to tidy up – and quick. By the time the boss arrives, the office is a model of calm efficiency. But the boss pauses. He's spotted one of his male employees wearing fishnet stockings. The earlier you arrive, the more you notice. That's why it's best to take the train.

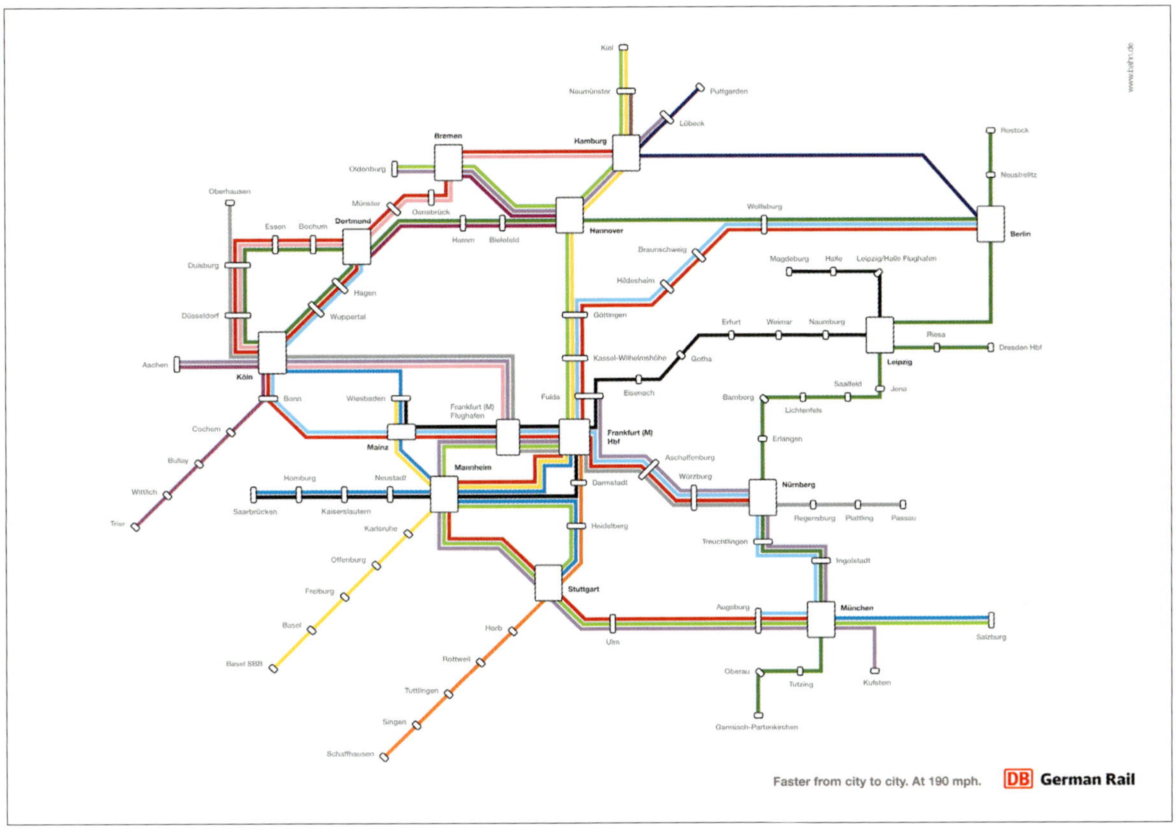
Faster from city to city. At 190 mph.
DB German Rail

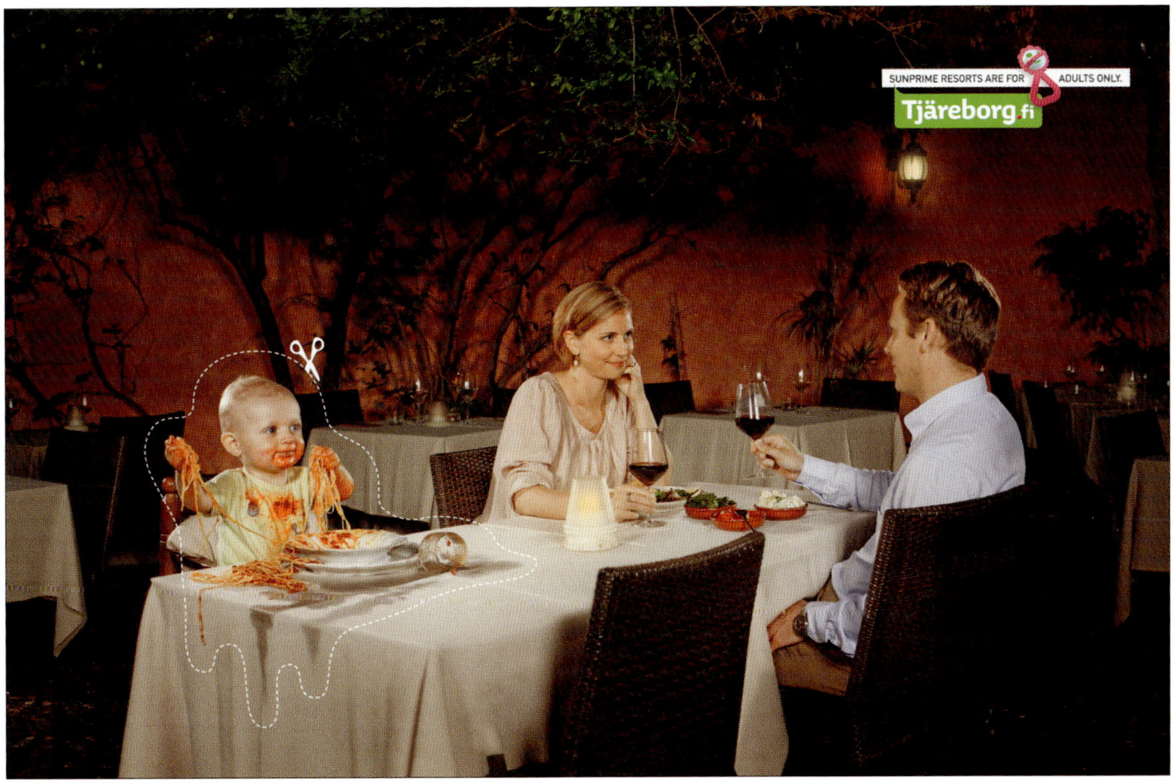
SUNPRIME RESORTS ARE FOR ADULTS ONLY.
Tjäreborg.fi

Agency	Ogilvy, Frankfurt
CCO	Stephan Vogel
Copywriter	Marcus Pfeiffer
Art Director	Daniel Schweinzer
Clients	Ulrich Klenke Gabriele Handel-Jung Gina P. Roeder
Acct. Supervisor	Martina Huschka
Advertiser	Deutsche Bahn (German Rail), "Germany is Getting Smaller"

Agency	358 Helsinki
Creative Director	Antero Jokinen
Copywriter	Taro Korhonen
Art Director	Maria Fridman
Photography	Rami Hanafi
Graphic Design	Joel Parsons
Typographer	Joel Parsons
Strategy	Milla Kokko
Client Director	Robert From
Producer	Krista Durchman
Advertiser	Tjäreborg Sunprime, "For Adults Only"

There's always a good reason to travel.

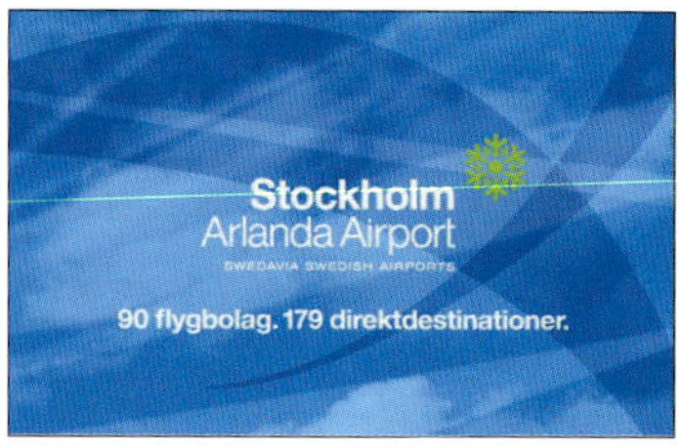
Stockholm
Arlanda Airport
SWEDAVIA SWEDISH AIRPORTS
90 flygbolag. 179 direktdestinationer.

Agency	Fältman & Malmén, Stockholm
Creative Director	Magnus Fältman
Copywriter	Viktor Olsson
Art Directors	Björn Nordfors Ellen Ström
Production	Lunatic Speed, Stockholm
Director	Calle Åstrand
Producer	Jeanette Albertsson
Photography	Aril Wretblad
Account Team	Carolina Thoors Fred Raaum
Advertiser	Stockholm Arlanda Airport, "There's Always a Good Reason to Travel"

A man is typing away in his office. Behind him, an annoying colleague reads over his shoulder, while noisily eating a banana. There's always a good reason to travel. Stockholm Arlanda Airport.

Try that in a car.

SJ
Swedish Rail. A smarter way to travel.

Try that in a car.

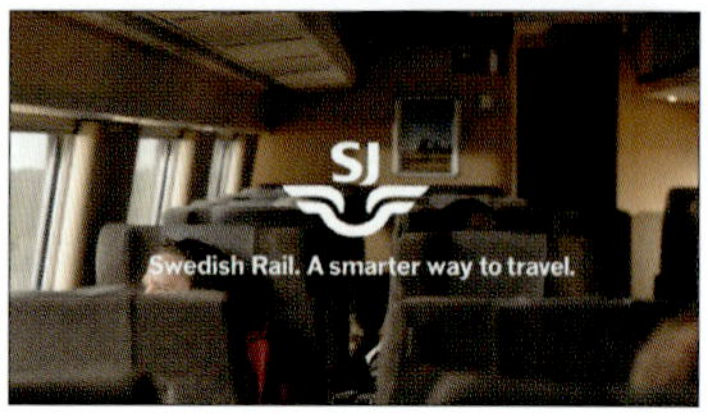
SJ
Swedish Rail. A smarter way to travel.

Agency	King, Stockholm
Creative Director	Frank Hollingworth
Copywriters	Hedvig Hagwall Bruckner Jens Englund
Art Director	Lotta Ågerup
Production	Traktor
Director	Mats Lindberg
Producer	Anders Gernandt
Advertiser	SJ (Swedish Rail), "A Smarter Way to Travel"

A couple are sitting on the train, both thinking dreamily about something. Almost by chance, they turn to look at one another, smiling tenderly. Perhaps they were both thinking about the same thing? They exchange a loving kiss. Try that in a car. Swedish Rail. A smarter way to travel.

A father and son are on the train. The son holds up his hand with a smile that has a slight challenge in it. "OK," says the dad. They begin to arm wrestle. The son is winning…no, now it's the dad…but wait, the son is using both hands. Finally dad prevails, with great effort. They burst out laughing. A perfect father and son bonding moment. Try that in a car. Swedish Rail. A smarter way to travel.

t
Go for next
to nothing.
99€
transavia.com

t
Go for next
to nothing.
Morocco
85€
transavia.com

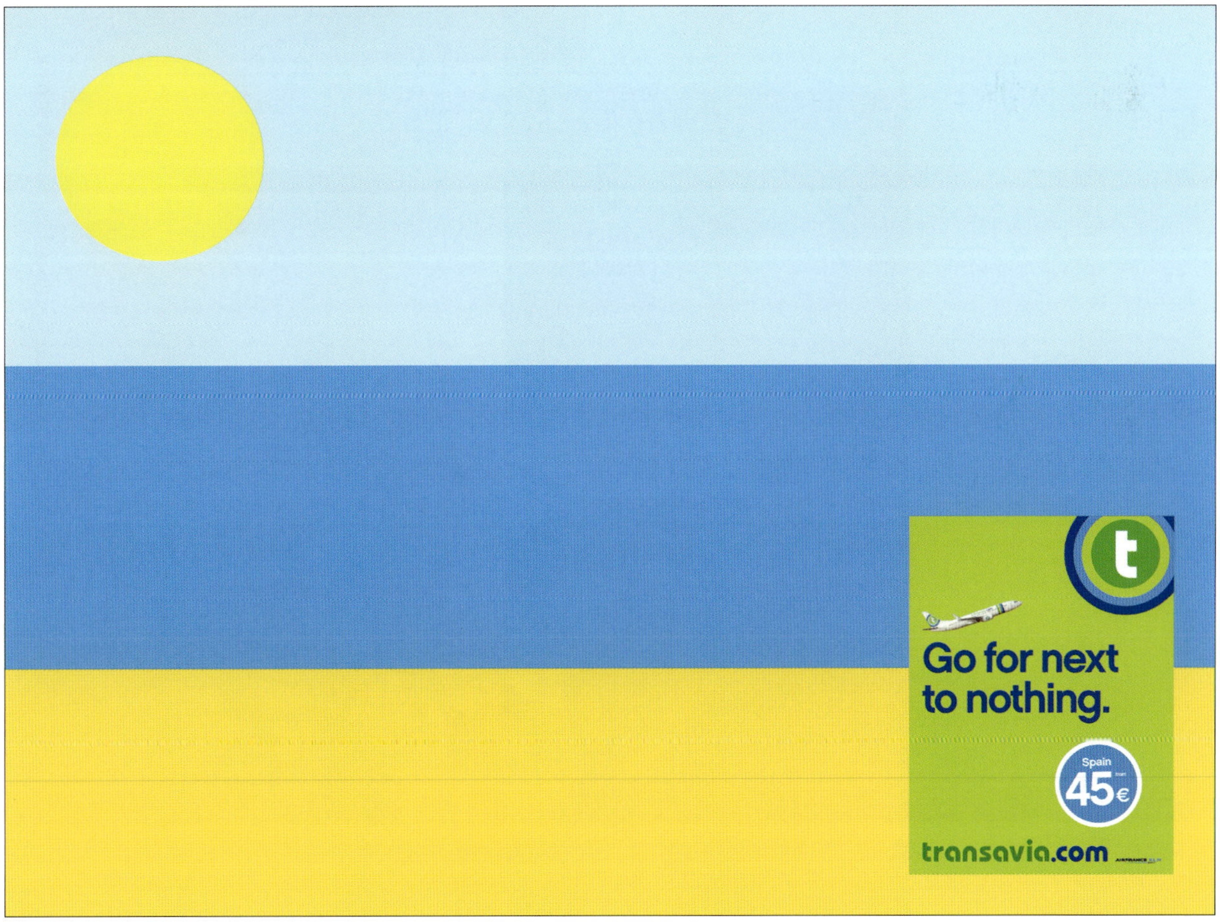
t
Go for next
to nothing.
Spain
45€
transavia.com

Agency	H, Suresnes
Creative Director	Gilbert Scher
Copywriter	Lilian Moine
Art Director	Julien Doucet
Advertiser	Transavia.com, "Go for Next to Nothing"

crosscountry
your search engine
To James Mum
Happy Birthday
Love Mom James
xxx
For train tickets just as cheap
crosscountrytrains.co.uk/nus

HAVE BETTER STORIES TO TELL WHEN YOU'RE OLD.
sudden rush

HAVE BETTER STORIES TO TELL WHEN YOU'RE OLD.
sudden rush
worldwide surfing trips

Agency McCann, Manchester
Creative Directors Dave Price, Neil Lancaster
Copywriter Neale Denaro
Art Director Parisa Shadi
Advertiser CrossCountry Trains, "Mum"

Agency Advico Young & Rubicam, Zurich
Creative Directors Dominik Oberwiler, Thomas Schöb
Copywriter Martin Stulz
Art Director Isabelle Hauser
Typographer Annik Weber
Advertiser Sudden Rush Surf Travel, "Grandparents"

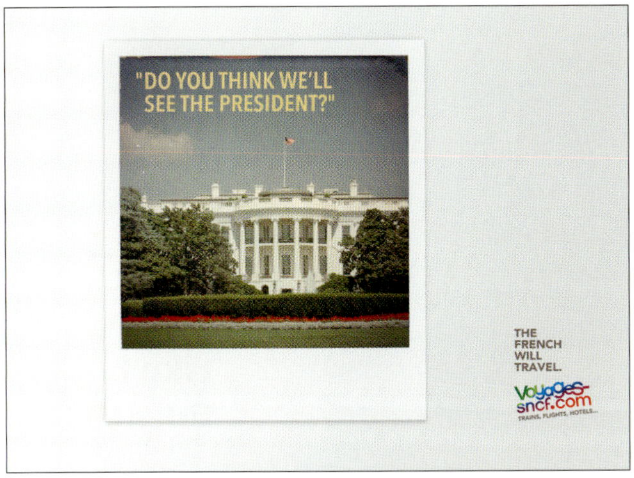
"DO YOU THINK WE'LL SEE THE PRESIDENT?"
THE FRENCH WILL TRAVEL.
voyages-sncf.com

"IT'S AS IF WE WERE AT EURODISNEY."
THE FRENCH WILL TRAVEL.
voyages-sncf.com

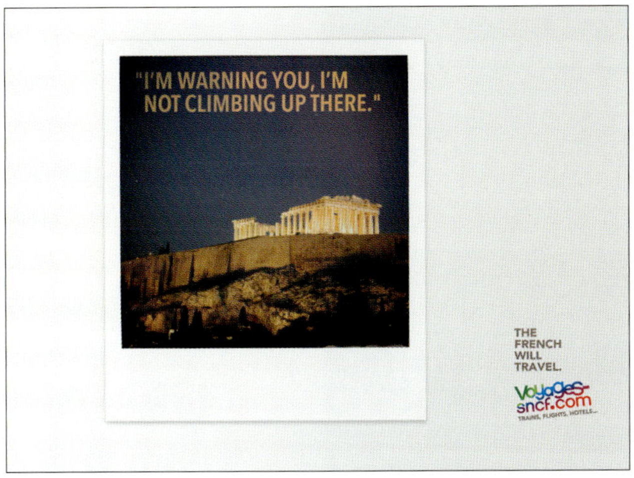
"I'M WARNING YOU, I'M NOT CLIMBING UP THERE."
THE FRENCH WILL TRAVEL.
voyages-sncf.com

"DO YOU HAVE BREAD ?"
THE FRENCH WILL TRAVEL.
voyages-sncf.com

Granny's birthday
Every journey is important. So we fix you fast.
RAC
the driving people

Agency	DDB Paris
Executive CD	Alexandre Hervé
Copywriter	Olivier Lefebvre
Art Director	Benjamin Marchal
Advertiser	Voyages-sncf.com, "The French Will Travel"

Agency	Abbott Mead Vickers BBDO, London
Executive CD	Paul Brazier
Creative Directors	Phil Martin Brian Campbell
Creatives	Sonny Adorjan Milo Campbell
Photography	Henrik Knudsen
Typographer	James Townsend
Art Producer	Kirstie Johnstone
Final Artwork	Stuart Calder
Advertiser	RAC Breakdown Service, "Granny"

PG TIPS 160 bags
£3.00
ALDI 160 bags
£1.99
Prices checked 18 May on mysupermarket.com. Details at aldi.co.uk.
In taste tests, 133 liked PG tips, 77% of them also liked Aldi Tea.

£3.00
£1.99
Prices checked 18 May on mysupermarket.com. Details at aldi.co.uk.
In taste tests, 133 liked PG tips, 77% of them also liked Aldi Tea.

Aldi.
Like brands.
Only cheaper.
aldi.co.uk
ALDI

In taste tests 151 liked Hellmann's, 87% of them also liked Aldi.

79p
In taste tests 151 liked Hellmann's, 87% of them also liked Aldi.

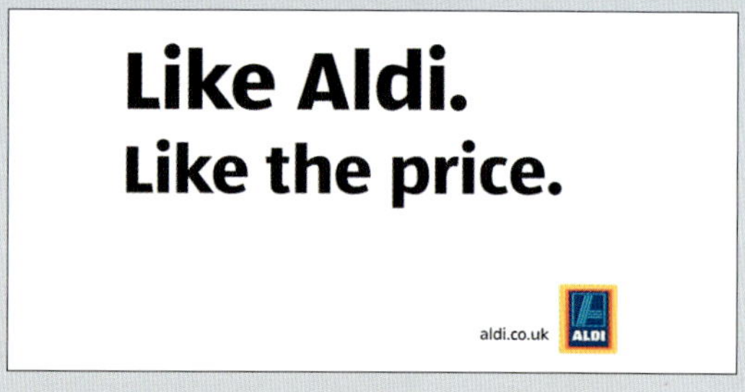
Like Aldi.
Like the price.
aldi.co.uk
ALDI

All in 1
COMPLETE
BEST BUY
In Which? tests (March 11) Finish scored 69%, Aldi scored 74%.

£3.99
In Which? tests (March 11) Finish scored 69%, Aldi scored 74%.

BEST BUY
All in 1
COMPLETE
Aldi.
2011 Which?
Best Buy.
aldi.co.uk
ALDI

Agency	McCann, Manchester
Creative Directors	Dave Price Neil Lancaster
Copywriter	Neil Lancaster
Art Director	Dave Price
Production	Love Commercial, London
Director	MJ Delaney
Producers	Jane Lloyd Sarah Martin Alex Cowley
Advertiser	Aldi Supermarkets, "Like Brands"

An elderly woman sits at her dining room table. "I buy this tea for my husband," she says, indicating a packet of PG Tips. The price flashes up: £3. "He likes tea. He also likes this one." She shows a packet of Aldi tea: £1.99. "I don't like tea," the woman admits. "I like gin." She sips from a glass. Aldi. Like brands. Only cheaper.

A young woman in her living room. "I like this mayonnaise," she says, indicating a jar of Hellman's on her coffee table. "And I like this mayonnaise." Aldi: 75p. "I like it on chicken, tuna, chips. I even like it on cornflakes." She laughs. "Anyone would think I was pregnant." Abruptly, she stops, frowns...Like Aldi. Like the price.

A little girl in a kitchen. "My mummy likes these dishwasher tablets," she says, indicating a pack of Finish. "She likes these ones too." Aldi dishwasher tablets, £3.99 for 40. "But I like cleaning them like this," adds the little girl, taking a plate and licking it. Aldi dishwasher tablets may be the next cheapest thing. They've also been voted "best buy" in their category by Which? magazine.

THE
HARVEY NICHOLS
SALE
STOP WINDOW SHOPPING

THE
HARVEY NICHOLS
SALE
STOP WINDOW SHOPPING

THE
HARVEY NICHOLS
SALE
STOP WINDOW SHOPPING

Agency	DDB London
Creative Director	Jeremy Craigen
Copywriter	Pablo Arellano
Art Director	Miguel Gonzalez
Photography	Marc Philbert
Advertiser	Harvey Nichols Winter Sale, "Window Shopping"

HARVEY NICHOLS SALE
DAYLIGHT ROBBERY STARTS 15TH JUNE

HARVEY NICHOLS SALE
DAYLIGHT ROBBERY STARTS 15TH JUNE

HARVEY NICHOLS SALE
DAYLIGHT ROBBERY STARTS 15TH JUNE

Agency	DDB London
Creative Director	Jeremy Craigen
Copywriter	Will Lowe
Art Director	Victor Monclus
Photography	Frederike Helwig
Advertiser	Harvey Nichols Summer Sale, "Daylight Robbery"

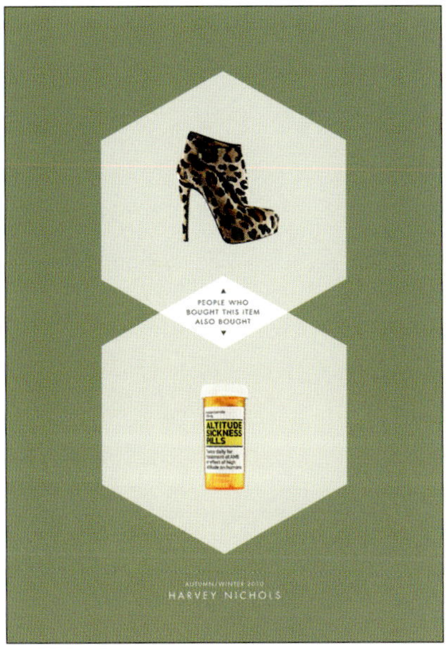
PEOPLE WHO
BOUGHT THIS ITEM
ALSO BOUGHT
ALTITUDE SICKNESS PILLS
HARVEY NICHOLS

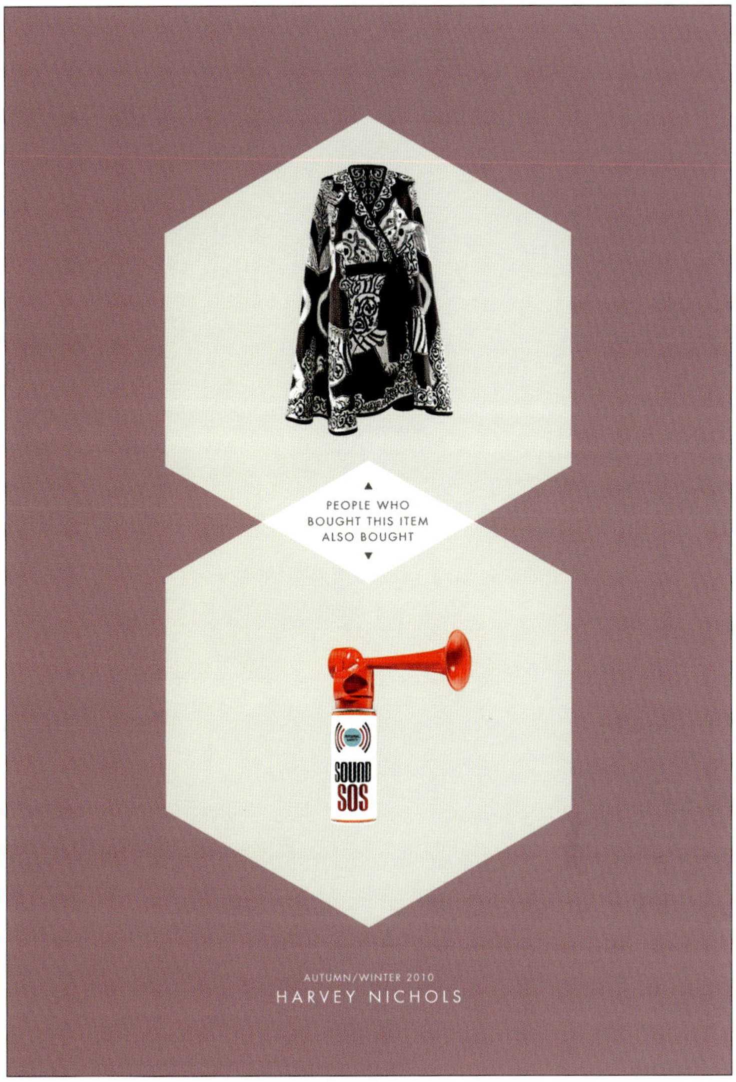
PEOPLE WHO
BOUGHT THIS ITEM
ALSO BOUGHT
SOUND SOS
AUTUMN/WINTER 2010
HARVEY NICHOLS

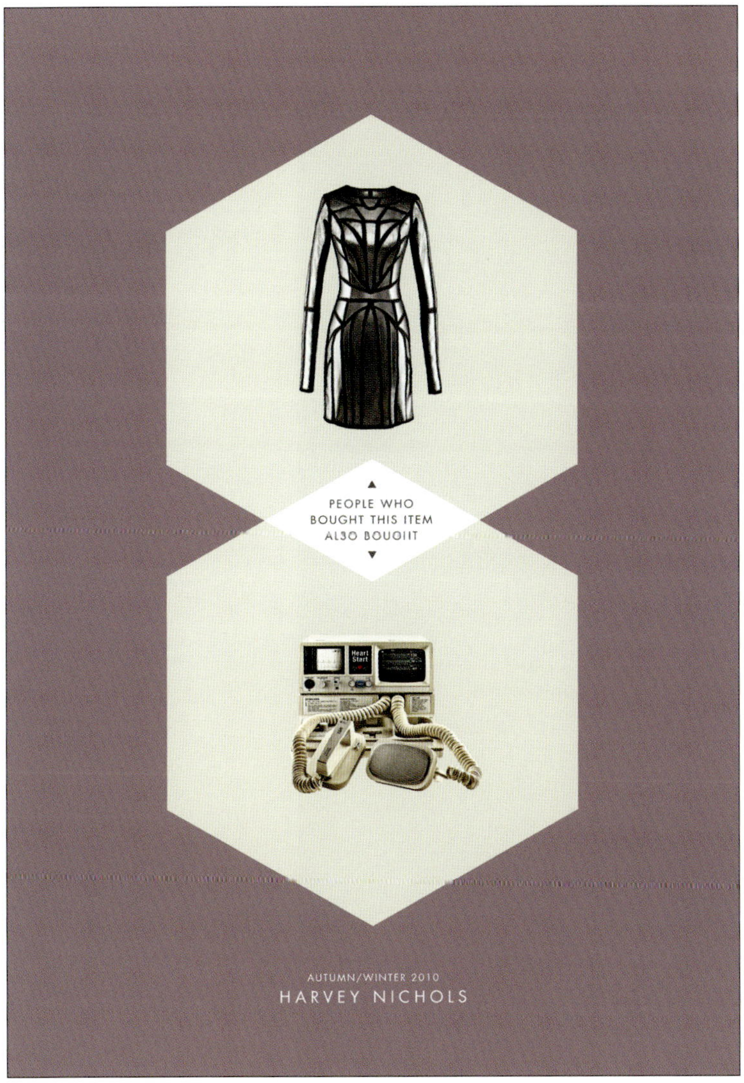
PEOPLE WHO
BOUGHT THIS ITEM
ALSO BOUGHT
Heart Start
AUTUMN/WINTER 2010
HARVEY NICHOLS

PEOPLE WHO
BOUGHT THIS ITEM
ALSO BOUGHT
HARVEY NICHOLS

Agency	Young & Rubicam, Dubai
Creative Directors	Shahir Zag Komal Bedi Sohal
Copywriter	Shahir Zag
Art Directors	Komal Bedi Sohal Shahir Zag
Photography	James Day
Graphic Design	Shahir Zag
Planner	Nadine Ghossoub
Advertiser	Harvey Nichols, "Accessories Required"

The power of flowers.
INTERFLORA
FLEUROP

 Retail Services

Agency	Spillmann/Felser/ Leo Burnett, Zurich
Creative Director	Peter Brönnimann
Copywriter	Diana Rossi
Art Director	Reto Clement
Photography	David Willen
Advertiser	Fleurop Interflora, "Broken Vase"

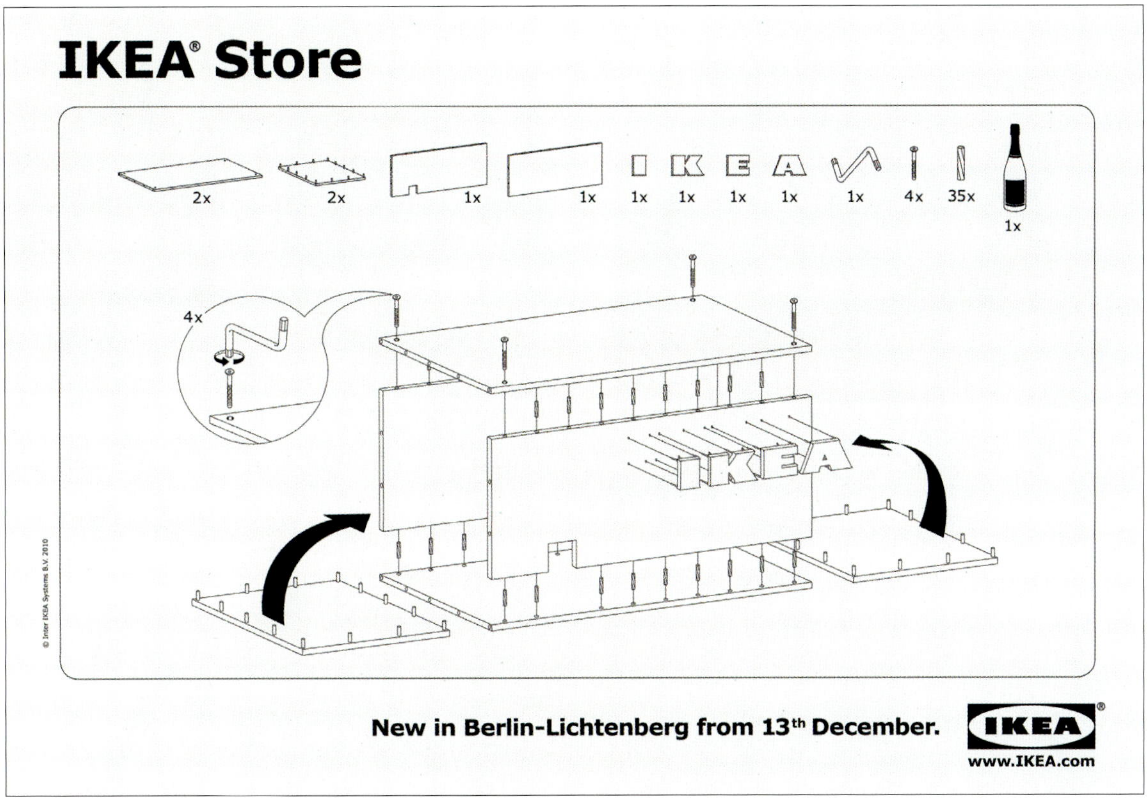
IKEA® Store
2x
2x
1x
1x
1x
1x
1x
1x
1x
4x
35x
1x
4x
© Inter IKEA Systems B.V. 2010
New in Berlin-Lichtenberg from 13th December.
IKEA
www.IKEA.com

GRRRROWL...
HUNGER'S A DRAG.
BURGER KING

Agency	Grabarz & Partner, Hamburg
Executive CD	Ralf Heuel
Creative Directors	Tom Hauser Dirk Siebenhaar
Copywriters	Ole Lisberg Martin Grass Tom Hauser
Art Directors	Tim Hartwig Djik Ouchiian Stefan Schoembs
Acct. Supervisor	Denise Ewald
Advertiser	Ikea, "Store Opening"

Agencies	Interone, Munich, Hamburg & Düsseldorf
Executive CDs	Thomas Pakull Marco Mehrwald
Creative Director	Gunnar Immisch
Copywriter	Felix Hennermann
Art Director	Felix Hennermann
Photography	Stefan Dokoupil
Account Team	Andreas Ernst Tony Bergmann Lara Timm Stephanie Weigand
Advertiser	Burger King, "Hungry"

DnB NOR
Bank of Norway

Financial Services

Agency	Try, Oslo
Copywriters	Janne Brenda Lysoe Jonas Grønnern
Art Directors	Stian Johansen Lars-Kristian Harveg
Production	Bacon, Oslo
Director	Martin Werner
Producers	Magne Lyngner Monika Augustsson Kristin Berge Jahr
Advertiser	DnB NOR (Bank of Norway), "Finally Married"

A pretty blonde woman wakes up with a hangover in a strange bed, dressed in a man's shirt. On her finger is a diamond wedding ring; there's a wedding dress on the floor. A Polaroid photo shows her with a disguised man. Unexpectedly, George Clooney enters the hotel room. "I was letting you sleep," he says. It seems she's somehow managed to marry the elusive actor. He tells the speechless girl that he's been looking for a home for them. Some people are lucky in life. For the rest of us, it's best to start saving with the Bank of Norway.

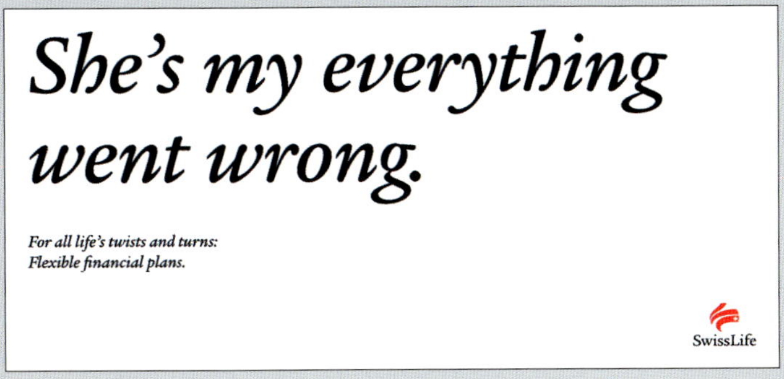
She's my everything
went wrong.
For all life's twists and turns:
Flexible financial plans.
SwissLife

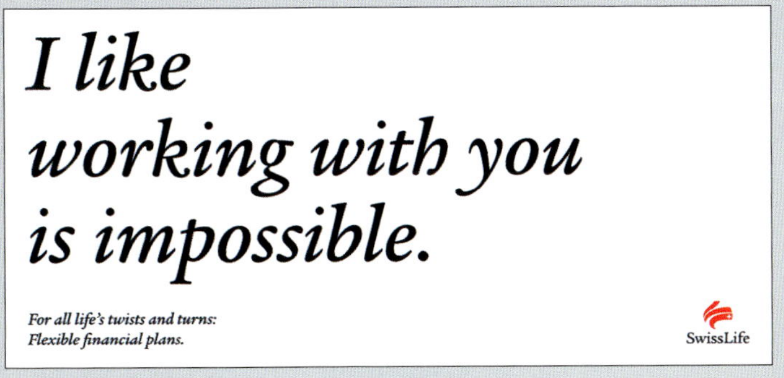
I like
working with you
is impossible.
For all life's twists and turns:
Flexible financial plans.
SwissLife

I never
want
children
are great.
For all life's twists and turns:
Flexible financial plans.
SwissLife

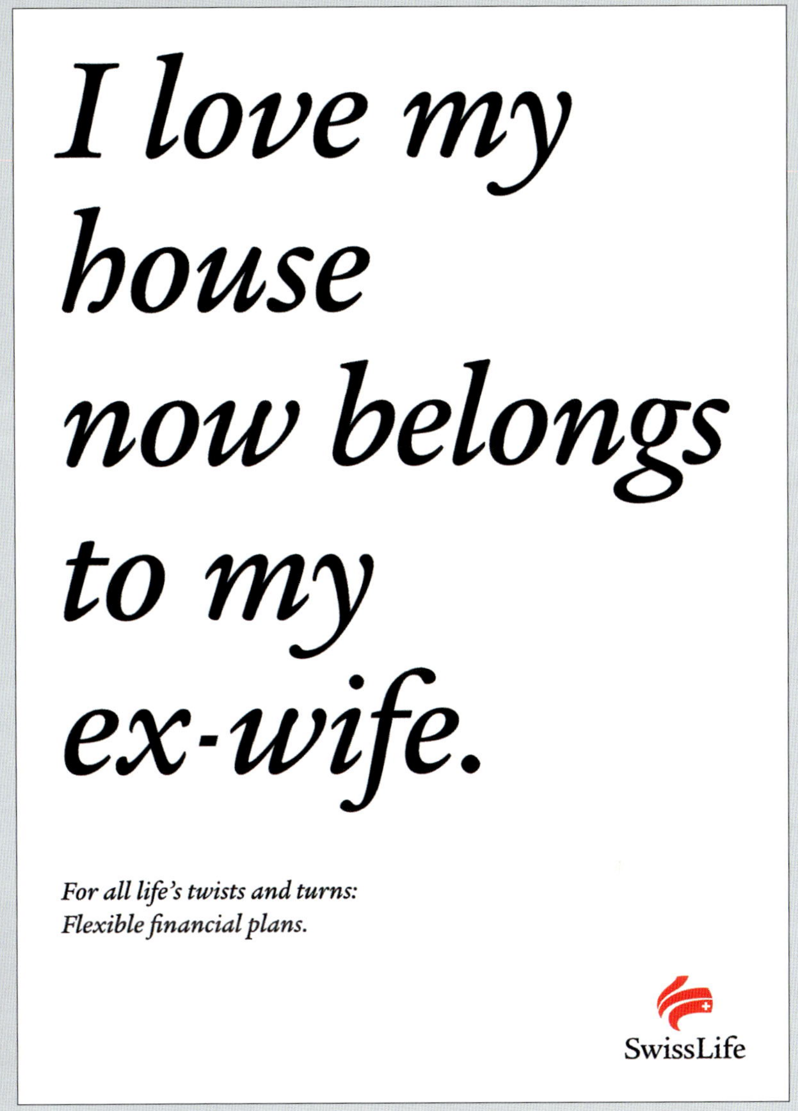
I love my
house
now belongs
to my
ex-wife.
For all life's twists and turns:
Flexible financial plans.
SwissLife

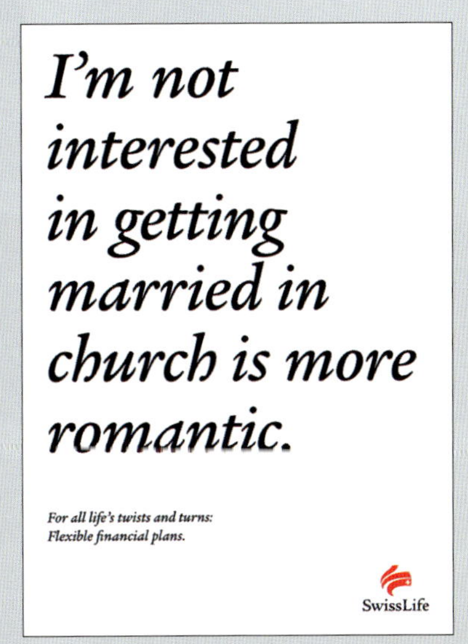
I'm not
interested
in getting
married in
church is more
romantic.
For all life's twists and turns:
Flexible financial plans.
SwissLife

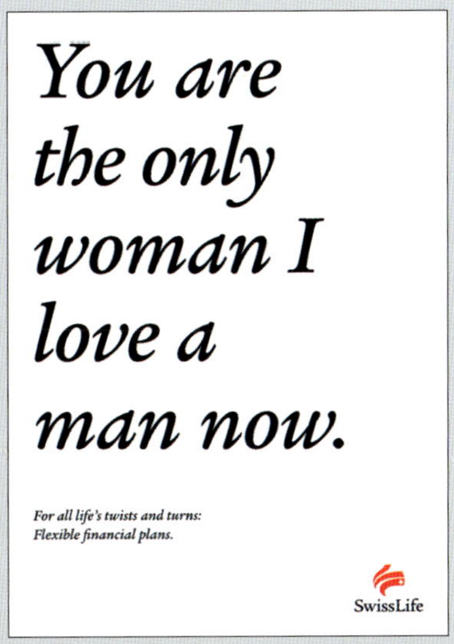
You are
the only
woman I
love a
man now.
For all life's twists and turns:
Flexible financial plans.
SwissLife

Agency	Spillmann/Felser/ Leo Burnett, Zurich
Creative Director	Peter Brönnimann
Copywriters	Thomas Schöb Simon Smit
Art Directors	Reto Clement Daniele Barbiero
Advertiser	Swiss Life, "Life's Turns in a Sentence"

MUSIC MAKES LIFE EASIER

SO MUSIC
CREDIT
CARD
VISA

Agency	Fred & Farid, Paris
Creative Directors	Fred Raillard
	Farid Mokart
Copywriters	Fred Raillard
	Farid Mokart
Art Directors	Fred Raillard
	Farid Mokart
	Romain Lehur
Production	Irene, Paris
Film Director	Alex Ogus
Producers	Guillaume de Bary
	Raphaèle Tanneur
Clients	Bénédicte Richard
	Nathalie Gouadain
	Nicolas Gobert
Account Team	Eudes Jover
	Anais Chounlamountri
Advertiser	Société Générale,
	"So Music"

A group of five young hikers reach a cliff edge and stop to admire the view. But they are cut off by a pack of snarling wolves. Just when all seems lost, one of the men turns into a human beat box. The wolves nod their heads appreciatively to the beat. The rest of the hikers join in, rapping the lyrics and calming the wolves. Music makes life easier. Introducing the So Music credit card, banking for young people with Universal Music mix collections thrown in.

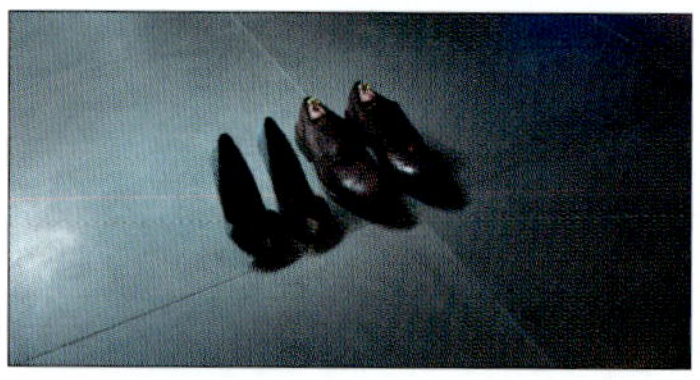

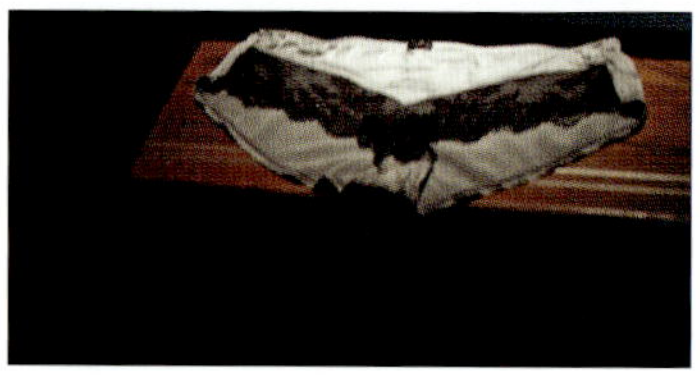

BANK FORUM
Commerzbank Group
Banking. German style.

BANK FORUM
Commerzbank Group
Banking. German style.

Agency	Ogilvy & Mather, Kiev
CDs	Will Rust
	Ferenc Benesch
Copywriters	Balazs Szaday
	Karolina Galacz
Art Director	Zoltan Visy
Production	Sauna International
	Feel Films, London
Director	Mikko Lehtinen
Producers	Nick Hirschkorn
	Dan Cleland
Planner	Martin Alles
Advertiser	Bank Forum

Germans are known for their no-nonsense efficiency, as these two spots indicate. In the first, a camera travels through a spotless apartment at night. We see two perfectly aligned champagne glasses. High heels and brogues, sitting neatly alongside one another. Neatly folded and hung clothing. Knickers, bra and boxer shorts perfectly arranged. The camera politely stops at the bedroom, but there is a glimpse of a spotless white duvet. Passion: German style. Their banks are equally efficient, as Bank Forum customers know.

In the second spot, a man is wrapping a Christmas gift as his coolly composed wife looks on, sipping a martini. He cuts each strip of paper with precision, at one point using a ruler and a scalpel. When he's finished, the present is wrapped too perfectly: we can see very well that it's a bicycle. Surprise: German style. German banks don't hide any surprises, either. Bank Forum.

Dies ist eine Pfeife.
Surrealism. German style.
Banking. German style.
www.forum.ua
BANK FORUM
Commerzbank Group

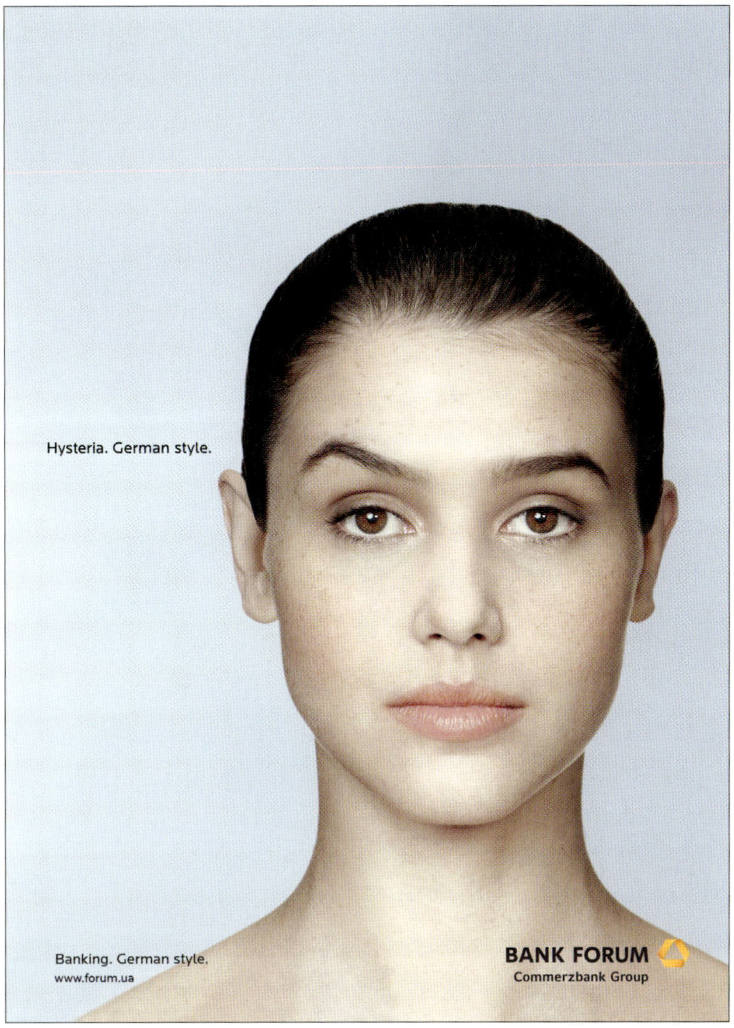
Hysteria. German style.
Banking. German style.
www.forum.ua
BANK FORUM
Commerzbank Group

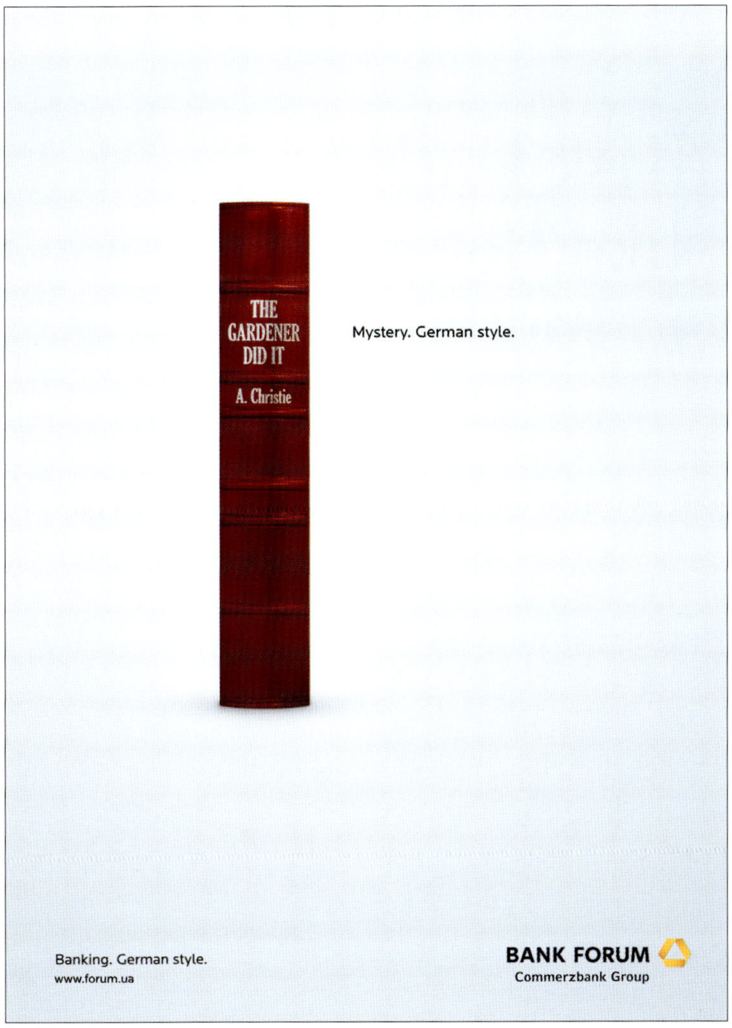
THE GARDENER DID IT
A. Christie
Mystery. German style.
Banking. German style.
www.forum.ua
BANK FORUM
Commerzbank Group

Agency Ogilvy & Mather, Kiev
Creative Directors Will Rust, Ferenc Benesch
Copywriters Karolina Galacz, Alexandra Doroguntsova, Sergey Kolos
Art Directors Zoltan Visy, Taras Dzendrovskii
Photographer David Lukacs
Strategic Planner Martin Alles
Account Team Alexandra Savonik, Svetlana Korytko, Svetlana Polyakova
Producer Irina Pigal
Advertiser Bank Forum, "Banking. German Style."

SARASIN
ALPEN
ISLAMIC BANKING. SWISS STANDARDS.

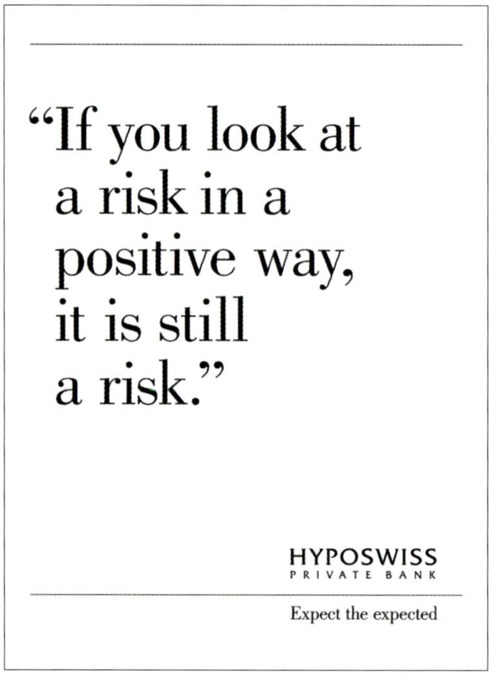
"If you look at
a risk in a
positive way,
it is still
a risk."
HYPOSWISS
PRIVATE BANK
Expect the expected

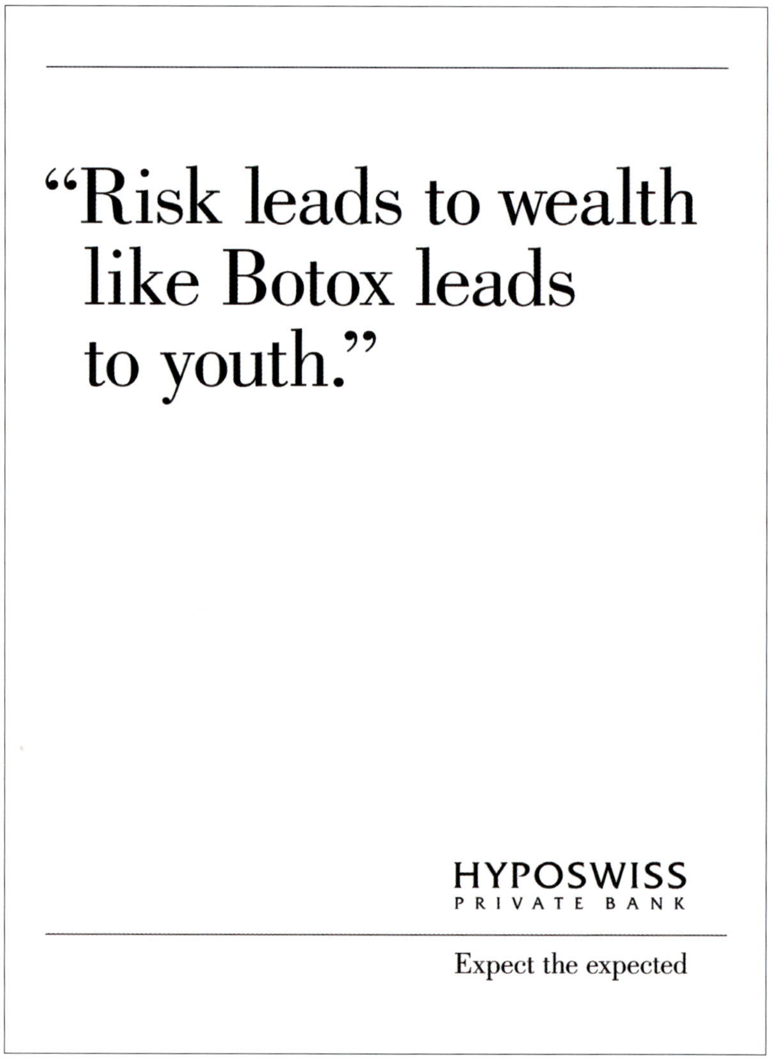
"Risk leads to wealth
like Botox leads
to youth."
HYPOSWISS
PRIVATE BANK
Expect the expected

Agency	Kobeso, Dubai
Creative Directors	Komal Bedi Sohal K.S. Gopal
Copywriter	K.S. Gopal
Art Director	Komal Bedi Sohal
Graphic Design	Komal Bedi Sohal
Typographer	Majid Alyousef
Advertiser	Bank Sarasin-Alpen, Islamic Banking, "Swiss"

Agency	Walker, Zurich
Creative Director	Pius Walker
Copywriters	Heinz Helle Martin Arnold Henning Müller-Dannhausen
Art Directors	Stefanie Huber Golf Nuntawat
Account Team	Lisa Binkert Cornelia Nünlist
Advertiser	Hyposwiss, "Expect the Expected"

In Turkey
they haven't known
the meaning of the word
steal for years.
If you forget your wallet
or expensive watch somewhere,
you can come back hours later
and still find them right where
you left them.
Believe it or insure yourself.
Union
Insurance
tel: 0850 111 211 www.union.sk sms:6655

ITALIANS
ARE THE MOST COURTEOUS
DRIVERS IN EUROPE.
TRAFFIC REGULATIONS
ARE SACRED TO THEM.
GO AHEAD AND GO FOR
A DRIVE IN A CAR OR HOP
ON A SCOOTER,
YOU'RE PERFECTLY SAFE
ON ITALIAN
ROADS.
BELIEVE IT
OR INSURE YOURSELF.
Union
Insurance
tel: 0850 111 211 www.union.sk sms:6655

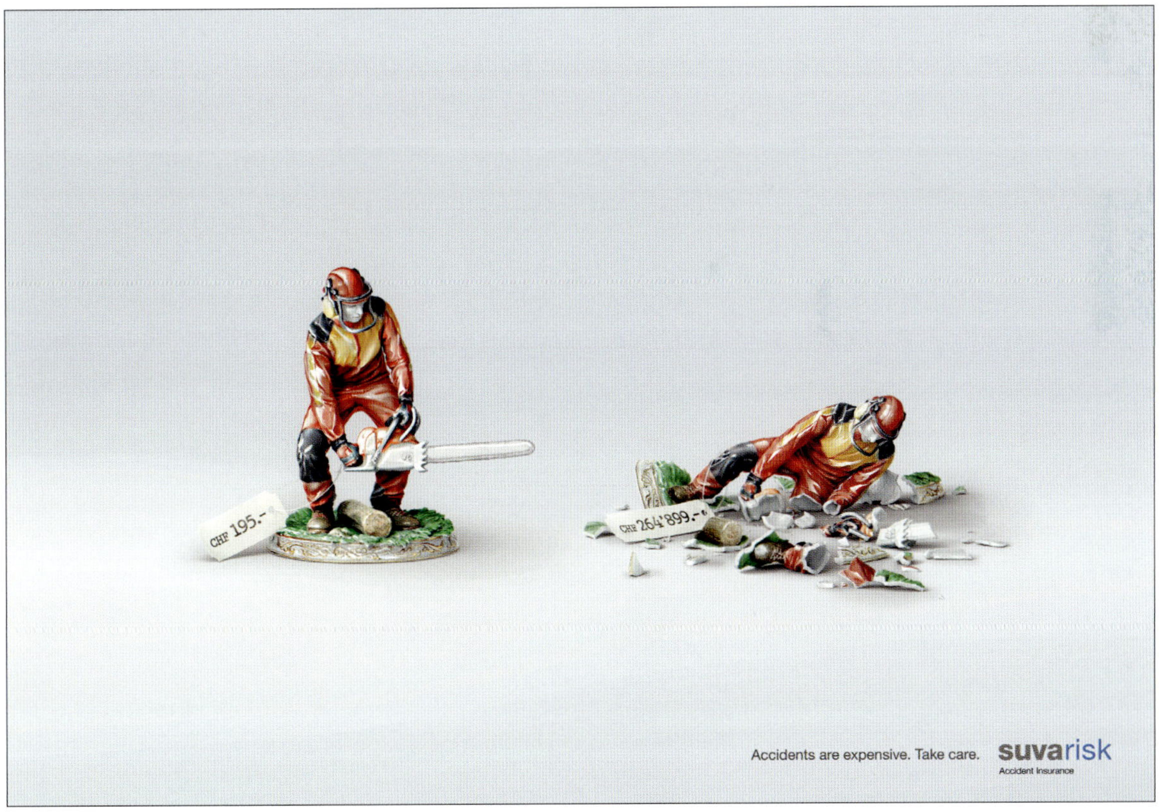
CHF 195.-
CHF 264'899.-
Accidents are expensive. Take care.
suvarisk
Accident Insurance

Agency	Wiktor Leo Burnett, Bratislava
Creative Directors	Peter Kacenka Martin Ondrusek
Copywriters	Peter Izo Vlado Cabak
Art Director	Stefan Andrejco
Graphic Design	Stefan Andrejco Peter Kacenka
Advertiser	Union Travel Insurance, "Truth Well Told"

Agency	Spillmann/Felser/ Leo Burnett, Zurich
Creative Directors	Martin Spillmann Dan Strasser Patrick Suter
Copywriter	Reto Vogler
Art Director	Sebastian Krayer
Illustration	Illusion, Bangkok
Digital Artwork	Illusion, Bangkok
Advertiser	Suva Risk Insurance, "Porcelain Workers"

FINANCIAL TRADING EVEN MORE SEXY
Invest differently with Certificats Bonus and Bonus Cappés.
BNP PARIBAS

Works for your business,
as well as
the environment.
İŞBANK
ENERGY PRODUCTIVITY
AND ENVIRONMENT
LOAN

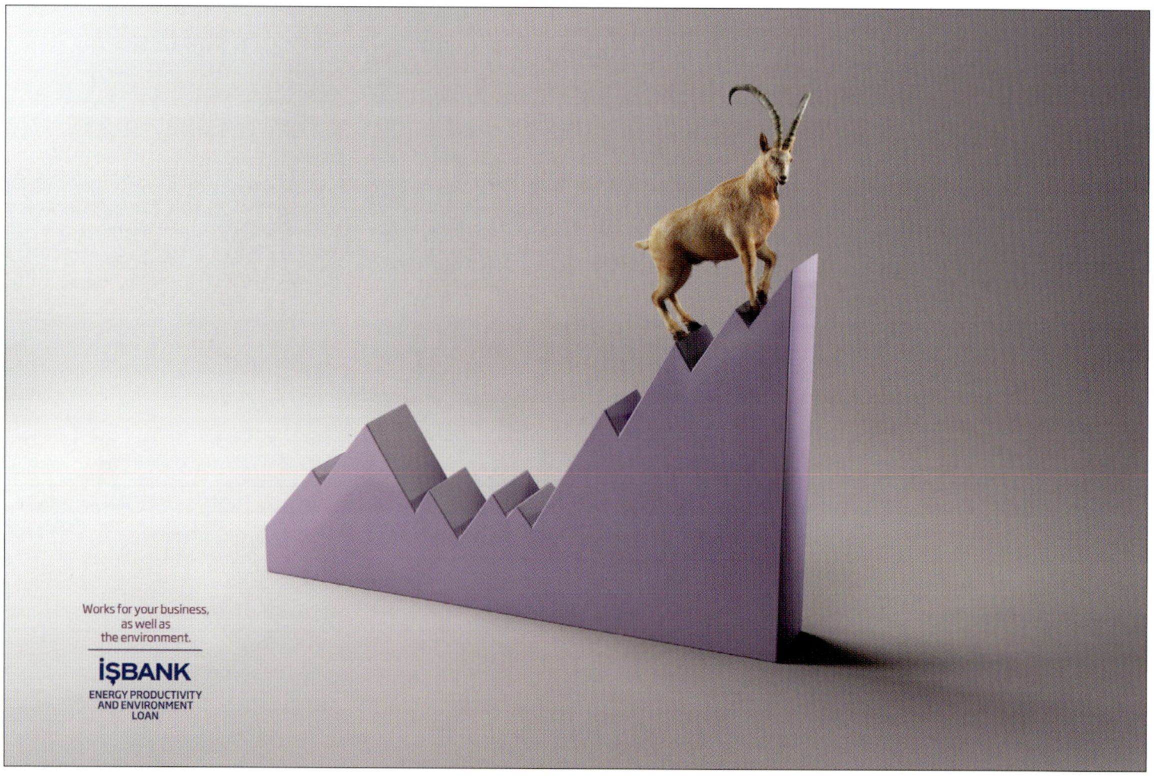
Works for your business,
as well as
the environment.
İŞBANK
ENERGY PRODUCTIVITY
AND ENVIRONMENT
LOAN

Agency Publicis Conseil, Paris
Creative Directors Olivier Altmann, Christian Vouhe
Copywriters Fabien Chiaffrino, Christophe Paviot
Art Directors Fabien Chiaffrino, Christophe Paviot
Photography Pierre Even
Art Buying Jean-Luc Chirio, Soone Riboud
Account Team Charles Georges-Picot, Donatien Souriau
Advertiser BNP Paribas, "CAC 40"

Agency Medina Turgul DDB, Istanbul
Creative Director Kurtcebe Turgul
Copywriters Talha Yuksel, Arda Erdik
Art Directors Mert Kunc, Baris Sarhan
Illustrators Ahmet Eken
Advertiser Işbank, "Goat" & "Penguin"

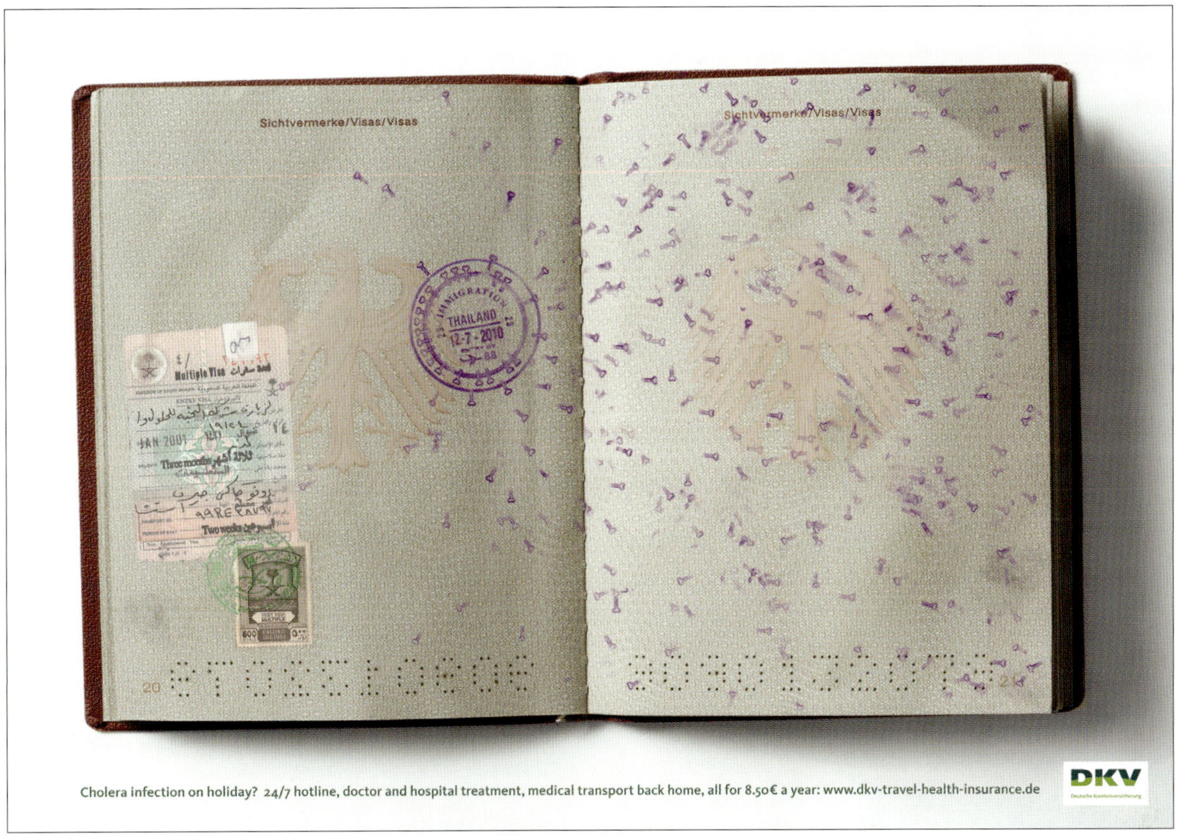
Sichtvermerke/Visas/Visas
THAILAND
12-7-2010
Cholera infection on holiday? 24/7 hotline, doctor and hospital treatment, medical transport back home, all for 8.50€ a year: www.dkv-travel-health-insurance.de
DKV

Sichtvermerke/Visas/Visas
EGYPT
13-02-2011
MUMBAI IMMIGRATION
13 FEB 2011
CSI AIRPORT
Malaria infection on holiday? 24/7 hotline, doctor and hospital treatment, medical transport back home, all for 8.50€ a year: www.dkv-travel-health-insurance.de
DKV

Agency	Ogilvy, Frankfurt
CCO	Stephan Vogel
Creative Director	Simon Oppmann
Copywriter	Peter Roemmelt
Art Director	Simon Oppmann
Clients	Wolfgang Kroul Peter Baumann
Account Team	Carola Romanus Daniela Loesch
Advertiser	DKV (German Health Insurance), "Infectious Passports"

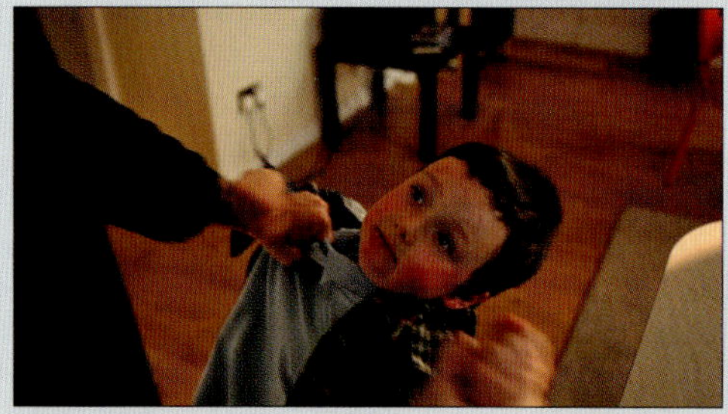

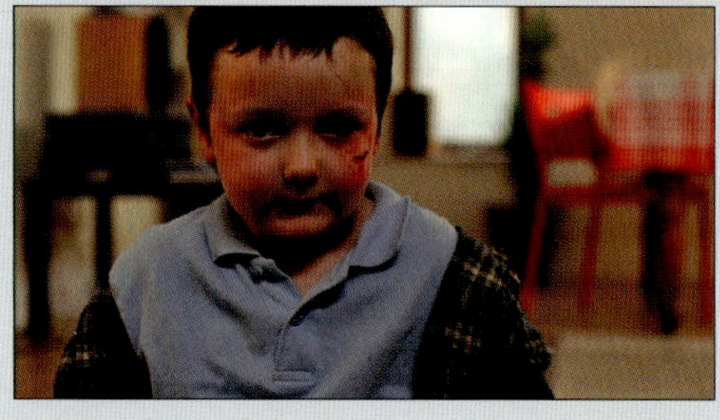

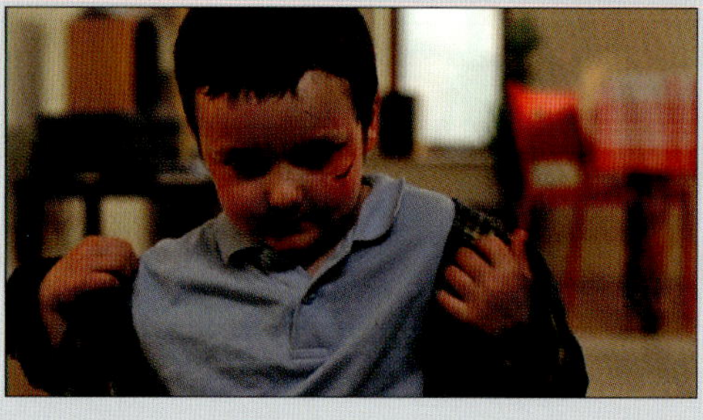

ISPCC
www.ispcc.ie

Agency	Ogilvy & Mather, Dublin
Creative Director	Colin Nimick
Copywriter	Des Kavanagh
Art Director	Laurence O'Byrne
Production	Blinder, Dublin
Director	Richie Smyth
Producers	Michael Duffy Derek Doyle
Advertiser	ISPCC, "I Can't Wait"

"I can't wait until I grow up," says a little boy with a scarred face. We see him cowering from his father, who hits him. "I have the right to be kept safe, to be kept warm." He chants the words like a mantra, but they can't protect him from his father's brutality. "To feel loved, to be listened to, to be heard." As the sickening violence continues, he pledges to "fight for the rights of children like me, who don't have a childhood. I can't wait until I grow up." Join the ISPCC (Irish Society for the Prevention of Cruelty to Children) and give children back their childhood.

SIRE
Your mother ruined us all
WHAT YOU SAY DURING DIVORCE LASTS FOREVER.

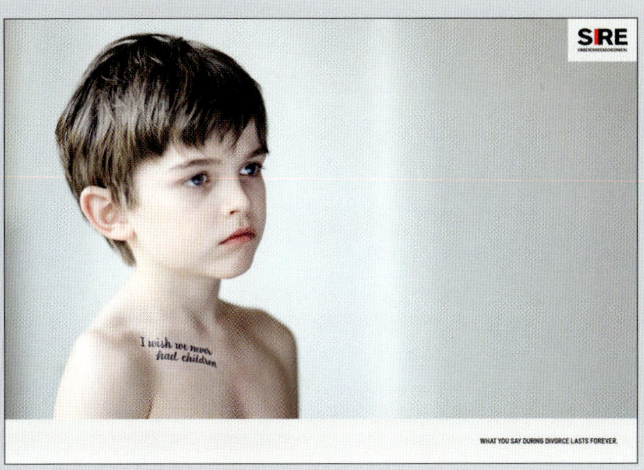

SIRE
I wish we never had children
WHAT YOU SAY DURING DIVORCE LASTS FOREVER.

SIRE
KINDERENINEENSCHEIDING.NL
Forget your Dad. He's already forgotten you.
WHAT YOU SAY DURING DIVORCE LASTS FOREVER.

Public Interest

Agency	180 Amsterdam
Creative Director	Andy Fackrell
Copywriters	Marianne Riphagen Jessica Hartley
Art Director	Andy Fackrell
Photography	Laura Pannack
Illustrator	Jan Willem Dijkstra
Typographers	Yomar Augusto Jan-Paul Jansen
Digital Artwork	Markus Sablatnik
Advertiser	SIRE, "Marked for Life"

Denk maar niet dat papa je nog wil zien
Forget your Dad. He's already forgotten you.

SIRE
KINDERENINEENSCHEIDING.NL

Agency 180 Amsterdam
Creative Director Andy Fackrell
Copywriters Marianne Riphagen, Jessica Hartley
Art Director Andy Fackrell
Production Partizan, London
Director Ariel Kleiman
Producers Martin Poyner, Chayenne de Witte
Advertiser SIRE, "Marked for Life"

We see young children tattooed with hurtful phrases. "If you go to your dad now, you can stay there," on a little boy's chest. "Your mother ruined us all," on the arm of a little girl. "If you take the house," on one brother, "I'll take the boys," on another. On a girl's back: "Forget your dad. He's already forgotten you." We see a tattooist inking onto a little boy: "I wish we'd never had children." Bitter words spoken by divorcing parents mark kids – for life. Watch what you say. SIRE is the Dutch foundation for idealism in advertising.

There, there.. How come I always forget how beautiful you are?

Let me give you a squeeze.

Was your childhood affected by alcohol?
lasinenlapsuus.fi

SOLIDARITÉS INTERNATIONAL
www.solidarites.org

Agency Euro RSCG, Helsinki
Creative Director Marko Vuorensola
Copywriter Juha Koivisto
Art Director Marko Vuorensola
Production Kennel, Helsinki
Director Teemu Niukkanen
Producer Petteri Lehtinen
Account Director Nina Myllyharju
Coordinator Janne Takala
Sound Design Humina, Helsinki
VFX Anders Helle
Advertiser Lasinen Lapsuus, "Voice for a Child"

Two kids are playing in a sandpit. The little boy lifts the bucket as if he's drinking. "Starting to feel the buzz," he says, in an adult voice. "You're one sweet dumbass," says the girl. They're reproducing the conversation of their alcoholic parents. "Did you make the kids something to eat?" asks the girl. "No, I did not." The girl accuses him of peeing in his pants. Recriminations and violence ensue, until they both collapse. In her normal voice, the girl asks: "Why do they have to behave like that?" The bottle shape around them provides the answer.

Agency BDDP Unlimited, Paris
CD Guillaume-Ulrich Chifflot
Copywriter Fabien Duval
Art Director Fabien Nunez
Production Hush, Paris
Director Clement Beauvais
Producers Nicolas Lhermitte, Arthur De Kersauson, Christophe Guyot
Account Team Marco de la Fuente, Irache Martinez, Anne-Celine Bloch
Advertiser Solidarités International

To mark World Water Day, Solidarités International created a spot revealing the invisible threat of polluted water. An artist "paints" clear water onto a page and introduces drops of black ink to form symbolic images: a small boy, carrion crows, gravestones, a skull. The narrator says: "Water may seem harmless. Colourless, odourless, transparent. But it kills millions every year all around the world. Just like that. Silently, quietly…when only a little bit of ink can reveal this terrible truth." Dirty water is the leading cause of death in the world.

VERF
Afwas
Vloeibare Ontstopper
CHILDREN SEE
THINGS DIFFERENTLY
PREVENT ACCIDENTS. READ THE LABEL.

Snoep
CHILDREN SEE
THINGS DIFFERENTLY
PREVENT ACCIDENTS. READ THE LABEL.

don't condemn him
to a life of loneliness
helpautism.ro

Agency	Lemz, Amsterdam
Copywriter	Chester de Vries
Art Director	Bram Tervoort
Illustrator	INDG, Amsterdam
Advertiser	Stichting Consument Veiligheid & VWA, "Children See Things Differently"

More than 7,000 accidents involving household chemicals occur in the Netherlands each year. In most cases, the victims are children under 5. Showing a kitchen cupboard through the eyes of a child allowed parents to see the potential danger of household products. The lenticular technique – in which the image changes depending on the angle it's seen from – enabled the viewer to switch between an adult's view and that of a child. Where we see plastic containers of noxious substances, a child sees playthings.

Agency	Mercury360, Bucharest
Creative Group Director	Ciprian Banica
Creative Director	Liviu Turcanu
Copywriter	Ciprian Banica
Art Director	Emanuel Borcescu
Illustrator	Emanuel Borcescu
Advertiser	HelpAutism.ro, "The Shadow"

Roll up the ad to see how thick a tree gets in only six months.
The trees in the Vi Agroforestry Programme grow really fast. After just six months, they are big enough to bear fruit, feed the animals and fertilize the land for peasants in eastern Africa. That is why the planting of trees in the Vi Agroforestry Programme is a fast but long-term aid helping families to become self-sufficient. And planting a tree is only €2.
Plant your tree at www.viskogen.se/planteratrad and see it grow for six months.
VI AGROFORESTRY PROGRAMME

Välkommen!
Ett civilkurage långt utöver det vanliga
Under alla dessa månader och år har de levt på flykt.
KURORTEN BIE BRUNN

HELP WWF SAVE ENDANGERED SPECIES BEFORE THEY BECOME JUST A MEMORY
WWF

wwf.org
HELP WWF SAVE ENDANGERED SPECIES BEFORE THEY BECOME JUST A MEMORY.
WWF

Agency Pool, Stockholm
Copywriter Ulf Rönnbäck
Art Director Johan Pödra
Graphic Design Emma Sandler
Digital Artwork Patrik Zachrisson
Account Director Hanna Steiner
Advertiser VI Agroforestry Programme, "Tree Stem"

Agency Y&R Brands, Milan
Group ECD Vicky Gitto
Copywriter Gabriele Caeti
Art Director Alessandro Stenco
Photography Maartje Jaquet
Account Marco Ruggeri
Client Barbara Franco
Advertiser WWF, "Animals"

EVERY 60 SECONDS A SPECIES DIES OUT.
BUND

BUND

EVERY 60 SECONDS A SPECIES DIES OUT.
EACH MINUTE COUNTS. EACH DONATION HELPS: BUND.NET
BUND
FRIENDS OF THE EARTH

Agency	Scholz & Friends, Berlin
CCO	Martin Pross
Executive CO	Matthias Spaetgens
Creative Directors	Florian Schwalme Mathias Rebmann
Art Directors	René Gebhardt Bjoern Kernspeckt Ksenia Slavcheva Sebastian Frese
Illustrator	Peppermill, Berlin
Account Team	Christine Scharney Susanne Kieck
Advertiser	BUND, "Time Up, Life Over"

"WOULD YOU CARE MORE
IF I WAS A RHINO?"

"WOULD YOU CARE MORE
IF I WAS A GORILLA?"

"WOULD YOU CARE MORE
IF I WAS A PANDA?"
The Bluefin Tuna is being fished to extinction
So like a few other species, it would appreciate your help
WWF

Public Interest

Agency	Ogilvy France, Paris
Creative Director	Chris Garbutt
Copywriter	Arnaud Vanhelle
Art Director	Benoît Raynert
Photography	Thomas Mangold
Digital Artwork	Thomas Mangold
Account Team	Nathalie Avedissian Benoît de Fleurian
Client	Jacques-Olivier Barthes
Strategic Planner	Loic Mercier
Advertiser	WWF, "Red Tuna"

DESERTIFICATION DESTROYS 6.000 SPECIES EVERY YEAR.
WWF

DESERTIFICATION DESTROYS 6.000 SPECIES EVERY YEAR.
WWF

Agency	Contrapunto BBDO, Madrid
Executive CDs	Carlos Jorge Félix Del Valle
Copywriters & ADs	Aurora Hidalgo Raúl López
Producers	Javier Luján Raúl López
General Manager	Paco Ribera
Account Team	Verónica Félez Dalal Solaiman
Advertiser	WWF Adena Spain, "Desertification"

Скрой
несовершенства
кожи
Скрой
несовершенства
кожи
АННА
Национальный центр
по предотвращению насилия
или обратись за помощью
8 800 7000 600

Будь стильной
в любой ситуации
Fixit
или обратись за помощью
8 800 7000 600
АННА
Будь стильной
в любой ситуации
Fixit

Agency	Lowe Adventa, Moscow
Creative Directors	Pavel Mordioukov Mikhail Panteleev
Copywriter	Mikhail Panteleev
Art Directors	Ivan Lougovoy Maxim Trishin
Photography	Olga Tuponogova Volkova
Advertiser	Anna Help Center, "Domestic Violence"

Cover your skin imperfections...or call for help.

Be stylish in any situation...or call for help.

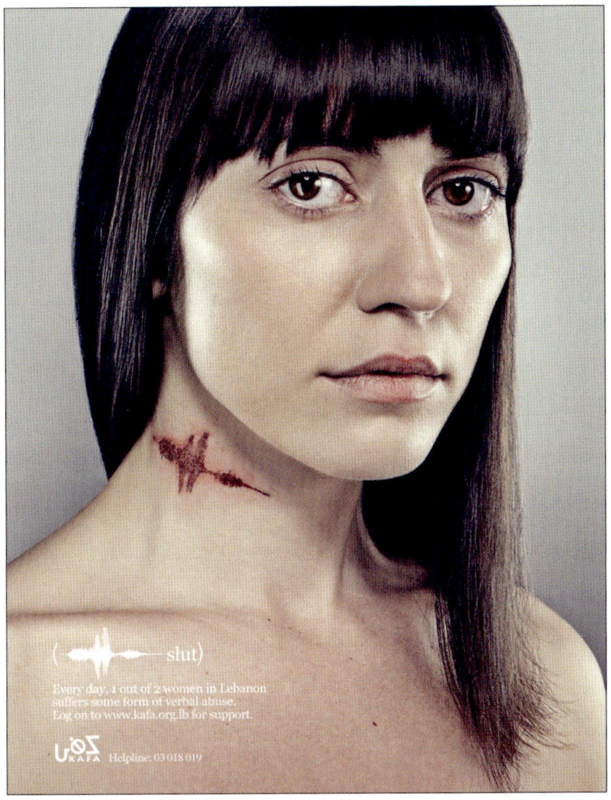
slut)
Every day, 1 out of 2 women in Lebanon
suffers some form of verbal abuse.
Log on to www.kafa.org.lb for support.
KAFA
Helpline: 03 018 019

whore)
Every day, 1 out of 2 women in Lebanon
suffers some form of verbal abuse.
Log on to www.kafa.org.lb for support.
KAFA
Helpline: 03 018 019

WHICH ONE OF YOU IS BEHIND
THE WHEEL TODAY?
ROAD SAFETY IS IN YOUR HANDS

Agency	Young & Rubicam, Dubai
Creative Directors	Shahir Zag Kalpesh Patankar
Copywriter	Shahir Zag
Art Director	Kalpesh Patankar
Photography	James Day
Planner	Nadine Ghossoub
Advertiser	Kafa, "Words Hurt"

Agency	Euro RSCG, Amsterdam
Creative Directors	Thijs de Boer Peter Hamelinck
Copywriter	Thijs de Boer
Art Director	Peter Hamelinck
Photography	Krijn van Noordwijk
Post Production	Wieger Poutsma
Acct. Supervisor	Budi Gonzalez de Chaves
Advertiser	Top Gear, "Heads"

AMNESTY
INTERNATIONAL
USTAVITE
NASILJE NA
WWW.AMNESTY.SI

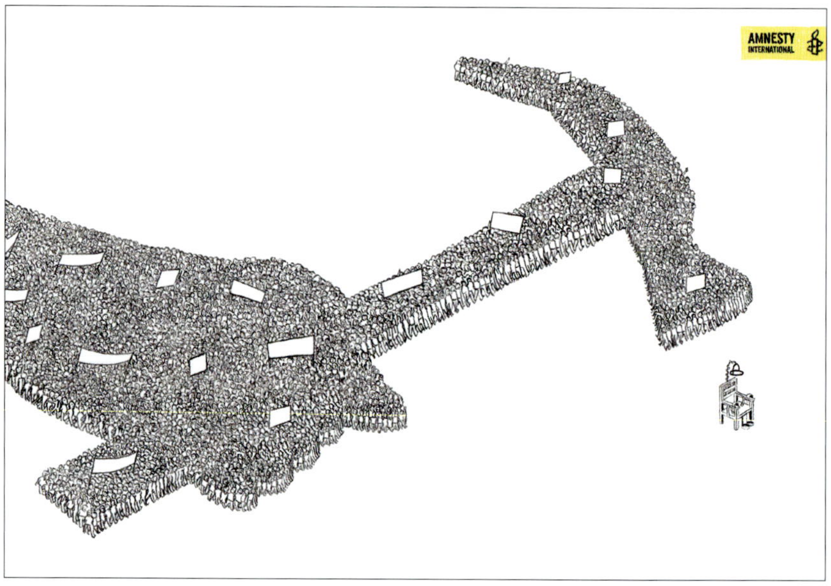
AMNESTY
INTERNATIONAL

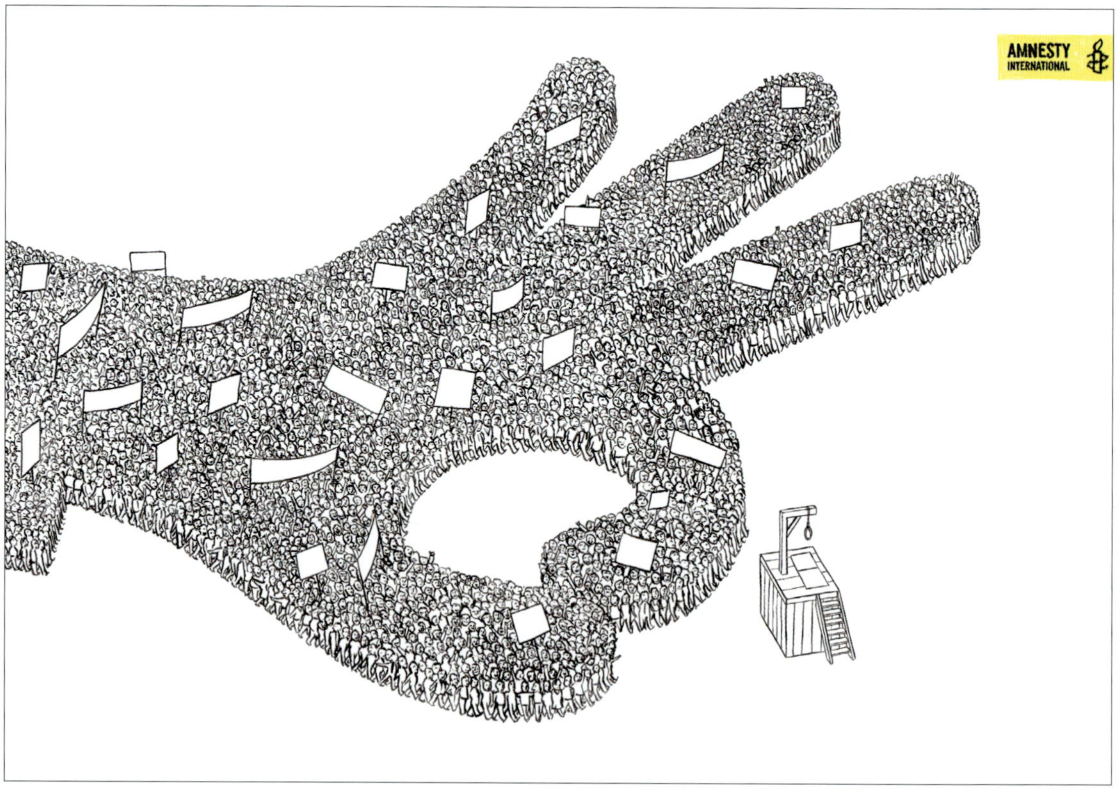
AMNESTY
INTERNATIONAL

Agency Pristop, Ljubljana
Creative Director Aljosa Bagola
Copywriter Drago Mlakar
Art Director Martina Kokovnik
Photography Shutterstock
Advertiser Amnesty International, “Plug Right”

Agency Contrapunto BBDO, Madrid
Executive CDs Carlos Jorge, Félix Del Valle
Copywriter Gonzalo Urriza
Art Director Gorka Fernández Iriso
Illustrator Iván Solbes
Producers Javier Luján, Daniel Rubio
Account Team Lorena Landau, Leticia Gutiérrez
Advertiser Amnesty International, “Protest”

18 WOZ DIE WOCHENZEITUNG

VERANSTALTUNGEN

OBAMAO
in: Die Kunst des Fälschens
Völkerkundemuseum der Universität Zürich
Ausserdem: Sofabilder aus Varanasi
Indien im Blick - Karikaturen aus Indien
Di-Fr 10-13, 14-17, Sa 14-17, So 11-17
www.musethno.uzh.ch
Pelikanstrasse 40 8001 Zürich

tonhalle orchester zürich
Do 11. März, 12.15 h
LUNCHKONZERT
Spuren der Romantik in den 20er-Jahren
Felix-Andreas Genner, Klarinette; Isabel Neligan, Violine
Mari Parz, Violine; Ursula Sarnthein, Viola
Anita Leuzinger, Violoncello; Marian Rosenfeld, Klavier
Prokofjew: Ouvertüre über hebräische Themen op. 34
Bloch: Klavierquintett Nr. 1
Fr 12. März, 19.30 h
Bach I
JULIA FISCHER, VIOLINE
J. S. Bach: Die drei Solo-Sonaten
So 14. März, 11.15 h
So 14. März, 14.15 h
Familienkonzert
EIN ELEFANT IM ORCHESTER
Jugend Sinfonieorchester Zürich; Massimiliano Matesic, Leitung
Timo Schlüssel, Konzept und Spiel
Britten: The Young Person's Guide to the Orchestra op. 34
Poulenc: L'histoire de Babar, le petit éléphant
So 14. März, 19.30 h
Kammermusik-Soiree, Bach II
JULIA FISCHER, VIOLINE
J. S. Bach: Die drei Partiten
Mo 15. März, 19.30 h
SÉRIE JEUNES
Francesco Piemontesi, Klavier
Händel: Suite Nr. 1 B-Dur HWV 434; Brahms: Variationen und Fuge über ein Thema von Händel B-Dur op. 24; Tognetti: Hommage an Schumann, UA; Schumann: Klaviersonate Nr. 1 fis-Moll op. 11
www.tonhalle-orchester.ch, Claridenstr. 7, 044 206 34 34

Frühling in Salecina
Das selbstverwaltete Haus im Bergell
Ferien, Begegnungen, Ideen, Bildung, Bewegung, Sport, eine besondere Erfahrung für Jung und Alt.
Drunter und Drüber
5.-12. Juni
Solidarische Ökonomie
Tagung 12.-19. Juni
Kletterwoche fortgeschrittene
20.-26. Juni
Fest: 100 Jahre Amalie
3.- 4. Juli
Mehr Infos auf unserer Homepage
Stiftung Salecina
Ferien- & Bildungszentrum
7516 Maloja
081 - 824 32 39
info@salecina.ch
www.salecina.ch

moods im schiffbau
So 7.3.
AROMA

Rote Fabrik
Seestrasse 395
8038 Zürich
www.rotefabrik.ch
Do. 4.3. Fabriktheater 20:00
HAPPY SYSTEMS
Ein Theaterabend von happysystem mit G. Ph. Telemann
Weitere Vorstellungen:
Fr. 5.3./ Sa. 6.3. und Di. 9.3./ Mi. 10.3., 20:00 Uhr
Do. 4.3. Clubraum 20:30
Fabrikjazz
ROB MAZUREK - SOUND IS
So. 7.3. Aktionshalle 20:30
A Thousand Leaves
*TOCOTRONIC
Dillon
*Vorverkauf: Zürich: Crazy Beat, Jamarico, Jelmoli (044 212 13 11), Migros City • Aarau: Dezibelle • Baden: Zero Zero • Bern: Olmo Tickets • St. Gallen: BRO • Winterthur: Jamarico

Ego
Elektriker-genossenschaft
Elektroanlagen und Telefon-Installationen
8408 Winterthur
Gewerbehaus Hard 4
Telefon 052 222 18 08
www.ego-elektro.ch
eGO

Die Shedhalle ist ein kreativer Think-Tank in welchem Konzepte und Strategien gesellschaftspolitischer Fragestellungen und Belange mit und durch die Mittel der künstlerischen experimentellen Praxis entwickelt werden. Künstlerische, kulturelle und wissenschaftliche Praktiken gesellschaftspolitischer Relevanz werden miteinander in Dialog gebracht.
Shedhalle
Verein Shedhalle, Rote Fabrik
Seestrasse 395, CH-8038 Zürich
phone +41 44 481 5950, fax +41 44 481 5951
info@shedhalle.ch, www.shedhalle.ch

HELFEN SIE UNS, DAMIT MENSCHENRECHTSVERLETZUNGEN NICHT IM HINTERGRUND VERSCHWINDEN. AUF AMNESTY.CH
AMNESTY INTERNATIONAL

Dynamo
Stadt Zürich
Jugendkulturhaus Dynamo

3FACH
WWW.3FACH.CH
KICK ASS RADIO

Weiterbildung – wie ich sie will
Das neue Kursprogramm ist da!
Mehr als 400 Kurse, Bildungsgänge und Beratungen – Beginn Mai
Persönlichkeitsbildung und Management
Kommunikation / Mediation / Selbstständigkeit / Nachhaltigkeit / Management / Führen / Projektmanagement / Marketing / Werbetexte / Journalismus / PR / Arbeitstechnik / Stress und Gesundheit / Standortbestimmung / Prüfungsvorbereitung BMS, KME
Deutsch für Deutschsprachige
Sicheres Deutsch / Rechtschreibung / Deutschdiplome / Schreibwerkstatt / Briefe, Protokolle, Konzepte schreiben
Deutsch als Zweitsprache
Standard- und Tagesintensivkurse / Zertifikat Deutsch ZD / telc / Goethe-Zertifikat C1 / ZOP / Alphabetisierungs- und Konversationskurse
Fremdsprachen
Englisch / Französisch / Italienisch / Spanisch / Portugiesisch-Brasilianisch / Neugriechisch / Russisch / Chinesisch
Informatik
PC-Kurse / Mac-Kurse / Office-Kurse / Internet / SIZ- und ECDL-Zertifikate / Video / CAD / Flash / 3D / Desktop-Publishing / Web-Publishing / Bildbearbeitung / Datenbanken / Programmieren / Betriebssysteme
Didaktik und Bildungsmanagement
Zertifikat für Berufsbildner/in / SVEB-Zertifikat / Eidg. Fachausweis Ausbilder/in / Eidg. Diplom Ausbildungsleiter/in / Ausbilder/in für Basiskompetenzen
Bestellen Sie jetzt kostenlos das neue Kursprogramm.
EB Zürich Kantonale Berufsschule für Weiterbildung
Bildungszentrum für Erwachsene BiZE
Riesbachstrasse 11, 8090 Zürich
Telefon 0842 843 844
www.eb-zuerich.ch / lernen@eb-zuerich.ch
EB Zürich

Franco, Kolumbien
„Ich brauche deine Solidarität, denn ich bin Sans-Papiers. Zusammen sind wir stärker!"
Anlaufstelle für Sans-Papiers
Rebgasse 1, 4058 Basel
www.sans-papiers.ch
PC 40-327601-1

AFRIKA PUR!
Im LaFourmi, 12. März 2010, 18.30 bis 3.00 Uhr mit Essen aus dem Togo und dem Maghreb
Nora - Oriental Dance
Alafia - Carneval africain
Daouda Coulibaly und Freunde
DJ Nathalie
Vorverkauf per sms: 078 688 01 73
Stadt Luzern FUKA-Fonds
SüdKulturFonds
THEATRE LA FOURMI

Agency Walker, Zurich
Creative Director Pius Walker
Copywriter Martin Arnold
Art Director Nik Hodel
Graphic Design Andrea Bissig
Advertiser Amnesty International, "Not Here but Now"

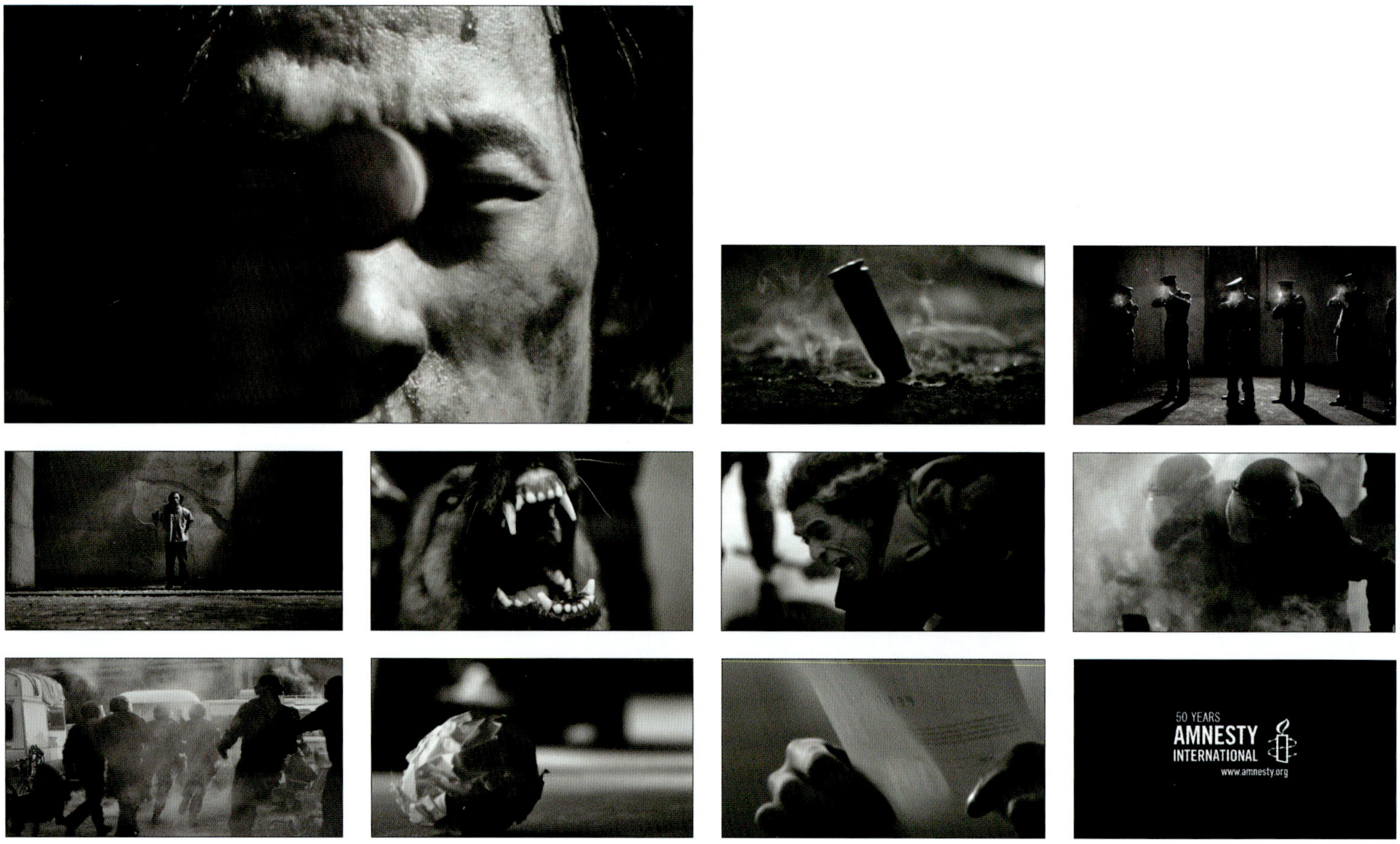
50 YEARS
AMNESTY
INTERNATIONAL
www.amnesty.org

International Alert.

Agency La Chose, Paris
Co-Founder & CD Pascal Grégoire
Copywriter & AD Mickael Krikorian
Production Wanda Productions, Paris
Director Wilfrid Brimo
Producers Claude Fayolle, Nicolas Buisset
Post Production Mikros Image, Paris
Sound The, Paris
PR Manager Barka Zerouali
Advertiser Amnesty International, "The Projection"

A bullet flies backwards from a man's head and returns to a gun. More scenes of violence are shown in reverse: gypsies return to their camp as the police retreat; reporters are freed by soldiers, who march away backwards. In the last scene, a balled-up petition jumps back into a man's hand, where it is smoothed out as he considers signing it. You can defend human rights, and right wrongs. Sign Amnesty International's petition.

Agency HMDG, London
Creative Director Paul Shearer
Production Great Guns, London
Director Paul Shearer
Post Production Rushes, London
Editing The Chop House, London
Advertiser International Alert, "Peace Talks"

Two men in black t-shirts, facing one another in a blank room. One opens his mouth as if to shout. Instead of sound, bullets emerge. They fly towards the other man, who's also silently shouting – but a string of words emerges from his mouth. The words meet the bullets and knock them to the ground. Peace-building NGO International Alert believes violence can be beaten by mere words. Peace, talks.

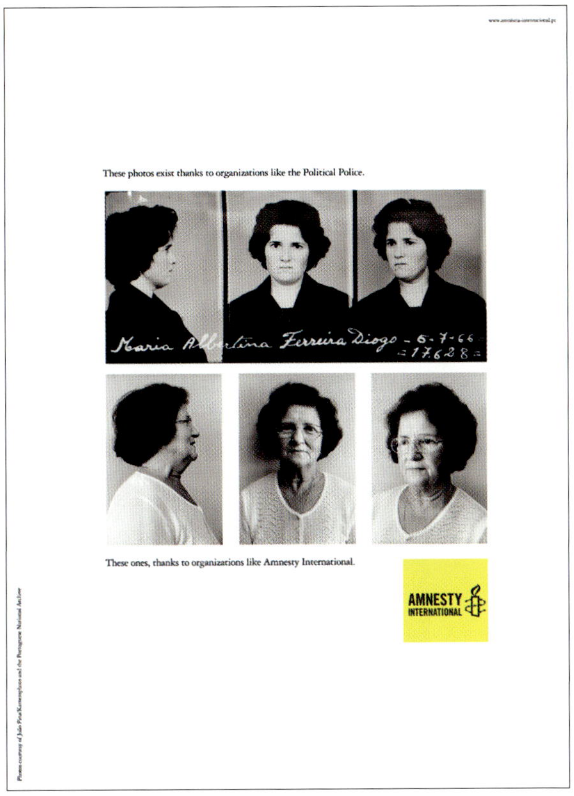
These photos exist thanks to organizations like the Political Police.
These ones, thanks to organizations like Amnesty International.
AMNESTY INTERNATIONAL

These photos exist thanks to organizations like the Political Police.
These ones, thanks to organizations like Amnesty International.
AMNESTY INTERNATIONAL

Ihre Kleider und Accessoires können helfen, den Hunger sozial benachteiligter Kinder in Deutschland zu stillen. www.fashionforfood.de
FASHION FOR FOOD

Agency	Fuel Euro RSCG, Lisbon
Creative Directors	Pedro Bexiga Marcelo Lourenço
Copywriter	Marcelo Lourenço
Art Director	Pedro Bexiga
Photography	João Pina
Advertiser	Amnesty International, "Mugshots"

Agency	Saint Elmo's, Munich
Creative Directors	Arwed Berendts Sebastian Vogel Marcel Koop
Copywriter	Christina Rauschan
Art Director	Francika Tidlacka
Photography	Sara Wilson
Advertiser	Fashion for Food

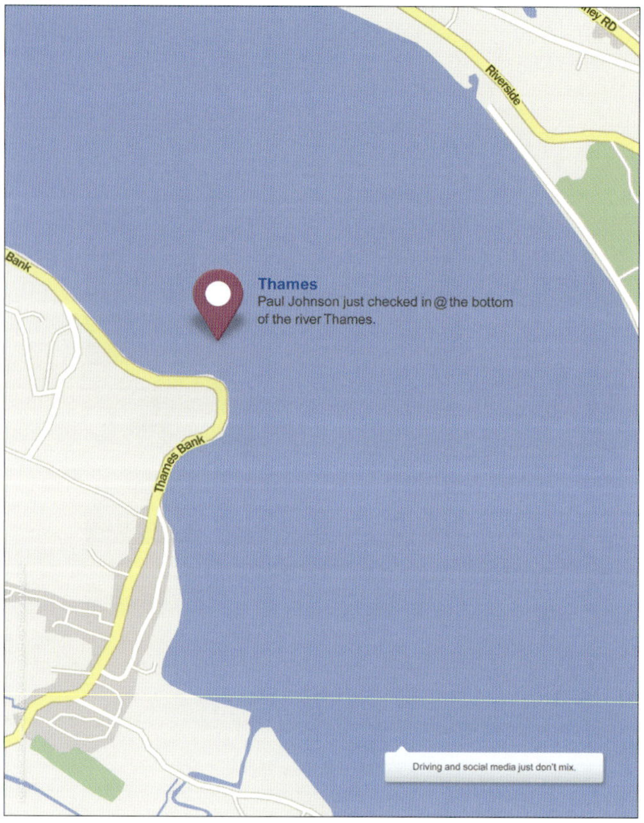
Thames
Paul Johnson just checked in @ the bottom of the river Thames.
Riverside
Thames Bank
Bank
Driving and social media just don't mix.

TEXT WHILE YOU'RE DRIVING
AND YOU'RE 23 TIMES MORE LIKELY
TO HAVE AN ACCIDENT

TOWER HAMLETS
MAYOR OF TOWER HAMLETS
TEXT WHILE YOU'RE DRIVING
AND YOU'RE 23 TIMES MORE LIKELY
TO HAVE AN ACCIDENT

Agency N=5, Amsterdam
Creative Directors Lukas van de Ven, Jeroen van der Sluis
Copywriter Thijs Bontje
Art Director Marco de Jong
Advertiser Top Gear, "River Thames"

Agency Abbott Mead Vickers BBDO, London
Executive CD Paul Brazier
Creative Directors Ant Nelson, Mike Sutherland
Creatives Ant Nelson, Mike Sutherland
Photography Trevor Ray Hart
Art Producer Simon Pedersen
Final Artwork Mark Deamer
Advertiser London Borough of Tower Hamlets, "Boys" & "Girls"

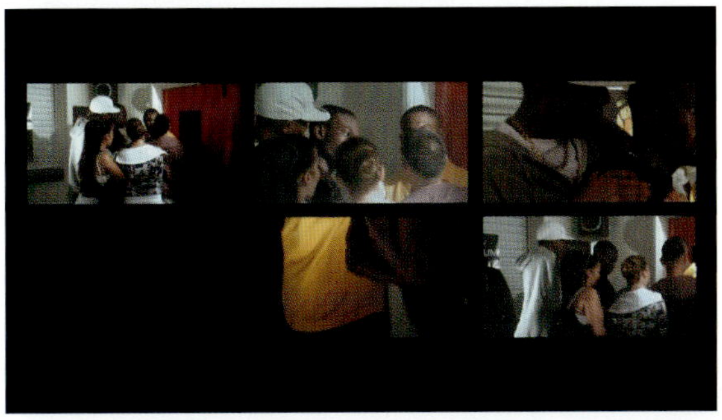

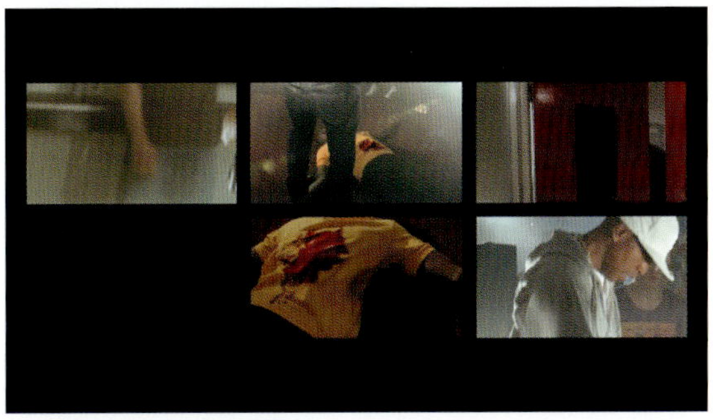

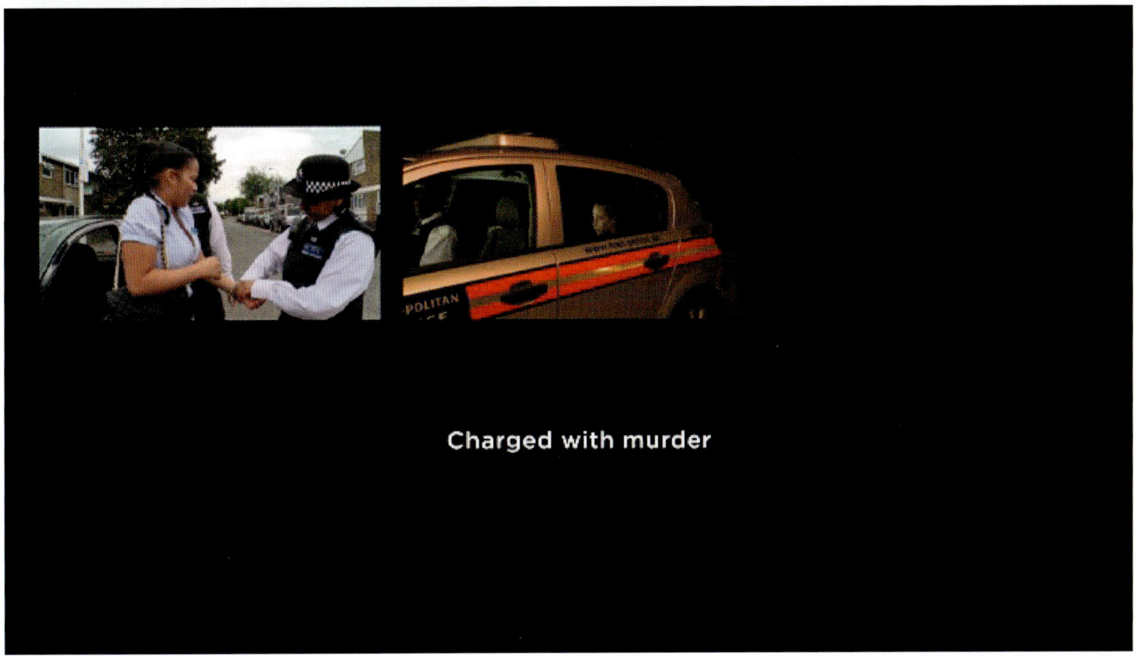
Charged with murder

Agency	Abbott Mead Vickers BBDO, London
Executive CD	Paul Brazier
Creative Directors	Steve Jones Martin Loraine
Creatives	Aidan McClure Laurent Simon
Production	Mad Cow Films, London
Director	Simon Ellis
Exec. Producer	Pete Chambers
Producers	Jonas Blanchard Rebecca Scharf Luke Solson
Editor	Matt Swanpoel
Post Production	The Mill, London
Sound Engineer	Ben Gulvin, 750mph, London
Advertiser	The London Metropolitan Police, "Who Killed Deon?"

In the UK, you don't have to be the one holding the knife or the gun to be convicted of murder. If you encouraged or aided the killer, you're guilty. To educate viewers about the law, the film shows the run-up to a murder at a party. A girl is jealous of her pretty friend, who's flirting with a good-looking guy. One crafty call to the pretty girl's boyfriend, another to the provider of a murder weapon, and the good-looking guy winds up dead. As a result, five people are charged with murder.

Like me.
Not everybody has a network of friends. Become a real life friend at www.redcross.fi
Finnish Red Cross

THOUSANDS OF PEOPLE OWE
THEIR LIVES TO ORGAN DONORS
FRANCE
ADOT

THOUSANDS OF PEOPLE OWE
THEIR LIVES TO ORGAN DONORS
FRANCE
ADOT
Sign up for your donor's card at france-adot.org

Agency	King, Helsinki
Copywriter	Julius Miikkulainen
Art Director	Kasimir Häiväoja
Graphic Design	Teemu Kurko
Advertiser	The Finnish Red Cross Friendship Network, "Like Me"

Agency	CLM BBDO, Paris
Creative Directors	Jean-Francois Sacco Gilles Fichteberg
Copywriter	Julien Perrard
Art Director	Lucie Vallotton
Photography	Deirdre O'Callaghan
Advertiser	France Adot Organ Donation, "The Ghost"

MUSIC TELEVISION
SEX IS NO ACCIDENT.
ALWAYS USE A CONDOM.

Agency	Grey Worldwide, Düsseldorf
Creative Directors	Andreas Henke Sacha Reeb
Copywriter	Janus Hansen
Art Directors	Reto Oetterli Frederico Gasparian Alphons Conzen
Advertiser	MTV, "Sexidents"

TV3
Join us in the fight against breast cancer.
Watch the fundraising gala, tonight on TV3.
Pink Ribbon
The Swedish Cancer Society

–What a glorious moment.
It rarely gets the appreciation it deserves – life, that is. But if you've survived cancer, that appreciation is always there – every minute, every second of every day. Support the fight against cancer and give more people the chance to experience house duties and other boring chores that are a natural part of life. Fight cancer on cancerfonden.se
Cancerfonden
The Swedish Cancer Society

–What an awesome feeling.
Rolf Melin, survived cancer
It rarely gets the appreciation it deserves – life, that is. But if you've survived cancer, that appreciation is always there – every minute, every second of every day. Support the fight against cancer and give more people the chance to experience house duties and other boring chores that are a natural part of life. Fight cancer on cancerfonden.se
Cancerfonden
The Swedish Cancer Society

Agency TBWA\Stockholm
Copywriter Johannes Ivarsson
Art Director Patrick Waters
Final Artwork Fanny von Pongrácz
Account Team Per Olholt, Charlotte Asplund
Advertiser Cancerfonden (The Swedish Cancer Society), "TV3"

Agency TBWA\Stockholm
Copywriter Johannes Ivarsson
Art Director Patrick Waters
Photography Petrus Olsson
Final Artwork Erika Hellström
Account Team Per Olholt, Charlotte Asplund
Planner Niclas Norström
Advertiser Cancerfonden (The Swedish Cancer Society), "Survivors"

"DO YOU BELIEVE CANCER CAN PUT UP WITH THE KIDS ALL SUMMER LONG ?"

I AM A PERSON, NOT A CANCER.
THE CANCER RESEARCH IS MOVING FORWARD.
LET'S CHANGE OUR VISION.
INSTITUT NATIONAL DU CANCER
www.e-cancer.fr

"DO YOU THINK CANCER CAN STILL NAIL THIS PROJECT ?"

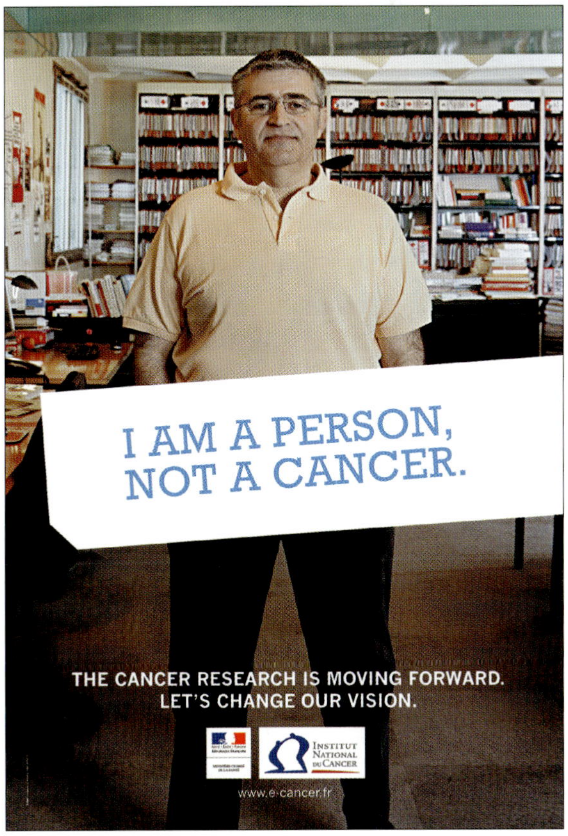
I AM A PERSON, NOT A CANCER.
THE CANCER RESEARCH IS MOVING FORWARD.
LET'S CHANGE OUR VISION.
INSTITUT NATIONAL DU CANCER
www.e-cancer.fr

Agency	La Chose, Paris
Creative Director	Pascal Grégoire
Copywriter	Ibrahim Seck
Art Director	Nathalie Foratier
Photography	Jean-Gabriel Barthélémy
Advertiser	Institut National du Cancer

Mum... when my soul goes to God, how's it going to get through the ceiling?
Childhood cancer is always posing new questions. A cure is the best answer. Help us make it a reality.
www.hilfe-fuer-krebskranke-kinder.de

Dad... if I held on to you very tight, would you go with me to heaven?
Childhood cancer is always posing new questions. A cure is the best answer. Help us make it a reality.
www.hilfe-fuer-krebskranke-kinder.de

Agency Leo Burnett, Frankfurt
CCO Andreas Pauli
Creative Directors Andreas Stalder, Ulf Henniger von Wallersbrunn
Copywriters Andreas Stalder, Marc-Anton Stalder, Leonardo Assad
Art Directors Ulf Henniger von Wallersbrunn, Benjamin Roeder, Juliana Paracencio
Illustrator Aki Roell
Account Director Martin Krauter
Advertiser Hilfe für Krebskranke Kinder Frankfurt, "Children's Cancer - Questions"

exit
DEUTSCHLAND
Help a neo-Nazi leave the scene.
For further information www.exit-deutschland.de

Censorship tells the wrong story.
REPORTERS WITHOUT BORDERS

Censorship tells the wrong story.
REPORTERS

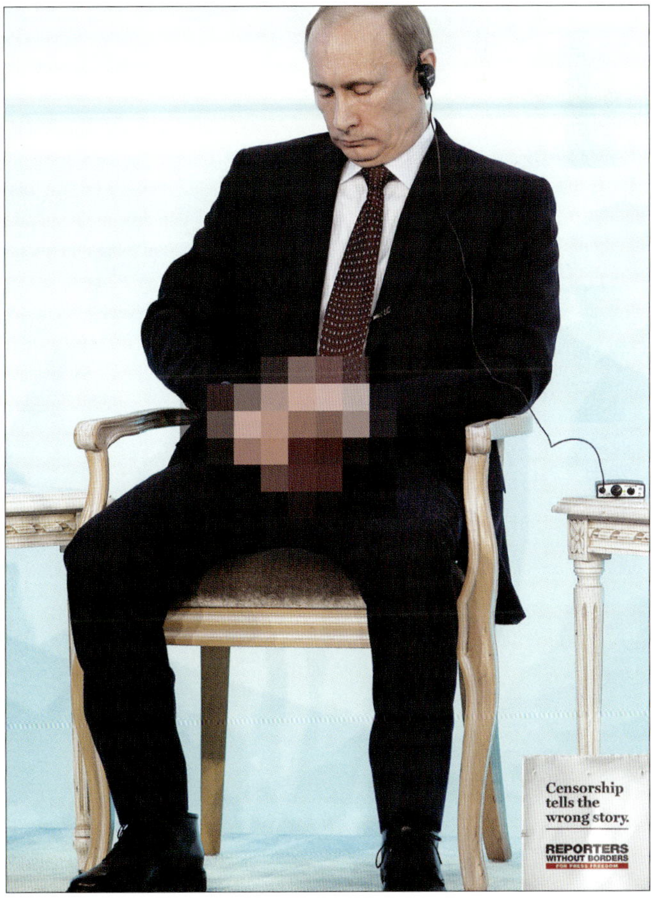
Censorship tells the wrong story.
REPORTERS WITHOUT BORDERS
FOR PRESS FREEDOM

Agency	Kolle Rebbe, Hamburg
Creative Directors	Jens Theil Sven Klohk Ingo Mueller Petra Cremer
Copywriter	Sascha Petersen
Art Director	Alexander Schmid
Photography	Imke Jansen
Graphic Design	Gerwin Schwaeger Florian Hoffmann
Account Team	Tina Jappsen Katharina Voss
Advertiser	Exit Deutschland, "Boot"

Agency	Memac Ogilvy & Mather, Dubai
Creative Directors	Steve Hough Ramzi Moutran
Copywriter	Sascha Kuntze
Art Directors	Sascha Kuntze Leonardo Borges Rafael Rizuto
Advertiser	Reporters Without Borders, "Pixelated Truth"

3D
world
Created by Sony

Home Electronics & Audiovisual Equipment

Agency Grey London
Creative Directors Nils Leonard, Dave Monk, Matt Waller
Copywriters Dave Monk, Matt Waller
Art Directors Dave Monk, Matt Waller
Production Spy Films, Toronto
Director Arev Manoukian
Producers Marcus Truilli, Jacqueline Dobrin
Cinematographer Bojan Bazelli
Editor Will Cyr
Music Leonard Cohen, Clint Mansell
Acct. Supervisor Anneliese St-Amour
Advertiser Sony 3D TVs, "Two Worlds"

This film uses the power of love to illustrate the extra drama provided by Sony's 3D technology. As a couple walk towards one another from opposite sides of a city street, all the obstacles in their path are blasted away by the force of their physical attraction. The gravelly voice of Leonard Cohen reciting "That's What I Heard You Say" adds to the romance. The lovers converge and finally kiss, leaving quite a mess in their wake. Don't just watch: feel.

The new Leica D-Lux 5
with face recognition.
Leica
SHOP

The new Leica D-Lux 5
with face recognition.
Leica
SHOP

Agency	Demner, Merlicek & Bergmann, Vienna
Creative Directors	Rosa Haider Tolga Buyukdoganay
Copywriters	Niki Peterson Nadja Nashef
Art Director	Dominika Babski
Photography	Oliver Gast
Account Team	Moana Merzel Heike Degen
Art Buying	Ilona Urikow
Final Artwork	Aron Cserveny
Advertiser	Leica, "Face Recognition"

elvis
lives
iPod shuffle.

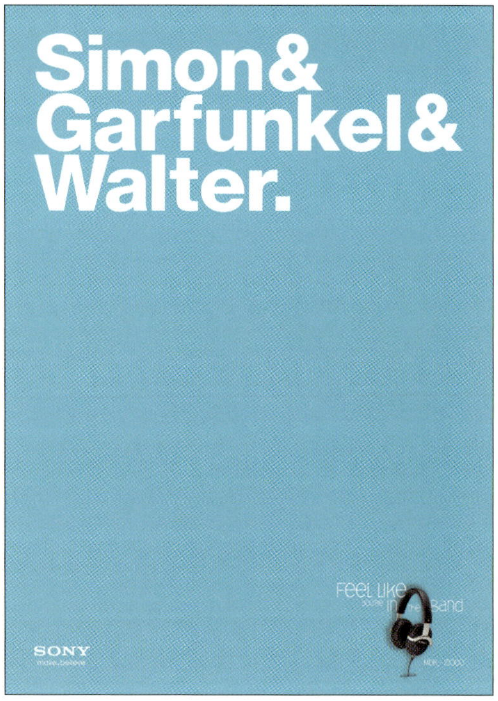
Simon&
Garfunkel&
Walter.
SONY

John&
Paul&
Ringo&
George&
Emma.
FeeL LIKe YOU'Re IN the Band
SONY
make.believe
MDR-Z1000

Agency	Bold Ogilvy & Mather, Athens
Creative Director	Giorgos Garefalakis
Copywriters	Giorgos Garefalakis Dimitris Peponis
Art Directors	Dimitris Peponis Giorgos Garefalakis
Advertiser	iPod Shuffle, "Elvis Lives"

Agency	PKP BBDO, Vienna
Creative Director	Christian Gosch
Copywriter	Christian Gosch
Art Director	Robert Dassel
Graphic Design	Robert Dassel
Advertiser	Sony Headphones, "Band Names"

PSP
ALCOHOL

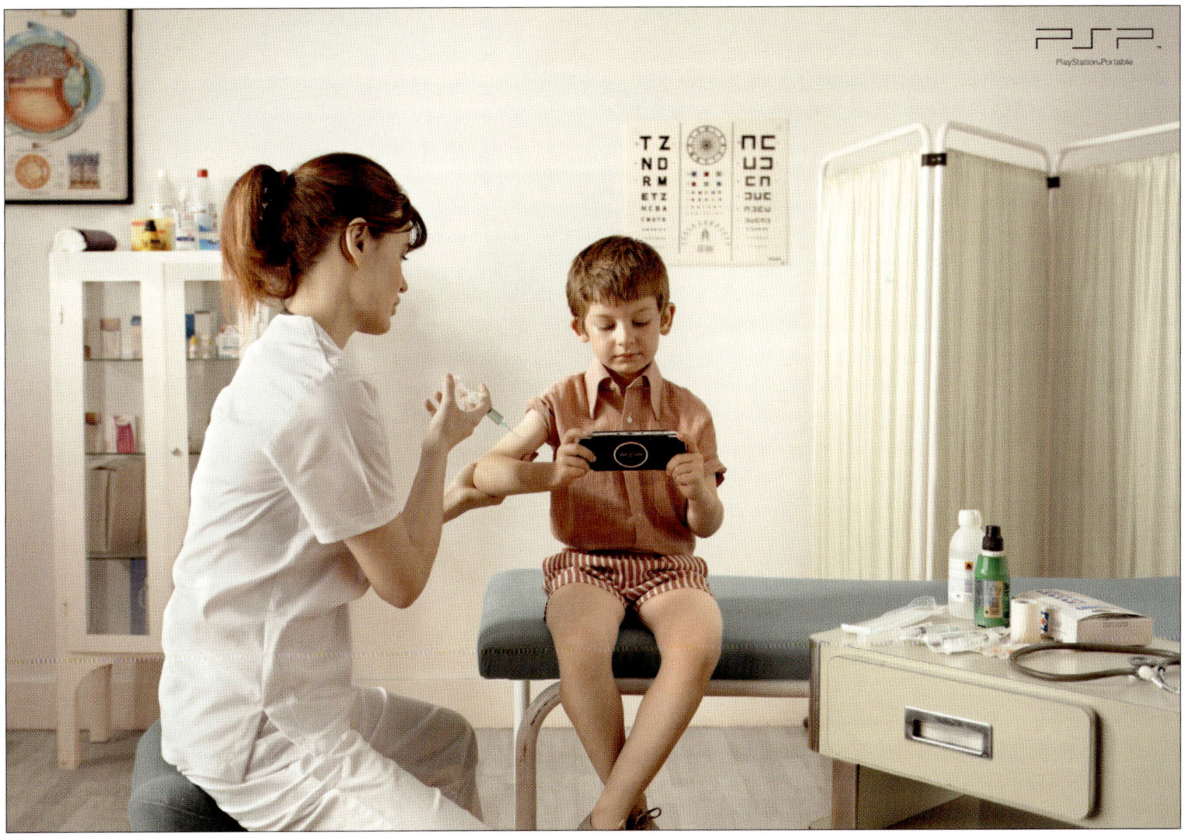
PSP

Agency TBWA\España, Madrid
Creative Directors Juan Sánchez
Guillermo Ginés
Vicente Rodríguez
Copywriter Vicente Rodríguez
Art Director Fran López
Photography Jesús Alonso
Graphic Design Fran López
Typographer Fran López
Advertiser Sony PlayStation, "Wound" & "Injection"

The USB recordable TV
BEKO

The USB recordable TV
BEKO

Agency	TBWA\Istanbul
Creative Directors	Ilkay Gurpinar Emre Kaplan
Copywriter	Ali Sener
Art Director	Burak Kunduracioglu
Illustrators	Omur Kokes Haluk Demirel
Advertiser	Beko TVs, “The Recorded Contents”

DON'T
be YOURSELF
inFAMOUS 2
PS3

DON'T
YOURSELF

DON'T
YOURSELF

DON'T
be YOURSELF
inFAMOUS 2
PS3

Agency	TBWA\España, Madrid
Creative Directors	Juan Sánchez Guillermo Ginés Montse Pastor
Copywriter	Pablo Farrés
Art Director	Gonzalo Vergara
Advertiser	Sony PlayStation, "Infamous"

05/03/2011 23:35:11
REC
INT CAM 2
LIVING ROOM 1
05/03/2011 23:35:15
REC
INT CAM 2
LIVING ROOM 1
05/03/2011 23:35:19
PAUSE
INT CAM 2
LIVING ROOM 1
05/03/2011 23:35:19
PAUSE
INT CAM 2
LIVING ROOM 1
SANTEC
security cameras
REC
INT CAM 7
PRISON CELL 5

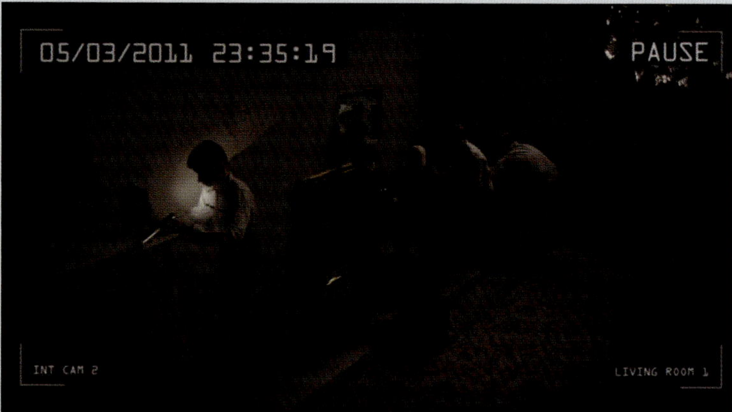

Homes, Furnishings & Appliances

Agency	Serviceplan, Munich	**Director**	Axel Laubscher
Creative Directors	Christoph Nann Maik Kaehler	**Producers**	Pieter Lony Tanja Bruhn Christoph Koehler
Copywriters	Marc Vosshall Rudolf Novotny	**Advertiser**	Santec Video Surveillance, "Santec Prison"
Art Director	Till Diestel		
Production	Cobblestone, Hamburg		

A couple of burglars are emptying the safe in an opulent house. Suddenly, one of them notices they're being observed by a Santec security camera. The men freeze – literally. Then a bunch of scene-shifters enter the room and change the décor around the paralysed burglars, transforming it into a prison cell. When the burglars are snapped out of their trance, they're astonished to find themselves behind bars. Once you're caught on a Santec surveillance camera, there's no escape.

dank!
The history is for free.
2nd HAND FURNITURE

dank!
The history is for free.
2nd HAND FURNITURE

dank!
The history is for free.
2nd HAND FURNITURE
dank-design.com
€25,70

Agency DDB&Co., Istanbul
Creative Director Karpat Polat
Copywriter Eduardo Marques
Art Director Lucas Zaiden
Advertiser Dank! Second-Hand Furniture Store, "History is for Free"

Don't let your partner
interrupt your dreams.
Pfiste
LUNA

GOODBYE AUTUMN.
HIGH POWER BLOWER.
STIHL

Agency Walker, Zurich
Creative Director Pius Walker
Copywriters Martin Arnold, Heinz Helle
Art Directors Golf Nuntawat, Stefanie Huber
Production Knucklehead, London
Director Ben Gregor
Producers Matthew Brown, Lisa Binkert, Cornelia Nünlist
Advertiser Pfister, "The Dinner"

A woman is eating a romantic sushi meal with a good-looking man some years her junior. From the way their eyes meet, we can tell they're attracted to one another. Even the other diners appear to pick up on their sexy chemistry. Suddenly, a middle aged bloke in pyjamas belly-flops onto the table between them. Don't let your partner interrupt your dreams: try Luna, the new movement absorbing bed from Pfister.

Agency Publicis Conseil, Paris
Creative Director Olivier Altmann
Copywriter Patrice Lucet
Art Director Philippe Boucheron
Photography Leo Caillard
Final Artwork Antoine Mairot
Account Team Edouard Pacreau, Stephane Gaillard, Eric Hazout, Sylvie Tavares
Clients Regis Guimont, Gilles Olleris
Advertiser Stihl, "Birds"

VARIÉR
YOUR COMFORT ZONE.
It's never too early to save your back

VARIÉR
YOUR COMFORT ZONE.
It's never too early to save your back

Agency	Alch1m1a ADV, Milan
Creative Directors	Viviana Leveghi Raul Riccardo Pisani
Copywriter	Viviana Leveghi
Art Director	Raul Riccardo Pisani
Photography	Bellocchio & Natalini
Advertiser	Variér, "Back Safeguard"

No overcharges.
IKEA

Shade
RENATE
29,95TL
Fixed prices all year long.
IKEA

Sofa
KARLSTAD
G206xD93xY80
Blekinge white
A range of coordinated covers makes it easy for you to give your furniture a new look.
100% cotton removable, washable cover.
Designer: Tord Björklund.
679TL
IKEA
Home Furnishings
Fixed prices all year long.
IKEA

110 **Homes, Furnishings & Appliances**

Agency TBWA\Istanbul
Creative Directors Ilkay Gurpinar, Volkan Karakasoglu
Copywriter Merve Gezer Subasi
Art Director Ozan Can Bozkurt
Photography Mustafa Nurdogdu
Illustrators Arman Senaz, Arda Senaz
Advertiser Ikea, "Dollar Bills"

Agency TBWA\Istanbul
Creative Directors Ilkay Gurpinar, Volkan Karakasoglu
Copywriter Cagri Saka
Art Director Tolga Ulkumen
Photography Yigit Gunel
Illustrator Tolga Ulkumen
Advertiser Ikea, "Fixed Prices"

SPLASH
Silence Force Vacuum Cleaner
EVERYTHING ELSE SEEMS LOUDER
Rowenta
INTELLIGENT BEAUTY

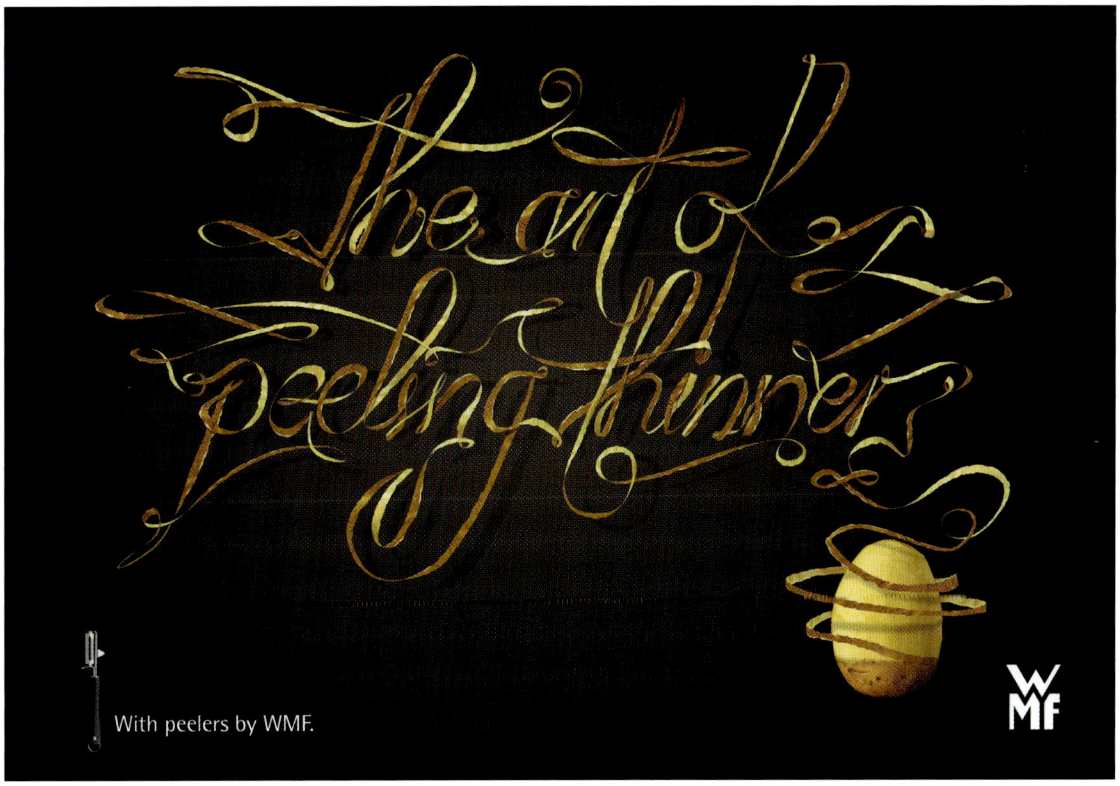
The art of peeling thinner
With peelers by WMF.
WMF

Agency	Publicis Conseil, Paris
Creative Directors	Olivier Altmann Frederic Royer
Copywriter	Mathieu Degryse
Art Directors	Yves-Eric Deboey Jean Weessa
Photography	Jean-Baptiste Begez
Art Buying	Jean-Luc Chirio
Account Team	Jean-Patrick Chiquiar Vincent Larnaudie Charlotte Baudry Jeanne Gauthier
Advertiser	Rowenta, "Big Noises"

Agency	KNSK, Hamburg
Creative Directors	Tim Krink Ulrike Wegert
Copywriter	Dieter Kolaja
Art Directors	Julian Heidt Thomas Thiele Oliver Fermer
Photography	Peter Backens
Graphic Design	Julian Heidt Sara Stowasser
Account Director	Kirsten Kohls
Advertiser	WMF Peelers, "Potato"

SECURITY
WINDOWS & DOORS BY
actual

BRÖKER
SICHERHEITSSYSTEME
SECURITY SYSTEMS
PERFECTLY INTEGRATED

BRÖKER
SICHERHEITSSYSTEME
SECURITY SYSTEMS
PERFECTLY INTEGRATED

Agency Demner, Merlicek & Bergmann, Vienna
Creative Directors Rene Pichler, Alistair Thompson
Photography Markus Thums
Graphic Design Lukas Hueter
Art Buying Ilona Urikow
Final Artwork Stefan Loeffler
Account Team Magda Schlegel, Stefanie Trauner
Advertiser Actual Security Windows, "Bedroom"

Agency Publicis, Frankfurt
CCOs Volkers Schrader, Stephan Ganser
Creative Director Diana Sukopp
Copywriter Daniel Steller
Art Director Christian Kuzman
Photography Sven Glage
Post Production Alphadog, Hamburg
Art Buying Katja Bonnert
Account Team Christian Emme, Claudia Giese
Advertiser Bröker Security Systems, "Piano" & "Horn"

€619
€2,235/pc
€85
€179
€3,459
€2,199
€99
€2,097
€1,670
€7,850
€325
€115,890
€439

€149
SAMSUNG

ROLF
BENZ

Agency	Ogilvy, Budapest
Creative Directors	Will Rust Ferenc Benesch
Copywriter	Karolina Galacz
Art Director	Zoltan Visy
Photography	David Lukacs
Advertiser	Samsung Modern Alarm, "Break-In"

Two consecutive double page ads pay homage to a certain Swedish home furnishings provider. The first shows the cost of replacing all the items damaged during a break-in. The second shows the single and much lower cost of installing a Modern Alarm home security system from Samsung.

Agency	Serviceplan, Munich
CCO	Alex Schill
Executive CD	Matthias Harbeck
Creative Director	Alexander Rehm
Copywriter	Frank Seiler
Art Directors	Julia Koch Sophia Puck
Graphic Design	Franz Röppischer
Advertiser	Rolf Benz, "What Trees Dream About"

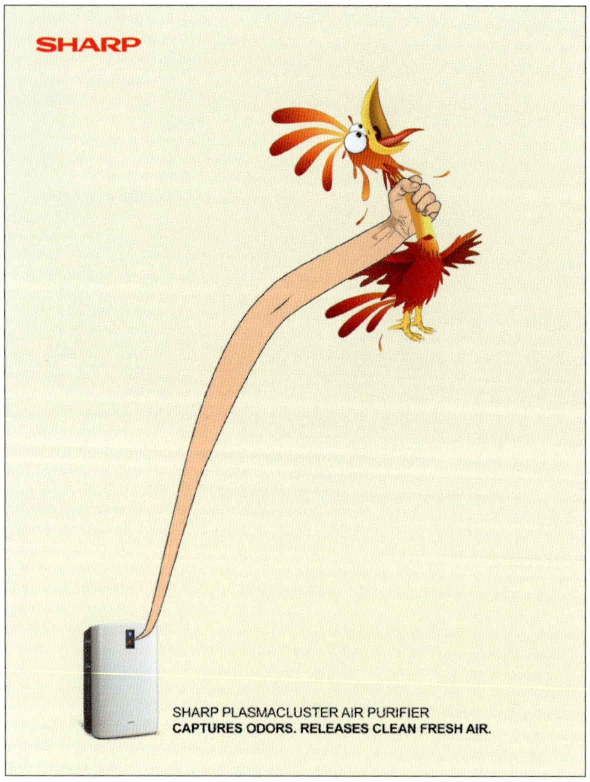
SHARP
SHARP PLASMACLUSTER AIR PURIFIER
CAPTURES ODORS. RELEASES CLEAN FRESH AIR.

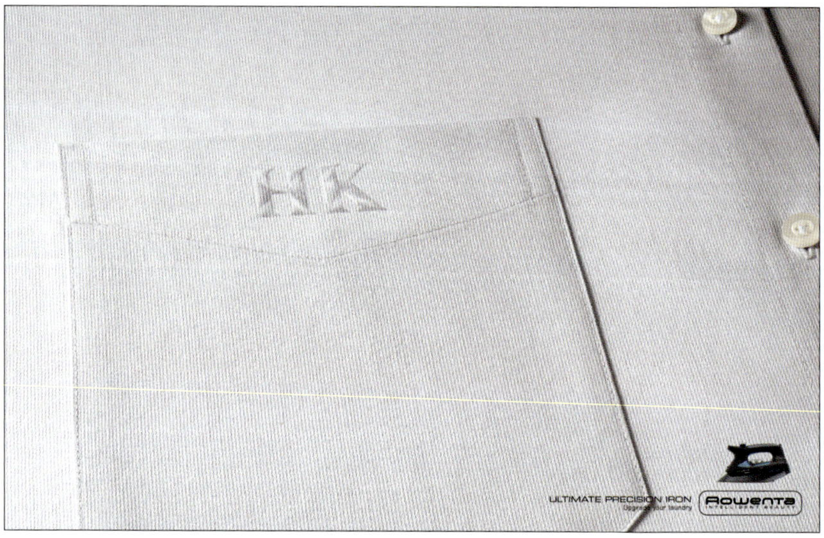
HK
ULTIMATE PRECISION IRON
Rowenta

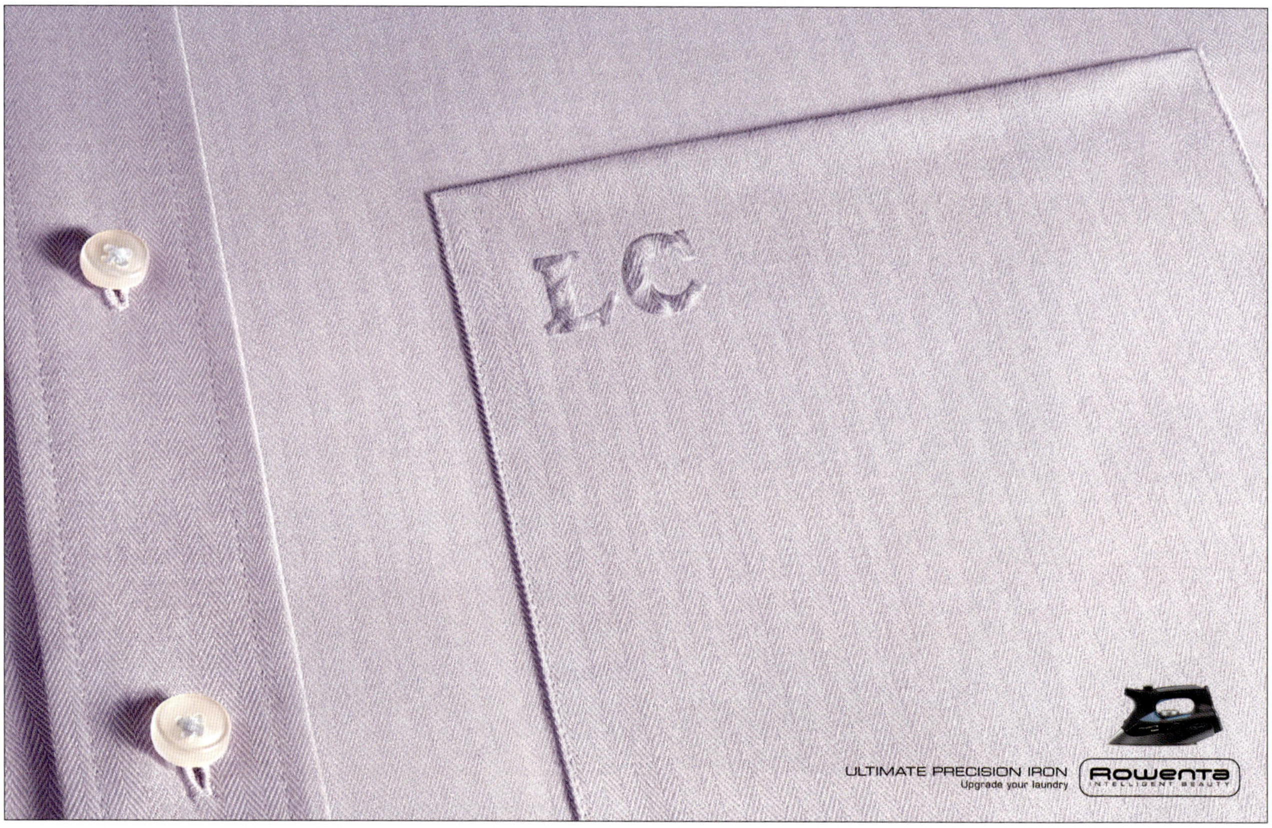
LC
ULTIMATE PRECISION IRON
Upgrade your laundry
Rowenta
INTELLIGENT BEAUTY

 Homes, Furnishings & Appliances

Agency	Ikon, Dubai
Creative Director	Shantesh Row
Assistant CD	Samson Dsouza
Art Director	Jayanand Pujari
Vice President	Lopamudra Kundu
Advertiser	Sharp Air Purifiers, "Captures Odors"

Agency	Publicis Conseil, Paris
Creative Directors	Olivier Altmann Frederic Royer
Copywriter	Olivier Dermaux
Art Directors	Mathieu Vinciguerra Melanie Pennec
Photography	Daniel Schweitzer
Art Buying	Alexandra Riviere
Account Team	Jean-Patrick Chiquiar Vincent Larnaudie Charlotte Baudry Jeanne Gauthier
Advertiser	Rowenta, "Monogrammes"

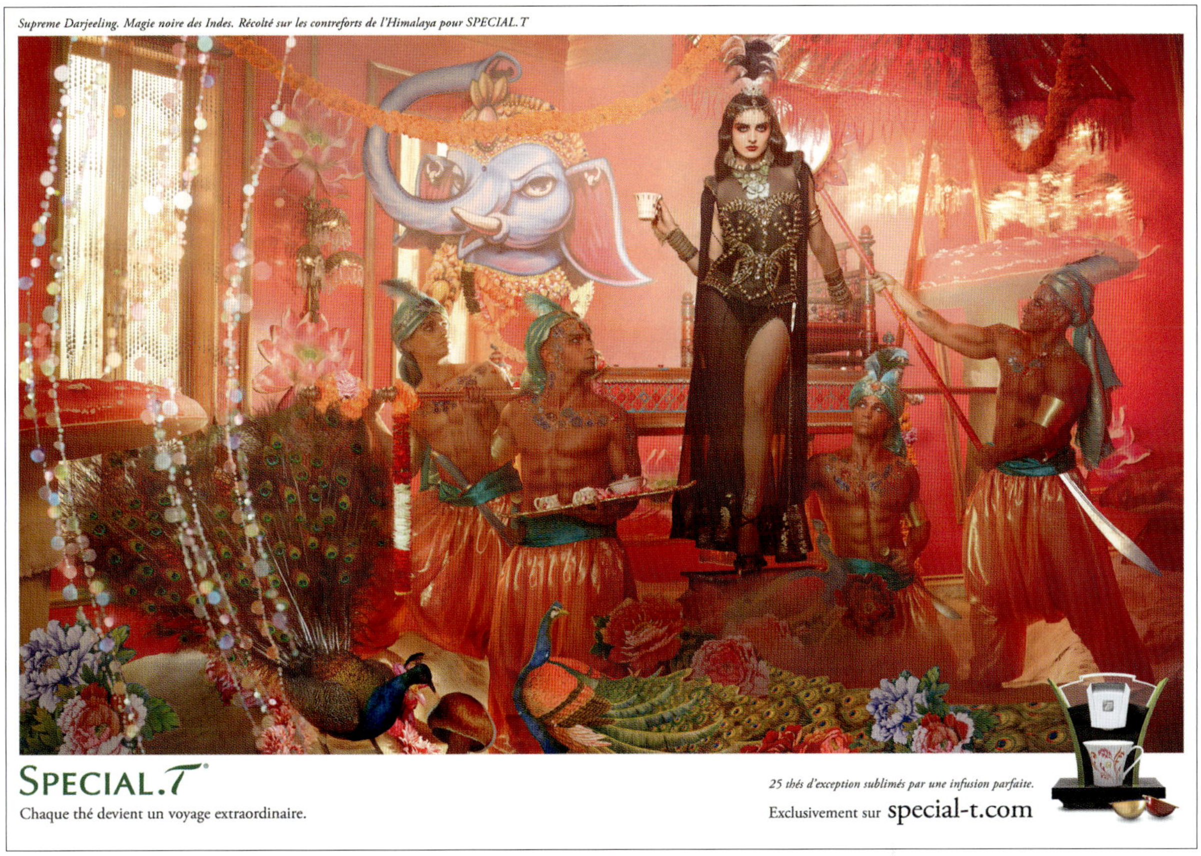
Supreme Darjeeling. Magie noire des Indes. Récolté sur les contreforts de l'Himalaya pour SPECIAL.T
SPECIAL.T
Chaque thé devient un voyage extraordinaire.
25 thés d'exception sublimés par une infusion parfaite.
Exclusivement sur special-t.com

KEEP YOUR DRINK HOT FOR HOURS
TIGER

Agency	Publicis Dialog, Paris
Creative Director	Michel Duval
Copywriter	Jean-Louis Zuber
Art Director	Jean-Christophe Esclafit
Photography	David LaChapelle
Art Buying	Nathalie Maudet
Account Team	Matthieu Faure Elise Gaiardo
Planner	Anne Dimier-Vallet
Advertiser	Nestlé Special.T, "Each Tea Becomes an Extraordinary Journey"

Agency	FP7/RUH, Riyadh
Executive CD	Ahmad Beck
Copywriter	Ahmad Beck
Art Directors	Ahmad Beck Ramero Firmeza
Photography	Steve Kozman
Digital Artwork	Amin Daou
CSD	Mohammad Abdel-Kader Baqalb
Client	Al Zahrani Trading
Advertiser	Tiger Vacuum Jar, "Always Hot"

Did you know that Colon 101 removes 101 stains?

101 stains. Got a little carried away, haven't they?

Removes

Household Maintenance

Agency	Euro RSCG, Tel Aviv
Creative Director	Ben Sever
Copywriters	Ilan Nachmian Yiftach Chozev
Art Director	Ben Sever
Production	Shoshi and Udi, Tel Aviv
Director	Adam Sanderson
Producers	Shoshi Sofer Dana Caro
Advertiser	Colon 101, "101 Stains"

Unloading their shopping from the car, a woman tells her husband that the product she's bought can remove "101 different stains." The husband scoffs: "Got a bit carried away, haven't they?" A second later he's carried away…by a runaway golf cart whose careering route causes him to pick up stains of orange juice, ice cream, garbage, barbecue sauce, soy sauce, cream, mud, clay…you name it. Stained from head to toe, the man returns to his wife. Wordlessly, he takes the stain remover from her hands.

TRUE COLOURS
FABER-CASTELL
since 1761

TRUE COLOURS
FABER-CASTELL
since 1761

Agency	Serviceplan, Munich
CCO	Alex Schill
Executive CD	Matthias Harbeck
Creative Director	Oliver Palmer
Copywriters	Nicolas Becker Lorenz Langgartner
Art Director	Andreas Balog
Graphic Design	Marijo Sanje
Advertiser	Faber-Castell, "True Colours"

Sopalin
THE ART OF CLEANING by Sopalin

Bissell
HAIRLESS CLEAN

Bissell
Experts in Home Cleaning
HAIRLESS CLEAN
ShedAway Pet vacuum attachment

Agencies	Révolutions, Paris Leo Burnett, Paris
Creative Director	Pascal Etchebarne
Copywriter	Lucas Bouneou
Art Directors	François-Xavier Barre Antoine Davy
Illustrator	Si Scott
Advertiser	Sopalin, "The Art of Cleaning"

Agency	FP7/DXB, Dubai
Creative Director	Fadi Yaish
Art Director	Supparat Thepparat
Photography	Illusion Bangkok: Anuchai Secharunputong Nok Pipattungkul
Illustration	Illusion Bangkok: Chanchay Aussawanuchit
Producer	Clarisse Mar Wai May
Advertiser	Bissell ShedAway Pet Vaccum Attachment, "Inside Out"

SEKUNDA GLUE. SUPER INSTANT

Agency	McCann Erickson, Istanbul
Creative Director	Gokhan Yucel
Copywriter	Ali Bozkurt
Art Director	Caglar Cengiz
Illustrator	Caglar Cengiz
Advertiser	3M Scotch-Brite Lint Roller, "Your Pet's Hair is Not a Problem."

Agency	BBDO, Moscow
Creative Director	Mihai Coliban
Copywriter	Andrey Sivkov
Art Directors	Max Kitaev Mihai Coliban
Acct. Manager	Ekaterina Konovalova
Post Production	Fiero Animals, Moscow
Advertiser	Sekunda Glue, "Bullets"

tempo
Super Absorbent Paper Towel

1. Place HAMMER in hand.
2. Earn back your SELF-RESPECT.
EVERY CHANGE NEEDS A BEGINNING.
HORNBACH
Home Improvement Superstores

1. Grip DRILL firmly.
2. Show your WIFE once and for all that you are the RIGHT one for her.
EVERY CHANGE NEEDS A BEGINNING.
HORNBACH
Home Improvement Superstores

Household Maintenance

Agency	THE, İstanbul
Creative Directors	Alper Pala Caglar Eser
Copywriter	Toygar Arat
Art Directors	Mustafa Ozmal Ugur Say
Photography	Engin Yıldız
Illustrator	Ugur Say
Advertiser	Tempo Paper Towel, "Tattoo"

Agency	Heimat, Berlin
Creative Directors	Guido Heffels Myles Lord
Copywriter	Sabina Hesse
Art Directors	Susanna Fill Jue Alt
Photography	Ragnar Schmuck
Illustrator	Viktor Koen
Graphic Design	Jue Alt
Typographer	Teresa Jung
Advertiser	Hornbach, "Every Change Needs a Beginning."

Extra Absorbent
vileda

UNIVERSAL
NEOSTIK

Agency	FP7/ MCT, Muscat
Creative Director	Noufal Ali
Copywriter	Noufal Ali
Art Director	Noufal Ali
Photography	Kailash K Sony
Graphic Design	Renjith Pillai
Advertiser	Vileda Kitchen Sponges, "Milking"

Agency	Agencija Imelda, Ljubljana
Creative Director	Jure Požun
Copywriter	Andrej Baša
Art Director	Branislav Milošević
Photography	Matjaž Tančič
Graphic Design	Jože Martinčič
Account Director	Nina Hočevar
Advertiser	Neostik Universal Glue, "Medic"

EFFORTLESS CLEANING
Flash

BECAUSE IT'S RARE
TO BE PROUD
OF A STAIN
K2r
Stain remover powder
Dangerous. Follow the precautions for use.

BECAUSE IT'S RARE
TO BE PROUD
OF A STAIN
K2r
Stain remover powder
Dangerous. Follow the precautions for use.

Agency	Leo Burnett, London
Executive CD	Justin Tindall
Creative Directors	Richard Brim Daniel Fisher
Copywriter	Daniel Fisher
Art Director	Richard Brim
Designer	Lance Crozier
Advertiser	Flash, "Effortless Cleaning"

Agency	TBWA\Paris
Creative Directors	Eric Holden Rémi Noël
Copywriter	Daniel Perez
Art Director	Mohamed Bareche
Photography	Sacha Goldberger
Art Buying	Carine Galluffo
Account Team	Siegrid Bourgois Teddy Notari
Advertiser	K2R, "Unexpected Stains"

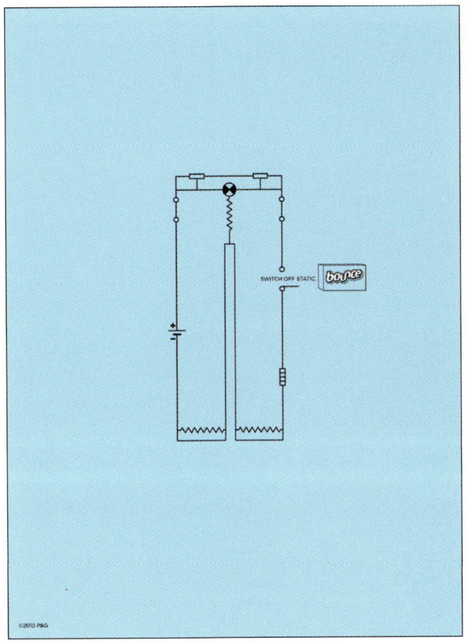
SWITCH OFF STATIC
bounce
©2010 P&G

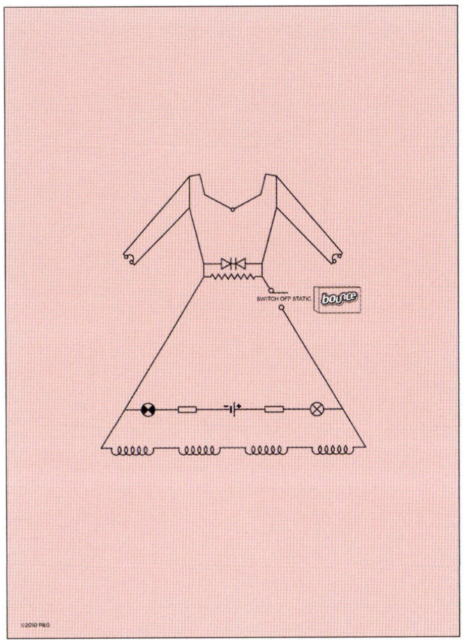
SWITCH OFF STATIC
bounce
©2010 P&G

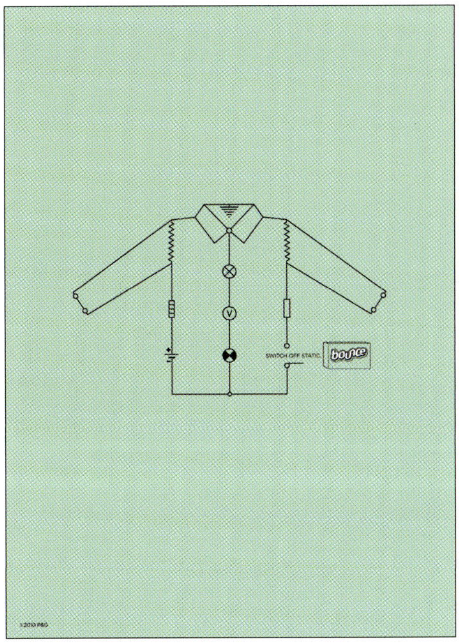
SWITCH OFF STATIC
bounce
©2010 P&G

OFFICIAL SPONSOR OF THE SWEDISH NATIONAL ICE HOCKEY TEAM
ALCRO

Agency Leo Burnett Iberia, Madrid
Creative Directors Chacho Puebla, Paulo Areas, Francisco Cassis
Copywriter Roberto Luque
Art Director Pouline Atencio
Advertiser Bounce Anti-Static Fabric Softener, "Switch Off"

Agency Lowe Brindfors, Stockholm
Creative Directors Rickard Villard, Martin Bartholf
Copywriter Peter Laurelli
Photography Ian Crawford
Graphic Design Jeanette Andersson
Account Team Maria Lundvall, Marie Klinte, Anette Nygårds, Karolina Jansson
Advertiser Alcro Paint, "Colour Tackle"

J'adore
Dior

Beauty Products & Services

Agency	TBWA\Paris
Creative Directors	Eric Holden Rémi Noël Sophie Guyon
Art Director	Stephanie Ragot
Production	Wanda Productions
Director	Jean-Jacques Annaud
Producers	Francois Lamotte Maxime Boiron Herve Dommange Patrick Barbier
Prod. Coordinator	Julien Floutard
Sound Design	Else
Post Production	Mikros Image, Paris Julien Meester Pascal Giroux Manuel Souillac Olivier Mitonneau Michael Nauzin Guillaume Terrien Stephane Pivron Benoit Holl
Account Team	Guillaume Pannaud Luc Bourgery
Planner	Vincent Garel
Advertiser	Dior, "J'Adore"

At Versailles, a fashion show is about to begin. A young woman dashes in: Charlize Theron, who's late for her opening slot on the catwalk. To our surprise, she's greeted by Grace Kelly – who seems impressed by her beauty. Backstage, she slips into a slinky gold dress while a feline Marlene Dietrich looks at her appraisingly. As Charlize fixes her hair, Marilyn Monroe borrows her bottle of Dior perfume. "J'Adore," pouts Marilyn, who's normally associated with Chanel. Charlize struts onto the runway, every bit the equal of these Hollywood legends as cameras flash around her.

CARRYING TOO MUCH WEIGHT?
pilateswithgerda

CARRYING TOO MUCH WEIGHT?
pilateswithgerda

Agency	Concept, Istanbul
Creative Directors	Kerem Altuntas Kerem Ozkut
Copywriter	Emre Kuzuoglu
Art Director	Fatih Senay
Illustrator	Fatih Senay
Graphic Design	Fatih Senay
Advertiser	Pilates with Gerda, "Belly Bag" & "Butt Bag"

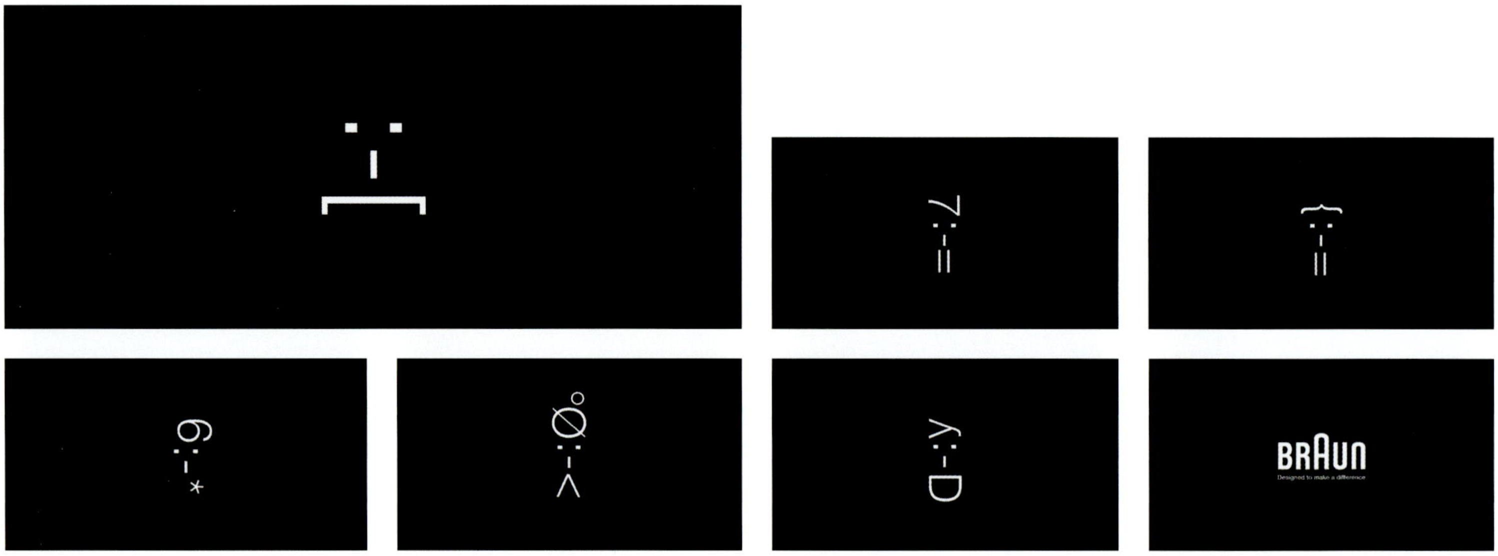
BRAUN

Because hair is your most beautiful accessory. Iam Haircare.

Agency BBDO Proximity, Düsseldorf
CCOs Christian Mommertz, Wolfgang Schneider
Copywriter Christopher Fink
Art Director Stephan Eichler
Post Production VCC, Düsseldorf
Directors Christian Mommertz, Steffen Gentis
Producer Christian Winnig
Designer Philipp Alings
Advertiser Braun Multistyler, "Hairmoticons"

"Emoticons" are the little faces we create in e-mails and texts using punctuation marks – a smiling face with a bracket mouth and colon eyes is the most common example. In this fast-paced animation we meet the "hairmoticons" – emoticons with hairstyles. Each style expresses a different mood. And you can change your own hairstyle just as easily with the Braun Satin Hair 5 Multistyler.

Agencies Exxtra Kommunikation, Zurich; Advico Y&R, Zurich
CCO Markus Gut
Creative Directors Dominik Oberwiler, Martin Stulz
Copywriters Marietta Mügge, Sascha Borsai
Art Director Benny Goldstein
Photography Chris Tribelhorn
Graphic Design Sarah Paul, Joelle Hauser
Advertiser Migros, "Precious Hair"

GARNIER
SKIN NATURALS
UltraLift
Anti-Aging Firming Cream

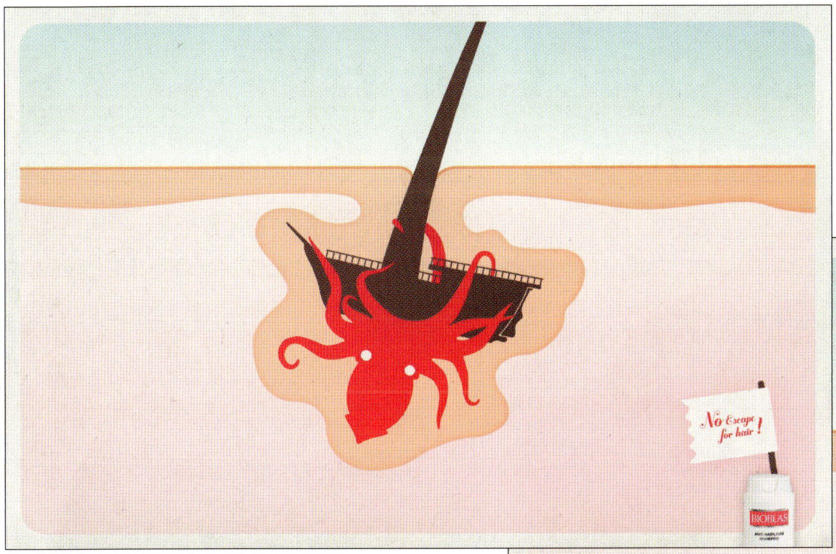
No Escape for hair!
BIOBLAS

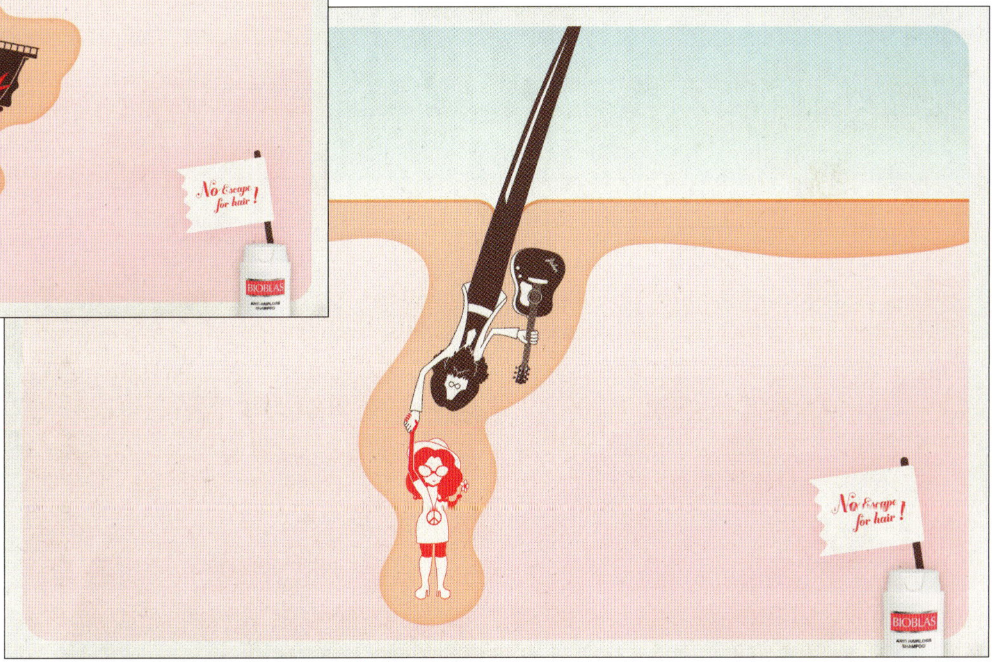
No Escape for hair!
BIOBLAS

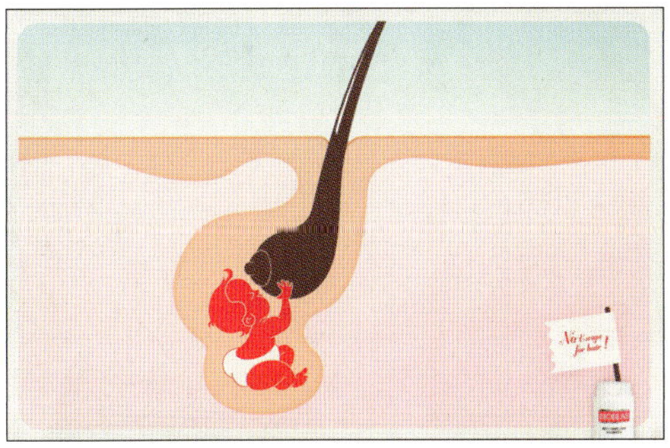

Agency	Publicis, Zurich
Creative Director	Peter Rettinghausen
Copywriter	Peter Rettinghausen
Art Director	Bruce Roberts
Photography	Scheffold Vizner
Account Team	Margrit Weber Jennifer Meier
Advertiser	Garnier, "Forever Young"

Agency	DDB&Co., Istanbul
Creative Director	Karpat Polat
Art Director	Edward Sedelius
Illustrator	Edward Sedelius
Advertiser	Bioblas, "No Escape for Hair"

"What are you thinking of up there at HQ?
It's chaos down here!"
How are the working conditions in your tummy?
"No, I don't think anyone wants to have it like this."
"What is it you do down here?"
"Aaah, so good getting rid of this shit,
feels like I've been waiting forever."
Kenneth Hill
Intestines
"Damn! I can't keep up."
How are the working conditions in your tummy?
"Stop it! You've got to stop now!"
apoteket
Sweden's Pharmacy

Agency	Forsman & Bodenfors, Gothenburg	**Account Team**	Leif Sorte
			Daniel Smedfors
Copywriter	Anna Qvennerstedt	**Planning**	My Troedsson
Art Director	Joakim Blondell		Tobias Nordström
Production	FLX, Stockholm	**Client**	Johan Landeström
Director	Felix Herngren		Susanne Lysholm
Producers	Ylva Axéll	**Advertiser**	Apoteket (Pharmacy of Sweden), "Stomach Test"
	Sandra Sohlman		
	Magnus Kennhed		

This funny campaign portrays the human digestive system as a small business. In documentary-style clips, we see the "workers" being interviewed. Susan Miller, "stomach", has to shred all the paperwork she receives from a hatch in her ceiling. Then she stuffs it through a tube to Kenneth Hill, "intestines". He bags it up and sends it down to Sheldon Baker, "rectum", who drops it out of a final hatch "once or twice a day". They all seem stressed out by their jobs. How are the working conditions in your stomach? Might be time to visit the Pharmacy of Sweden.

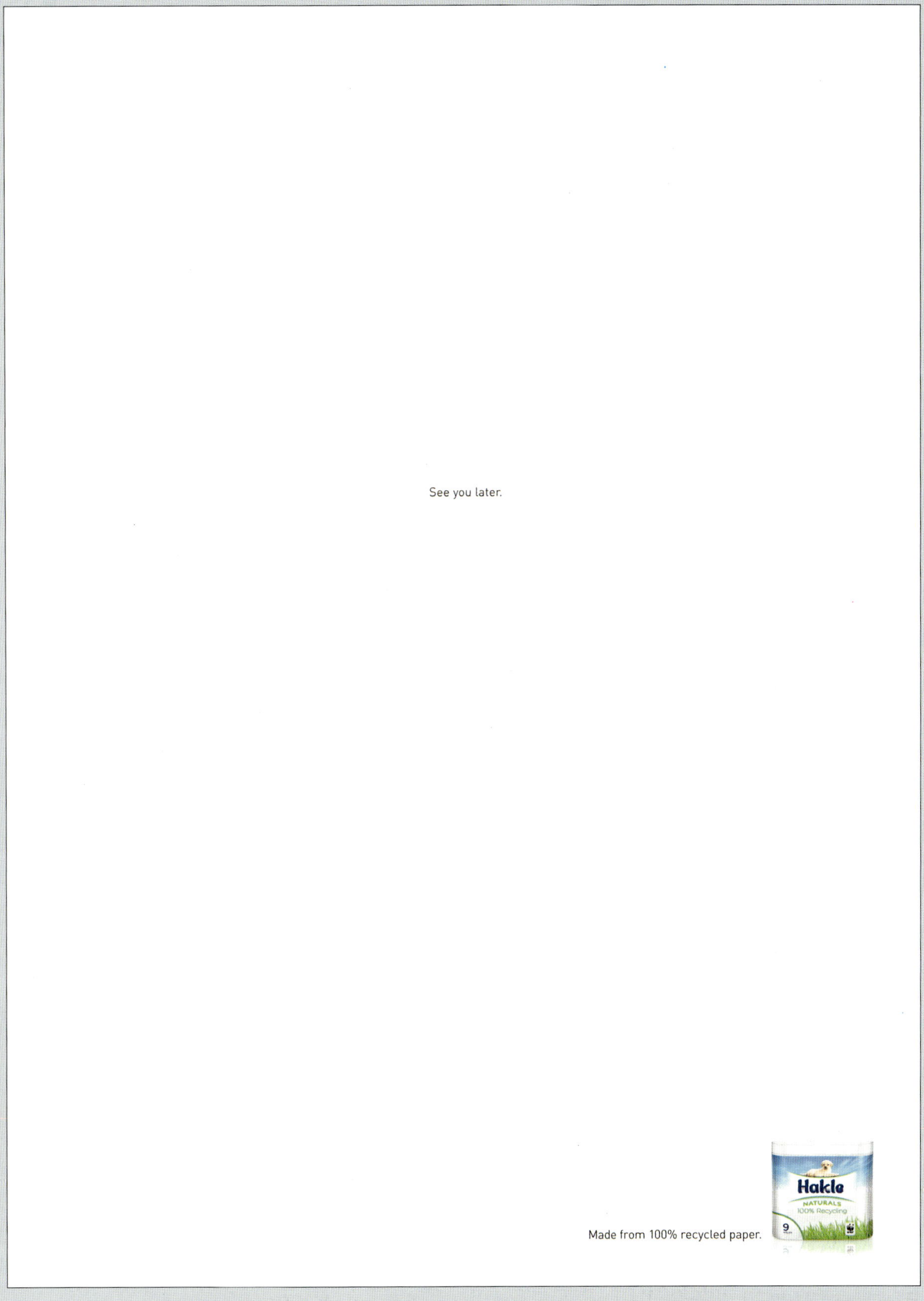
See you later.
Made from 100% recycled paper.
Hakle
NATURALS
100% Recycling

Agency	JWT/Fabrikant, Zurich
CCO	Remy Fabrikant
Creative Directors	Andreas Maedler Grischa Rubinick
Copywriter	Mathias Bart
Art Director	Roger Dobmann
Typographer	David Guntern
Acct. Supervisor	Vanessa Lehmann Spalleck
Planner	Rainer Buehler
Advertiser	Hakle Recycled Toilet Paper, “See you Later”

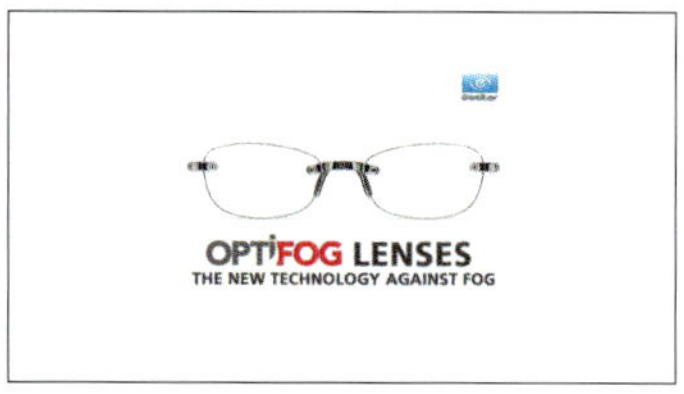
OPTIFOG LENSES
THE NEW TECHNOLOGY AGAINST FOG

Agency Herezie, Paris
Creative Director Andrea Stillacci
Copywriters Jean-Laurent Py, Edouard Dorbais
Art Directors Rémi Arnaud, Julian Brice, Sebastien Boutebel
Production Hard Citizen, Toronto
Director Christopher Hutsul
Producers Eva Preger, Jacinte Faria, Link York, Nick Sorbara, Barbara Vaira
Editor Ross Birchall
Post Production Alter Ego, Toronto
Cinematographer Tico Poulakakis
Planning Luc Wise, Celine Choueri
Advertiser Essilor Optifog Lenses, "Foggy Moments"

A man arrives home on a cold, snowy night. His little dog runs to greet him. He picks it up, then inexplicably begins rubbing his face against its furry arse. He wrinkles his nose – and we see that the lenses of his glasses are steamed up. He can't tell one end of his pooch from the other. Having a foggy moment? Try Essilor Optifog lenses, the new technology against fog.

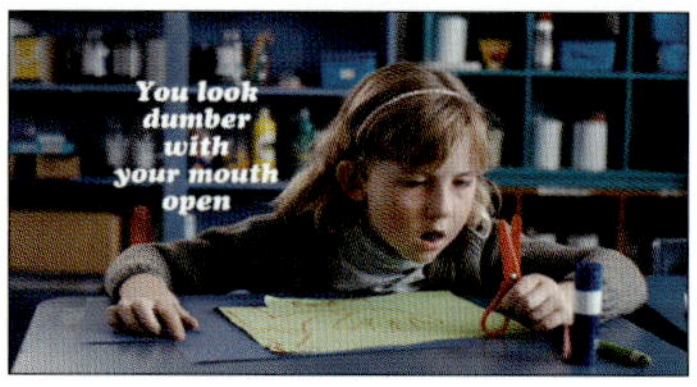
You look
dumber
with
your mouth
open

You look
dumber
with
your mouth
open

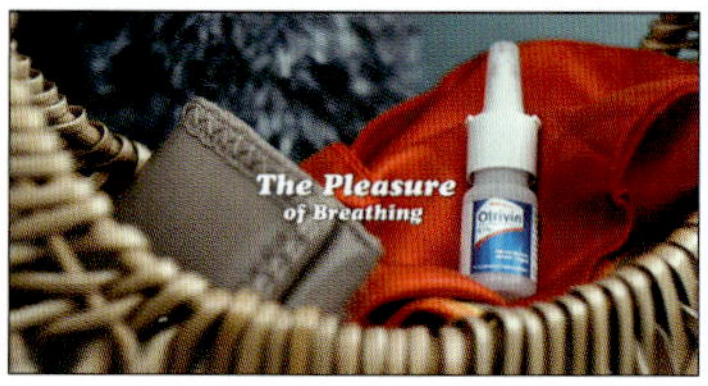
The Pleasure
of Breathing

Agency Saatchi & Saatchi, Geneva
CCOs John Pallant, Derek Green
Creative Director Leon Jacobs
Copywriters Maureen McCabe, Boris Declerck
Art Directors Lisa McLeod, Daniela Nedelschi, Lucy Crudgington
Production The Sweet Shop
Director Sam Holst
Advertiser Otrivin Nasal Spray

Two spots encouraging us to take nasal decongestant when we've got a cold. In the first, a teacher is handing out metal scissors so children can cut paper patterns during a craft lesson. Seeing one little girl's mouth hanging slackly open, the teacher gives her blunt plastic scissors. The girl looks faintly aggrieved. But you look dumber when your mouth's open. Otrivin would help her breathe through her nose.

A man stands at a bus stop. Shoulders hunched, one shoelace undone, mouth agape. A woman looks at him with a mixture of concern and pity. Unable to restrain herself, she crouches down and ties his shoelace for him. The man looks astonished. But after all, you look dumber when your mouth's open. Otrivin: the pleasure of breathing.

BRAUN
Silk·épil

BRAUN
Silk·épil

BRAUN
Silk·épil
precision trimmer

Agency	Impact BBDO, Dubai
Executive CD	Fouad Abdel Malak
Copywriter	Darren McCall
Art Directors	Mohammed Diaa
	Mark Held
	Andrej Arsenijevic
Photography	Andreas Franke
	Ricardo Salamanca
Illustrator	Mladen Penev
Art Buying	Mariam Moin
Account Team	Talal Sheikh Elard
	Noura Al Nazer
Advertiser	Braun Trimmers

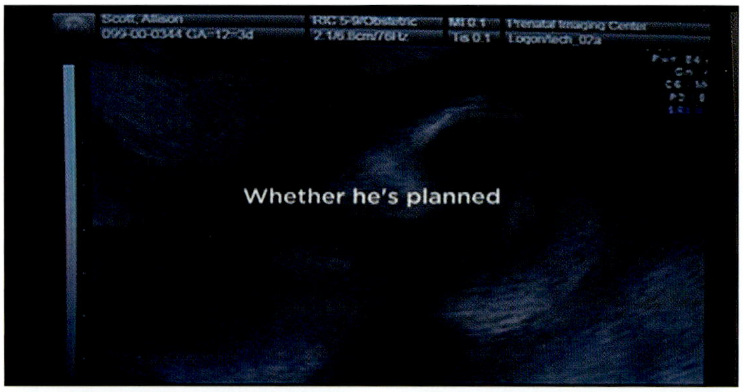
Whether he's planned

or not.

Whether she learns one language

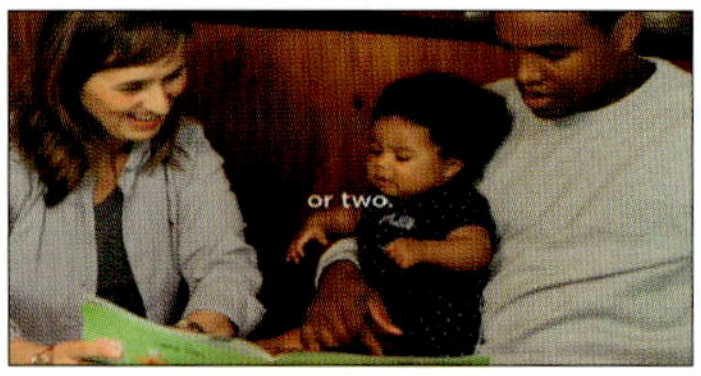
or two.

Pampers
For every little miracle.
facebook.com/pampers

Agency	Saatchi & Saatchi, New York
Worldwide P&G CD	Cliff Francis
Global CD	Tris Gates-Bonarius
CCO	Con Williamson
Creative Directors	Adam Kerj Jorg Riommi
Digital CD	James Cooper
Copywriter	Cliff Francis
Production	Twin Film, Munich
Director	Jan Gleie
Producers	Marc Stemmer Ryan Fitch, Michael von Schmidt-Pauli
Editor	Florian Hoger
Post Production	257 Productions, Munich Egi Seipler
Composer	Naren Rauch
Advertiser	Pampers, "Miracles"

Some babies are planned – and some are not, as a shot of a pregnant bride establishes. In a series of touching clips, the film shows us many different kinds of babies. Babies with older mums, younger mums and surrogate mums; adopted babies, triplets or babies with special needs. But no matter what kind they are, Pampers believes every baby is a little miracle who deserves to be celebrated, supported and protected without judgement.

IT'S THE
FOUNDATION
OF LIFE.

WE ALL NEED IT
EVERY DAY.

STOP
THE WATER
WHILE
USING ME!

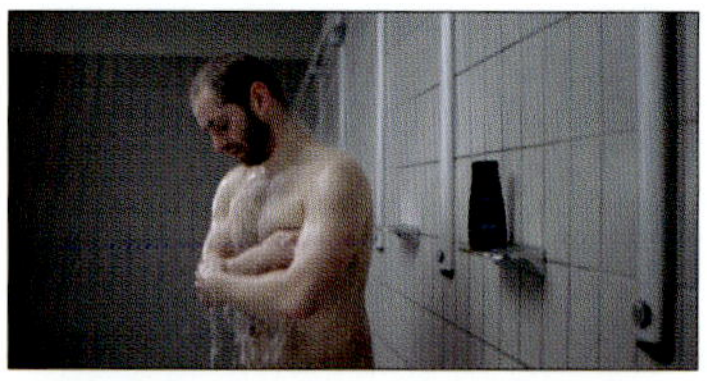

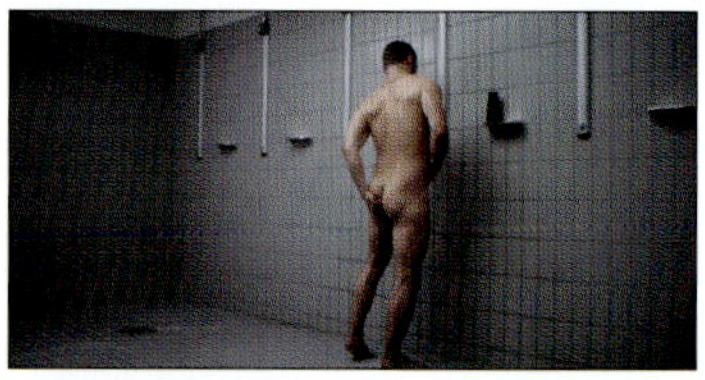

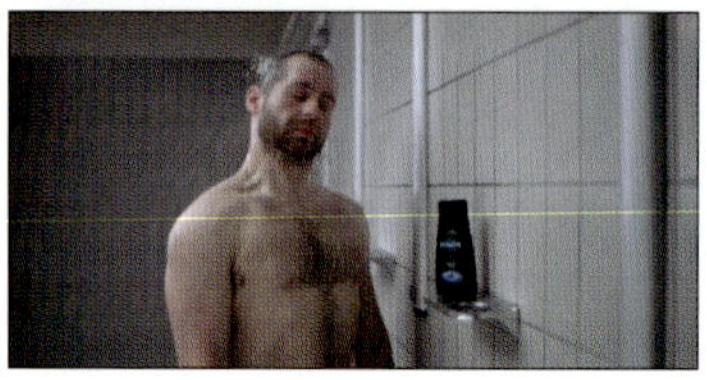

FOR MEN
HAIR BODY BALLS
asan

Agency	Kolle Rebbe/KOREFE, Hamburg
Creative Director	Katrin Oeding
Copywriters	Till Felber Thomas Voelker
Art Director	Christian Doering
Production	Tony Petersen Film Pixelbutik, Hamburg
Director	Jan Richter
Producers	Michael Duttenhoefer Bianca Mack
Illustration	Jan Richter
Advertiser	Stop the Water...

In this animated film, we're reminded that water is the foundation of life. But people use water wastefully. Why do we leave the tap running while brushing our teeth? Does the shower need to run while we're soaping up or applying shampoo? The film promotes a range of bathroom products called "Stop the water while using me!" We eliminate the water, they promise to eliminate artificial ingredients, colours and preservatives, animal testing, non-biodegradable ingredients and energy-hungry production techniques. Now turn off the tap.

Agency	Los&Co, Oslo
Copywriter	Marianne Knutsen
Art Director	Maria Myhre
Production	Einar Film & Fortellinger, Oslo
Director	Morten Tyldum
Producer	Guri Neby
Advertiser	Asan Trippel Shower Gel, "Shower Like a Man"

We see a rugged bloke who's about to take a shower. A languid female voiceover gives a clichéd beauty industry spiel about how his shower gel will make his hair beautiful (he hasn't got much), encouraging him to "inhale the aroma" (he snorts), while "gently massaging his body" (he flicks out a bit of navel fluff), even his "most intimate parts" (he vigorously washes his arse crack). Finally, our man takes a nice piss and leaves. Asan shower gel. For hair, body, balls. For men.

Colgate
MaxWhite
ONE
MAKE YOUR SMILE YOUR BEST ACCESSORY.

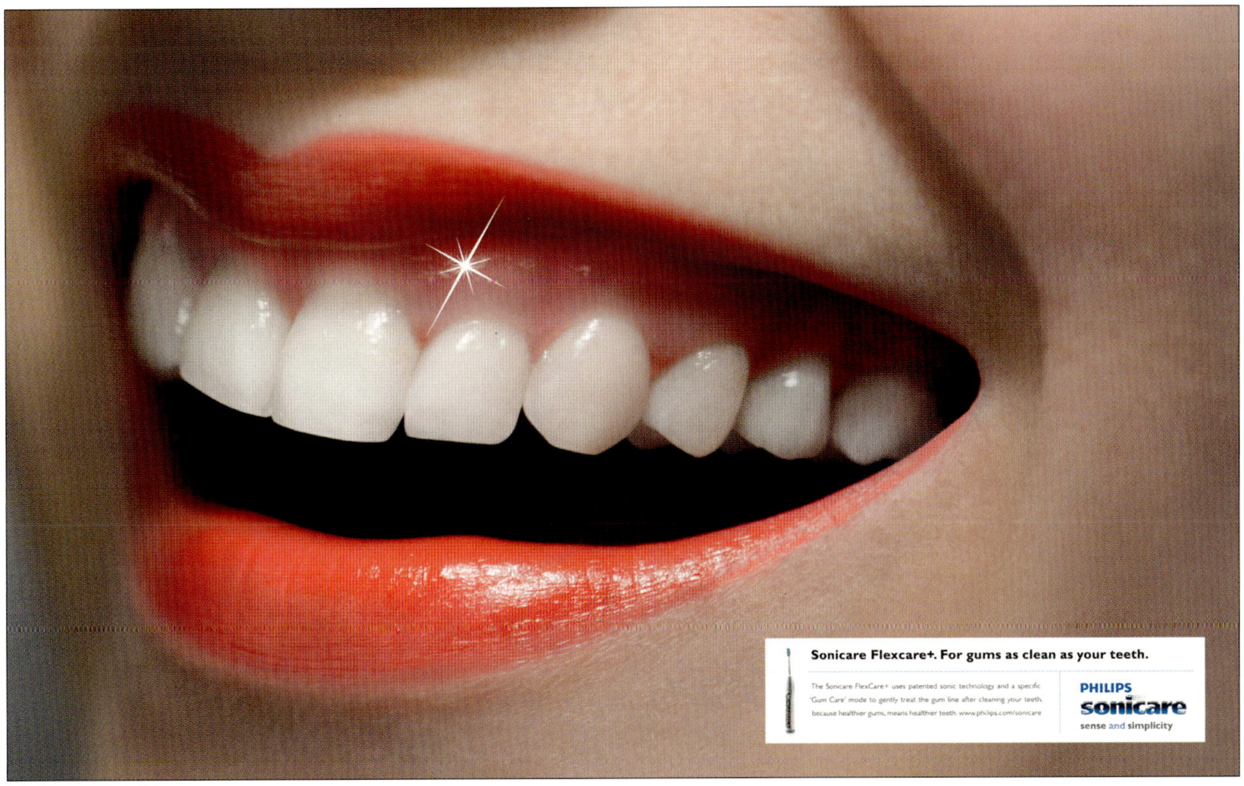
Sonicare Flexcare+. For gums as clean as your teeth.
The Sonicare FlexCare+ uses patented sonic technology and a specific 'Gum Care' mode to gently treat the gum line after cleaning your teeth. because healthier gums, means healthier teeth. www.philips.com/sonicare
PHILIPS
sonicare
sense and simplicity

Agency	Young & Rubicam, Paris
Creative Director	Carmine Coppola
Copywriters	Edward Selover Jaron Anderson
Art Director	Ricardo Turcios
Project Leader	Dominique Jeannin
Producer	Annapaola Rossi
Client	Florence Prevost
Advertiser	Colgate Max White One, "Best Accessories"

Agency	DDB London
Creative Director	Neil Dawson
Copywriter	Mike Crowe
Art Director	Rob Messeter
Photography	John Christian Lonningdal
Typographer	Trevor Slabber
Advertiser	Philips Sonicare Toothbrush, "Gum Sparkle"

Let the whoosh of fireworks be music to your ears.
www.phonak.com
PHONAK life is on
Hearing Aids

// BECAUSE WE DO THINGS WE'RE NOT BUILT FOR //
Voltaren

// BECAUSE WE DO THINGS WE'RE NOT BUILT FOR //
Voltaren
Pain Relief Gel

Agency	Wunderman, Zurich
CCD	Markus Gut
Creative Director	Roger Rüegger
Copywriters	Florian Tillmann Samuel Textor
Art Directors	Michael Gallmann Silke Heinzelmann
Photography	Ted Sabarese
Typographers	Nora Angstmann Christoph Krummenacher
Account Team	Renato Di Rubbo Rahel Güttler
Advertiser	Phonak Hearing Aids

Agency	Saatchi & Saatchi, Geneva
CCOs	John Pallant Derek Green
Creative Director	Leon Jacobs
Copywriter	Daniel Lunn
Art Director	Daniela Nedelschi
Photography	Carioca
Art Buying	Tania Retchisky
Account Team	Stéphanie Rupp Joan Flanagan Emma Jenkin
Client	Charlie Hough
Advertiser	Voltaren, “Transformers”

Durex Lubes.
Get in anywhere.
durex

Sales by Region
R1
R2
R5
R4
Hear twice as good.
hörwelt
digital hearing aids

Agency	McCann Erickson, Milan
Creative Directors	Marco Cremona Gaetano Del Pizzo
Copywriter	Marco Cremona
Art Director	Gaetano Del Pizzo
Photography	Vincent Dixon
Typographer	Marco Zilioli
Advertiser	Durex Gel Lubricant, "Club Crasher"

Agency	Demner, Merlicek & Bergmann, Vienna
Creative Director	Tolga Buyukdoganay
Art Director	Tolga Buyukdoganay
Copywriter	Niki Peterson
Photography	Karafiat Oliver Gast
Imaging	Mladen Penev
Account Manager	Stefanie Trauner
Advertiser	Hörwelt, "Hear Twice As Good"

NAZOL
Health Life
WAKES YOUR NOSE UP TO THE SMELLS OF THE WORLD.

FUEL
GAS
DIESEL
NAZOL
Health Life
WAKES YOUR NOSE UP TO THE SMELLS OF THE WORLD.

Agency	BBDO, Moscow
Creative Directors	Luis Tauffer Andres Vergara
Copywriters	Luis Tauffer Christian Balivet
Art Directors	Luis Tauffer Teco Cipriano
Illustrator	Teco Cipriano
Advertiser	Bayer Nazol, “Smells of the World”

BAYER

BAYER

Agency	BBDO, Moscow
Creative Directors	Luis Tauffer Andres Vergara
Copywriter	Pedro Levier
Art Directors	Luis Tauffer Paulo Garcia
Illustrator	Paulo Garcia
Advertiser	Bayer Aspirin, "Before & After"

we all need warmth

Quechua
mountain hardware

Agency	Fred & Farid, Paris
Creative Directors	Fred Raillard Farid Mokart
Copywriters	Fred Raillard Farid Mokart
Art Directors	Fred Raillard Farid Mokart Julien Boulard
Production	Irene, Paris
Directors	François Alaux Hervé de Crécy
Music Composer	Jonsi
Producers	Guillaume de Bary Stéphanie Huguenin Raphaèle Tanneur
Post-Production	Mikros Image, Paris Benoit Armstrong
Account Team	Emmanuel Ferry Bérengère Mangin Bénédicte Muller
Clients	Christian Ollier Thomas Bevilacqua
Advertiser	Quechua, "We All Need Warmth"

A bear leaves its cave. Wolves lope through the mist. As we look on, the wolves approach campers outside their tent – and snuggle up to them. Similarly, the bear snuggles up to a lone trekker. Owls land on another pair of hikers and appear to seek comfort from their body heat. Maybe it's something to do with the Quechua fleece jackets they're all wearing? Quechua: we all need warmth.

Wrangler

Wrangler
WE ARE ANIMALS

Wrangler
WE ARE ANIMALS

Agency	Fred & Farid, Paris
CDs & Copywriters	Fred Raillard Farid Mokart
Art Directors	Fred Raillard Farid Mokart Juliette Lavoix
Photography	Cass Bird
Clients	Adam Kakembo Yasemin Akkaya
Account Manager	Emmanuel Ferry
Advertiser	Wrangler, “Stunt” Campaign

FIGHT ACNE
DRDENIM JEANSMAKERS

BEST OF 60'S CLOTHING
at SECOND CHANCE
VINTAGE BOUTIQUE
secondchanceist.com

BEST OF 70'S CLOTHING
at SECOND CHANCE
VINTAGE BOUTIQUE
secondchanceist.com

140 Clothing & Fabrics

Agency	Dragster Kommunikation, Gothenburg
Creative Director	Dan Stendahl
Copywriter	Sara Dobareh
Art Director	Dan Stendahl
Photography	Jonatan Fernström
Graphic Design	Martin Joelsson
Typographer	Martin Joelsson
Acct. Manager	Hanna Littorin
Advertiser	Dr. Denim Jeans, "Fight Acne"

Note: Acne is also a popular brand of jeans in Sweden.

Agency	TBWA\Istanbul
Creative Director	Ilkay Gurpinar
Copywriter	Evren Dograr
Art Director	Caglar Biyikoglu
Production	212 Production, Istanbul
Photography	Emre Dogru
Illustrator	Yasin Aktasgil
Advertiser	Second Chance, "Taken Clothes"

ATHENA
UNDERWEAR
PROUD PARTNER OF THE FRENCH ATHLETICS TEAM

ATHENA
UNDERWEAR
PROUD PARTNER OF THE FRENCH ATHLETICS TEAM

ATHENA
UNDERWEAR
PROUD PARTNER OF THE FRENCH ATHLETICS TEAM

Agency	Euro RSCG 360, Paris
Creative Director	Hugues Pinguet
Copywriter	Dimitri Hekimian
Art Directors	Thomas Derouault Hakim Idriss
Photography	Jean-Yves Lemoigne
Digital Artwork	Asile Studio, Paris
Art Buying	Isabelle Baud
Account Team	Vanessa Bernard-Granger Anne-Flore Seringe
CEO	Pascal Allard
Advertiser	Athena Underwear, "Partnership"

ENGLAND IN ROO-INS!

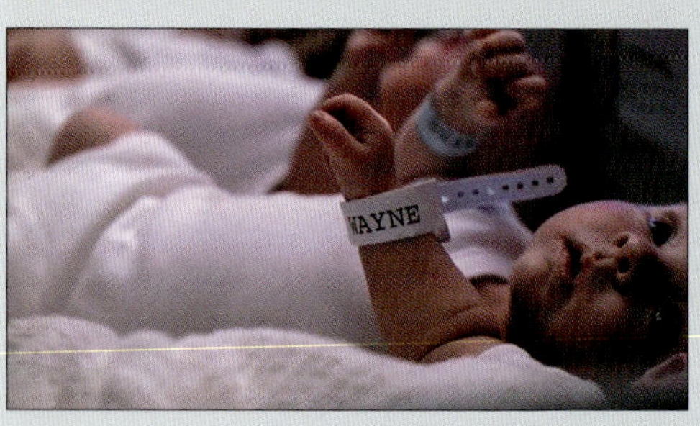

WRITE THE FUTURE

Agency	Wieden+Kennedy, Amsterdam
Executive CD	Jeff Kling
Creative Directors	Mark Bernath Eric Quennoy
Copywriters	Stuart Harkness Freddie Powell
Art Directors	Stuart Harkness Freddie Powell
Production	Independent Films
Director	Alejandro Gonzalez Inarritu
Producers	Jani Guest Richard Packer Dave Morrison
Agency Producers	Elissa Singstock Olivier Klonhammer
Head of Broadcast	Erik Verheijen
Account Team	Gene Willis Jordi Pont David Anson Marco Palermo
Clients	Enrico Balleri Colin Leary
Advertiser	Nike, "Write the Future"

During the soccer World Cup, glory or disaster can hinge on one goal, one pass, one tackle – or one mistake. This lengthy but gripping spot dramatizes that idea by showing soccer stars at pivotal moments and imagining the potential outcomes. For instance, we see Wayne Rooney visualizing catastrophic failure – or iconic status if only he can save the day. Other stars featured include Didier Drogba, Fabio Cannavaro, Franck Ribéry, Ronaldhino and Cristiano Ronaldo.

THE MIKROGRAPH. PRECISE TO 1/100TH OF A SECOND.
TAGHeuer

THE MIKROGRAPH. PRECISE TO 1/100TH OF A SECOND.
TAGHeuer

Agency	CLM BBDO, Paris
Creative Directors	Jean-Francois Sacco Gilles Fichteberg Fabien Mouillard
Copywriter	Jamie Standen
Art Director	Mark Forgan
3D Production	Mécanique Générale, Paris
3D Designer	Baptiste Masse
Art Buying	Sylvie Etchemaite
Advertiser	Tag Heuer, "Precision"

GÖTTE
customized eyeware
Cut TO FIT your face

Don't give the wrong gift again.
TROLLBEADS

Don't give the wrong gift again.
TROLLBEADS
ORIGINAL JEWELLERY

Agency	Jung von Matt/Limmat, Zurich
Creative Directors	Alexander Jaggy Fernando Perez Livio Dainese
Copywriters	Thomas Engeli Daniel Pieracci
Art Directors	Adrian Merz Barbara Suter-Bläsi
Photography	Patrick Rohner
Art Producer	Sabrina Transiskus
Lithographer	Blue Horizon
Advertiser	Götte Eyewear

Agency	Advico Young & Rubicam, Zurich
Creative Directors	Dominik Oberwiler Martin Stulz
Copywriter	Andy Lusti
Art Director	Oliver Glutz von Blotzheim
DTP Artist	Elias Zurbuchen
Photography	Schaub Stierli
Editor	Ferco Dregelyvari
Account Team	Claus Bornholt Sonja Wyss
Advertiser	Trollbeads, "Wrong Gifts"

Men over 180cm earn 10% more money.*
GO GET THEM!
DEICHMANN
* Institute for Employment Research (IAB), Guido Heineck

80% of all top managers are over 180cm tall.*
GO GET THEM!
DEICHMANN
* Institute for Employment Research (IAB), Guido Heineck

Looking at the world through children's eyes.
cam

Agency Grey Worldwide, Düsseldorf
Creative Directors Andreas Henke, Sacha Reeb
Copywriter Sissi Schneider
Art Director Stella Bittner
Advertiser Deichmann Graceland, "High Heels"

Agency DLV BBDO, Milan
Creative Directors Stefania Siani, Federico Pepe
Copywriter Dennis Casale
Art Director Matteo Pozzi
Illustrator Davide Calluori
Advertiser CAM, "The Children's World"

MAX
SHOES

MAX
SHOES

MAX
SHOES

MAX
SHOES

MAX
SHOES

MAX
SHOES

Footwear & Personal Accessories

Agency Jung von Matt/Limmat, Zurich
Creative Director Lukas Frei
Copywriter Samuel Christ
Art Director David Hanselmann
Photography Anti Wendel
Graphic Design André Hermetschweiler
Advertiser Max Shoes, "Eye Catcher"

39.90
VŌGELE | SHOES

35.90
VŌGELE | SHOES
voegele-shoes.com

59.90
VŌGELE | SHOES
voegele-shoes.com

59.90
VŌGELE | SHOES

Agency	Jung von Matt/Limmat, Zurich
Creative Director	Lukas Frei
Copywriter	Samuel Christ
Art Director	Inken Rohweder
Photography	Jonathan Heyer
Illustrator	Gabriel Moreno
Graphic Design	Adrian Merz
Digital Artwork	Moser Fernandes Ben Fernandes
Advertiser	Vögele Shoes, "Box Models"

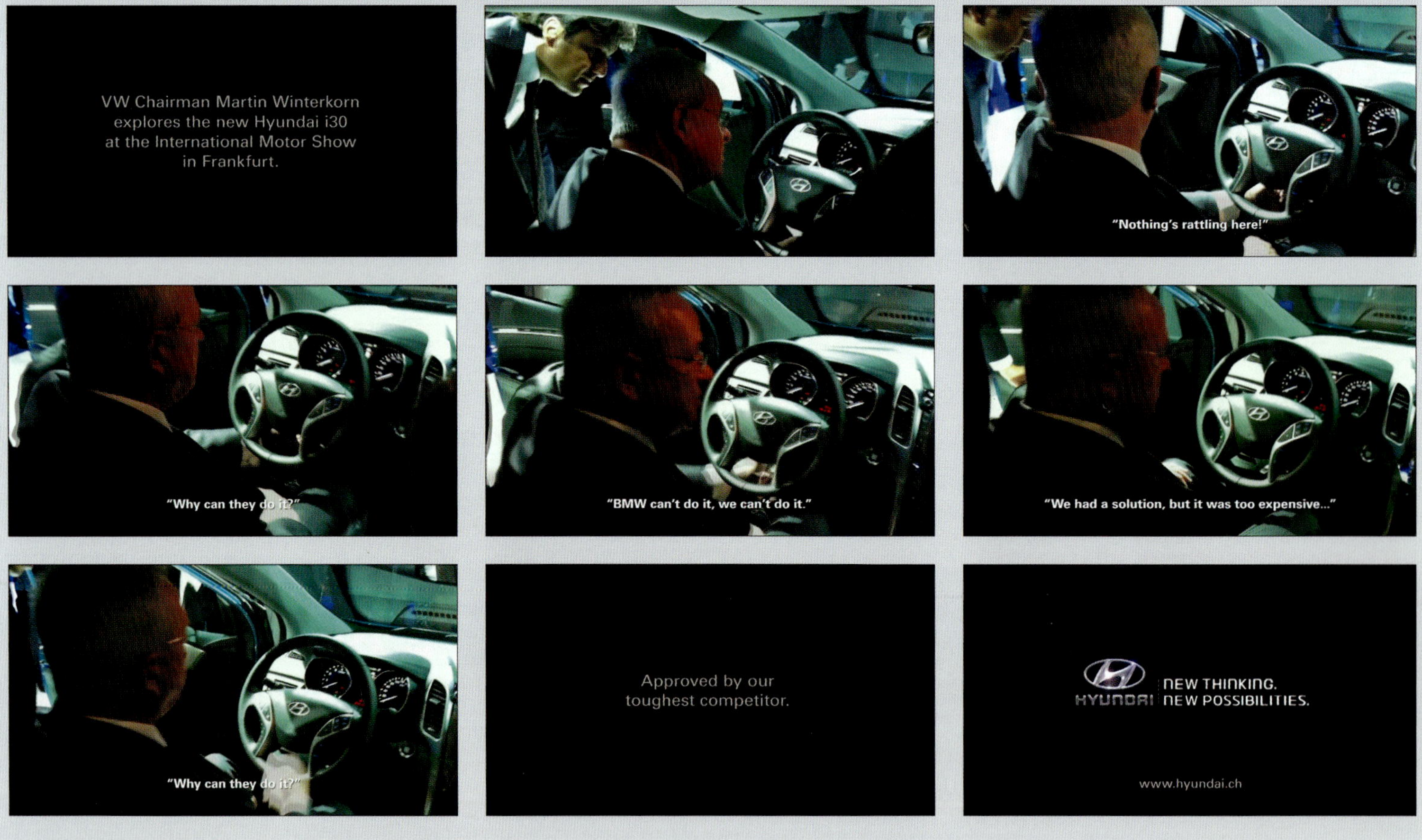
VW Chairman Martin Winterkorn explores the new Hyundai i30 at the International Motor Show in Frankfurt.
"Nothing's rattling here!"
"Why can they do it?"
"BMW can't do it, we can't do it."
"We had a solution, but it was too expensive..."
"Why can they do it?"
Approved by our toughest competitor.
HYUNDAI
NEW THINKING.
NEW POSSIBILITIES.
www.hyundai.ch

Agency	Ruf Lanz, Zurich
Creative Directors	Danielle Lanz Markus Ruf Marcel Schlaefle
Copywriter	Maren Beck
Art Director	Marcel Schlaefle
Production	Manifesto Films, Zurich
Producer	Daniela Berther
Editor	Michael Graf
Account Team	Heike Rindfleisch Sabrina Luck
Advertiser	Hyundai i30, "Approved by VW Chairman"

At the International Motor Show in Frankfurt, a camera captures Volkswagen Chairman Martin Winterkorn as he examines the new Hyundai i30. When he gets inside, he tests the steering wheel adjustment. Suddenly, he angrily summons a colleague. "Nothing's rattling here! BMW can't do it. We can't do it. Why can they do it?" His colleague protests that they had a solution – but it was too expensive. The VW chief looks disgruntled. The Hyundai i30: approved by its toughest competitor.

DEFENDER
GO BEYOND

Agency	Rainey Kelly Campbell Roalfe/Y&R, London
Creative Directors	Mark Roalfe Graham Lang
Copywriter	Phil Forster
Art Director	Tim Brookes
Photography	Carl Warner
Typographer	Lee Aldridge
Advertiser	Land Rover Defender, "Passport Stamps"

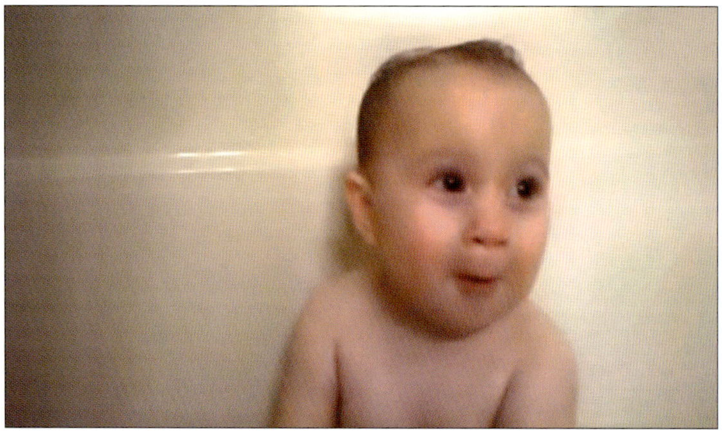

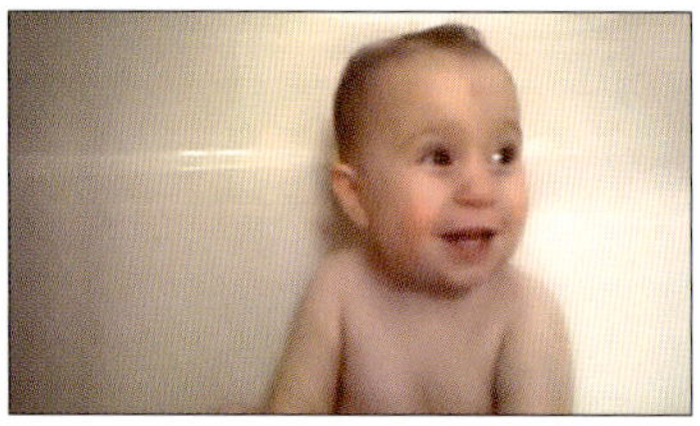

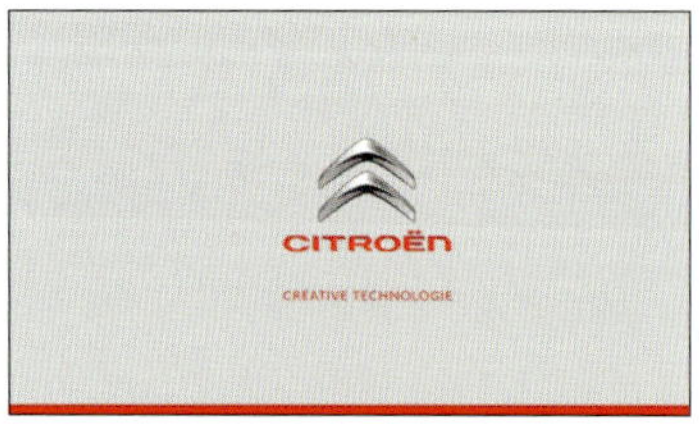
CITROËN
CRÉATIVE TECHNOLOGIE

Agency	H, Suresnes
Creative Directors	Gilbert Scher Marco Venturelli Luca Cinquepalmi
Copywriter	Marco Venturelli
Art Director	Luca Cinquepalmi
Production	Hercule, Suresnes
Producer	Julie Malet
Advertiser	Citroën DS4, "Baby"

A little girl is taking a bath. Meanwhile, her father asks her if she'd like a tricycle? "No!" she replies, smiling. "D'you want a pony?" "No!" "A car?" "No!" The game continues as dad lists several possibilities of car, from an SUV to a limousine. "No! No!" Learn to say "no" again. Instead of settling for any old car, visit www.ds4.citroen.com and check out the radically different new Citroën DS4.

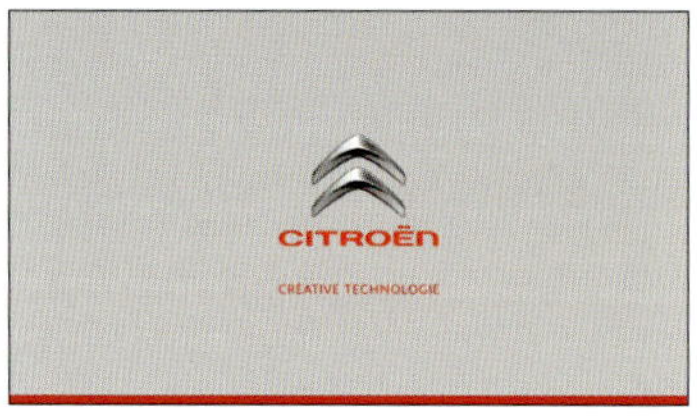
CITROËN
CRÉATIVE TECHNOLOGIE

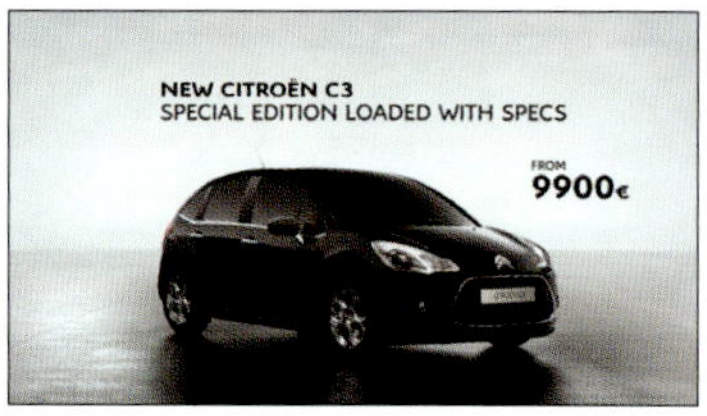
NEW CITROËN C3
SPECIAL EDITION LOADED WITH SPECS
FROM
9900€

Agency	H, Suresnes
Creative Directors	Gilbert Scher Marco Venturelli Luca Cinquepalmi
Copywriter	Marco Venturelli
Art Director	Luca Cinquepalmi
Production	Henry de Czar, Paris
Director	Lieven van Baeler
Producers	Jean Ozannat Christopher Thiery Julie Malet
Advertiser	Citroën C5, "Work for Nothing"

In extreme close-up, we see the workings of the Citroën C5's "Hydractive" suspension as it negotiates a rough and potholed country road. It all looks extremely jarring and violent. But when we cut to the interior of the car, we see that its occupants are not affected at all. The ride is as smooth as silk – to the extent that a young woman in the passenger seat is fast asleep.

Agency	H, Suresnes
Creative Directors	Gilbert Scher Marco Venturelli Luca Cinquepalmi
Copywriter	Lilian Moine
Art Director	Julien Doucet
Production	La Pac, Paris
Director	Thorsten Herken
Producers	Fabien Roques Ingrid Vasseur
Advertiser	Citroën C3, "Bip Bip"

The owner of a very old car imitates the sounds a far newer model would make. "Toot toot" – he mimics an electronic door lock. "Zhhhhh" – the electric windows. "Bing bing" – seat belt warning. Once on the road, he imitates a GPS: "In 50 metres, turn left…" He "electronically" adjusts the seat and the wing mirror. And of course when he's parking he makes the "bip bip beeeep" warning noises. While in a café overlooking the car, he even imitates its alarm when a pedestrian leans on it. If he wants so many features, he should invest in a new Citroën C3.

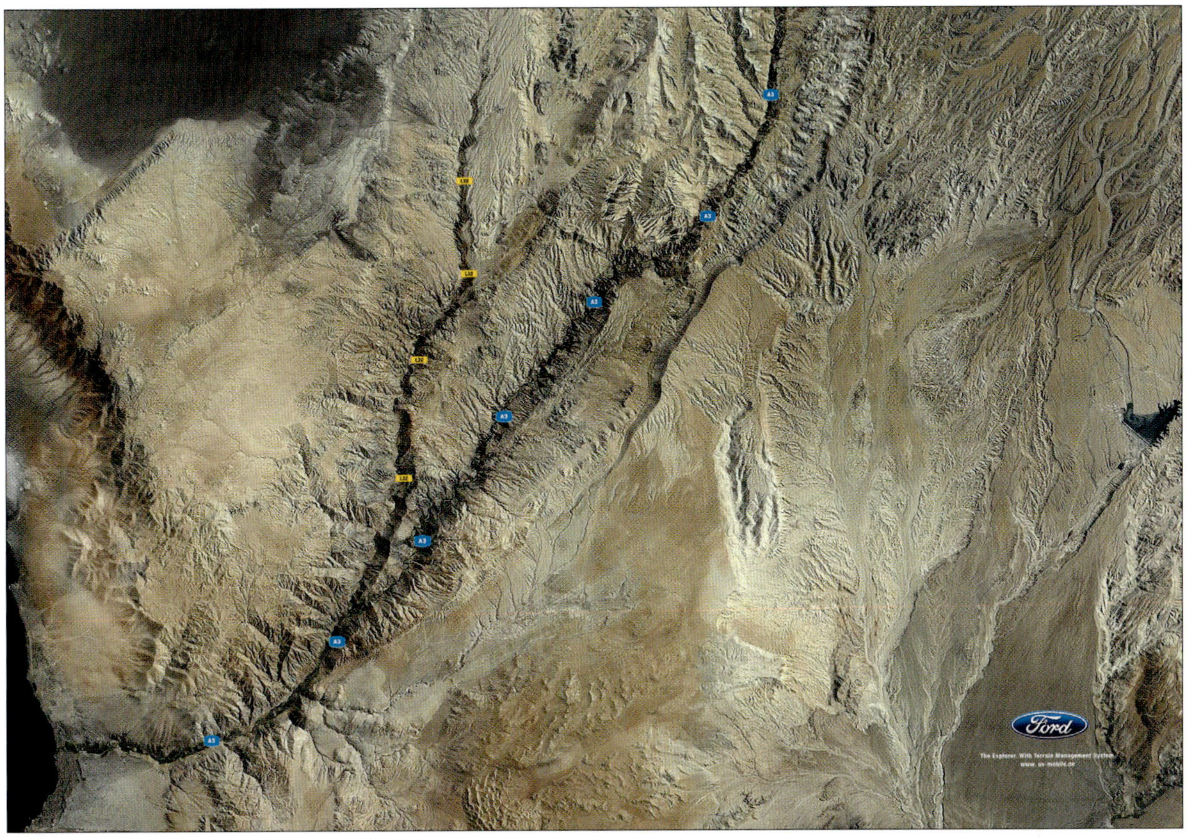
The Explorer. With Terrain Management System.
www.us-mobile.de

Agency	Ogilvy, Frankfurt
CCO	Stephan Vogel
Creative Director	Helmut Meyer
Copywriters	Peter Regnery Stephan Vogel
Art Director	Helmut Meyer
Account Team	Michael Fucks Stefanie Ta
Art Buying	Valerie Opitz Caroline Walczok
Imaging	Bing Maps
Client	Thomas Pfaeffle
Advertiser	US-Mobile.de, Ford

TE KOOP

You cannot trust every old lady.

Agency DDB Amsterdam
Creative Directors Dylan de Backer, Joris Kuijpers
Copywriter Dylan de Backer
Art Director Joris Kuijpers
Production Czar, Amsterdam
Director Bart Timmer
Producers Hein Scheffer, Yuka Kambayashi
D.O.P. Wouter Westendorp
Editing The Ambassadors
Clients Jasper van der Bijl, Menno van de Gronden
Advertiser Volkswagen Golf, "Old Lady"

A father and son go to buy a used Volkswagen Golf. The dad is delighted to see that it belongs to a little old lady. But in a series of flashbacks, we see that the granny thrashed hell out of the car: screeching off at the traffic lights, taking a hump-backed bridge at a leap, performing a handbrake turn to whip the vehicle into a parking space. Nevertheless, the dad sees that the car is in great shape and buys it for his son. You can't trust every old lady. But you can trust every Golf.

MINI
MINI.COM

EFTIRLYSTUR
WANTED.

Agency BSUR, Amsterdam
Creative Director Jason Schragger
Copywriter Gian Carlo Lanfranco
Art Director Rolando Cordova
Production Camp David, Stockholm
Director Robert Jitzmark
Producers Anna Adamson, Niko Koot, Niels Scheide
Advertiser Mini Family Range, "Mini vs Monster"

In a floodlit stadium, a monster truck prepares to leap over the entire Mini Family range – now bigger than ever. Slow motion captures the stunt, as well as the appalled expressions of spectators. Even the driver of the truck cringes as its gigantic tyres bear down on the adorable little vehicles. It looks like the truck will make it to the other side, but we're left in suspense as the tagline reads: "Introducing 15.52 metres of new Mini". The ad was shown in 3D in cinemas, but in 2D on TV and the web

Agency BSUR, Amsterdam
Creative Directors Jason Schragger, Karl Dunn
Copywriter Jason Schragger
Art Director Thomas Jullien
Production Thomas Thomas Films, London
Director Kevin Thomas
Producers Philippa Thomas, Jeremy Barnes, Oscar Thomas
Advertiser Mini Coupé, "Hitchhiker"

Tuesday in Iceland. Two men in a Mini Coupé. It becomes obvious that the passenger is a hitchhiker: the conversation is awkward and stilted. They stop at a gas station and when the driver goes inside to get coffee, he spots a WANTED poster on the wall. It looks exactly like his passenger. He squints out at the man in his car. The hitcher grins. Mind you, another man leaving the café also looks a bit like the criminal. The mystery is not resolved…but it's clear that adventure begins when you get behind the wheel of a Mini Coupé.

Shortens your reaction time. Brake Assist PLUS.
125! years of innovation
Mercedes-Benz
The best or nothing.

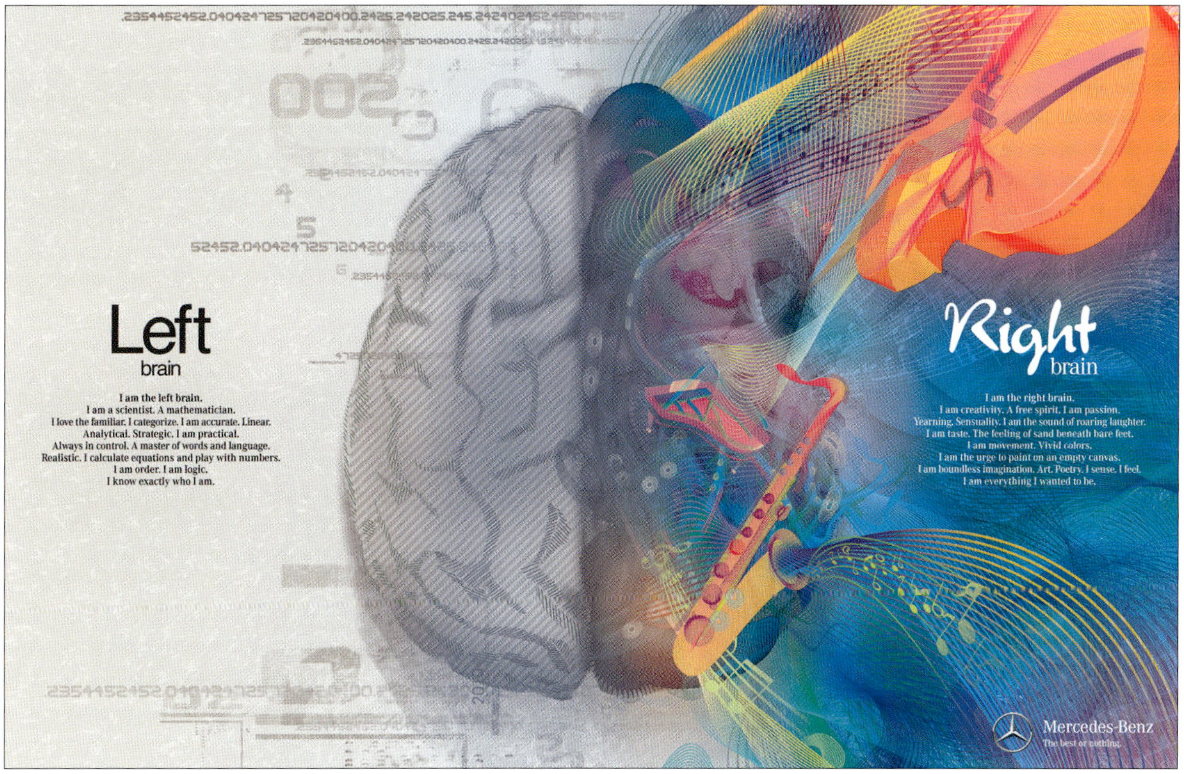
Left
brain
I am the left brain.
I am a scientist. A mathematician.
I love the familiar. I categorize. I am accurate. Linear.
Analytical. Strategic. I am practical.
Always in control. A master of words and language.
Realistic. I calculate equations and play with numbers.
I am order. I am logic.
I know exactly who I am.
Right
brain
I am the right brain.
I am creativity. A free spirit. I am passion.
Yearning. Sensuality. I am the sound of roaring laughter.
I am taste. The feeling of sand beneath bare feet.
I am movement. Vivid colors.
I am the urge to paint on an empty canvas.
I am boundless imagination. Art. Poetry. I sense. I feel.
I am everything I wanted to be.
Mercedes-Benz
The best or nothing.

Agency	Jung von Matt/Limmat, Zurich
Creative Directors	Alexander Jaggy Fernando Perez Livio Dainese
Photography	Hannes Kutzler
Graphic Design	Laura Grümann
Advertiser	Mercedes-Benz, "Braking Heads"

Agency	Shalmor Avnon Amichay/ Y&R Interactive Tel Aviv
CCO	Gideon Amichay
Executive CDs	Tzur Golan Zeev Ravid
Creative Director	Yariv Twig
Copywriters	Oren Meir Sharon Refael
Art Directors	Gil Aviyam Dror Nachumi
Exec. Client Director	Adam Polachek
Head of Strategy	Yoni Lahav
Advertiser	Mercedes-Benz

HAVE A WILD XMAS.
BE MINI.
MINI

SHIFT_ the way you move
NISSAN
IMPRESSIVELY SPACIOUS.
THE NISSAN NOTE.

SHIFT_ the way you move
NISSAN
IMPRESSIVELY SPACIOUS.
THE NISSAN NOTE.

Agency	Bcube, Milan
Creative Director	Francesco Bozza
Associate CD	Alessandro Sabini
Copywriter	Martino Lapini
Art Director	Maria Piccinini
Advertiser	Mini, "Have a Wild Xmas"

Agency	TBWA\Düsseldorf
Executive CD	Jörg Herzog
Creative Directors	Stefan Rehne Jörg Bruns
Copywriter	Matthias Hardt
Art Director	Simon Hattrup
Photography	David Maurer
Digital Artwork	Aaron Wienand Jürgen Hein
Production Manager	Meo Suzuki-Roeder
Producer	Malte Keller
Advertiser	Nissan Note, "Impressively Spacious"

DEFENDER The best tool for the job.
LAND ROVER

NEW CHEVROLET VOLT. 150 ELECTRIC HP.
CHEVROLET
MAKE IT HAPPEN

Agency	Rainey Kelly Campbell Roalfe/Y&R, London
Creative Director	Graham Lang
Copywriter	Adrian Lim
Art Director	Steve Williams
Photography	Andy Green
Typographer	Lee Aldridge
Advertiser	Land Rover Defender, "The Best Tools for the Job"

Agency	Herezie, Paris
Creative Director	Andrea Stillacci
Copywriter	Jean-Laurent Py
Art Director	Sebastien Boutebel
3D Artwork	Gregory Pierrain
CSD	Daniela Knecht
Producer	Evelyne Luce
Head of Planning	Luc Wise
Advertiser	Chevrolet Volt, "The Slingshot"

Library-Quiet interior
2011 SRX
cadillac.com
Cadillac

Library-Quiet interior
2011 SRX
cadillac.com
Cadillac

Agency	Futatsu Industries, Oslo
Creative Director	Aris Theophilakis
Art Directors	Frode Bjerved Niri von Bøyesen
Illustrator	Børge B. Bredenbekk
Advertiser	Smart Fortwo, "Air"

Agency	Leo Burnett, Dubai
Regional ECD	Malek Ghorayeb
Creative Director	Munah Zahr
Copywriter	Simon Raffaghello
Art Directors	Samer Lahoud Ziad Aouad
Advertiser	Cadillac SRX, "Library-Quiet Interior"

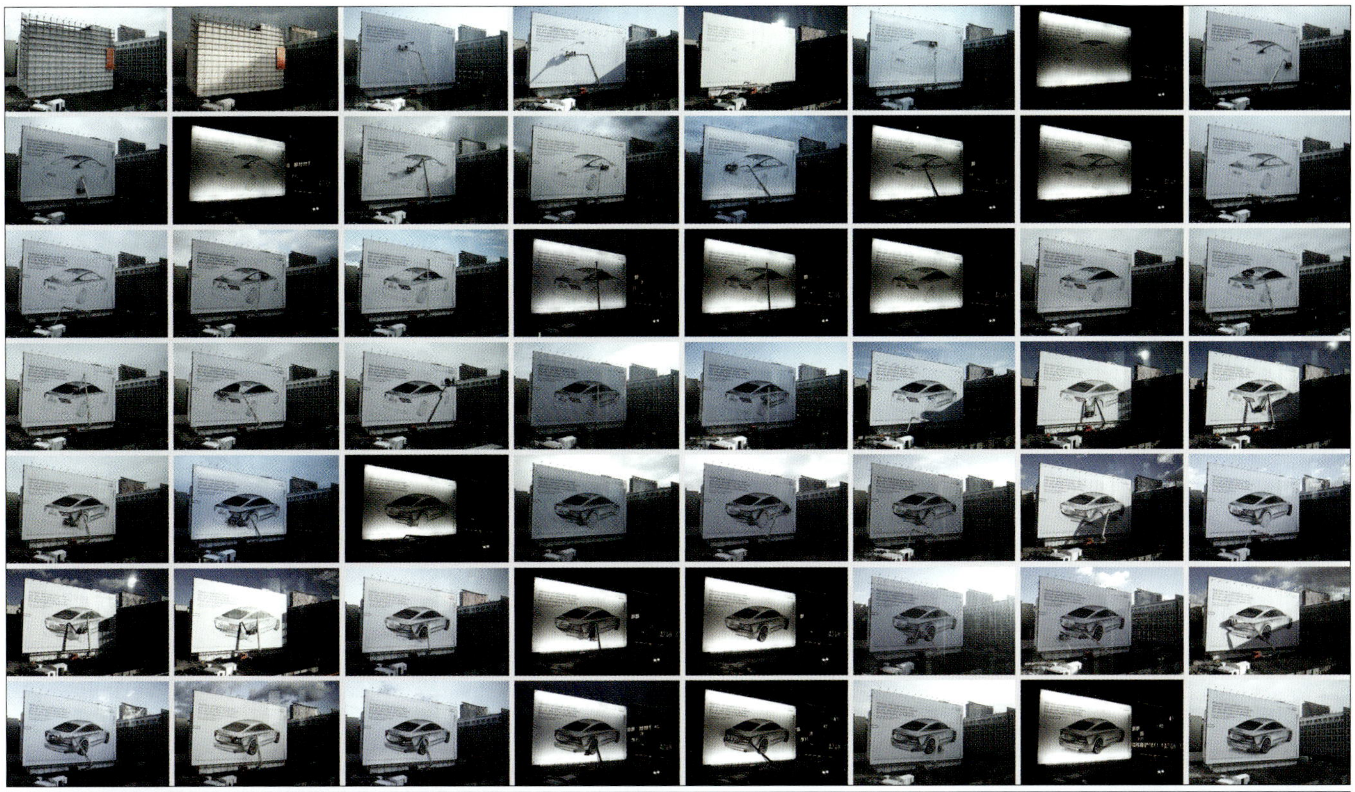

Audi
Vorsprung durch Technik
Nichts ist inspirierender als ein weißes Blatt Papier. Es ist die Chance, etwas Einzigartiges zu kreieren.
Der Audi A7 Sportback.
www.audi.de/a7
IN RL 954

Agencies	kempertrautmann, Hamburg kempertrautmann west, Düsseldorf	**Production**	Romey von Malottky, Hamburg
Creative Director	Fabian Kirner	**Producers**	Felipe Ascacibar Kai Branss
Copywriters	Michael Manke Stefano Sciolti	**Post Production**	Pirates 'N Paradise, Düsseldorf
Art Director	Rilana von Werne	**Account Team**	Jan Rütten Hendrik Heine Niklas Kruchten
Illustrator	Oliver Kray		
Graphic Design	Bastian Adam	**Advertiser**	Audi A7, "Live Billboard"
Art Buying	Susi Kastner-Linke		

Audi launched the new Audi 7 Sportback with the idea "nothing is more liberating than a blank sheet of paper – it's a chance to create something original". To bring this thought to life, Audi and its agency stuck a giant sheet of paper to a wall at Munich International Airport and gave graffiti artist Oliver Kray and his team 14 days. Over that period, thanks to the talent of the artists and 200 aerosol cans, the car "emerged" live on the wall.

The Financial Times.

DON'T BE THE LAST
TO CHANGE WITH THE TIMES.
TO RESERVE YOUR RENAULT ELECTRIC VEHICLE
GO TO RENAULT-ZE.COM
Z.E.
DRIVE THE CHANGE
RENAULT
FINANCIAL TIMES
Are we one people?
Irish face €50bn bank rescue
Greece ignores IMF and grants de facto tax amnesty to millions

NEWS-WEEK

DON'T BE THE LAST
TO CHANGE WITH THE TIMES.
TO RESERVE YOUR RENAULT ELECTRIC VEHICLE
GO TO RENAULT-ZE.COM
Z.E.
DRIVE THE CHANGE
RENAULT
WATER: THE NEW OIL
MADE FOR CHINA
Newsweek
THE TERROR THREAT
WHY AL QAEDA HAS MADE EUROPE FAR MORE DANGEROUS NOW THAN AT ANY TIME SINCE 2001

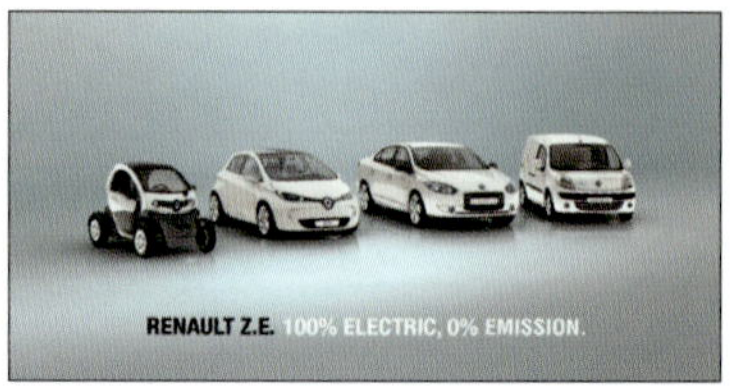
RENAULT Z.E. 100% ELECTRIC, 0% EMISSION.

RENAULT
DRIVE THE CHANGE

Agency Publicis Conseil, Paris
Creative Director Olivier Altmann
Copywriter Patrice Lucet
Art Directors Philippe Boucheron
Antoine Dezes-Richard
Account Team Edouard Pacreau
Aurore Duhamel
Jean-Jacques Hubert
Aurelie Fretti
Carine De Oliveira
Clients Stephen Norman
Patrick Fourniol
Advertiser Renault ZE

A time travelling effect was created to get people talking about the Renault ZE electric car. Readers of well-known newspapers and magazines like Newsweek, the Financial Times and the International Herald Tribune found themselves staring at front covers from 50 years ago. As they turned the page to return to the present, they saw the words: “Don't be the last to change with the times”, with a picture of the car and its web address.

Agency Publicis Conseil, Paris
Creative Director Olivier Altmann
Copywriter Thierry Lebec
Art Director Bénédicte Potel
Production Nose Ph, Paris
Blink, London
Director Dougal Wilson
Producers Juliette Desmarescaux
Pierre Marcus
Anne Boucher
Account Team Edouard Pacreau
Aurore Duhamel
Advertiser Renault ZE

An ordinary domestic scene: a man is shaving while his wife dries her hair. But the appliances have something strange in common: they're powered by petrol engines. In this odd world, lots of everyday objects are powered by petrol: office equipment, appliances, toys, vending machines – they all have exhaust pipes. Even a waiter must refuel his credit card machine. Voiceover: “You already switched to electric for many things, so why not for travelling?” We see a woman filling her Renault ZE – with electricity.

smart
open your mind.
>> Smallest turning circle. smart fortwo.
www.smart.com
smart – a Daimler brand

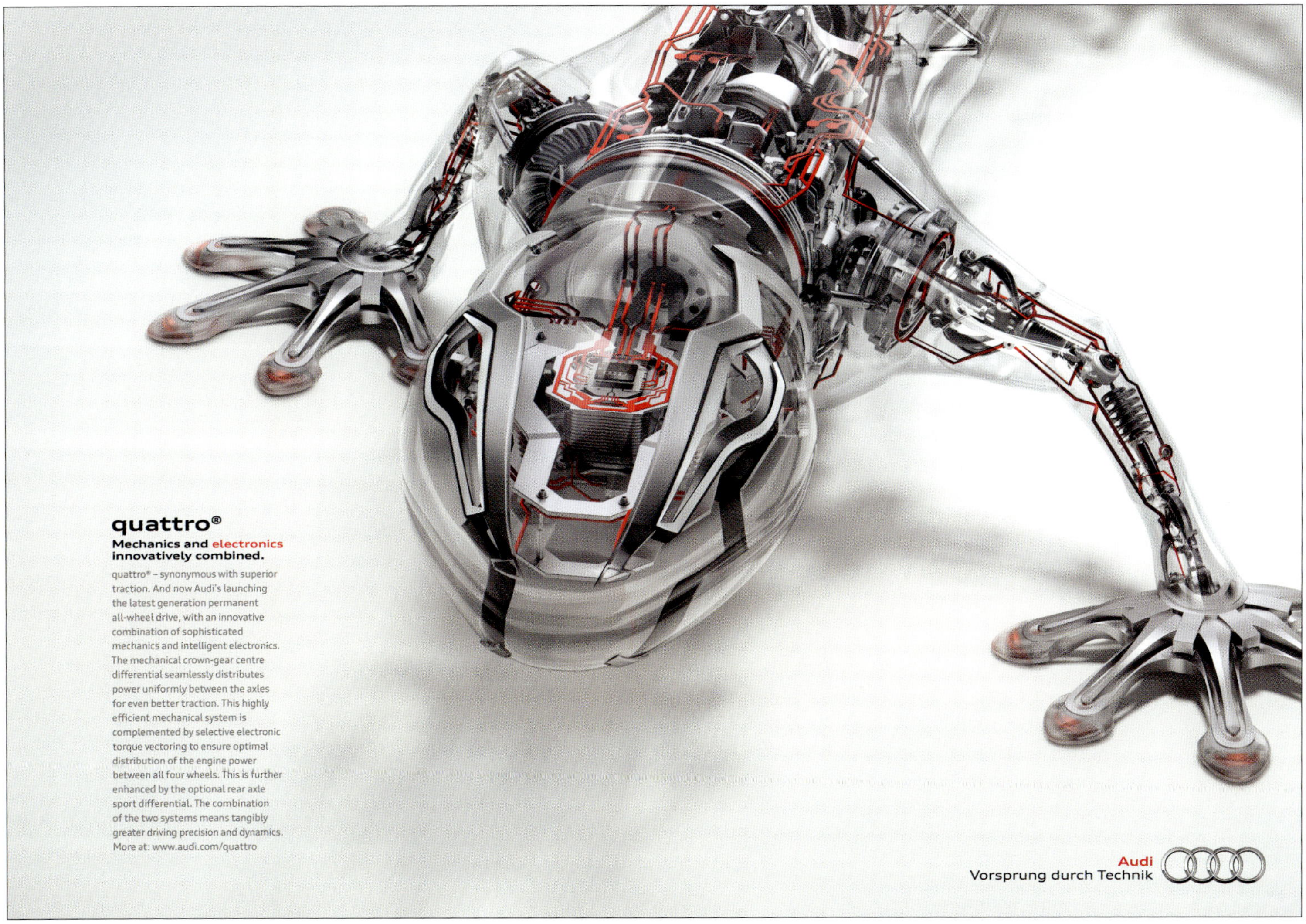
quattro®
Mechanics and electronics innovatively combined.
quattro® – synonymous with superior traction. And now Audi's launching the latest generation permanent all-wheel drive, with an innovative combination of sophisticated mechanics and intelligent electronics. The mechanical crown-gear centre differential seamlessly distributes power uniformly between the axles for even better traction. This highly efficient mechanical system is complemented by selective electronic torque vectoring to ensure optimal distribution of the engine power between all four wheels. This is further enhanced by the optional rear axle sport differential. The combination of the two systems means tangibly greater driving precision and dynamics. More at: www.audi.com/quattro
Audi
Vorsprung durch Technik

Agency	BBDO Proximity, Düsseldorf
CCOs	Toygar Bazarkaya Sebastian Hardieck
Copywriter	Peter Engelbrecht
Art Directors	Karolina Bukowiecka Gustavo Vieira-Dias
Photography	Robert Eickelpoth
Art Buying	Joana Uhlaczky
Production	Zerone, Düsseldorf Tom Stein
Account Team	Dirk Spakowski Sebastian Schlosser
Advertiser	Smart Fortwo, “360 Degrees”

Agency	kempertrautmann, Hamburg
Creative Directors	Heiko Freyland Mathias Lamken Gerrit Zinke Christian Fritsche
Copywriters	Heiko Freyland Sven Nagel
Art Directors	Mathias Lamken Maria Sommer
Graphic Design	Jan Behn
Production	Liga_01, Hamburg
Advertiser	Audi Quattro, “Gecko”

XCTRAVELS.COM
VOLVO

XCTRAVELS.COM
VOLVO

XCTRAVELS.COM
VOLVO

 Automobiles

Agency	Forsman & Bodenfors, Gothenburg
Copywriter	Fredrik Jansson
Art Directors	Staffan Lamm Andreas Malm
Designer	Mikko Timonen
Account Team	Anders Bothén Anna Levegård
Client	Bengt Junemo
Advertiser	Volvo XC, "XC Travels"

Never miss a sign
NEW FORD FOCUS with Traffic Sign Recognition
Feel the difference

VOLVO V70
DETECTING PEDESTRIANS
BEFORE YOU DO

VOLVO V70
DETECTING PEDESTRIANS
BEFORE YOU DO

Agency Bold Ogilvy & Mather, Athens
Creative Director Lazaros Nikiforidis
Copywriter George Kouveliotis
Art Director Vangelis Tolias
Photography Vassilis Michail
Illustrator Tereza Ferentinou
Account Team Rebecca Salmona, Maggie Adamou
Advertiser Ford Focus, "Human Traffic Signs"

Agency Forsman & Bodenfors, Gothenburg
Copywriter Jacob Nelson
Art Directors Johan Eghammer, Andreas Malm
Art Designer Mikko Timonen
Client Bengt Junemo
Account Team Anders Bothén, Anna Levegård
Advertiser Volvo V70, "Pedestrian"

In this clever media placement, the man crossing the street at the centre of this double-page spread isn't visible until the reader fully opens up the page. The words on the upper right hand side explain the benefits of the Volvo V70's safety technology: "Detecting pedestrians before you do."

Arrive in better shape.
The Phaeton with adaptive air suspension.
Das Auto.

Arrive in better shape.
The Phaeton with adaptive air suspension.
Das Auto.

Arrive in better shape.
The Phaeton with adaptive air suspension.
Das Auto.

Agency	Grabarz & Partner, Hamburg
Executive CD	Ralf Heuel
Creative Directors	Timm Weber Christoph Stricker Christoph Breitbach
Copywriter	Christoph Breitbach
Art Directors	Jasmin Remmers Barbara Dirscherl Yvonne Reinsch
Illustrators	Die Illustratoren: Silke Bachmann Corinna Hein
Account Team	Reinhard Patzschke Peter Stroeh Jasmin Schwarzinger Katja Fredriksen
Clients	Luca De Meo Giovanni Perosino Achim Glogowski
Advertiser	Volkswagen Phaeton, "Cubism"

ל-100 ב-6.9 שניות
Golf GTI.
מ-0

A fuel tank has never felt so big.
The Polo BlueMotion®. Only 3.3 l/100 km.
Das Auto.

Agency ACW Grey, Tel Aviv
CCO Tal Riven
Creative Director Moti Roubinstein
Copywriter Uri Marek
Art Director Irena Moravin
Advertiser Volkswagen Golf GTI, "0 to 100 kph in 6.9 secs"

While most automobile advertising expresses acceleration in terms of the time it takes to reach 100 kph from a standing start, this outdoor execution also shows the actual distance a Golf GTI will cover before reaching that speed.

Agency Grabarz & Partner, Hamburg
Executive CD Ralf Heuel
Creative Directors Timm Weber, Christoph Stricker, Christoph Breitbach
Copywriter Leander Schmalfuß
Art Director Jasmin Remmers
Photography Tom Mennemann
Graphic Design Barbara Dirscherl
Account Team Reinhard Patzschke, Katja Fredriksen
Advertiser Volkswagen Polo BlueMotion, "Ocean"

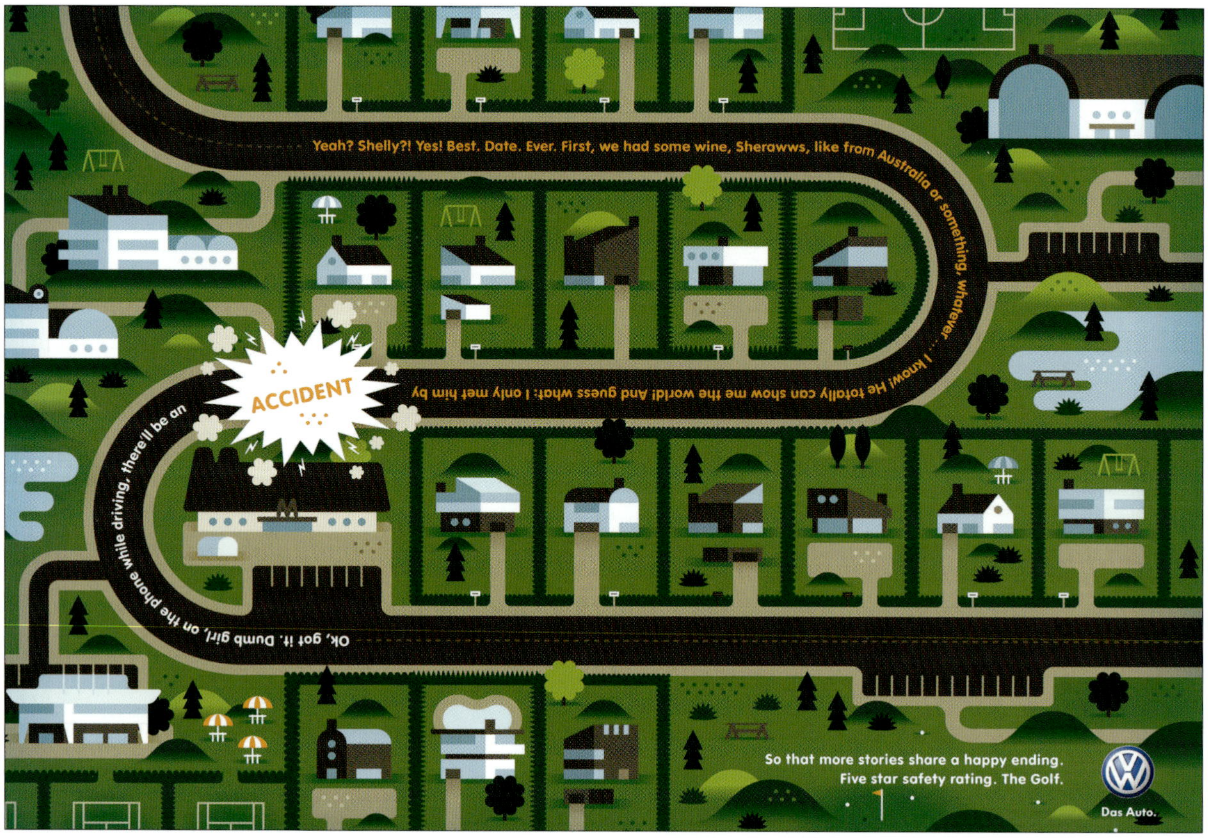
Yeah? Shelly?! Yes! Best. Date. Ever. First, we had some wine, Sherawws, like from Australia or something, whatever ... I know! He totally can show me the world! And guess what: I only met him by
ACCIDENT
Ok, got it. Dumb girl, on the phone while driving, there'll be an
So that more stories share a happy ending.
Five star safety rating. The Golf.
Das Auto.

Sweet Jesus! This has to be a joke. Hey you! Watch the stoplight, bloody fool of a motorist, I swear to God, we're gonna
CRASH
Still one magnificent edifice! Remember, how they fired me. Said, I was too outspoken ... But I was right! Nobody but me foresaw that market
So that more stories share a happy ending.
Five star safety rating. The Golf.
Das Auto.

 Automobiles

Agency	DDB Tribal Group, Düsseldorf
CCO	Eric Schoeffler
Creative Directors	Dennis May Kristine Holzhausen
Copywriter	Tobias Hecking
Art Director	Maya Darli
Illustration	Khuan+Ktron: Steebz
Acct. Supervisor	Silke Lagodny
Advertiser	Volkswagen Golf, "Crashes"

Precision parking.
The Touran with Park Assist.
Das Auto.

55
Precision parking.
The Tiguan with Park Assist.
Das Auto.

Agency	Grabarz & Partner, Hamburg
Executive CD	Ralf Heuel
Creative Directors	Tom Hauser Timm Weber Christoph Stricker Christoph Breitbach
Copywriter	Christian Moehler
Art Director	Tim Hartwig
Graphic Design	Rebecca Leiner
Photography	Waldmann Solar, Hamburg: Patrice Lange
Account Team	Reinhard Patzschke Peter Stroeh Katja Fredriksen
Clients	Luca De Meo Giovanni Perosino Achim Glogowski
Advertiser	Volkswagen Tiguan, "Parking Precision"

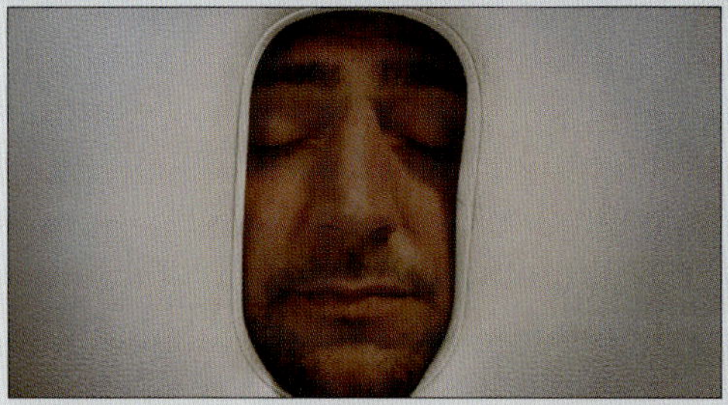

NUDIST
BEACH

Pleasure
BMW
BECAUSE YOUR HEAD IS NOT
ALWAYS IN THE RIGHT PLACE.

Agency	Serviceplan, Munich
CCO	Alex Schill
Creative Directors	Christoph Nann Maik Kaehler
Copywriters	Jan Kesting Marc Vosshall
Art Directors	Mo Whiteman Till Diestel
Production	Bakery Films, Hamburg
Director	Florian Sigl
Producers	Axel Doepner Stefan Schuh Christoph Koehler
D.O.P.	Thomas Wildner
Advertiser	BMW Lane Departure Warning, "Heads"

A man is enjoying himself at the beach. He seems a perfectly normal bloke – except that he's literally disembodied. He's just a head. The head snorkels, water-skis, relaxes on a lounger with his beautiful girlfriend. Suddenly, there's a vibrating noise. We cut to the inside of a BMW, where the man – his head now fully attached to his body – is alerted by the car's lane departure warning. BMW has installed this safety feature, because your head is not always in the right place.

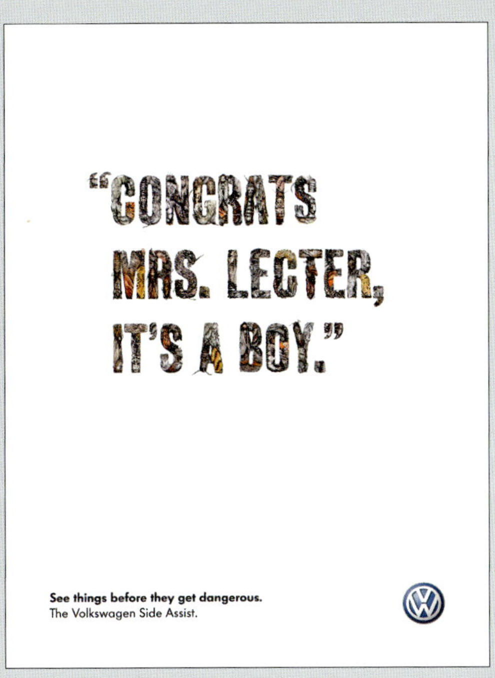
"CONGRATS MRS. LECTER, IT'S A BOY."
See things before they get dangerous.
The Volkswagen Side Assist.

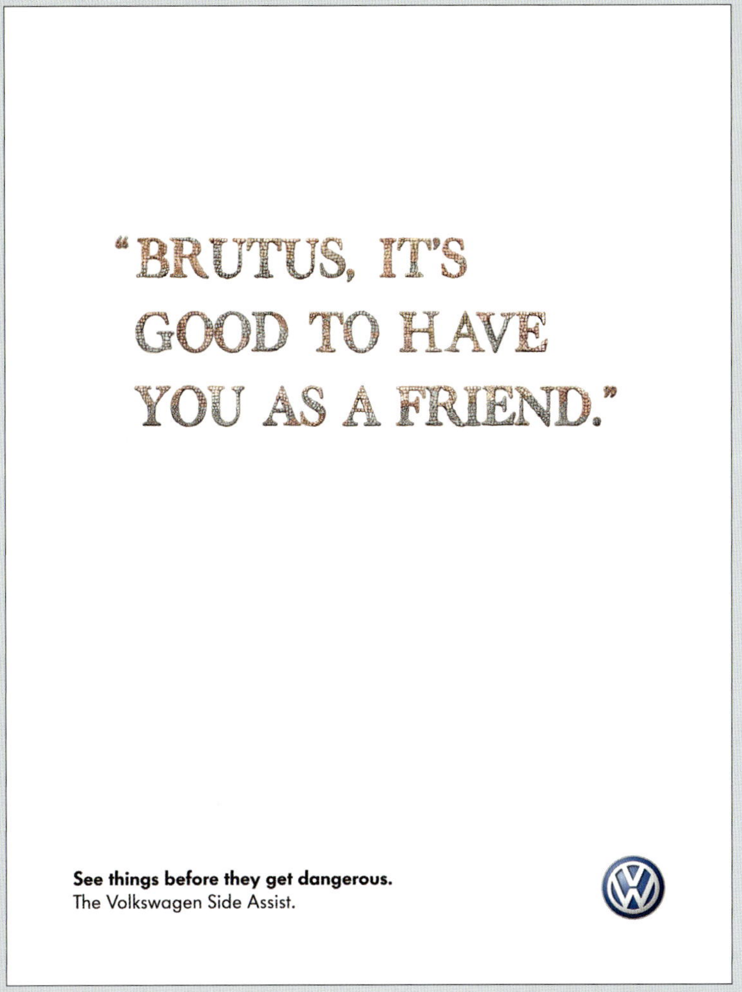
"BRUTUS, IT'S GOOD TO HAVE YOU AS A FRIEND."
See things before they get dangerous.
The Volkswagen Side Assist.

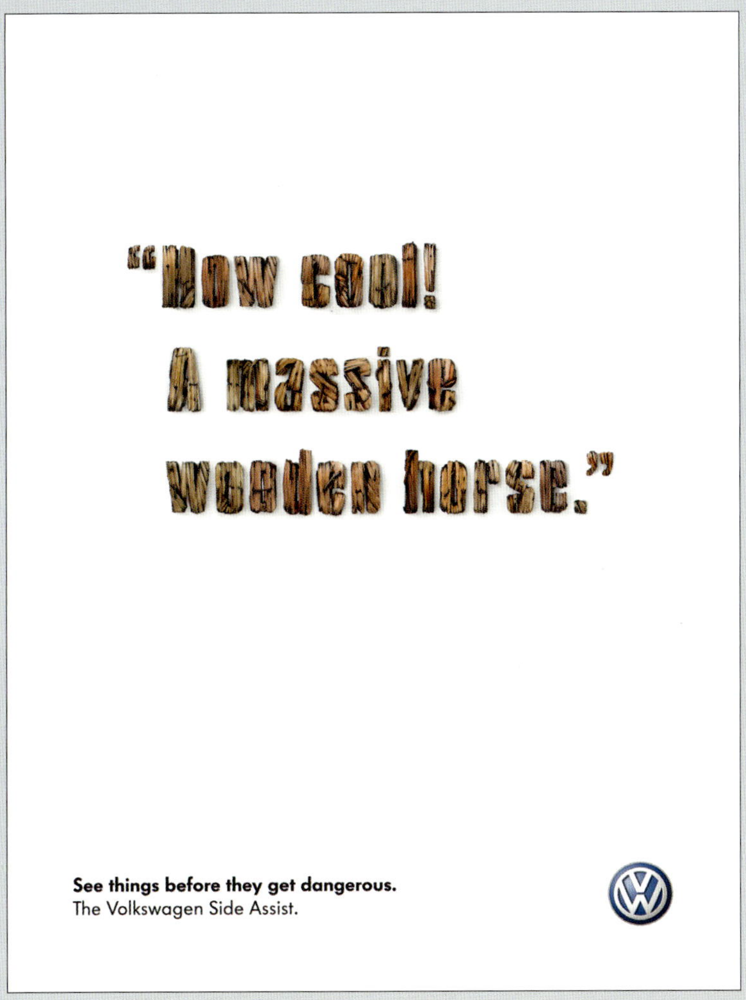
"How cool! A massive wooden horse."
See things before they get dangerous.
The Volkswagen Side Assist.

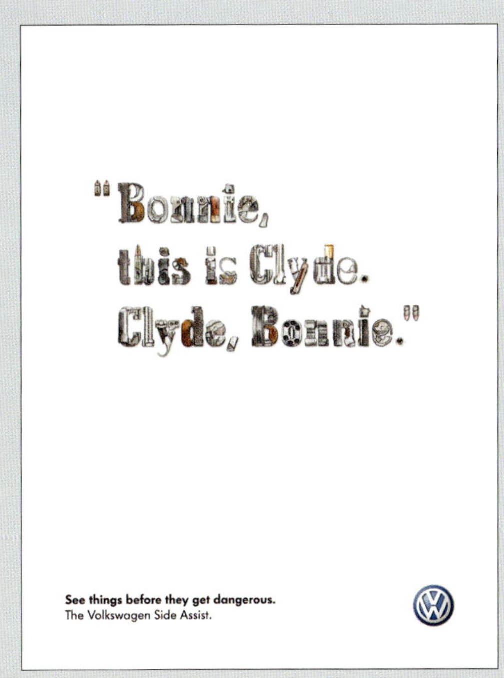
"Bonnie, this is Clyde. Clyde, Bonnie."
See things before they get dangerous.
The Volkswagen Side Assist.

Agency	DDB Tribal Group, Berlin
CCO	Eric Schoeffler
Creative Director	Johannes Hicks
Copywriter	Rachel Hutchinson
Art Director	Jack Christensen
Illustrator	Sebastian Hudert
Account Team	Jan Isterling Silke Lagodny
Advertiser	Volkswagen Side Assist, "Early Warning"

SURPRISINGLY
SURPRISINGLY SPACIOUS.
DUCATO
FIAT

Finds a space anywhe the Fox.
Has space for anything: the Crafter.

Agency	Leo Burnett, Istanbul
Executive CD	Idil Akoglu Ergulen
Creative Director	Guven Haktanir
Copywriter	Selcuk Akyuz
Art Director	Selim Unlusoy
Production	Dinamo, Istanbul
Producers	Sevinc Oktem Eser Firat
Advertiser	Fiat Ducato, "Surprisingly Spacious"

At a dockside, a pair of freight handlers are talking beside their white Fiat Ducato van, sorting out the paperwork for a couple of crates they've just offloaded. They can barely hear themselves speak over the sounds of screeching gulls, ships' foghorns, chugging engines, sirens, lapping waves and so on. Annoyed, one of the men shuts the Ducato's rear doors. The noises abruptly cease. Ducato: surprisingly spacious.

Agency	DDB Tribal Group, Berlin
CCO	Eric Schoeffler
Executive CD	Till Eckel
Creative Director	Johannes Hicks
Copywriter	Lennart Frank
Art Director	Michael Janke
Graphic Design	Vincent Schaublin
Account Team	Jan Isterling Silke Lagodny Kathrin Thiele
Advertiser	Volkswagen Fox & Crafter, "Fox in Crafter"

www.volkswagen-commercial-vehicles.com
The "Rear Assist" rear-view camera.
Now also available in the Caravelle.
Commercial Vehicles

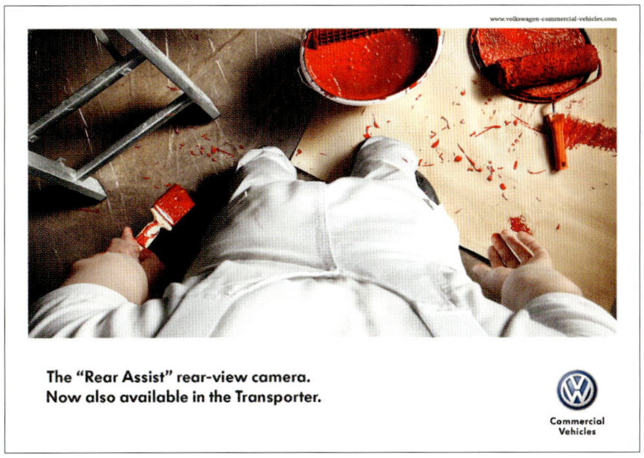
www.volkswagen-commercial-vehicles.com
The "Rear Assist" rear-view camera.
Now also available in the Transporter.
Commercial Vehicles

www.volkswagen-commercial-vehicles.com
The "Rear Assist" rear-view camera.
Now also available in the Crafter.
Commercial Vehicles

Agency Grabarz & Partner, Hamburg
Executive CD Ralf Heuel
CDs Timm Weber, Goesta Diehl, Oliver Heidorn
Copywriter Kerstin Correll
Art Director Thomas Schmiegel
Graphic Design Milena Pfannkuche
Art Buying Anna Simdon
Photography Christa Klubert, Düsseldorf
Tom Mennemann
Account Team Reinhard Patzschke, Stefanie Kirsch, Jennifer Fabian
Clients Ramsis Moussa, Stefan Pfeiffer
Advertiser Volkswagen Rear Assist, "All-Round Safety"

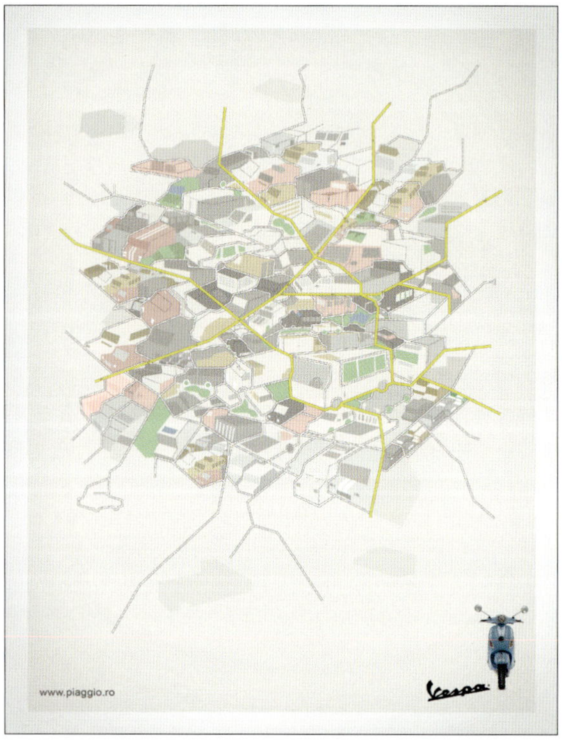
www.piaggio.ro
Vespa

Individual power distribution for each wheel.
The Vito. Now with four-wheel-drive 4x4 and Electronic Traction System 4ETS.
60
80
70
50
Mercedes-Benz

Individual power distribution for each wheel.
The Vito. Now with four-wheel-drive 4x4 and Electronic Traction System 4ETS.
Mercedes-Benz

Agency	Three, Bucharest
Creative Director	Andrei Tripsa
Copywriter	Sabin Staicu
Art Director	Nicu Duta
Illustrator	Nicu Duta
Account Team	Miruna Pop
Advertiser	Vespa, "The Map"

Agency	Scholz & Friends, Berlin
CCO	Martin Pross
Executive CO	Matthias Spaetgens
Creative Directors	Robert Krause David Fischer Philipp Woehler
Copywriter	Stefan Sohlau
Art Director	Melanie Specht
Account Team	Anna Gabriel Stefanie Wurst
Art Buying	Kirsten Rendtel
Advertiser	Mercedes-Benz Vito

BICYCLE
See things going backwards and forwards. The new Park Assistant from Renault.
RENAULT

CARAVAN
See things going backwards and forwards. The new Park Assistant from Renault.
RENAULT

SPORTSCAR
See things going backwards and forwards. The new Park Assistant from Renault.
RENAULT

Agency	Publicis, Zurich
Creative Director	Ralph Halder
Copywriter	Cyrill Wirz
Art Director	Bruce Roberts
Typographer	Bruce Roberts
Advertiser	Renault Park Assistant, "Bicycle", "Caravan" & "Sportscar"

B-SM 9372
B.SM9372H
Sorry, you are not a Volkswagen.
Volkswagen Classic Parts.

B.HE5845H
Sorry, you are not a Volkswagen.
Volkswagen Classic Parts.

Agency	DDB Tribal Group, Berlin
CCO	Eric Schoeffler
Executive CD	Till Eckel
Creative Director	Johannes Hicks
Copywriters	Philip Bolland Andres Blumenthal
Art Director	Gabriel Mattar
Photography	Hans Starck
Graphic Design	Bruno Luglio Alexey Fedorenko
Account Team	Jan Isterling Silke Lagodny
Advertiser	Volkswagen Classic Parts

HEADMASTER
HAND-PICKED BY THE ESTABLISHMENT

HAND-PICKED BY THE ESTABLISHMENT

BIKEKING24

Agency	McCann, Birmingham
Creative Director	Vince McSweeney
Copywriter	Vineet Raheja
Art Director	Shaun Loynds
Photography	Martin Brent
Graphic Design	Adam Humphries
Typographer	Adam Humphries
Account Team	Jamie Heath Greg Burch
Advertiser	Harley-Davidson, "Hand Picked by the Establishment"

Agency	Scholz & Friends, Berlin
CCO	Martin Pross
Executive CO	Matthias Spaetgens
Creative Directors	Michael Winterhagen Nils Busche
Copywriter	Michael Schoepf
Art Director	Walter Ziegler
Photography	Idris Kolodziej
Account Team	Joris Jonker Josef Hoehnow
Art Buying	Kirsten Rendtel
Advertiser	BikeKing24, "Twisted Motorcycle"

RENAULT VANS
4 MILLION FANS IN EUROPE
RENAULT

RENAULT VANS
4 MILLION FANS IN EUROPE
RENAULT

Agency Publicis Conseil, Paris
Creative Director Olivier Altmann
Copywriter Patrice Lucet
Art Directors Philippe Boucheron, Antoine Dezes Richard
Photography Frieke Janssen
Planner Sophie Benkemoun
Art Buying Gael Cheval, Jean Luc Chirio, Soone Riboud
Account Team Eric Hazout, Thibault Repelin, Adeline Blanc, Edouard Pacreau
Clients Stephen Norman, Bruno Travade, Dominique Musset, Olivier Dupuis
Advertiser Renault Vans, “Fans”

Total de plată
(col.5+col.6)
KRISTIN
SHOT J.R.
14-4-10/A
NO SURPRISES ON YOUR SERVICE BILL.
FIXED-PRICE PACKAGES ONLY AT RENAULT SERVICE!
DRIVE THE CHANGE
RENAULT

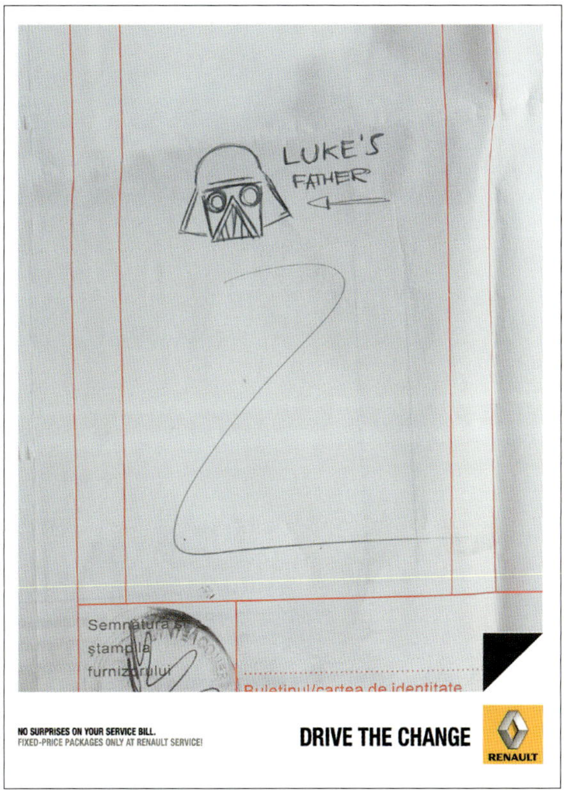

LUKE'S
FATHER
Semnătura și
ștampila
furnizorului
Buletinul/cartea de identitate
NO SURPRISES ON YOUR SERVICE BILL.
FIXED-PRICE PACKAGES ONLY AT RENAULT SERVICE!
DRIVE THE CHANGE
RENAULT

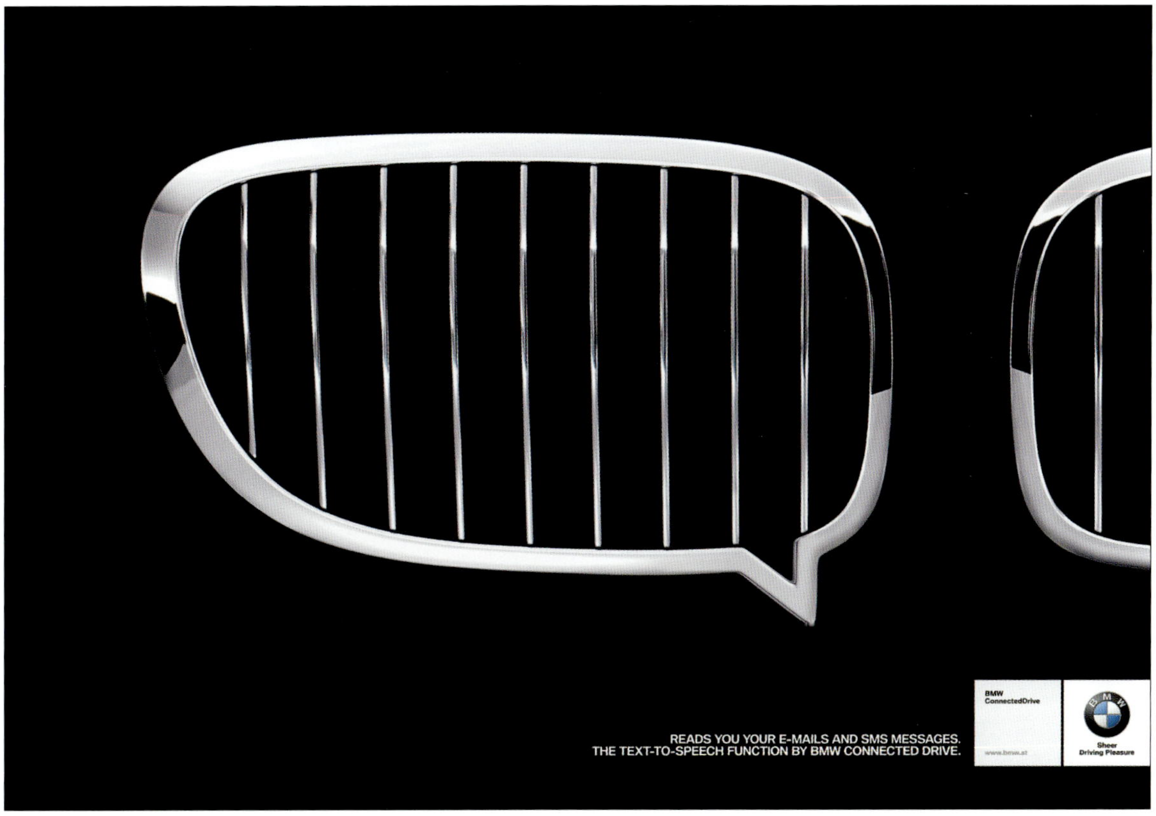

READS YOU YOUR E-MAILS AND SMS MESSAGES.
THE TEXT-TO-SPEECH FUNCTION BY BMW CONNECTED DRIVE.
BMW
ConnectedDrive
Sheer
Driving Pleasure

Agency	Publicis, Bucharest
Creative Director	Razvan Capanescu
Copywriter	Cezar Panait
Art Director	Dragos Ometita
CSD	Catalin Albu
Advertiser	Renault Service, "No Surprises"

Agency	Demner, Merlicek & Bergmann, Vienna
Creative Directors	Francesco Bestagno Alexander Hofmann
Copywriter	Isabelle Stadler
Graphic Design	Lilli Reich
Account Team	Christin Herrnberger Markus Dammelhart
Imaging	Vienna Paint, Vienna
Final Artwork	Dominik Source
Advertiser	BMW, "Text-to-Speech"

LIVE
NCB
T PEACE TALKS
SonntagsZeitung
THE INSIGHT STORY

Agency Advico Young & Rubicam, Zurich
CCO Markus Gut
Creative Directors Martin Stulz, Dominik Oberwiler
Copywriter Martin Stulz
Art Director Lukas Wietlisbach
Production Markenfilm, Zurich
Director Stephan Usteri
Producer Jens Derler
Graphic Design Annik Weber
Post Production Universal Production Partner, Prague
Editor Wolfgang Weigl
Account Team Julia Kull, Pablo Koerfer
Advertiser SonntagsZeitung, "Peace Talks"

Media coverage today is often superficial – but Swiss newspaper SonntagsZeitung gets to the heart of things. This idea is illustrated when leaders, in this case Israel's Benjamin Netanyahu and Palestine's Mahmoud Abbas, are revealed for what they really are in a Russian doll effect. Here, we see Netanyahu and Abbas behaving like a couple of bratty kids taunting one another while Hillary Clinton, playing the role of a school teacher, tries to keep them in order.

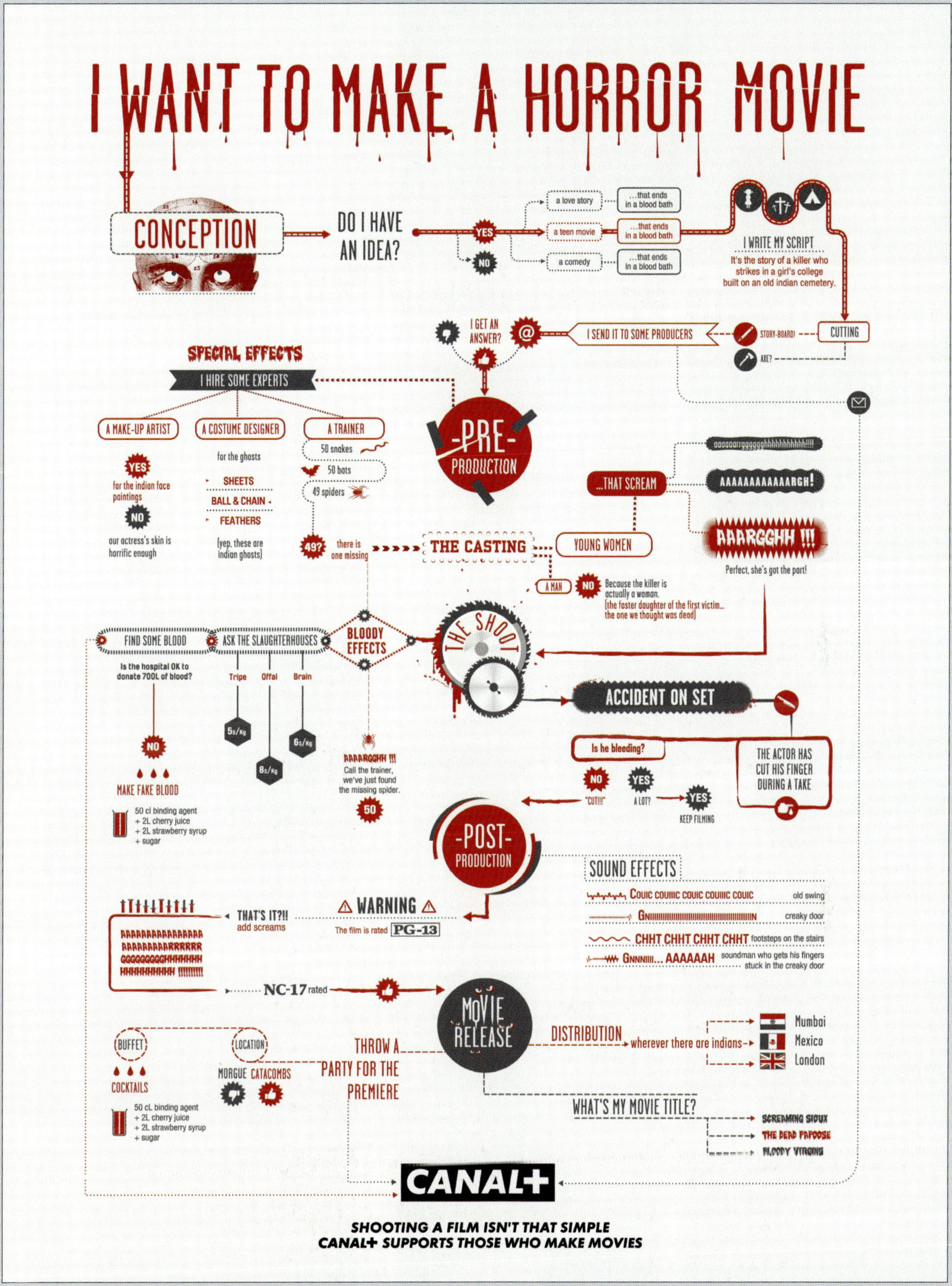
I WANT TO MAKE A HORROR MOVIE
CONCEPTION
DO I HAVE AN IDEA?
YES
NO
a love story
a teen movie
a comedy
...that ends in a blood bath
...that ends in a blood bath
...that ends in a blood bath
I WRITE MY SCRIPT
It's the story of a killer who strikes in a girl's college built on an old indian cemetery.
CUTTING
STORY-BOARD!
I SEND IT TO SOME PRODUCERS
I GET AN ANSWER?
SPECIAL EFFECTS
I HIRE SOME EXPERTS
A MAKE-UP ARTIST
A COSTUME DESIGNER
A TRAINER
YES
for the indian face paintings
NO
our actress's skin is horrific enough
for the ghosts
SHEETS
BALL & CHAIN
FEATHERS
(yep, these are indian ghosts)
50 snakes
50 bats
49 spiders
49?
there is one missing
-PRE-
PRODUCTION
...THAT SCREAM
AAAAAAAAAAARGH!
AAARGGHH !!!
Perfect, she's got the part!
THE CASTING
YOUNG WOMEN
A MAN
NO
Because the killer is actually a woman.
(the foster daughter of the first victim... the one we thought was dead)
FIND SOME BLOOD
ASK THE SLAUGHTERHOUSES
BLOODY EFFECTS
Is the hospital OK to donate 700L of blood?
Tripe
Offal
Brain
NO
MAKE FAKE BLOOD
50 cl binding agent
+ 2L cherry juice
+ 2L strawberry syrup
+ sugar
Call the trainer, we've just found the missing spider.
50
THE SHOOT
ACCIDENT ON SET
Is he bleeding?
THE ACTOR HAS CUT HIS FINGER DURING A TAKE
NO
"CUT!!"
YES
A LOT?
YES
KEEP FILMING
-POST-
PRODUCTION
SOUND EFFECTS
Couic couic couic couic couic
old swing
creaky door
CHHT CHHT CHHT CHHT
footsteps on the stairs
GNNNIIII... AAAAAAH
soundman who gets his fingers stuck in the creaky door
THAT'S IT?!!
add screams
WARNING
The film is rated PG-13
NC-17 rated
MOVIE RELEASE
DISTRIBUTION
wherever there are indians
Mumbai
Mexico
London
WHAT'S MY MOVIE TITLE?
SCREAMING SIOUX
THE DEAD PAPOOSE
BLOODY VIRGINS
BUFFET
LOCATION
COCKTAILS
MORGUE
CATACOMBS
50 cL binding agent
+ 2L cherry juice
+ 2L strawberry syrup
+ sugar
THROW A PARTY FOR THE PREMIERE
CANAL+
SHOOTING A FILM ISN'T THAT SIMPLE
CANAL+ SUPPORTS THOSE WHO MAKE MOVIES

Agency	BETC Euro RSCG, Paris
Creative Directors	Stéphane Xiberras Olivier Apers
Copywriters	David Troquier Gregory Ferembach
Art Directors	Gregory Ferembach David Troquier
Illustrator	Les Graphiquants, Paris
Advertiser	Canal+, "Movie Flowcharts"

n-tv
The News Channel.

Agency Euro RSCG, Düsseldorf
CDs Felix Glauner, Martin Breuer, Martin Venn
Copywriters Sigi Zwar, Christian Kroll
Art Director Ingmar Krannich
Production VCC, Duesseldorf
Producer Eva Peschkes
Editor Peter Georgi
CSD Harald Jaeger
Advertiser N-tv News Channel, "Nothing Moves you More than Reality"

News channel n-tv believes that the news is often more dramatic than a Hollywood film. To prove it, we see a montage of political meetings in which the participants have ended up hurling paper at one another, scrapping, slugging each other in the face, or dealing with lobbed smoke bombs. "We don't need stunts", says the tagline. "All we show is real." n-tv – the news channel.

Everything seem fine to me. The figures look good.

-You got the handicap parking licenses?
-You mean these?

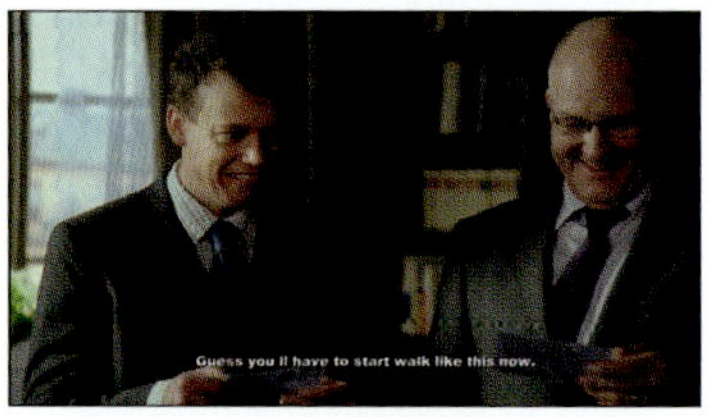

EXPRESSEN

EXPRESSEN
REVEALING NEWS

 Media

Agency King, Stockholm
Creative Director Frank Hollingworth
Copywriters Pontus Thorén, Jens Englund
Art Director Nima Stillerud
Production Esteban, Stockholm
Directors Markus Ernerot, Alex Brügge
Producer Sofia Wall
Advertiser Expressen, "Revealing News"

These two spots show how the press can not only expose corruption, but prevent it. In the first, a local government meeting draws to a close. The chairman suggests ending the day by going to a porn club: "a taxpayers' treat". They all get excited, baying like animals, until one of them says: "This is not a good idea, guys." "Why not?" A rolled-up copy of Expressen newspaper appears on the screen. Expressen: revealing news.

In the second spot, we meet our corrupt government officials again. One of them hands out "handicap parking" passes, which will enable them to park their cars wherever they like – all over Europe. They begin making tasteless remarks and imitating handicapped people. Finally, as if he's remembering something, the chairman comes to his senses. "Guys! Wait! Let's forget about this." "Why?" Expressen – revealing news.

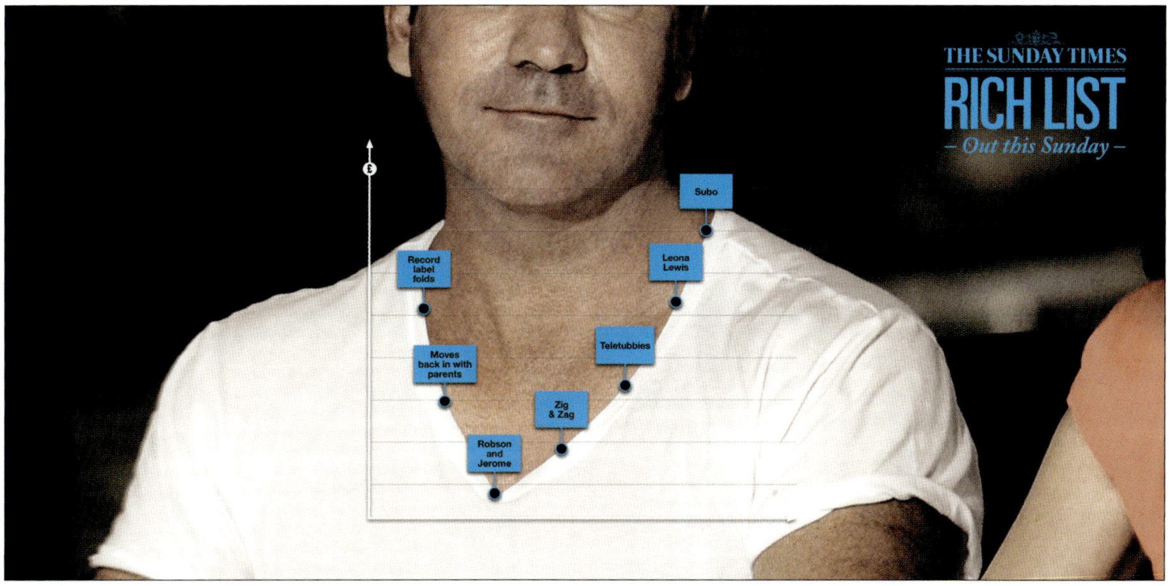
THE SUNDAY TIMES
RICH LIST
– Out this Sunday –
£
Record label folds
Moves back in with parents
Robson and Jerome
Zig & Zag
Teletubbies
Leona Lewis
Subo

THE SUNDAY TIMES
RICH LIST
– Out this Sunday –
£
Forms The Beatles
Splits from The Beatles
Mull of Kintyre
Heather Mills
The Beatles on iTunes

THE SUNDAY TIMES
RICH LIST
– Out this Sunday –
Honoured at The Brits
Monitored at The Priory
Honoured at The MOBOs

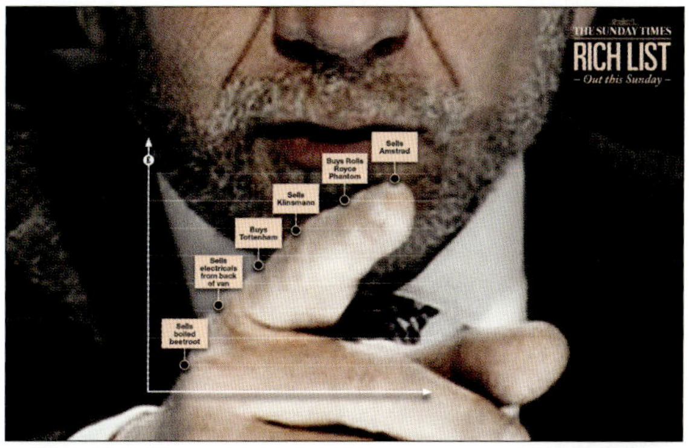
THE SUNDAY TIMES
RICH LIST
– Out this Sunday –
£
Sells boiled beetroot
Sells electricals from back of van
Buys Tottenham
Sells Klinsmann
Buys Rolls Royce Phantom
Sells Amstrad

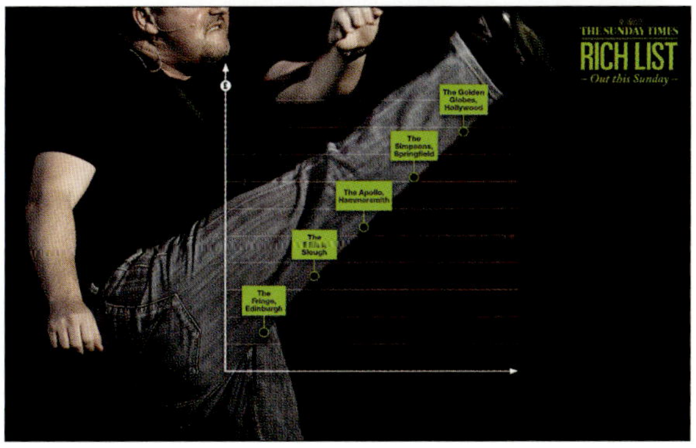
THE SUNDAY TIMES
RICH LIST
– Out this Sunday –
£
The Fringe, Edinburgh
The Apollo, Hammersmith
The Simpsons, Springfield
The Golden Globes, Hollywood

THE SUNDAY TIMES
RICH LIST
– Out this Sunday –
Wins Formula 3
Wins GP2
Wins F1 World Title
Wins over Pussycat Doll

Agency	CHI & Partners, London
Executive CD	Jonathan Burley
Creative Director	Micky Tudor
Copywriters	Matt Collier Wayne Robinson
Art Directors	Matt Collier Wayne Robinson
Graphic Design	Dan Beckett Rob Petrie
Art Buying	Emma Modler
Advertiser	The Sunday Times, "Rich List"

A drop, I have seen a drop of sweat in HD...

Miracles happen only on Sky sport.

sky
Liberi di...

Miracles happen only on Sky Sport
sky

Miracles happen only on Sky Sport
sky

Miracles happen only on Sky Sport
sky

Miracles happen only on Sky Sport
sky

Media

Agency 1861 United, Milan
Creative Directors Federico Ghiso, Giorgio Cignoni
Copywriter Federico Ghiso
Art Director Giorgio Cignoni
Production Akita Film, Milan
Director John O'Hagan
Producers Paolo Zaninello, Carla Beltrami
Advertiser Sky Sport, "Miracles"

To some people, sport is a religion. Maybe that's why fans expect their heroes to perform miracles. We see a few here, as sports stars hover in the air ("the Miracle of the Live Pause"), make church bells ring with a well-aimed strike, cause the afflicted to perform stunts, fill fishing nets with soccer balls, part water in a pool and enable the "blind" to see. One woman claims to see a statue of Roma soccer squad captain Francesco Totti sweating "in HD". But these miracles only happen on Sky Sport.

Agency 1861 United, Milan
Creative Directors Federico Ghiso, Giorgio Cignoni
Copywriter Federico Ghiso
Art Director Giorgio Cingnoni
Photography Garrigosa Studio, Barcelona
Digital Artwork Alex Torrens, Alvaro Torrens
Art Buying Maria Benenati
Advertiser Sky Sport, "Miracles"

Youth's got future letudiant.fr
ARE YOU SURE
YOUR CAREER CHOICE
IS THE BEST FIT?

21 METER
HÄRIFRÅN:
Massiva protester mot
SDU-tåget
NU FÅR DU NYHETERNA I
AVSTÅNDSORDNING PÅ GP.SE
GP

Agency	Young & Rubicam, Paris
Creative Director	Eric Hélias
Copywriter	Eric Lavenac
Art Directors	Guillaume Auboyneau Cédric Quissola
Art Buying	Claire Nicaise-Schindler
Final Artwork	Guillaume Auboyneau Cédric Quissola
Account Team	Clément Chovin Amandine Frery
Clients	Jean Weiss Delphine Cantat
Advertiser	L'Etudiant, "Astronaut"

Agency	Forsman & Bodenfors, Gothenburg
Copywriters	Anders Hegerfors Elisabeth Christensson
Art Directors	Staffan Forsman Lars Johansson Ferhat Deniz Fors
Photography	Emil Larsson
Designer	Staffan Håkanson
Account Team	Ann Spennare Bengtsson Åsa Pedersen
Client	Charlotte Odbjer
Advertiser	Göteborgs-Posten

Göteborgs-Posten aims to be the most local newspaper in the world. To this end it produced the world's most local news campaign. Breaking news stories were posted on billboards that showed the exact distance between each poster site and the source of its news. For example, "25 metres from here: Massive protests against SDU demonstration."The messages were updated twice a day to keep the campaign fresh.

Get closer with Sydsvenskan in your iPad.
SYDSVENSKAN

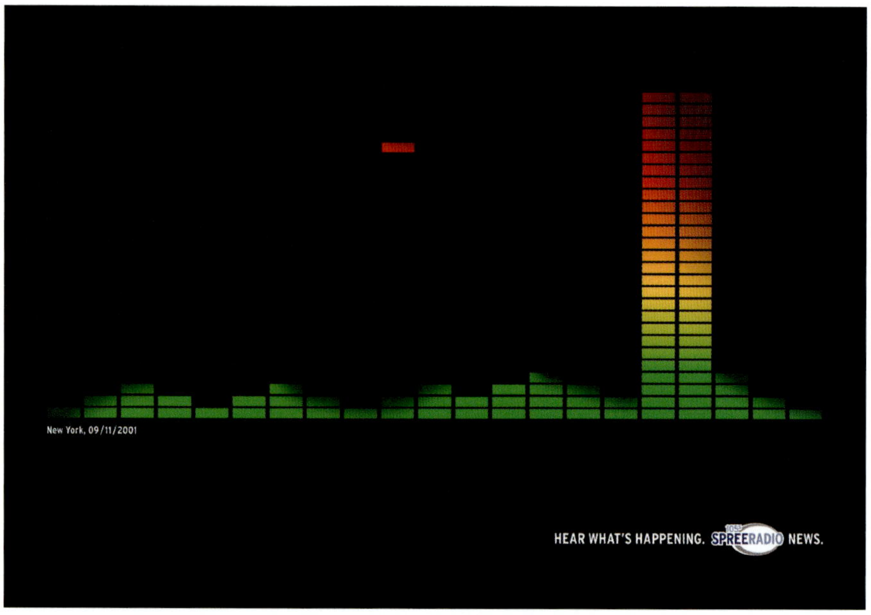
New York, 09/11/2001
HEAR WHAT'S HAPPENING. SPREERADIO NEWS.

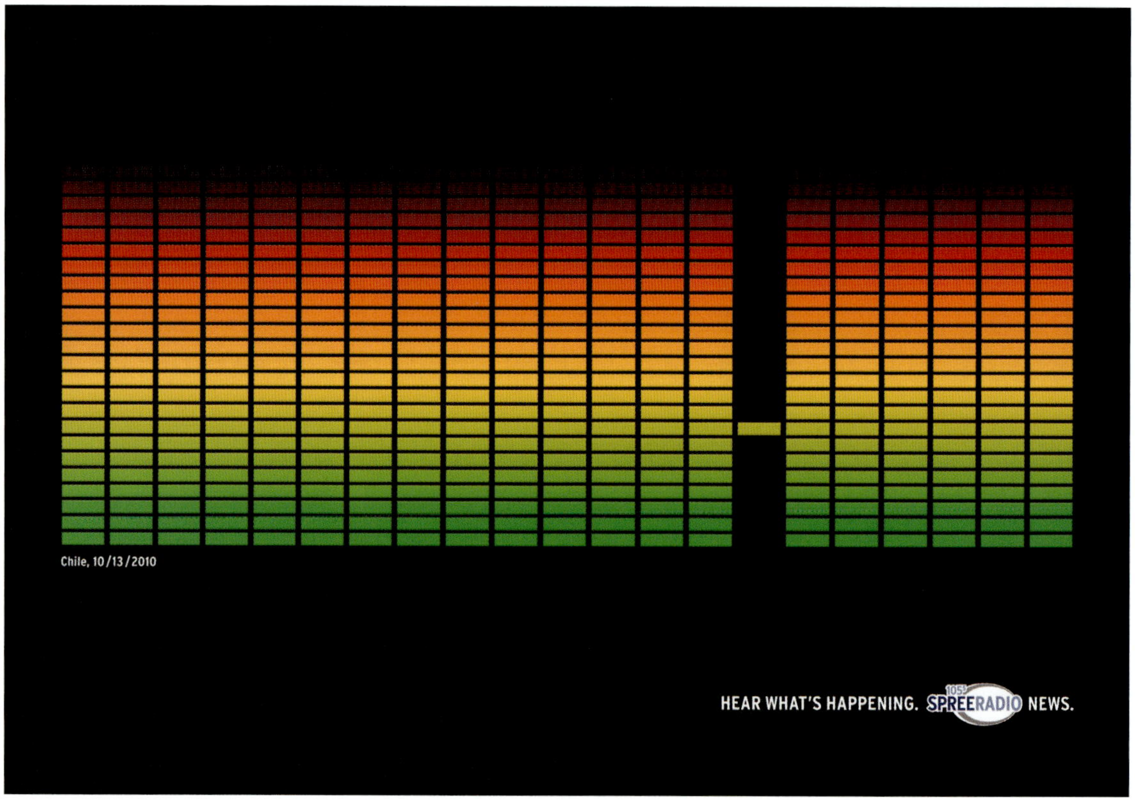
Chile, 10/13/2010
HEAR WHAT'S HAPPENING. SPREERADIO NEWS.

Agency	The Fan Club, Malmö
Creative Directors	Christian Barrett Ola Obrant Andreasson
Copywriters	Ola Obrant Andreasson Martin Rynvik
Art Director	Christian Barrett
Graphic Design	Helena Ivarsson
Final Artwork	Christian Ekeblom
Account Team	Ulla-Karin Barrett Peter Füle Rebecka Hjorth
Advertiser	Sydsvenskan Daily News, "Get Closer with Sydsvenskan"

Agency	BBDO Proximity, Berlin
CCOs	Wolfgang Schneider Jan Harbeck David Mously
Copywriters	Dana Wolf Daniel Ridderskamp
Art Directors	Simone Kiening Vothana Khieu Max Marohn
Account Team	Mark Andree Gülcan Demir
Producer	Michael Pflanz
Advertiser	Spree Radio News, "Equalizers"

Live from the source.
FOREIGN POLITICS Mon - Fri at 2 PM

Live from the source.
FOREIGN POLITICS Mon - Fri at 2 PM

Live from the source.
FOREIGN POLITICS Mon - Fri at 2 PM

Live from the source.
FOREIGN POLITICS Mon - Fri at 2 PM

THIS IS ENGLAND
THE LONG GOOD FRIDAY
TONITE LET'S ALL MAKE LOVE IN LONDON
ANDREI RUBLEV
laundrette
SOLARIS
DUTCHMAN
THE ACADEMY CINEMA
BFI LONDON FILM FESTIVAL
13 - 28 October 2010
SIDEWAYS
Lost In Translation
QUEENS
FOR A DREAM

Agency DDB&Co., Istanbul
Creative Director Karpat Polat
Copywriter Can Faga
Art Director Hande Guler
Photography Bora Subakan
Advertiser CNN Türk, "Live From the Source"

Agency Leo Burnett, London
Creative Directors Jonathan Burley, Jim Bolton
Copywriters Richard Brim, Daniel Fisher, Rob Tenconi, Mark Franklin
Art Directors Richard Brim, Daniel Fisher, Rob Tenconi, Mark Franklin
Illustration Village Green, London
Advertiser BFI London Film Festival

This outdoor execution was made up of a selection of iconic film posters from the festival's archives that were torn away to reveal the London skyline.

SonntagsZeitung
THE INSIGHT STORY

SonntagsZeitung
THE INSIGHT STORY

Media

Agency	Advico Young & Rubicam, Zurich
Creative Directors	Martin Stulz Dominik Oberwiler
Copywriter	Martin Stulz
Art Director	Lukas Wietlisbach
Photography	Scheffold Vizner
Graphic Design	Annik Weber
Account Team	Pablo Koerfer Julia Kull
Advertiser	SonntagsZeitung, "The Insight Story"

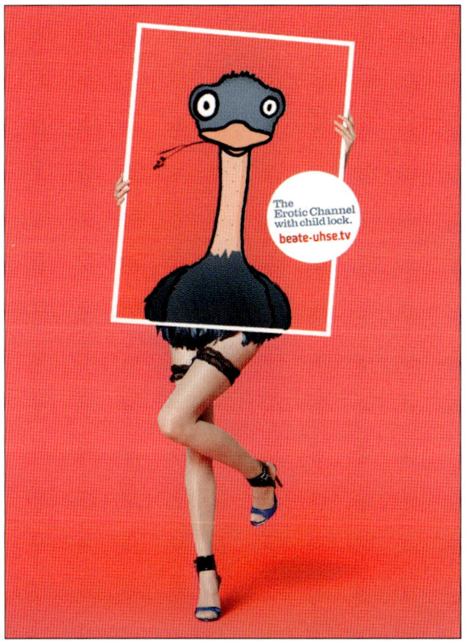
The Erotic Channel with child lock.
beate-uhse.tv

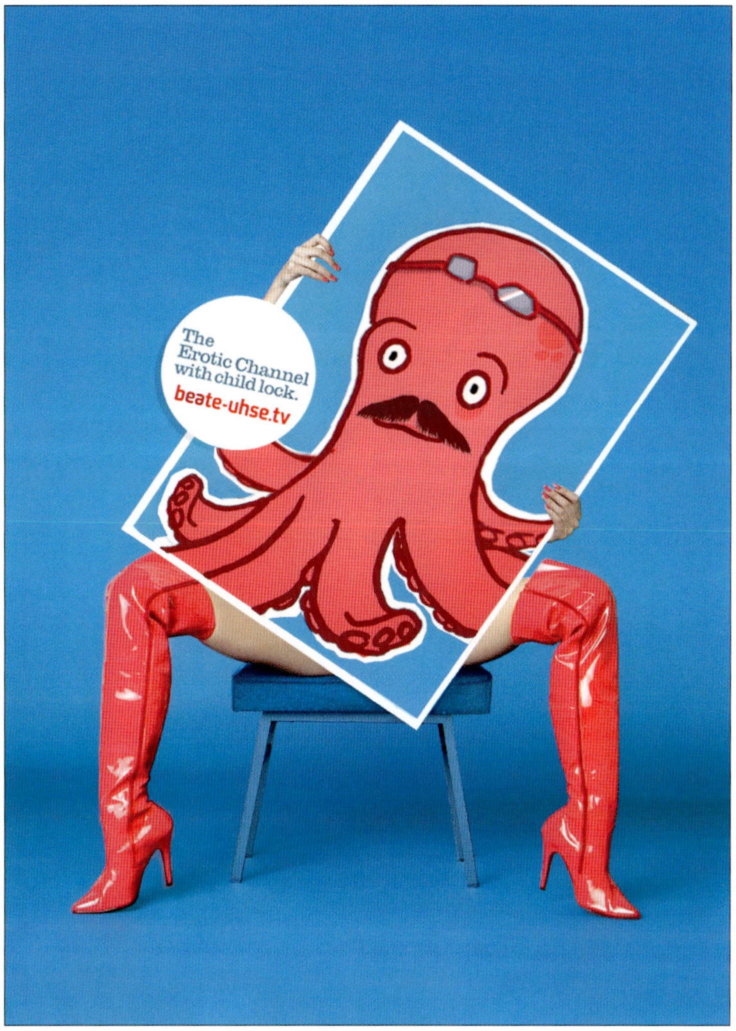
The Erotic Channel with child lock.
beate-uhse.tv

The Erotic Channel with child lock.
beate-uhse.tv

The Erotic Channel with child lock.
beate-uhse.tv

Agency	kempertrautmann, Hamburg
Creative Directors	Gerrit Zinke Christian Fritsche
Copywriter	Christoph Gähwiler
Art Director	Simon Jasper Philipp
Photography	Lisa Krechting
Illustrator	Julia Schonlau
Art Buying	Lina Eggers
Account Team	Jan Rütten Joana Gläscher
Advertiser	Beate Uhse TV, "Child Lock"

3-6 MAY
PRESENTS:
BEST
HOLLYWOOD
MOVIES ABOUT
CORRUPTION

Become
someone
else
Don
Quixote
PICK
YOUR HERO
AT
MintVinetu

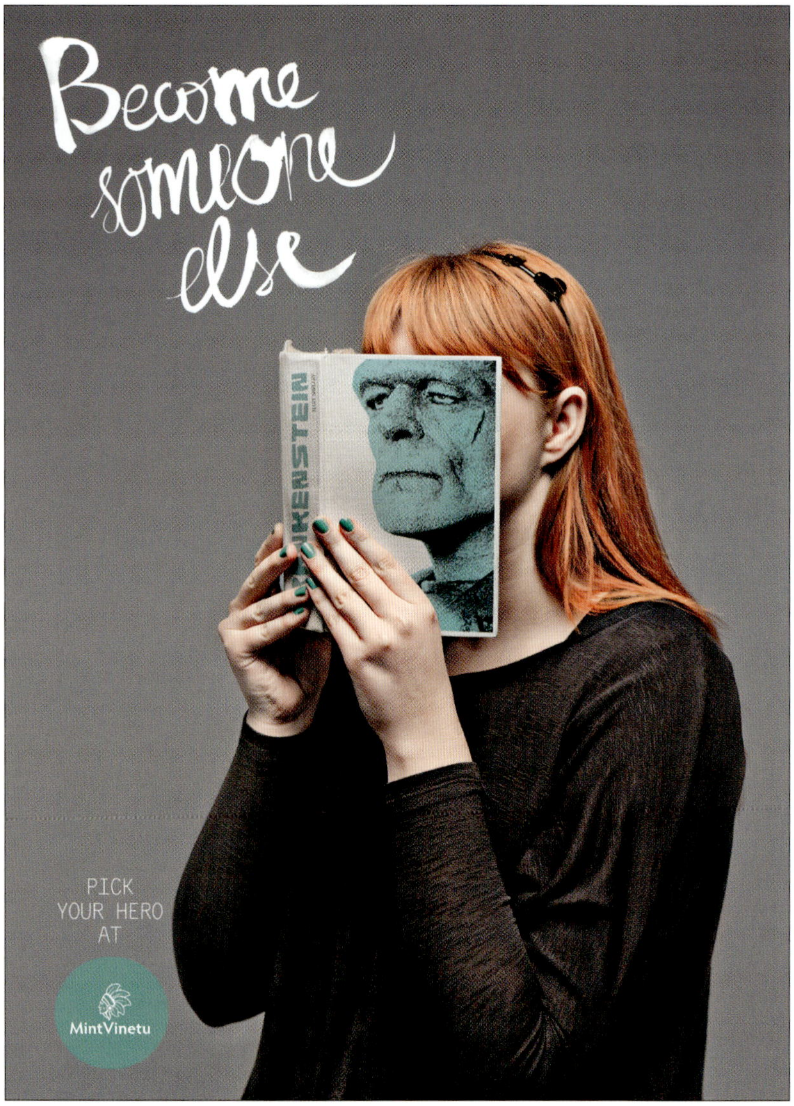
Become
someone
else
PICK
YOUR HERO
AT
MintVinetu

Agency	Box, Vilnius
Creative Director	Paulius Rymeikis
Copywriter	Lukas Šidlauskas
Art Director	Gabrielius Mackevičius
Illustrator	Antanas Dubra
Advertiser	Brave Word Film Festival, "Titanic"

Agency	Love, Vilnius
Creative Director	Tomas Ramanauskas
Art Director	Gediminas Saulys
Photography	Tomas Kauneckas
Advertiser	Mint Vinetu Bookshop, "Become Someone Else"

Updated every second.
stern.de

Updated every second.
stern.de

Updated every second.
stern.de

Updated every second.
stern.de

Agency	Kolle Rebbe, Hamburg
Creative Directors	Ingo Mueller Sven Klohk Jens Theil
Copywriter	Sascha Petersen
Art Director	Alexander Schmid
Graphic Design	Gerwin Schwaeger
Art Buying	Katrin Gruen
Post Production	POP, Hamburg
Account Manager	Tina Jappsen
Advertiser	Stern.de, "Updated Every Second"

Is it harder than ever to protect children from bullies?
LET'S TALK BULLYING
Irish Examiner
Thursday, September 29

How is porn affecting today's teens?
A SPECIAL INVESTIGATION
Irish Examiner
Starts Friday, July 8.

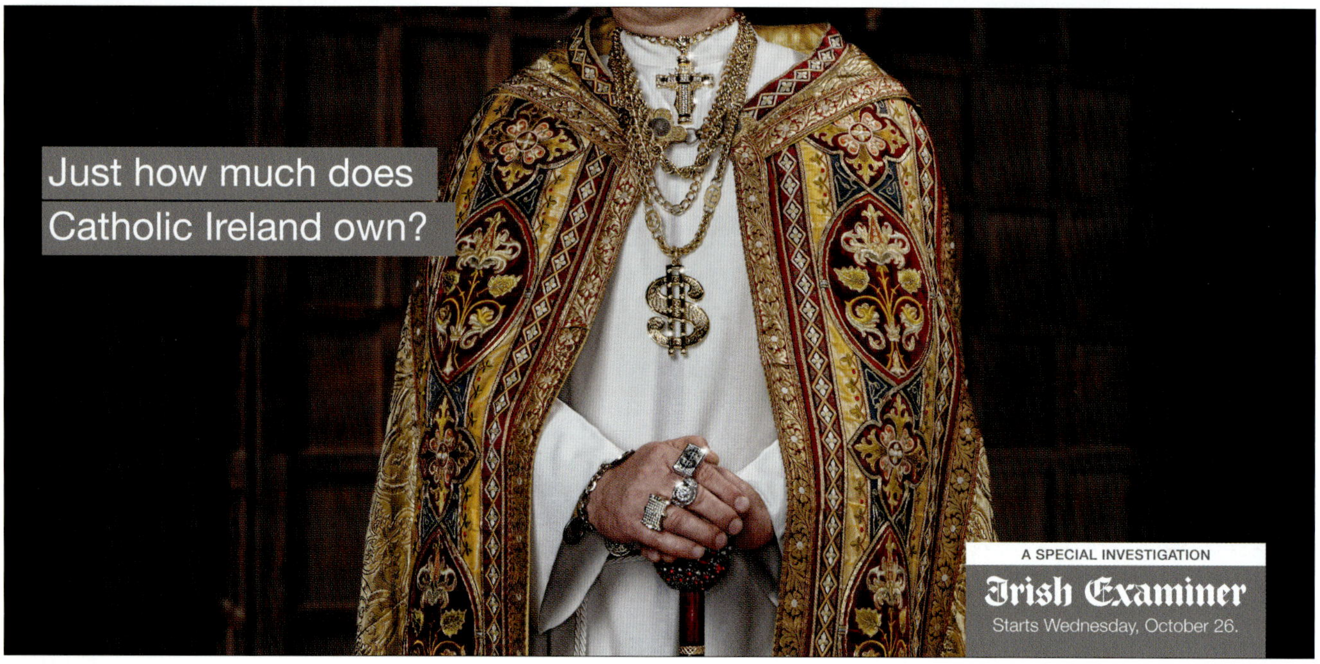
Just how much does Catholic Ireland own?
A SPECIAL INVESTIGATION
Irish Examiner
Starts Wednesday, October 26.

HAS DRINKING COME TO DEFINE OUR NATIONAL IDENTITY?
ALCOHOL AND IRELAND
Irish Examiner
Starts Friday, May 6

 Media

Agency	Chemistry, Dublin
Creative Director	Mike Garner
Copywriter	Anne Fleming
Art Directors	Adrian FitzSimon Nicole Sykes
Photography	Kevin Griffin Trevor Hart
Illustrator	PJ Lynch
Advertiser	The Irish Examiner

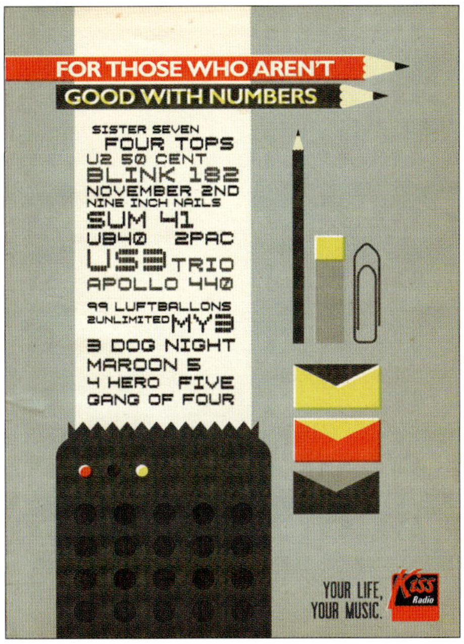

FOR THOSE WHO AREN'T
GOOD WITH NUMBERS
SISTER SEVEN
FOUR TOPS
U2 50 CENT
BLINK 182
NOVEMBER 2ND
NINE INCH NAILS
SUM 41
UB40 2PAC
US3 TRIO
APOLLO 440
99 LUFTBALLONS
2UNLIMITED MY3
3 DOG NIGHT
MAROON 5
4 HERO FIVE
GANG OF FOUR
YOUR LIFE,
YOUR MUSIC.
Kiss Radio

FOR THOSE WITH A PICKY TONGUE
HOT CHOCOLATE
MILK & TOAST & HONEY
CRANBERRIES
COLD TURKEY
PEARL JAM
SALT -N- PEPA
HONEY PIE
RED HOT CHILI PEPPERS
SMASHING PUMPKINS
CREAM
DAMIEN RICE
LEMON JELLY
MEAT LOAF
HOT BUTTER
POPCORN
YOUR LIFE,
YOUR MUSIC.
Kiss Radio

Polythene Pam
Michelle
Mary Mary
Lola
Layla
Mary Jane
Penny Lane
Jesus and Mary Chain
Laura a její tygři
Julia Says
Angie
Ecstasy of Saint Theresa
Alice In Chains
Roxanne
Marilyn Manson
Hey Jude
Tlustá Berta
Lucy In The Sky With Diamonds
Polly
Duffy
Lovely Rita
Jane's Addiction
Julia
Lucie
Belle and Sebastian
For those looking for the right name
YOUR LIFE,
YOUR MUSIC.
Kiss Radio

FOR THOSE WITH NO SENSE OF DIRECTION
TEXAS
LONDON CALLING
VIENNA CALLING
SWEET HOME ALABAMA
J.A.R.
NEW YORK CITY
AMERICA
MANCHESTER
JAPAN
VIENNA
EUROPE
ASIAN DUB FOUNDATION
VIVA LAS VEGAS
ATLANTIS
RIO
ASIA
STREETS OF PHILADELPHIA
NEVADA TAN
CONGO
CHICAGO
BRIGHTON ROCK
POLSKA BOYZ
WIENERBLUT
NAZARETH
ANGEL OF HARLEM
WATERLOO
TOKIO HOTEL
KASHMIR
MISS SARAJEVO
BARCELONA
YOUR LIFE,
YOUR MUSIC.
Kiss Radio

Agency	Jandl, Bratislava
Creative Director	Pavel Fuksa
Copywriter	Adam Rovný
Art Directors	Pavel Fuksa Matúš Nemčík
Illustrators	Pavel Fuksa Matúš Nemčík
Advertiser	Kiss Radio, "Your Life, Your Music"

New
SCRABBLE
trickster

Agency Ogilvy France, Paris
Creative Directors Chris Garbutt, Christian Reuilly
Copywriters Baptiste Clinet, Nicolas Lautier, Florian Bodet
Art Directors Baptiste Clinet, Nicolas Lautier, Florian Bodet
Production Paranoid, Paris
Directors Les Vikings
Producer Laure Bayle
Sound Producer Evelyne Callot
Music Apollo Studio, Montreal
Head of Digital Frederic Levron
Account Team Christine Dupetitmagneux, Marie-Charlotte Lafront, Xavier Delaporte
Clients Matéo Romano, Daphné Gerenton
Advertiser Scrabble Trickster, "Block Project"

How do you promote Scrabble Trickster, the classic board game with crazy new rules? You create an event by filling a huge apartment block in Berlin with bizarre characters: a brass band, a gorilla, a caped avenger, a giant (who takes up several windows), a fire-breathing dragon, comical policemen, a sea creature, a princess, and more. As the audience looks on, the building transforms into a giant Scrabble board, and we realise that the participants represent clues to the interlocking words that unfurl across the facade.

EXPERIMENTAL CLASSICAL CONCERTS. LUCERNE FESTIVAL

Agency	Ruf Lanz, Zurich
Creative Directors	Danielle Lanz Markus Ruf
Copywriter	Maren Beck
Art Director	Isabelle Hauser
Photography	Felix Schregenberger Philipp Ruault
Account Team	Heike Rindfleisch Sabrina Luck
Clients	Theresa Twachtmann Inés Maloigne
Advertiser	Lucerne Music Festival, “Emergency Exits”

The Earth Doesn't Need Cars.

btwin

Agency	Fred & Farid, Paris
Creative Directors	Fred Raillard Farid Mokart
Copywriters	Fred Raillard Farid Mokart
Art Directors	Fred Raillard Farid Mokart Eric Landowski
Production	Henry de Czar, Paris
Director	Lionel Goldstein
Producers	Jean-Luc Bergeron Michel Moniot
Clients	Olivier Robinet Yann Thomas Olivier Leblanc
Account Team	Emmanuel Ferry Eudes Jover
Advertiser	B'Twin Bicycles, "Everywhere"

A man wakes up in bed – next to his bicycle. He showers with it. In fact, he's never off it. As he leaves his building, he's joined by more people on bikes. The crowd of riders swells as they head into a very green-looking town. They perform little tricks and even flirt a little. The metro, libraries, schools, offices, sports fields: they're all filled with bikes. At the end of the day, the two flirting cyclists ride home together. The earth doesn't need cars. Do you?

THE HAMBURG THEATRE.
Has come under criticism for 110 years.

54th BFI LONDON FILM FESTIVAL
13 – 28 October 2010

Agency	Leagas Delaney, Hamburg
Creative Director	Hermann Waterkamp
Copywriter	Michael Okun
Art Director	Patrik Hartmann
Production	Deli Pictures
Director	Michael Reissinger
Producers	Patrick Plogstedt Claudia Remming
Graphic Design	Bjoern Byns
Animation	Robert Rhee Johannes Lippert
Advertiser	The Hamburg Theatre

This surreal spot – which resembles Terry Gilliam's creations for Monty Python – features a flying dolphin who guides us through a storm. On his journey he encounters the disembodied heads of critics, winged typewriters spewing reams of articles, clapping hands, clacking mouths and a hail of thumbs held both up and down. Finally, the dolphin guides us inside the Hamburg Theatre to the sound of cheers. The Hamburg Theatre has weathered thunderous applause and hails of criticism for 110 years.

Agency	Leo Burnett, London
Creative Directors	Jonathan Burley Jim Bolton
Copywriters & ADs	Daniel Fisher Richard Brim Rob Tenconi Mark Franklin
Production	Gorgeous
Director	Chris Palmer
Producer	Michaela Johnson
Advertiser	BFI London Film Festival, "Dialogue"

The BFI London Film Festival brings the world's best new films to London. So what could be more appropriate than showing ordinary Londoners speaking some the best lines of movie dialogue in entirely different contexts? The acting is equal to the task: but do you recognise the brilliant lines? Viewers who can't quite place them will want to watch again and again. "I've seen things you people wouldn't believe..." It sounds horribly familiar, doesn't it?

LEGO
Builders of Tomorrow.

LEGO
Builders of Tomorrow.

LEGO
Builders of Tomorrow.

Agency	Serviceplan, Munich
CCO	Alex Schill
Executive CD	Matthias Harbeck
Creative Director	Oliver Palmer
Copywriter	Frank Seiler
Art Directors	Sandra Loibl Julia Koch
Photography	Kristina Korb, Munich Susanne Dittrich
Graphic Design	Franz Röppischer
Advertiser	Lego, "Builders of Tomorrow"

NO GUTS NO GLORY
SOÖRUZ
Wakeboard - Summer 2011 collection

NO GUTS NO GLORY
SOÖRUZ
Snowboard - Winter 2011 collection

Agency Publicis Conseil, Paris
CDs Olivier Altmann, Frederic Royer
Copywriter Didier Aerts
Art Director Alexandra Offe
Photography Jean-Marie Vives
Art Buying Jean-Luc Chirio
Account Team Jean-Patrick Chiquiar, Laetitia Vitalis, Sophie Gustinelli
Clients Yann Dalibot, Matthieu Barat
Advertiser Sooruz, "Jump"

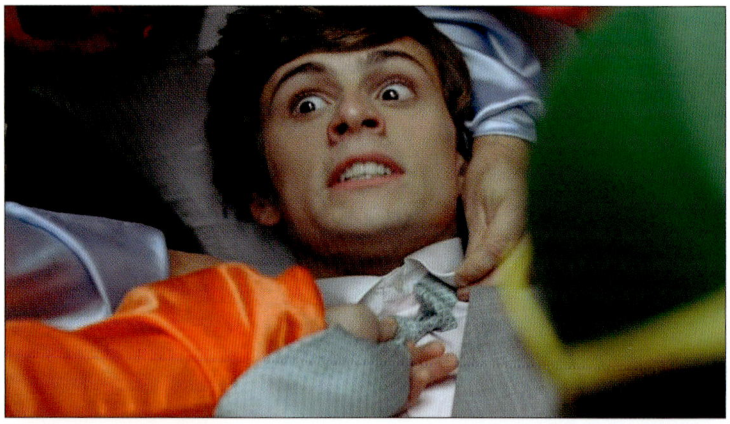

PMU

 Recreation & Leisure

Agency Publicis Conseil, Paris
Creative Director Olivier Altmann
Copywriter Marc Rosier
Art Director Jean-Marc Tramoni
Production Les Telecreateurs, Paris
Director Chris Palmer
Producers Amy Appleton, Pierre Marcus, Timothe Rosenberg
Music Les Avions, "Nuit Sauvage"
Sound Prod. Laurent Favard, Boris Jeanne
Post Production The Mill, London
Account Team Jean-Patrick Chiquiar, Eleonore Mabille
Clients Benoit Cornu, Cyrille Giraudat, Pascal Drai, Martin Terrier
Advertiser PMU, "The Jockeys are Back!"

The PMU is where French people go to bet on horse races. In the first spot, a group of tiny jockeys drag a man from his old car – along with the litter on the passenger seat, the CD he's playing and a photo of his wife – and deliver him to a flashy sports car. They even place posh driving gloves on his hands before running off, leaving him at the wheel with a bemused smile on his face. It's scary how the PMU could change your life.

In the second spot, the jockeys appear to mug a scruffy young man. They bundle him to the floor, rip off his clothes, snatch the cards from his wallet and chuck away his plastic watch. Then they dress him in a chic suit and silk socks, place his cards in a crocodile skin wallet, strap on a very expensive wristwatch, drape a cashmere coat over him and leave him holding a posh briefcase. Peeking inside, he sees it contains a gold bar. It's scary how the PMU could change your life.

THE GREAT HORROR CLASSICS.
PROFONDO ROSSO
Movies, books and more.

THE GREAT HORROR CLASSICS.
PROFONDO ROSSO
Movies, books and more.

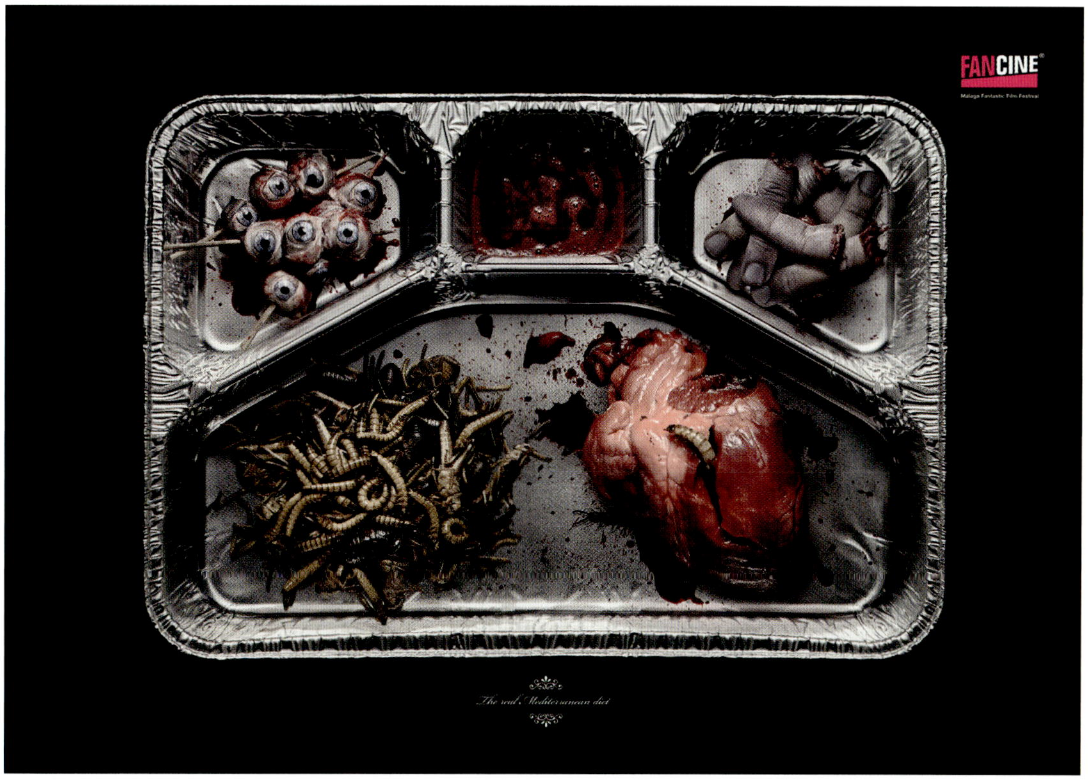
FANCINE
The real Mediterranean diet

Agency	Y&R Brands, Milan
Executive CD	Vicky Gitto
Copywriter	Gabriele Caeti
Art Director	Alessandro Stenco
Photography	Jessica Harrison
Illustrator	Jessica Harrison
Account Mgr.	Marco Ruggeri
Clients	Maria Letizia Sercia Luigi Cozzi
Advertiser	Profondo Rosso Shop & Museum

Agency	Tapsa, Madrid
Creative Directors	Antonio Botella Manuel Pérez de Camino
Photography	Eduardo Diaz-Bourgeot
Account Manager	Sylvia de Sienes
Advertiser	Fancine Fantastic Film Festival, "Tray"

PREMIERE!
OPERA IN 3D.
Tomorrow Folkoperan will broadcast Sweden's first opera in 3D, live at Filmhuset in Stockholm. The opera is Faust by Charles Gonoud. In December you can watch it at Folkets Hus 3D cinemas around Sweden. Book your tickets at fhp.nu/folkoperan and experience opera in a way you've never experienced it before.
FOLKOPERAN

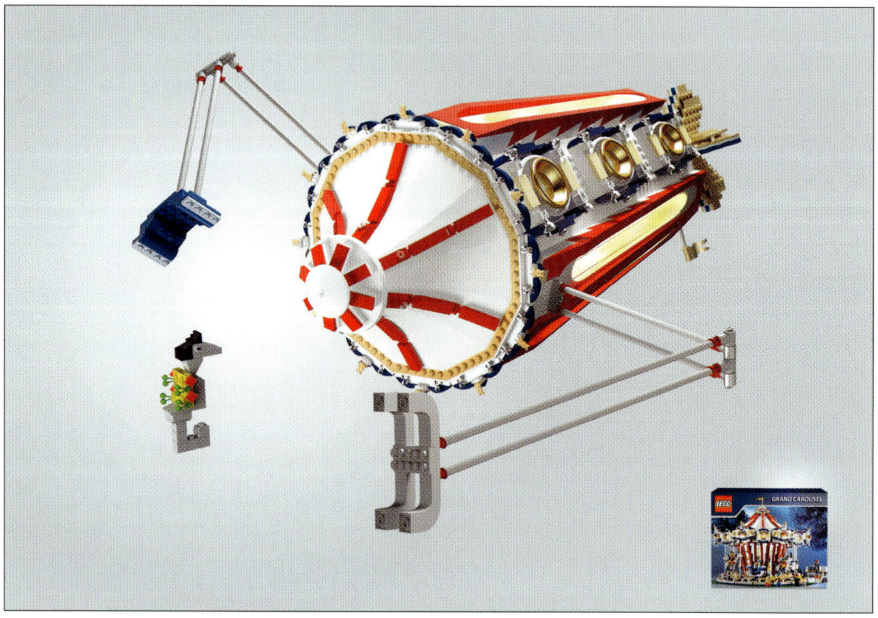
LEGO
GRAND CAROUSEL

LEGO
TAJ MAHAL

 Recreation & Leisure

Agency	Lowe Brindfors, Stockholm
Copywriter	Stefan Pagreus
Art Director	Kalle dos Santos
Photography	Pål Allan
Typographers	Margaretha Ekstrand-Almér Jeanette Andersson
Art Buying	Caroline Agné
Final Artwork	Roland Lindgren
Account Team	Pelle Holm Tina de Geer
Client	Elenor Wolgers
Advertiser	Folkoperan Opera, “3D”

Agency	Leo Burnett, Moscow
Creative Directors	Mikhail Kudashkin Dmitry Jakovlev
Copywriter	Rodrigo Linhares
Art Director	Arina Avdeeva
Illustrator	Ninjafilms Studio, Moscow
Graphic Design	Asya Boukhnina Viktoria Prokopavichute
Advertiser	Lego, “Taj Mahal” & “Batiskaf”

from joy through
self doubt to
resignation and back.
the face of
the marathon.
adidas.com/running

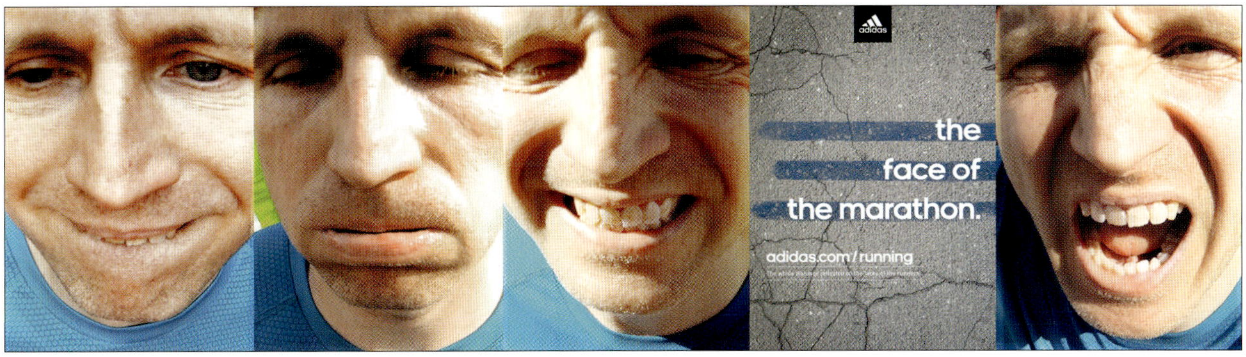
adidas
the
face of
the marathon.
adidas.com/running

ZURICH
CHAMBER
ORCHESTRA
ZKO

Agency Heimat, Berlin
Creative Directors Guido Heffels, Ove Gley, Ole Vinck
Copywriters Dominik Maas, Lucas Schneider
Art Directors Patrick Düver, Franziska Kriehn
Photography Acne, Berlin
Graphic Design Franziska Kriehn
Advertiser Adidas, "The Face of the Marathon"

These posters were the result of a much larger operation that Adidas mounted at the 2011 Berlin marathon. 15 runners were equipped with special cameras that were attached to their heads and recorded their changing facial expressions over the entire 42.195 km distance. The images were screened live to the world on a microsite and to digital screens along the marathon route. A handsome coffee-table book, embedded in asphalt, was also produced to commemorate the event.

Agency Euro RSCG, Zurich
Creative Director Axel Eckstein
Copywriter Rob Hartmann
Art Director Isabelle Bühler
Photography Julia Hetta
Advertiser Zurich Chamber Orchestra, "Touched By"

VELO
at
SPORTPLAUSCH
WIDER
BIKES TO FALL IN LOVE WITH – SPORTPLAUSCH WIDER – WALLISELLEN
RACING BIKES – MOUNTAIN BIKES – TOURING BIKES – CITY BIKES – ELECTRIC BIKES

MUSEUM OF
COMMUNISM
OPEN DAILY
FROM 9:00-21:00

MUSEUM OF
COMMUNISM
OPEN DAILY
FROM 9:00-21:00

Agency Advico Young & Rubicam, Zurich
CCO Markus Gut
Creative Directors Daniel Bieri, Thomas Engeli
Art Director Michael Gallmann
Advertiser Sportplausch Wider Sports Store, "Custom Bikes"

The letters in Robert Indiana's iconic painting "Love" are slightly re-arranged to read "Velo", French for "Bike", thereby communicating the store's love of cycling.

Agency Young & Rubicam, Prague
Creative Director Jaime Mandelbaum
Copywriter Conor Barry
Art Director Thiago Jacon
Photography Miro Minarových
Head of Art Marco Antonio do Nascimento
Final Art Asile, Paris
Advertiser Museum of Communism, "Escaping"

OVERPAID
LOSER
All you need is an opinion.
ODDSET
Sports betting

MATCHBOX

Agency TBWA\Stockholm
Copywriters Johannes Ivarsson, Kalle Widgren
Art Directors Alexander Fredlund, Carl Dalin
Typograpy C2, Stockholm
Final Art Stefan Gallon
Account Team Jonas Andersson, Annika Molnár
Advertiser Oddset, "All you Need is an Opinion"

Agency Bold Ogilvy & Mather, Athens
Creative Director Lazaros Nikiforidis
Copywriter Katerina Tsoumpa
Art Director Vangelis Tolias
Photography Vassilis Michail
Illustrator Tereza Ferentinou
Advertiser Matchbox Diecast Models, "Straw"

CONCERTS FOR BABIES
tickets — 0848 84 88 44 — billettkasse@zko.ch
ZURICH CHAMBER ORCHESTRA
ZKO

Uncage your kids.

Uncage your kids.
TIER | PARK | GOLDAU

Agency Euro RSCG, Zurich
Creative Director Axel Eckstein
Copywriter Urs Zwyssig
Art Director Rob Hartmann
Photography Annette Fischer
Digital Artwork Pixelprinz, Zurich: Linus Schneider
Advertiser Zurich Chamber Orchestra, "Babyconcerts"

Agency Advico Young & Rubicam, Zurich
CCO Markus Gut
Creative Directors Dominik Oberwiler, Martin Stulz
Copywriter Martin Stulz
Art Director Sandro Tissi
Account Manager Julia Kull
Advertiser Tierpark Goldau, "Cages"

ANYTHING CAN HAPPEN
WHEN CREATIVE MINDS CLASH AT MADE.
www.made-blog.com

ANYTHING CAN HAPPEN
WHEN CREATIVE MINDS CLASH AT MADE.
www.made-blog.com

ANYTHING CAN HAPPEN
WHEN CREATIVE MINDS CLASH AT MADE.
www.made-blog.com

ANYTHING CAN HAPPEN
WHEN CREATIVE MINDS CLASH AT MADE.
www.made-blog.com

ANYTHING CAN HAPPEN
WHEN CREATIVE MINDS CLASH AT MADE.
www.made-blog.com

ANYTHING CAN HAPPEN
WHEN CREATIVE MINDS CLASH AT MADE.
www.made-blog.com

Agencies	TBWA\Berlin, Che*Che, Berlin
Executive CDs	Nico Zeh Tatjana Stein Kurt Georg Dieckert Stefan Schmidt
Creative Directors	Dirk Henkelmann Philip Borchardt
Copywriter	Nadine Nedreboe
Art Director	Andy Tran
Graphic Design	Andrew Morgan
Advertiser	Absolut Vodka, "MADE - Clash of Objects"

STIHL® MS 880
EXTREMELY STRONG POWER
THE STRONGEST CHAINSAWS IN THE WORLD. STIHL.com

STIHL® MS 361
EXTREMELY DYNAMIC POWER
THE STRONGEST CHAINSAWS IN THE WORLD. STIHL.com

Agency	Scholz & Friends, Berlin	**Post Production**	Recom, Berlin: Simon Geis Lars Wittmaak
CCO	Martin Pross		
Executive CO	Matthias Spaetgens	**Account Team**	Benjamin Baader Sven Weiche
Creative Director	Michael Winterhagen		
Copywriter	Felix John	**Advertiser**	Stihl Chainsaws, "Warriors"
Art Director	Philipp Weber		
Illustrator	Valerij Mueller		

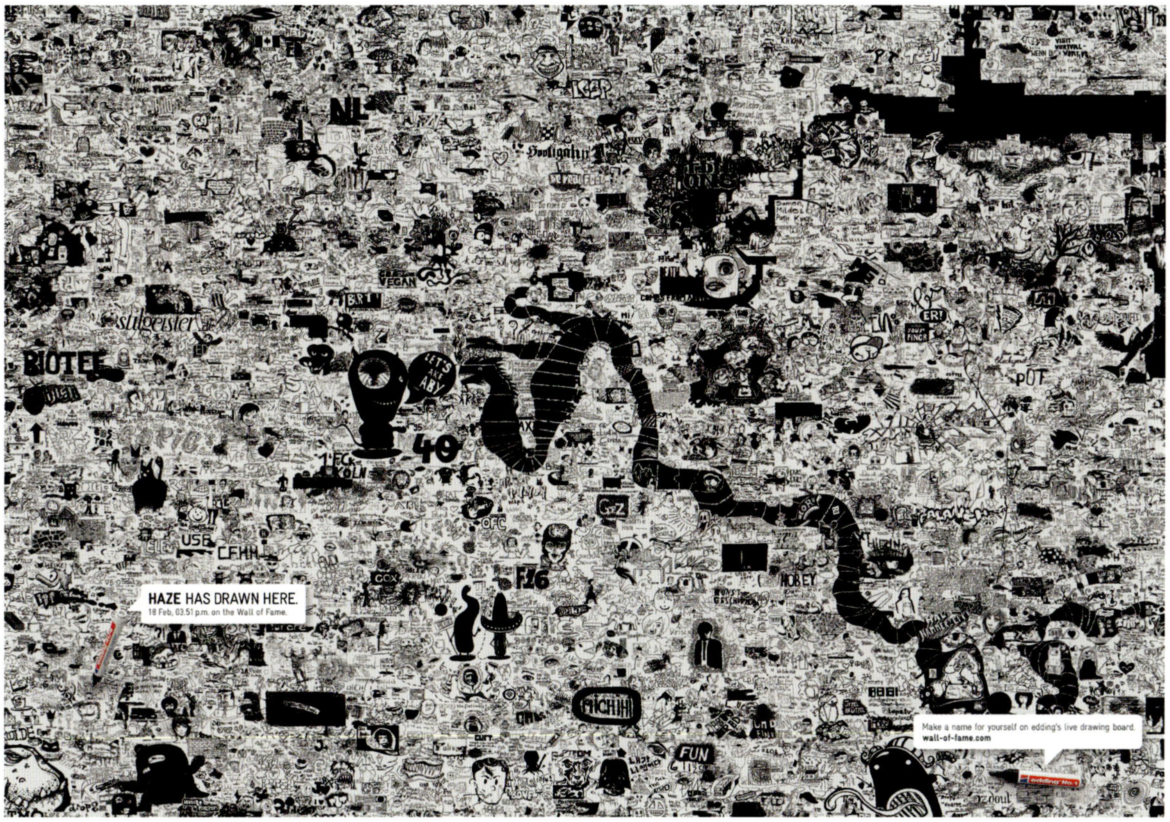
HAZE HAS DRAWN HERE.
18 Feb, 03:51 p.m. on the Wall of Fame.
Make a name for yourself on edding's live drawing board.
wall-of-fame.com

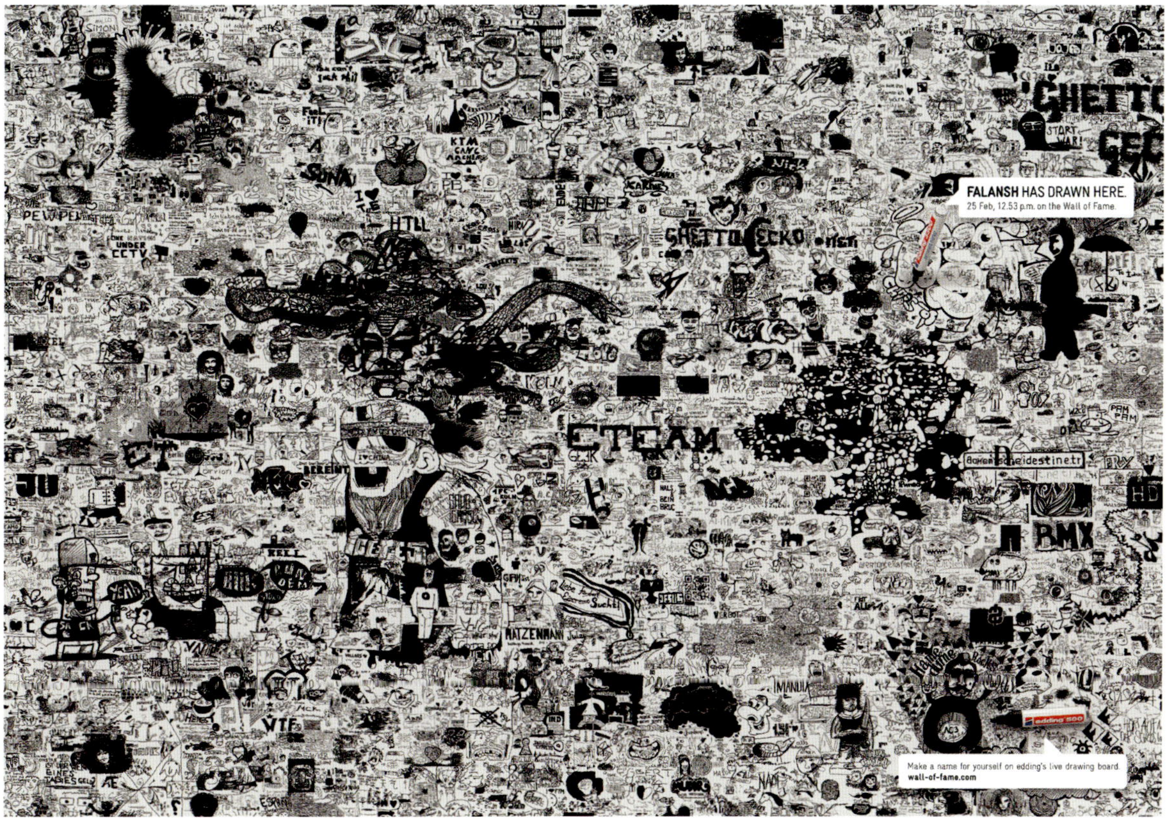
FALANSH HAS DRAWN HERE.
25 Feb, 12:53 p.m. on the Wall of Fame.
Make a name for yourself on edding's live drawing board.
wall-of-fame.com

Agency kempertrautmann, Hamburg
Creative Directors Simon Jasper Philipp, Christoph Gähwiler, Stefan Walz
Copywriters Christoph Gähwiler, Samuel Weiß, Michael Götz
Art Directors Simon Jasper Philipp, Stefan Walz, Florian Schimmer
Graphic Design David Scherer, Tobias Lehment
Production Demodern Digital Design Studio, Cologne; Appel Grafik
Art Buying Susi Kastner-Linke, Lina Eggers
Account Team Niklas Kruchten, Elisabeth Einhaus, Andrea Bison, Dorothea Feurer
Advertiser Edding, "Wall of Fame"

BRITAIN'S
MOST MEMORABLE
Snopake
STICKY NOTES
NOW IN THE UAE

Correction Fluid, 20 ml, colour: white
1,49€
Cheap fun in the office.
Herlitz

Magnum Permanent Marker, water resistant
3,99€
Cheap fun in the office.
Herlitz

Agency Impact BBDO, Dubai
Executive CD Fouad Abdel Malak
Creative Director Amit Kapoor
Associate CD Dinesh Tharippa
Art Directors Sameer Ketkar, Marie Claire Maalouf
Photography Adam Browning Hill
Final Artwork Byju Ravindran
Business Unit GM Talal Sheikh Elard
Account Manager Noura Al Nazer
Advertiser Snopake Sticky Notes, "Churchill"

Agency KNSK, Hamburg
Creative Directors Tim Krink, Ulrike Wegert
Copywriter Dieter Kolaja
Art Director Oliver Fermer
Graphic Design Julian Heidt
Advertiser Herlitz Office Supplies, "Cheap Fun in the Office"

Supersonic turbo sausage.
Sausage production now up to 90 percent faster.
CDS Hackner GmbH | Rossfelder Straße 52/5 | 74564 Crailsheim Germany | www.cds-hackner.de | natural casings | animal-by-products | frozen food logistics
CDS
For World Class Sausage.

You can just forget it.
The maintenance-free business printers from Samsung.
Reliable, high performance and easy to operate: Samsung business printers like the SCX-3205-W expect jobs, not attention. Find out more at www.samsung.de
SAMSUNG

Agency	Wensauer & Partner, Ludwisgburg
Creative Director	Norbert Graf
Copywriters	Stefan Mattes Kai Kemmler
Art Directors	Thomas Maguin Rainer Jagmann
Photography	Martin Baitinger
Graphic Design	Yvonne Schweizerhof
Digital Artwork	Arsmedicom, Ostfildern: Jörg Macha
Advertiser	CDS Hackner, "Supersonic Turbo Sausage"

Agency	Cheil Germany, Schwalbach am Taunus
Creative Directors	Roland Rudolf Thomas Schroeder Joern Welle
Copywriters	Gerrit Kleinfeld Thilo Mueller-Ohldach
Art Director	Heide Kotzyba
Photography	Tom Nagy
Illustrator	Mark Hassenpflug
Digital Artwork	Mark Gmehling
Advertiser	Samsung Printers, "Just Forget It"

Nokia, Vodafone?...
Microsoft, HP, Xerox, Post-it...

Tuborg? Stella Artois?

Avon! Nescafe, Novotel, Durex?

Domestos, Ariel, Whirlpool...

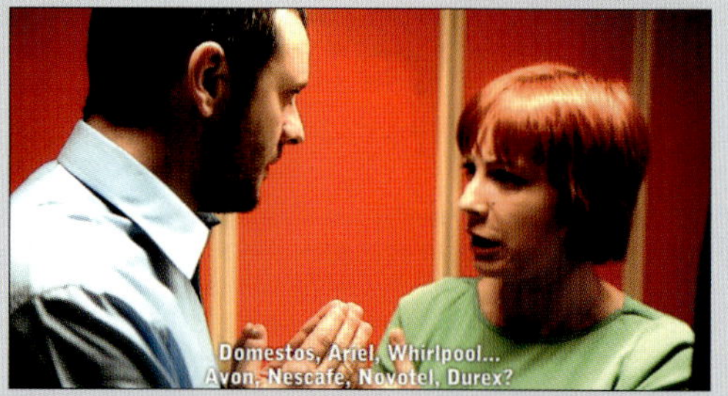
Domestos, Ariel, Whirlpool...
Avon, Nescafe, Novotel, Durex?

Novotel?

Novotel?
Toyota, Novotel!

IQads
www.IQads.ro
TOTUL DESPRE PUBLICITATE
Advertising is part of our life.
IQads.ro - All about advertising.

Agency Next, Bucharest
Creative Director Liviu David
Copywriters Mihaela Stefanica, Mihaela Neatu, Liviu David, Radu Olteanu, Semida Duriga
Art Director Catalin Baciu
Production Reload Film, Bucharest
Director Liviu David
Producer Traian Ardac
Advertiser IQads.ro, "Jealousy"

Meet the couple who converse in brand names. The man arrives home late from work. "Nokia? Vodafone?" his wife complains. He protests: "Microsoft, HP, Xerox, Post-It…" His wife suggests the truth is closer to "Tuborg," "Stella Artois" or "Bergenbier". Then she sees the lipstick on his collar. "Avon!" She challenges him: "Nescafé, Novotel, Durex?" Meanwhile, her life is full of "Domestos, Ariel, Whirlpool..." She shows him the door. "Toyota, Novotel!" Advertising is part of our lives, suggests IQads – a website about advertising.

ADVERTISING
HERE IS SWELL
IF YOU WANT TO REACH
MEN WHO WILL NOT
REMEMBER ONE BIT OF
YOUR ADVERTISING.
KVÄLLSPRESSEN
IMPACT

ADVERTISING
HERE IS PEACHY IF
YOU WANT TO REACH
PEOPLE WHO
LIKE STARING AT
BIKE SEATS.
If you'd rather reach 3,988,000 people with other
interests you should buy the Impact Tabloid Package,
now offering an extra placement in the tabloids this summer.
Call 08-6540500 and book!
KVÄLLSPRESSEN
IMPACT

ADVERTISING
HERE IS REALLY
CLEVER IF YOUR
TARGET GROUP
CONSISTS SOLELY
THE PEOPLE THAT USE
THIS PARTICULAR STAIRCASE.
If you'd rather reach 3,988,000 people
all over the place, you should buy the
Impact tabloid package, now offering an
extra placement in the tabloids this summer.
Call 08-6540500 and book!
KVÄLLSPRESSEN
IMPACT

BONJOUR!
ADVERTISING HERE
IS GREAT
IF YOU WANT TO REACH SOME
AD PEOPLE
"WORKING" IN CANNES.
KVÄLLSPRESSEN
IMPACT

Agency	Abby Norm, Stockholm
Creative Director	Emil Frid
Copywriter	Peter Fjäll
Art Directors	Helena Lonaeus Oskar Hellqvist
Photography	Lasse Burell
Account Team	Ebba Kilman Andreas Morne Sophie Wesslau
Advertiser	Kvällspressen Impact, "A Really Unalternative Media"

Google Analytics
google.com/analytics

Agency Google Creative Lab, London
Creative Director Tom Uglow
Copywriter Misha Manson Smith
Art Director Anna Deamer
Production Across The Pond, London
Director Misha Manson Smith
Producers Julie Cohen, Alexia Merrington, Beki Gard
Advertiser Google Analytics, "Online Checkout - In Real Life"

What if real life shopping was like shopping online? A man arrives at a supermarket checkout to pay for a loaf of bread. He's asked for his password – which he's forgotten. He has to agree to a stream of conditions. Soon the cashier freezes – the customer has "timed out". Once "online" again, he is asked to read a "captcha". Then he discovers his bread is outrageously expensive, due to express delivery and insurance. To get it cheap, he must wait five days. Frustrated, he leaves. Google Analytics can help retailers understand what online shoppers really need.

Translate a block of text
(Enter up to 150 words)
Would you like to meet my mama?
Select from and to languages
Chinese-simp to English
Chinese-simp to Chinese-trad
Chinese-trad to English
Chinese-trad to Chinese-simp
English to Chinese-simp
English to Chinese-trad
English to Dutch
English to French
Translate
Translate

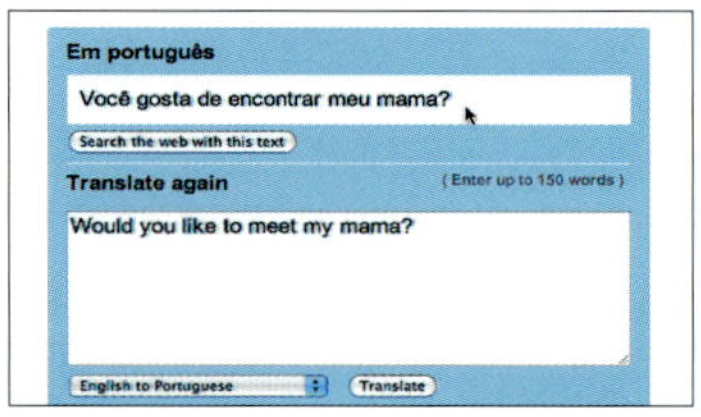
Em português
Você gosta de encontrar meu mama?
Translate again
Would you like to meet my mama?

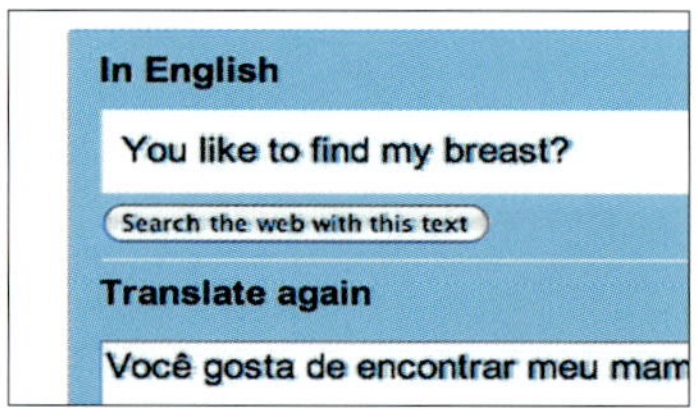
In English
You like to find my breast?
Search the web with this text
Translate again
Você gosta de encontrar meu mam

In English
You like to find my breast?
Translate again
If you want to speak a language properly, speak to us.
Berlitz Language Center

www.berlitz.com

Wrong job?

jobsintown.de

Agency Memac Ogilvy & Mather, Dubai
Creative Directors Steve Hough, Ramzi Moutran
Copywriters Jeremy Southern, Sascha Kuntze
Art Directors Jeremy Southern, Sascha Kuntze
Director Sara Abu Zahra
Producer Sara Abu Zahra
Advertiser Berlitz Language School, "Google Translates"

Translation sites still have a way to go. Here we see a genuine translation from English to Portuguese. The user types in: "Would you like to meet my mama?" A translation appears. But when it's cut, pasted and translated back into English, it mysteriously becomes: "Would you like to find my breast?" In a second spot, the exercise is repeated on another site, this time from English to Japanese and back to English. "Please don't shoot me. Here take my wallet." becomes "Please shoot me. Here take my purse." To speak a language properly, better go to Berlitz.

Agency Grabarz & Partner, Hamburg
Creative Directors Timm Weber, Goesta Diehl, Oliver Heidorn
Copywriter Kerstin Correll
Art Director Thomas Schmiegel
Director Robert Nylund
Producers Philipp Schmalriede, Alexa-Sophia Schaefer
Acct. Supervisor Reinhard Patzschke
Advertiser Jobsintown.de, "Fisherman"

We're on a trawler out at sea. It's bleakly beautiful. The narrator describes his life as a fisherman, denying that the job is lonely, frustrating or boring. We watch the men hauling in the nets. "Only sometimes," the narrator admits, "I wonder if there's something bigger in life for me." As we look on, he grabs an eel from the net and deftly twists it into a funny balloon animal. He seems pleased with himself, but his crew mates are aghast. Wrong job? Find the right one at jobsintown.de

Don't Be An Alien
In A Foreign Country
Berlitz

Bab Al-Bahrain Hotel
Don't Be An Alien
In A Foreign Country
Berlitz

Agency	FP7/DXB, Dubai
Creative Director	Fadi Yaish
Copywriter	Aunindo Anoop Sen
Art Director	Gautam Wadher
Photography	Remix Studio, Bangkok: Anuchai Secharunputong Nok Pipattungkul
Illustration	Remix Studio, Bangkok: Chanchay Aussawanuchit
Integrated Producer	Clarisse Mar Wai May
Advertiser	Berlitz Language School, "UFO"

SHE WANTS QUICK RESULTS
YOU NEED THEM TO LAST
Patients often want results quickly but at the expense of real long-term acne control. With Epiduo, you can start to clear their acne up quickly[1] and give them the long-term control they really need.[2]
Epiduo® 0.1% / 2.5% Gel
adapalene / benzoyl peroxide
Rapid action, long-term control
GALDERMA
Committed to the future of dermatology

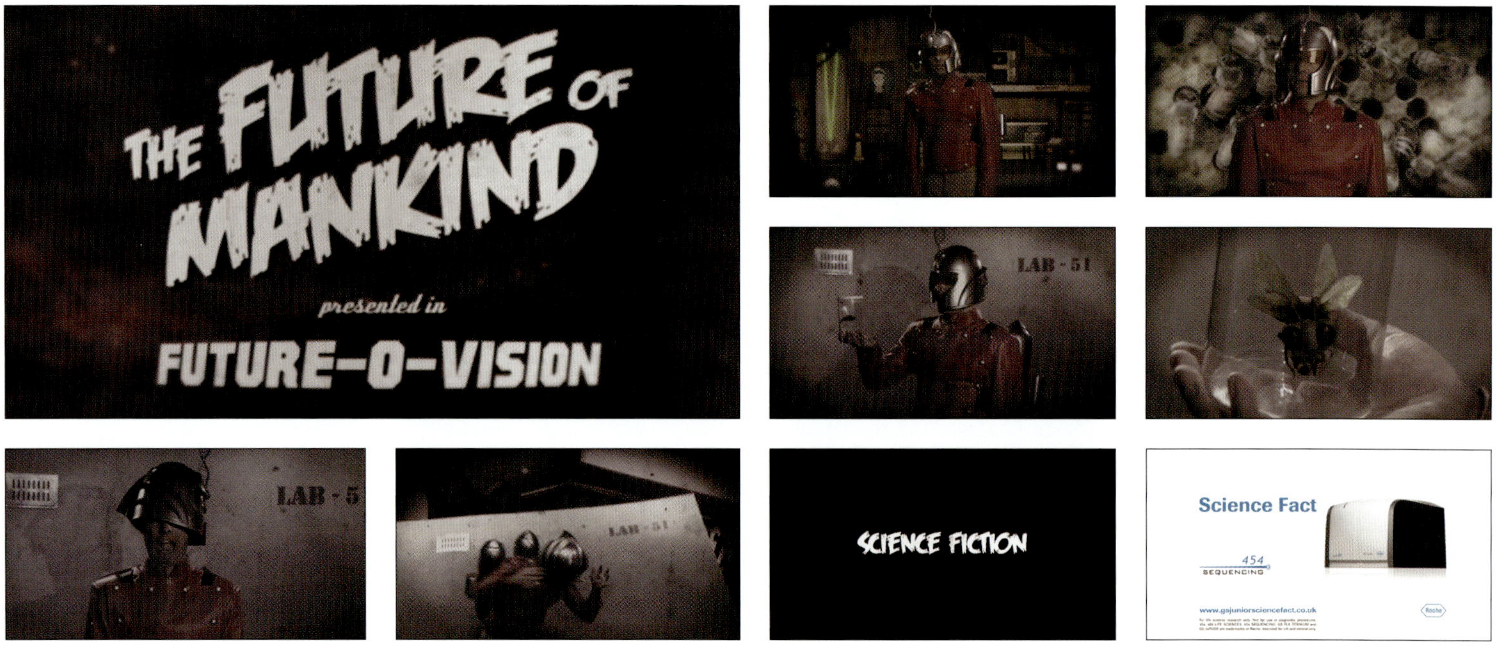
THE FUTURE OF MANKIND
presented in
FUTURE-O-VISION
LAB - 51
SCIENCE FICTION
Science Fact
454
SEQUENCING

Agency Torre Lazur McCann, London
Creative Director Adrian Parr
Copywriter Jonathan Moore
Art Director Thomas Dirnberger
Photography Jillian Lochner
Designer Steven Woodliffe
Advertiser Epiduo, "A Change of Face"

Agency TBWA\Paling Walters, London
Executive CD Dick Dunford
Creative Director Russell Speed
Copywriter Gavin Finney
Art Director Paul Byrne
Production One Hand Clapping
Director Christian De Vita
Producers Ben Campbell
Nicholas Kurs
Advertiser Roche GS Junior Sequencer, "Science Fiction, Science Fact"

In the style of a 1950's low-budget science fiction film, a mad scientist reveals "The Future of Mankind." With his jet-pack sequencer he promises to propagate life itself by harnessing the essence of a humble bee. The count-down ends and the sequencing commences, but at the same time the bee escapes. It takes refuge in the man's space helmet and panic ensues, resulting in the destruction of the set. That's science fiction. Science fact: the GS Junior genetic sequencer delivers fast and accurate results to help laboratories answer today's most pressing scientific questions.

Protect them from the
dangers of glucose toxicity
Glucobay®

Protect them from the
dangers of glucose toxicity
Glucobay®

Protect them from the
dangers of glucose toxicity
Bayer HealthCare
Bayer Schering Pharma
Glucobay®
Protecting their future meal by meal

Agency	Sudler & Hennessey, Milan
Creative Directors	Angelo Ghidotti Bruno Stucchi
Copywriter	Mair Dilworth
Art Director	Sinead Murphy
Photography	Patrice de Villiers
Advertiser	Glucobay, "Protecting Against Toxicity"

nettbuss

 Corporate Image

Agency Los&Co, Oslo
Copywriter Ragnar Roksvåg
Art Director Jo Espen Johansen
Production Social Club, Stockholm
Directors Jesper Ericstam, Giulio Musi Wennergren
Advertiser Nettbuss, "Whoever you Are"

The film celebrates the lives of various people who take the bus every day. We follow five very different travellers on the same bus. The commercial ensures that these misfits seem lovable, even if they cheat on their wives with men and abandon their school kids for an afternoon romp. Whoever you are, wherever you're going, we drive for you: Nettbuss.

CNN
GET A NEW PERSPECTIVE ON GERMANY.
WATCH CNN'S GERMANY SPECIAL "I-LIST". FEBRUARY 21ST - 26TH
cnn.com/ilist CNN

Agency	Heimat, Berlin
Creative Directors	Guido Heffels Myles Lord
Copywriter	Ramin Schmiedekampf
Art Director	Frank Hose
Producers	Florian Hoffmann Jessica Valin
Advertiser	CNN International, "Mirror Lakes"

CNN's i-List series takes viewers to a different country each month, showcasing its people, places and culture. In order to promote the Germany edition, CNN wanted German people to tune in and get a new perspective on their own country. So it placed giant "mirror lakes" – 2,500 stainless steel panels covering up to 400 square metres – at key locations in cities across Germany. The mirrors provided unusual perspectives as well as opportunities for interaction via photography and sharing images online.

HORNBACH
Home Improvement Superstores

LEVI STRAUSS & CO.
SAN FRANCISCO
CAL.
ORIGINAL RIVETED
QUALITY CLOTHING
PATENTED
MAY 20 1873
XX
501®
W33 L34
JOHN Q. SMITH
VP, LSA MARKETING
T 415.123.4567
F 415.123.7654
JSMITH@LEVI.COM
LEVI'S® BRAND
1155 BATTERY STREET
SAN FRANCISCO, CA 94111
LEVI.COM

Agency Heimat, Berlin
Creative Directors Guido Heffels, Myles Lord
Copywriters Sabina Hesse, Pep Bosch
Art Director Hendrik Schweder
Production Trigger Happy Productions, Berlin
Director Pep Bosch
Producer Stephan Vens
Advertiser Hornbach, "Every Change Needs a Beginning"

A town is falling apart because its citizens have forgotten how to use their hands. They've found other ways of doing things: heading footballs, drinking through straws and so on. One day, a giant walnut lands on the town. The people have no idea how to get rid of it, until it cracks and a man ventures inside. He emerges with a hammer. Suddenly, the citizens' hands come to life: all the tools they need to fix the town are inside the mysterious object. There are several ways of cracking a nut – but you have to get started. Hornbach home improvement stores can help.

Agencies Turner Duckworth Design, London & San Francisco
Creative Directors David Turner, Bruce Duckworth, Sarah Moffat
Art Directors Brian Steele, Britt Hull
Advertiser Levi's Visual Identity System

Jeans brand Levi's wanted to create an international visual identity that would draw on its heritage while positioning it for the future. The key lay in the brand's iconic "batwing" logo, which the agency refined by removing the brand name and adding the cropped ® found on the garments' famous red tab. The agency also updated the "two horses" leather patch and logo, as well as devising an in-house code for their use. The result: an historic brand is refreshed for the 21st century.

FOR BOTANISTS:
The Yalda Snow Lotus is found at altitudes of 3,500 to 4,300 metres. The leaves are arranged in a rosette pattern on the ground. Has many medicinal properties.
FOR LAND ROVER OWNERS:
Handy substitute to toilet paper.
GO BEYOND

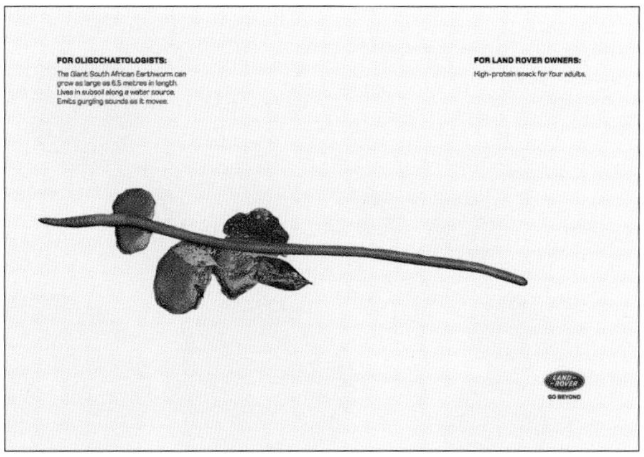
FOR OLIGOCHAETOLOGISTS:
The Giant South African Earthworm can grow as large as 6.5 metres in length. Lives in subsoil along a water source. Emits gurgling sounds as it moves.
FOR LAND ROVER OWNERS:
High-protein snack for four adults.
GO BEYOND

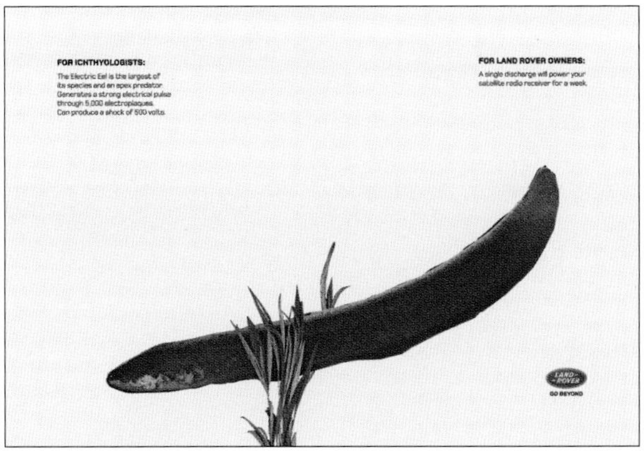
FOR ICHTHYOLOGISTS:
The Electric Eel is the largest of its species and an apex predator. Generates a strong electrical pulse through 5,000 electroplaques. Can produce a shock of 500 volts.
FOR LAND ROVER OWNERS:
A single discharge will power your satellite radio receiver for a week.
GO BEYOND

FOR ZOOLOGISTS:
The Bosavi Giant Woolly Rat was discovered in an extinct volcano. Considered to be the largest in the widespread Muridae family. An active nocturnal forager.
FOR LAND ROVER OWNERS:
Tastes like chicken.
GO BEYOND

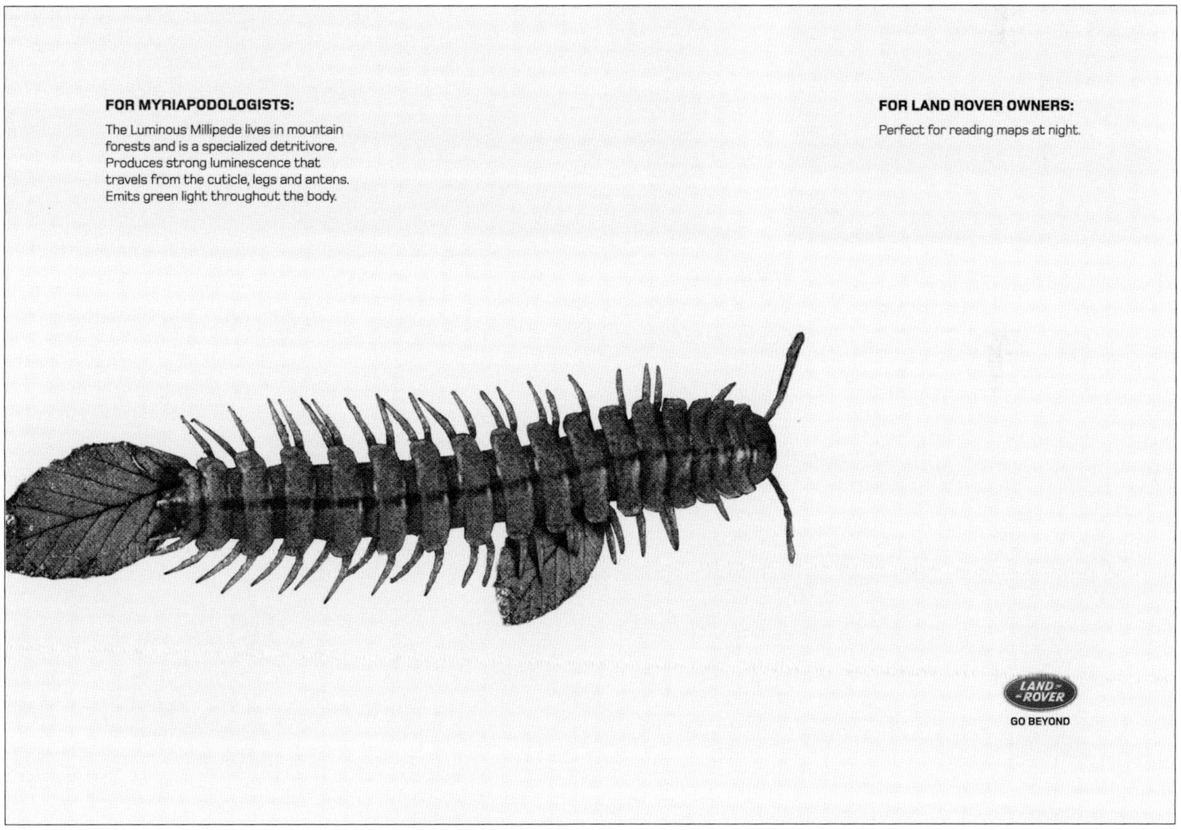
FOR MYRIAPODOLOGISTS:
The Luminous Millipede lives in mountain forests and is a specialized detritivore. Produces strong luminescence that travels from the cuticle, legs and antens. Emits green light throughout the body.
FOR LAND ROVER OWNERS:
Perfect for reading maps at night.
LAND ROVER
GO BEYOND

Agency Young & Rubicam, Dubai
Creative Directors Shahir Zag, Kalpesh Patankar
Copywriter Shahir Zag
Art Director Kalpesh Patankar
Illustrator Jomy Varghese
Planner Nadine Ghossoub
Advertiser Land Rover, "Rare" Campaign

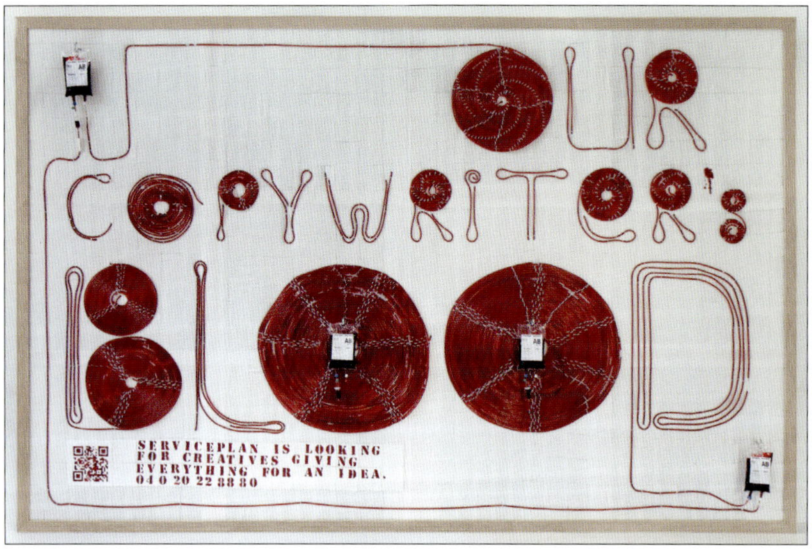
OUR COPYWRITER'S BLOOD
SERVICEPLAN IS LOOKING
FOR CREATIVES GIVING
EVERYTHING FOR AN IDEA.
040 20 22 88 80

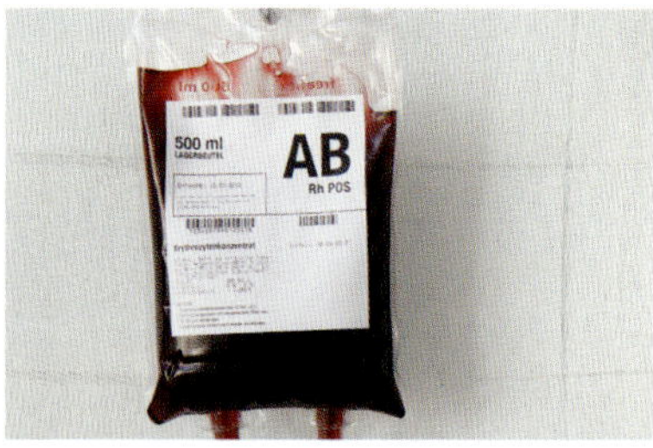
500 ml
AB
Rh POS

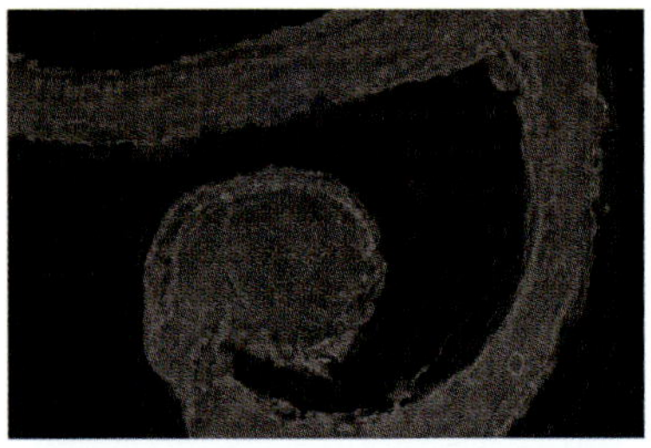

our Designers' Sweat
SERVICEPLAN IS LOOKING
FOR CREATIVES GIVING
EVERYTHING FOR AN IDEA.
040 20 22 88 80

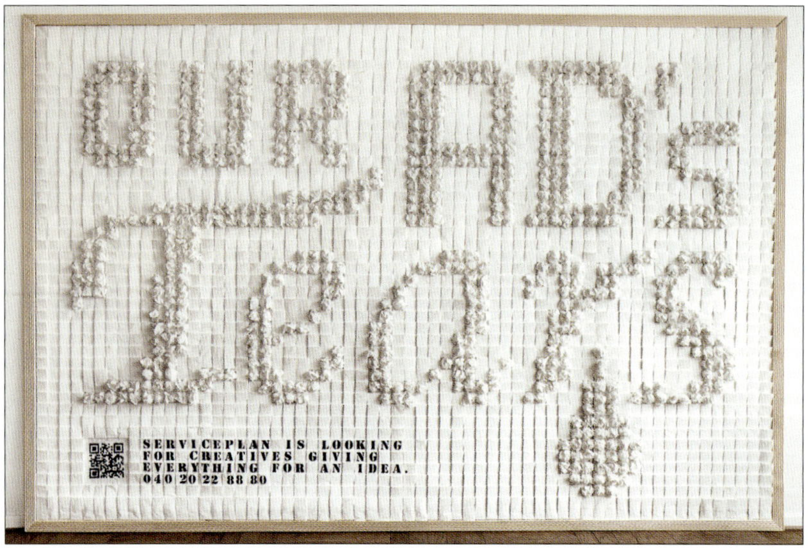
OUR AD's Tears
SERVICEPLAN IS LOOKING
FOR CREATIVES GIVING
EVERYTHING FOR AN IDEA.
040 20 22 88 80

SERV
FOR
EVER
0402

Agency	Serviceplan, Munich
CCO	Alex Schill
Creative Directors	Christoph Nann Maik Kaehler
Art Directors	Manuel Wolff Savina Mokreva
Typographers	Maik Kaehler Manuel Wolff Savina Mokreva
Programmer	plan.net: Steffen Knoblich
Advertiser	Serviceplan, "Posters of Passion"

The agency wanted to recruit creatives who were prepared to sacrifice everything for a good idea: blood, sweat and tears. Three posters were designed using these materials. A copywriter donated blood, which was pumped through small tubes to create the lettering on the first poster. For the second one, the agency rented a mobile sauna in which its designers collected their sweat. This was then sprayed onto black fabric, the salt residues leaving the message. Three kilos of raw onions produced enough tears for the final poster. These were collected on tissue papers and attached to the billboard. The three unique posters were exhibited in universities and other places where potential talent assembled.

A single journey can change the course of a life. Cambodia, May 2011.
Follow Angelina Jolie at louisvuittonjourneys.com
LOUIS VUITTON

PIRACY

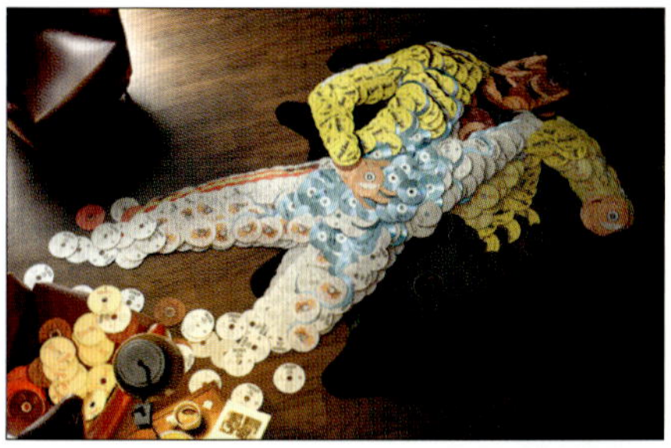

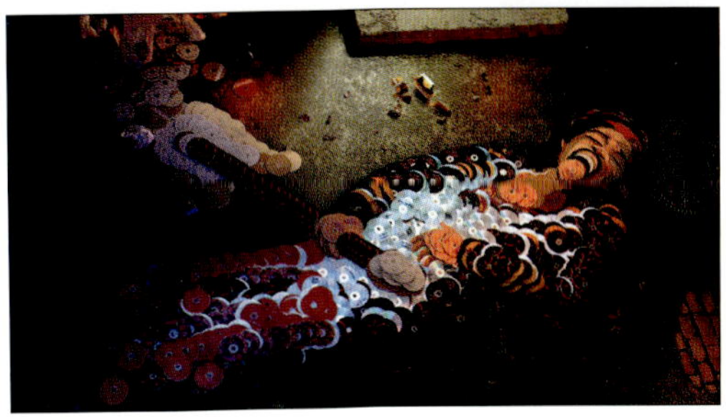

Agency	Ogilvy France, Paris
Creative Directors	Chris Garbutt Christian Reuilly
Copywriter	Luc Chomarat
Art Director	Christian Reuilly
Photography	Annie Lebovitz
Account Team	Laurent Janneau Bruno Britsch
Advertiser	Louis Vuitton, “Angelina Jolie’s Journey to Cambodia”

Agency	TBWA\Italia, Milan
Creative Directors	Nicola Lampugnani Francesco Guerrera
Copywriter	Mirco Pagano
Art Director	Moreno De Turco
Photography	FM: Matteo Bottin Fabio Orefice
Advertiser	First Floor Under (Online Magazine), “Piracy Art Exhibit”

Dad
Hello! I've sent you a message that will arrive in 20 years.
To recieve the message, go to amf.se/Recieve or keep this code:
ZWFUBNYP8C
Close
Answer
I have secretly loved you for ages. Let me know if you feel the same way...
/Andrew from work
HI MOM!

Send a message to the future!
Hi gramps! I've hidden a bottle of vintage wine in your back yard. Start digging south of the plum tree.
Hugs / Pete
Add receiver
AMF

Joakim Blondell
I just sent a really cute message to Åsa Plahn that will arrive in 20 years.
7 minutes ago • Like • Comment • Share

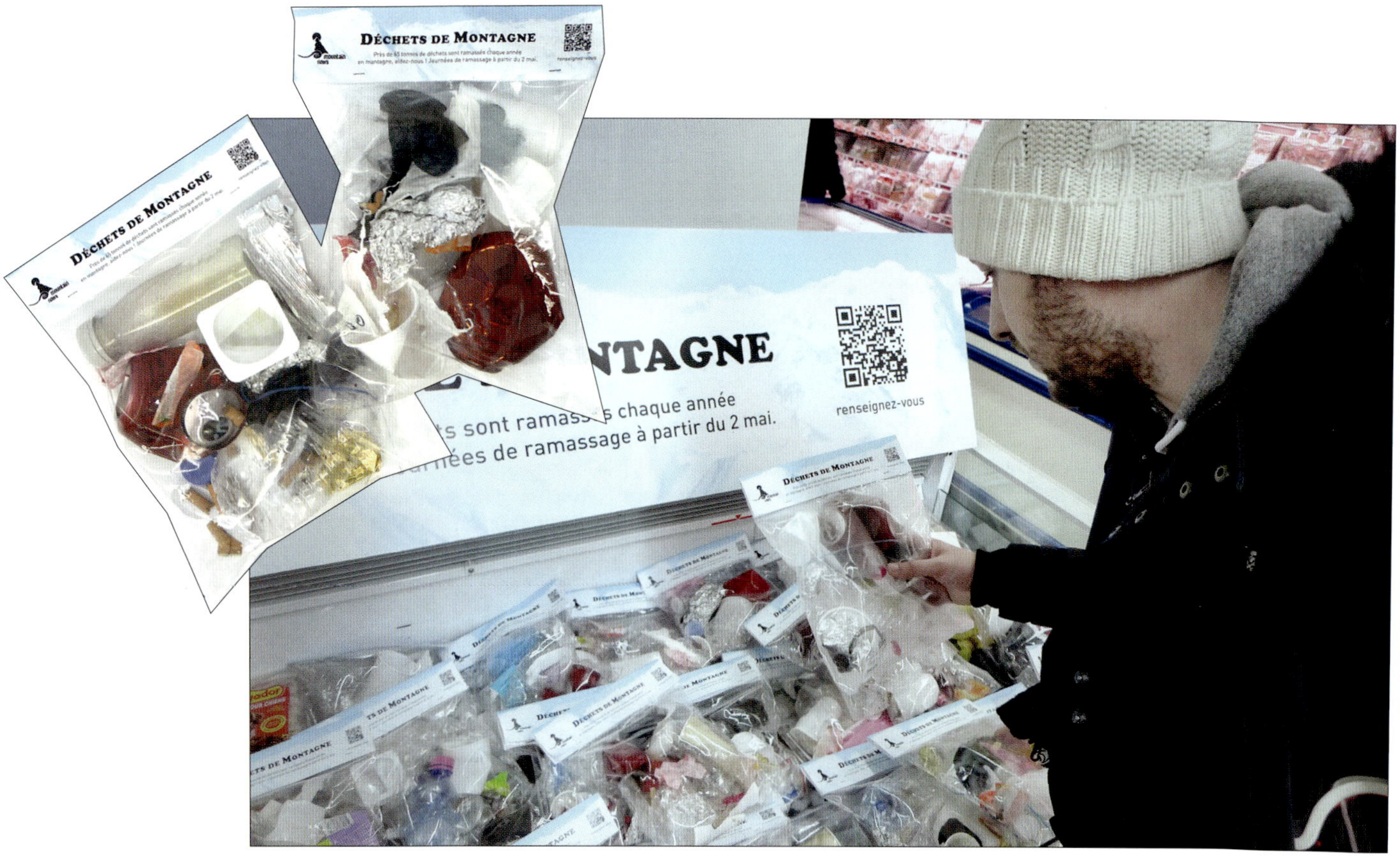
DÉCHETS DE MONTAGNE
DÉCHETS DE MONTAGNE
NTAGNE
s chaque année
s à partir du 2 mai.
renseignez-vous

Agency	Forsman & Bodenfors, Gothenburg
Copywriter	Jacob Nelson
Art Director	John Bergdahl
Art Designers	Åsa Plahn Axel Söderlund
Production	Camp David, Stockholm Mobiento, Stockholm Fantasy Interactive, NY
Producer	Magnus Kennhed
Web Producer	Peter Gaudiano
Acct. Supervisor	Leif Sorte
Advertiser	AMF Pensions

AMF wanted to remind people about the importance of planning for the future. Pensions are a dry subject – but the future is exciting! So the agency created a website enabling people to send a message to friends and family, with the catch that they wouldn't be able to open it until 2030. "Dad: Hello, I've sent you a message that you will receive in 20 years." Directed to the site by a traditional ad campaign, 300,000 people sent advice, pictures, videos and "let's get together" invitations, accessible via a code in 20 years, but for now stored safely on AMF's servers.

Agency	Publicis Conseil, Paris
Creative Directors	Olivier Altmann Emmanuel Lalleve Florent Imbert
Copywriter	Didier Aerts
Art Director	Alexandra Offe
Production	WAM, Paris Sequencis, Paris
Director	Heddy Dechicha
Producers	Pierre Marcus Laurent Sequaris
Account Manager	Celine Colin
Advertiser	Mountain Riders

Winter sports enthusiasts often leave litter in their wake. This gets buried in the next snowfall and doesn't appear until spring. In order to draw attention to the problem – and recruit volunteers for the clean-up – packets of trash were placed in frozen food containers at supermarkets in French towns near the Alps. Labelled "Mountain Litter", the packs were presented as real products. A QR code on the packs led to a website about Mountain Rider's clean-up project.

EYNULLA FATULLAYEV
Journalist
AUSTRIA
55

10.12.2010 · 1010 WIEN
TAG DER
MENSCHEN
RECHTE

TAG DER
MENSCHEN
RECHTE
AUSTRIA

Magdalena Zelasko
Mommsengasse 6/17
1040 Wien

Agency	Serviceplan, Munich
CCO	Alex Schill
Creative Directors	Christoph Everke Cosimo Möller Alexander Nagel
Art Directors	Elena Ressel Annalena Bottmann
Advertiser	Reporters Without Borders, "Human Rights Postmark"

Reporters Without Borders wanted to raise awareness of the plight of imprisoned journalists. So it created stamps featuring the faces of real incarcerated reporters and worked with the post office to design a suitable postmark. When the portraits of the journalists were stamped with the postmark, it gave the impression that they were behind bars. This drew dramatic attention to the problem before recipients opened the letter and read the full story.

Agency	Leo Burnett, Frankfurt
CCO	Andreas Pauli
CD	Hans-Juergen Kaemmerer
Copywriter	Hans-Juergen Kaemmerer
Art Director	Claudia Boeckler
Producer	Gabi Eikam
Project Mgr.	Bernd Mau
Advertiser	NAJU (German Society for Nature Conservation), "Genetically Modified Balloons"

A German youth organisation wanted the government to rethink its stance on genetically modified plants. Their effects on health remain uncertain and, thanks to seeds and pollen, there's a risk they could spread uncontrolled. To dramatize its message, the organisation created 2,000 helium-filled "GM tomato balloons" and set them free to drift like pollen. People who found them could read an attached postcard and record their exact location on a website thereby showing how far the GM balloons had travelled.

Schwarzkopf
got2b
THIS WOULD HAVE NEVER HAPPENED IF YOU USE GOT2B GLUED

BEFORE FLASH AFTER

FOTOBUDKA
00:01

vtm
SAMSUNG

Agency Kijjaa! Digital Miracles, Moscow
Creative Director Rob Ikki
Copywriter Vera Karpova
Art Director Olga Midlenko
Producer Lisa Nikolova
Head of Strategy Katya Bazilevskaya
Tech. Director Alexander Babaryko
Clients Natalia Markova, Olga Zapryatkina
Advertiser Schwarzkopf Got2BGlued, "Prankish Photo-Booth"

To promote super strong hair gel Got2B-Glued, a free photo booth was installed in a shopping mall. When people got their photo taken, a strong fan whipped their hair into a mess. The resulting snap made it look as if they'd been photographed in the middle of a gale. A message on the picture read: "This would never happen if you use Got2B-Glued". A QR code led to more info about the product. The images were streamed to online banners and could be shared via social media. Some were even used as part of a poster campaign.

Agency LDV United, Antwerp
Creative Directors Kristof Snels, Sam De Vriendt
Copywriter Pieter Staes
Art Director Manuel Ostyn
Production Make, Antwerp
Illustration dobson.be: Konrad Dobson
Digital Strategy Kristof Janssens
Account Executive Tim Janssens
CSD Ann Hostens
Advertiser Come a Casa, "Dinnertime!"

How do you get your kids to come to the dinner table when they're glued to the TV? Ready-made meal brand Come a Casa came up with the ultimate solution. Mums and dads could record their very own TV commercials telling their kids it was time for dinner. Via the brand's website, they could upload a video from their webcam. Then they could select their kids' favourite channel and an exact time for the broadcast. Imagine the kids' surprise when their parents popped up the middle of their favourite TV show.

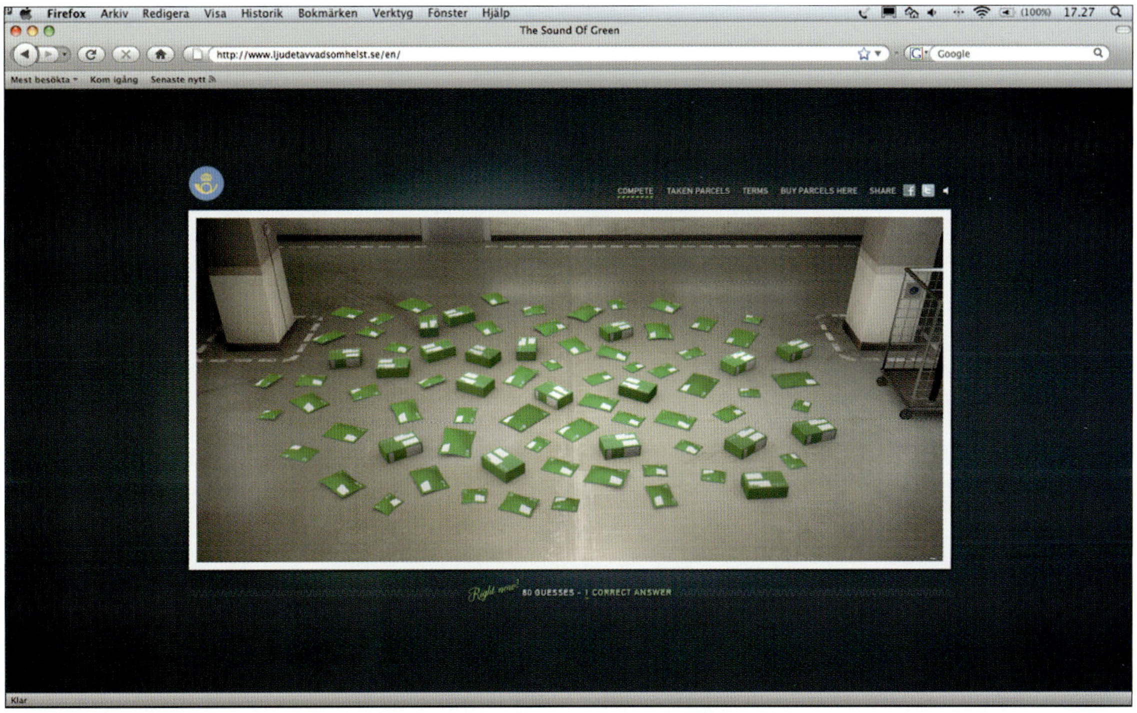
Firefox Arkiv Redigera Visa Historik Bokmärken Verktyg Fönster Hjälp
The Sound Of Green
http://www.ljudetavvadsomhelst.se/en/
Google
Mest besökta Kom igång Senaste nytt
COMPETE TAKEN PARCELS TERMS BUY PARCELS HERE SHARE
Right now!
80 GUESSES - 1 CORRECT ANSWER
Klar

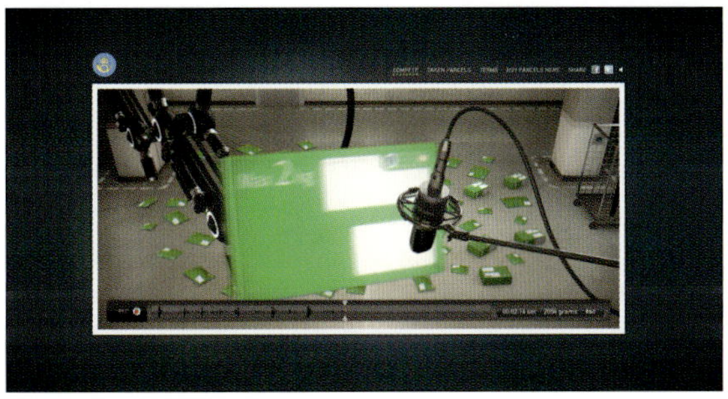
Max 2 kg

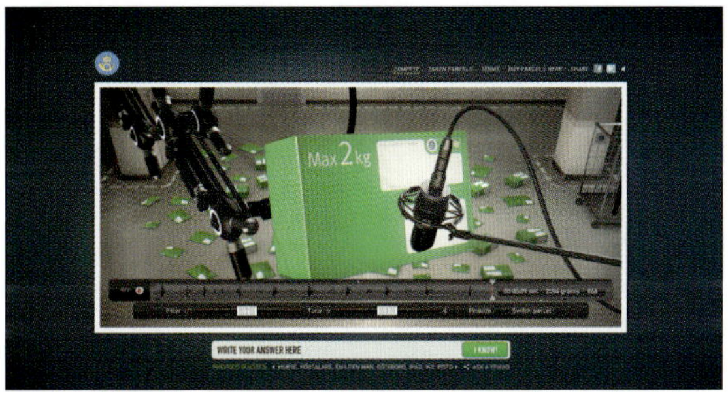
Max 2 kg

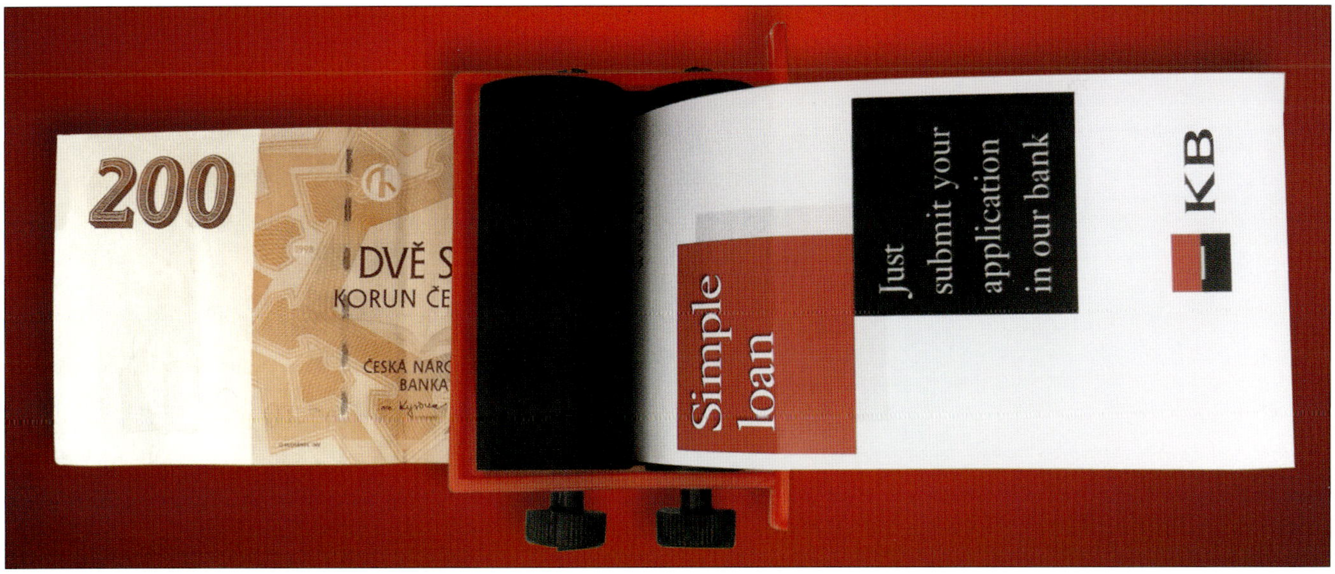
200
DVĚ S
KORUN ČE
ČESKÁ NÁR
BANKA
Simple loan
Just submit your application in our bank
KB

Agency Åkestam Holst, Stockholm
Creative Director Andreas Ullenius
Copywriter Hanna Bjork
Art Directors Lars Holthe, Kristoffer Larberg
Production From Stockholm With Love, Stockholm
Account Team Jacob Stjarne, Goran Akestam
Planner Lars Friberg
Advertiser The Swedish Post, "The Sound of Green"

The Swedish Post has a selection of pre-stamped green parcels that make it easier for people to send things. To show that it was possible to send almost anything overnight in these parcels, it created a special online competition. Using live streaming and an automated mechanical arm, visitors to the bespoke website could "shake" one a selection of 80 parcels and guess what was inside. If they guessed correctly, they won the parcel! After 12 days and over 140,000 guesses, only one parcel was left. It contained a Panama hat.

Agency Euro RSCG, Prague
Creative Directors Eda Kauba, Pavel Sobek
Copywriter Robert Valentin
Art Directors Jakub Kolarik, Tereza Janeckova
Advertiser KB Bank, "Moneymaker"

Getting a loan from your bank needn't be complicated. To prove it, KB bank sent selected customers a magical device. Simply feed in the "loan application" document, turn the wheel, and a banknote emerges from the other side! The message was simple: getting a loan really can be this easy, so visit your bank and apply for one.

Business to Business Direct

Agency	Scholz & Friends, Hamburg
CCO	Matthias Schmidt
Creative Directors	Marc Kittel Pedro Sydow
Copywriter	Christopher Nothegger
Art Director	Stefan Schabenberger
Graphic Design	Kathrin Fach
Technical Director	Andreas Maser
Web Developer	Aleksandr Lossenko
Post Production	Alireza Rashidi
Account Manager	Jessica Modschiedler
Advertiser	Scholz & Friends Hamburg Recruiting, "Pizza Digitale"

Being creative often means working late nights and dining on takeaway food like pizza. Ad agency Scholz & Friends deployed this insight when it launched a recruitment drive for new digital creatives. In cooperation with the delivery service Croque Master, the agency created the "Pizza Digitale": a special pizza which for four weeks was added to every order from rival agencies' employees. The tasty topping was a QR-Code that directly linked to an online ad describing the agency's hunger for new digital creatives. The feast resulted in lots of job interviews and some new teams for the agency's digital department.

YONSHI&SON
IF WE ARE ABLE TO SELL FLIES, WE ARE ABLE TO SELL ANYTHING – SELF PROMOTION CAMPAIGN.
on&on

MAKE iT BiG
TBWA\
is looking for creatives

Agency	On&On, Barcelona
Creative Director	David Garriga
Copywriters	Nico Pera Marta Lorente
Art Directors	Lluís Mora Ángela Cabal
Advertiser	On&On, "Yon-shi & Son"

In order to prove its effectiveness and raise its profile, the agency launched a campaign to sell the unsellable: flies. That's right: it created a fictitious Japanese company called Yon-shi & Son that sold flies as domestic pets. A convincing website went online and the message was spread through social media. Pretty soon, mainstream media picked up on the story. The website got 60,000 visits and many orders. The conclusion was simple: if the agency could sell flies, it could sell anything.

Agency	TBWA\Düsseldorf
Executive CD	Jörg Herzog
Copywriter	Matthias Hardt
Art Director	Simon Hattrup
Illustrator	Jean-Baptiste Chuat
Advertiser	TBWA Recruiting, "Hijack the Wall of Fame"

An ad within an ad. In order to target creatives for a recruitment drive, TBWA made use of pen brand Edding's "wall of fame". It's an online drawing board that has won a host of prizes and become a fun way of killing time for creative types. To get their attention, TBWA's illustrator "hijacked" the wall by drawing a huge job ad in a 13-hour session. Creative visitors to the wall were impressed: the first job application arrived within a few minutes.

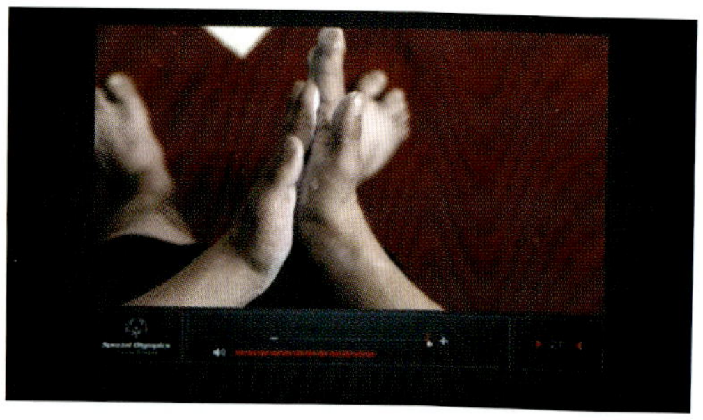

Special Olympics
Great Britain
It's life changing.

DAS
LEGAL SERVICES
The answer to
all the things
you didn't ask for.
das.nl
JCDecaux

Agency JWT, London
CDs Philip Meyler, Darren Keff
Production Gorgeous Enterprises, London
Director Johnny Green
Producers Spencer Dodd, Jack Bayley
Advertiser Special Olympics, "Encourage Omar"

All children need encouragement, especially children with disabilities. The Special Olympics took this insight as the basis for an interactive film capturing the extraordinary willpower of its athletes. In the film, a gymnast is seen approaching the mat in a stadium. By using their mouse to augment the sound of the crowd, users boost the athlete's confidence, until he's ready to go ahead with his impressive gymnastic routine. The film was initially hosted on parenting website netmums.co.uk, but quickly garnered wider coverage.

Agency N=5, Amsterdam
Copywriter Thijs Bontje
Art Director Marco de Jong
Advertiser DAS Insurance

BÄTTRE SÖMN
ÅT ALLA.

Byssan Lull
SULTAN SALHUS/SULTAN TAFJORD

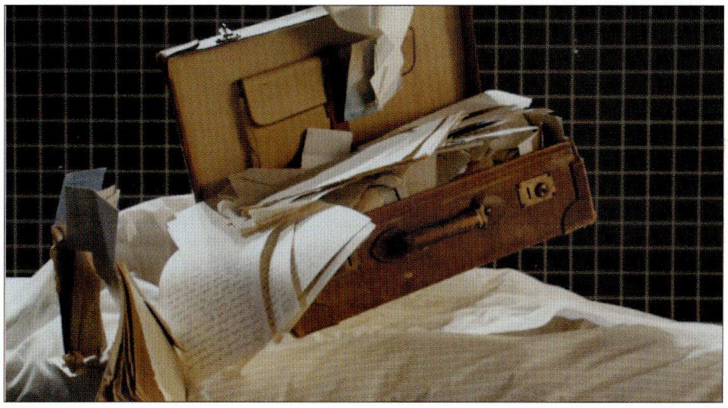

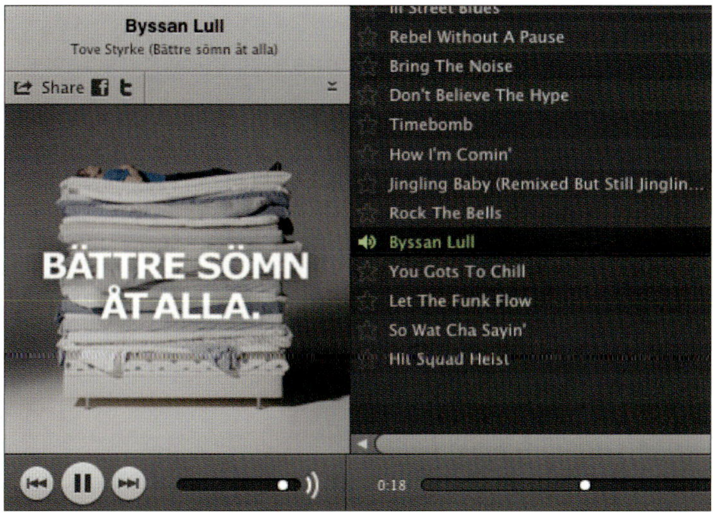
Byssan Lull
Tove Styrke (Bättre sömn åt alla)
Share
Rebel Without A Pause
Bring The Noise
Don't Believe The Hype
Timebomb
How I'm Comin'
Jingling Baby (Remixed But Still Jinglin...
Rock The Bells
Byssan Lull
You Gots To Chill
Let The Funk Flow
So Wat Cha Sayin'
Hit Squad Heist
BÄTTRE SÖMN
ÅT ALLA.
0:18

Jag finns kvar här
Maia Hirasawa — Bättre sömn åt alla – EP
BÄTTRE SÖMN
ÅT ALLA.
Bättre sömn åt alla - EP
Various Artists & Various Artists
Trollmors vaggsång
Brahms vaggvisa
Jag finns kvar här
Air On the G String
Vaggvisa

Agency Forsman & Bodenfors, Gothenburg
Copywriters Fredrik Jansson, Elisabeth Christensson
Art Directors Adam Ulvegärde, Andreas Malm
WW Producer Stefan Thomson
Photography Carl Nilsson
Production Social Club, Stockholm; KokoKaka, Stockholm
Producer Alexander Blidner
Art Designer Christoffer Persson
Planner Tobias Nordström
Account Team Katarina Klofsten, Hans Andersson
Client Christine Eliasson
Advertiser Ikea, “Lullabies”

Ikea wanted to show that it helps the world to sleep better. So it invited six of Sweden's top musicians to reinterpret the country's most popular lullabies. Music videos featuring the singers in Ikea beds were shown in ad slots. On Ikea's site, users could find out more about the artists and their beds. Radio stations played the songs, while bloggers chatted about the initiative. Then the songs were released as an album, with a cover that looked a lot like an Ikea ad. Users effectively bought ads for 99 cents each. And approving Tweets rolled in from around the world.

eFA.com/playerpass
ASTRA GTC

VAUXHALL
SUPPORT FOR OUR WOUNDED
ASTRA GTC

THE HUFFINGTON POST UK
HARPER SEVEN? KICK OFF THE DEBATE.
BLOG ALL ABOUT IT
For the full story go to
WWW.HUFFINGTONPOST.CO.UK

THE HUFFINGTON POST UK
WILL AND KATE IN LA. DON'T KEEP YOUR VIEWS CONFIDENTIAL.
BLOG ALL ABOUT IT
For the full story go to
WWW.HUFFINGTONPOST.CO.UK

THE HUFFINGTON POST UK
UNIVERSITY FEES? WHAT'S THE REAL COST?
BLOG ALL ABOUT IT
For the full story go to
WWW.HUFFINGTONPOST.CO.UK

THE HUFFINGTON POST UK
WHO WILL WIN THE APPRENTICE? FIRE AWAY.
BLOG ALL ABOUT IT
For the full story go to
WWW.HUFFINGTONPOST.CO.UK

THE HUFFINGTON POST UK
WHAT WILL YOU READ NOW? GIVE US YOUR VIEWS OF THE WORLD.
BLOG ALL ABOUT IT
For the full story go to
WWW.HUFFINGTONPOST.CO.UK

THE HUFFINGTON POST UK
GOT AN OPINION ON INDUSTRIAL ACTION? DON'T CROW, TWEET.
BLOG ALL ABOUT IT
For the full story go to the
WWW.HUFFINGTONPOST.CO.UK

Agency McCann, Birmingham
Creative Director Vince McSweeney
Copywriters James Cross, Tim Jarvis
Art Directors Tim Jones, Barrie Robinson
Production Chief Productions
Producer Bernadette Griffin
Director Dom Murgia
Account Team Paul Dean, Charlotte Manns
Advertiser Vauxhall Astra GTC, "St George"

To launch the new Astra GTC, the agency placed 3D mats beside the pitch during an England vs Wales football match, giving the impression that real cars were parked there. The special effect became reality during half-time, when a bit of trickery made it look as if live TV coverage had continued. A flag-waving spectator in a knight's outfit ran onto the pitch, got into a very solid Astra, and took it for a spin before being escorted off. When the second half began, the 3D Astra had changed position, with the flag of St George draped over its boot.

Agency MBA, London
Creative Directors Robin Garton, Graham Kerr
Advertiser The Huffington Post, "Blog All About It"

The Huffington Post is an interactive online newspaper written by bloggers. The launch campaign for the UK version of the site used outdoor digital posters incorporating live Twitter feeds. Headlines were updated daily with a punning but topical idea, igniting opinion and inviting Twitter contributions from the public. Instead of "read all about it", people were encouraged to turn citizen journalist and "blog all about it".

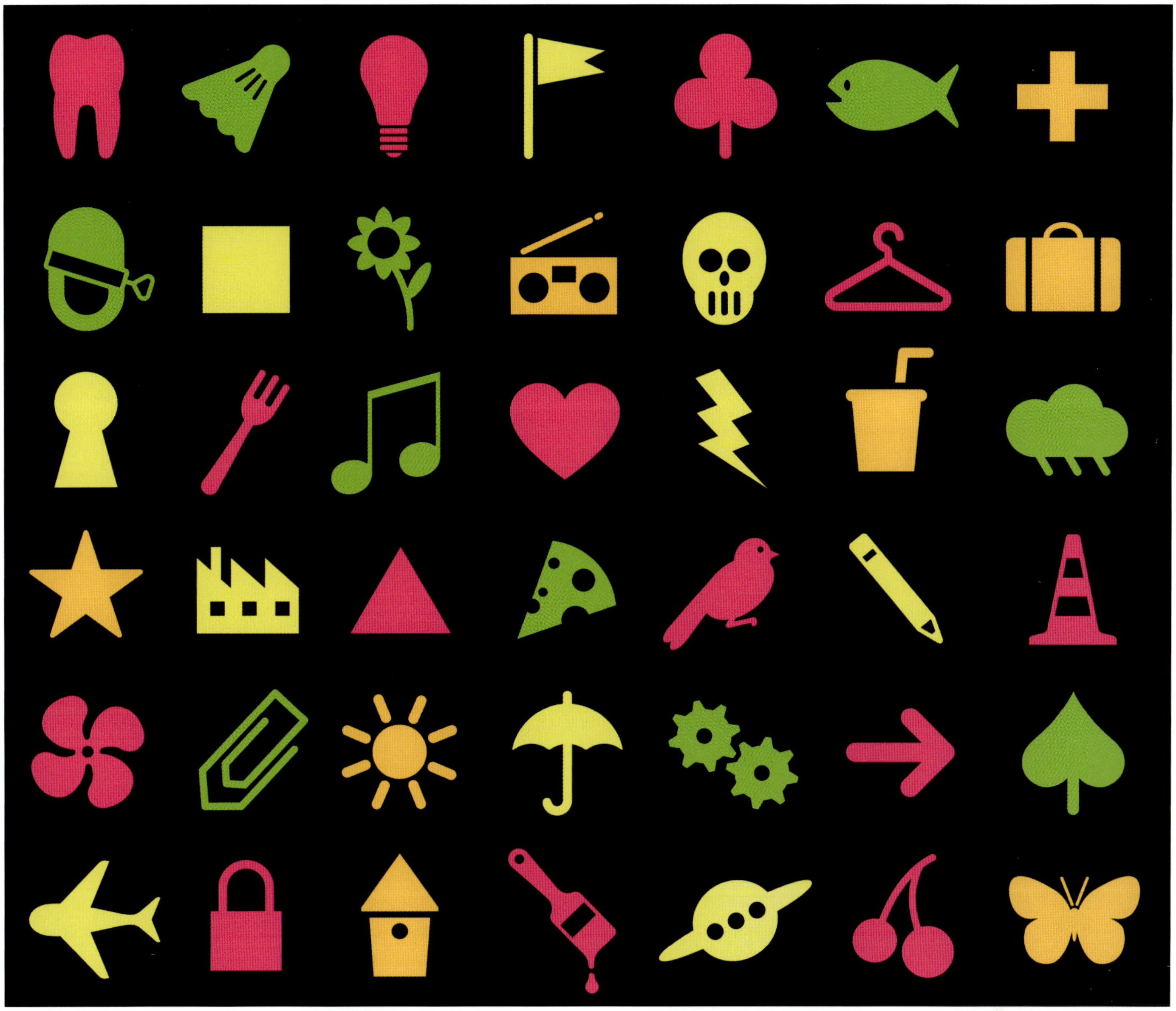

Utmana din hjärna.
För varje figur du memorerar får du
2% rabatt på utställningen TILT!
universeum

Utmana din hjärna.
För varje figur du memorerar får du
2% rabatt på utställningen TILT!
universeum

Utmana din hjärna.
För varje figur du memorerar får du
2% rabatt på utställningen TILT!
universeum

Utmana din hjärna.
För varje figur du memorerar får du
2% rabatt på utställningen TILT!
universeum

Agency	Forsman & Bodenfors, Gothenburg
Copywriter	Leo Magnusson
Art Director	Pål Eneroth
Art Designer	Magnus Almberg
Account Team	Jerk Zander Erica Berghagen
Media	Bright
Advertiser	Universeum, "Tilt"

To promote an exhibition called "Tilt – Challenge Your Brain", the Universeum science centre challenged the whole of Gothenburg to a giant memory game. Fifty symbols – such as a musical note or a skull – were shown on posters around the city. Each one was worth a 2% discount. If you could remember all 50 symbols, you got a free entry. The catch: you had to list them all within 60 seconds at the admissions desk. Only one man managed it, in 58 seconds, without cheating.

NEU
Extra
PROFESSIONAL
POLAR-FRISCH
Zahnpflegekaugummi – ohne Zucker
Schmeckt überraschend frisch.

 Media Innovation - Alternative Media

Agency	BBDO Proximity, Düsseldorf
CCOs	Christian Mommertz Sebastian Hardieck
Executive CD	Carsten Bolk
Copywriter	Isabel Campagna
Art Directors	Michael Plückhahn Gustavo Vieira-Dias
Production	Sytwala TV, Düsseldorf
Head of TV	Steffen Gentis
Account Mgr.	Sonja Struß
Advertiser	Wrigley's Extra, "Mint Parking Ticket"

Every driver knows the situation: when you drive into the parking lot, you haven't got a free hand for the parking ticket, so you put it between your lips as you look for a parking space. Based on this observation, Wrigley decided to make parking a more pleasant experience – by creating the world's first mint-flavoured parking ticket. It captured the attention of drivers and efficiently passed on the brand message: Oral care to go.

HASTIGHETS
LOTTERIET
DU KÖR
24
KM/H

Production Bakery Films, Hamburg
Director Florian Sigl
D.O.P. Moritz Anton
Producer Sunna Pilz
Post Production Musion, London: Oliver Gingrich
Music Production Yessian Music: Ingmar Rehberg
Visual Artist Tim Jockel
Advertiser Stefan Eckert, "3D Holographic Fashion Show"

A 3D holographic fashion show was performed at the Kampnagel arts centre in Hamburg in March 2011 for designer Stefan Eckert's "haute couture" collection. The goal was to communicate the inspiration, idea and philosophy behind the collection in a more creative way than a normal catwalk show. Behind the technology was a Victorian theatre trick called "Pepper's Ghost", which uses projections on a giant mirror to create an optical illusion that appears to break the rules of time and space.

Agency DDB Stockholm
Creative Director Andreas Dahlqvist
Copywriter Martin Lundgren
Art Director Simon Higby
Designer Rasmus Kellerman
Graphic Design Niklas Andersson
Web Producer Linda Eriksson
Social Media Michael Bugaj
Producer Joakim Kromnér
Business Director Jerker Fagerström
Planner Michael Bugaj
Advertiser Volkswagen, "The Speed Camera Lottery"

VW believes fun can change behaviour for the better. Its Fun Theory campaign included "piano" stairs that play a tune and a bottle bank arcade game. VW then introduced the Fun Theory award. Over 700 entries later, a winner was chosen: the Speed Camera Lottery. A camera snaps speeders and they are fined. But motorists who stick to the limit are also snapped. Their details go into a lottery, enabling them to win some of the speeders' money! When the idea was tested in Stockholm average speeds dropped by 22%.

Classic
Pattex
KRAFTKLEBER

K5
Überzeugen Sie sich selbst von der Pattex Klebkraft. Und sichern Sie sich 50% Rabatt!

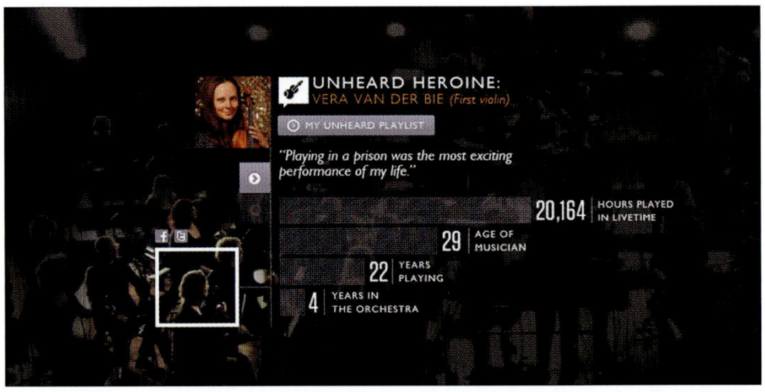
UNHEARD HEROINE:
VERA VAN DER BIE (First violin)
MY UNHEARD PLAYLIST
"Playing in a prison was the most exciting performance of my life."
20,164 HOURS PLAYED IN LIVETIME
29 AGE OF MUSICIAN
22 YEARS PLAYING
4 YEARS IN THE ORCHESTRA

Visit our Facebook page
See our products
UNITED KINGDOM/ENGLISH
SHARE
HD
SINGLE OUT EACH MUSICIAN
VERA VAN DER BIE
FIRST VIOLIN
Rhythm/Singers
Woodwinds/Reeds
Brass
Strings

Media Innovation - Alternative Media

Agency Serviceplan, Munich
CCO Alex Schill
ECD Matthias Harbeck
Creative Director Alexander Rehm
Copywriters Nicolas Becker, Lorenz Langgartner
Art Director Andreas Balog
Production Saurus Filmbauten, Munich
Producer Simon Feichtl
Advertiser Pattex, "Pattex Crane"

Most people know that Pattex glue is very effective. This initiative showed just how strong it is! The agency mounted a giant tube of Pattex on a construction crane, giving the impression that the glue was lifting extremely heavy objects. QR codes around the construction site explained the operation and offered a 50% discount so people could try the glue for themselves. The event created buzz, traffic on the Pattex site increased by 43% and over 1750 vouchers were downloaded.

Agency Tribal DDB, Amsterdam
Creative Director Chris Baylis
Copywriter Pol Hoenderboom
Art Director Bart Mol
Design Robbin Cenijn
Creative Tech. Ian Bauer
Strategy Director Henk Rijks
Director Rob Chiu
Producers Marcel Komblum, Mark Pytlik
Planner Niels Bellaar
Advertiser Philips Audio Range

An interactive video demonstrates that Philips is "obsessed with sound". The brand collaborated with the Grammy Award-winning Metropole Orchestra, recording a new composition on 55 separate tracks. On the site, viewers could experience the music video as a whole, played by the entire orchestra, or single out individual musicians to hear every detail. The event was also backed by a music competition. An "unheard" musical talent got their track specially adapted for the orchestra and recorded by U2 producer Steve Lillywhite.

Rauchen hinterlässt Teer in den kleinsten Verästelungen Ihrer Lunge.

LEGO

BUILDING PHANTASY
LEGO

Agency Serviceplan, Munich
CCO Alex Schill
CDs Christoph Nann, Maik Kaehler
Copywriters Christoph Nann, Maik Kaehler
Art Directors Savina Mokreva, Manuel Wolff
Advertiser Barmer GEK Insurance, "The Smoker's Lung"

German health insurance company Barmer GEK launched a New Year's resolution campaign encouraging smokers to give up. To dramatise its message, it chose a breathing organism as complex as a lung: a tree. Using black rubber balls, the tree in the centre of Hamburg was transformed into a giant contaminated lung. A sign below the tree read: "Smoking leaves tar in the smallest branches of your lungs." Press coverage and internet buzz ensured that the message spread widely.

Agency Serviceplan, Munich
CCO Alex Schill
Creative Directors Christoph Everke, Cosimo Möller, Alexander Nagel
Art Director Matthias Noesel
Advertiser Lego, "The Lego Stereoscope"

What kind of effect can be produced by 378,428 Lego bricks, assembled seemingly at random on a 12 square metre area? How about a 3D image that's invisible at first glance? To underline Lego's promise of "building phantasy", a stereoscopic billboard was created with the bricks and put on display at the entrance of the international toy trade fair in Nuremberg. When viewers focused on the poster, the bricks slowly began to blur and form an image: a Lego dinosaur.

KAIZERS ORCHESTRA
"HJERTEKNUSER"
THIS SONG DOES NOT EXIST
DOWNLOAD THE NOTESHEETS AND MAKE YOUR VERSION
OF THE UNRELEASED KAIZERS SONG "HJERTEKNUSER"
WWW.PETRE.NO/URORT

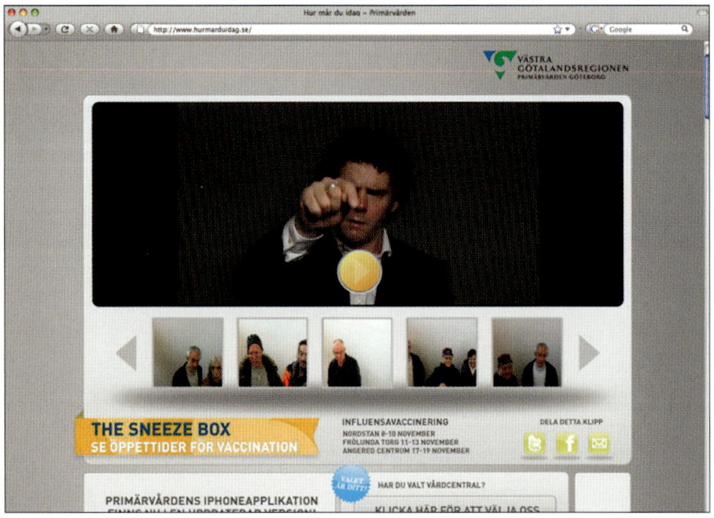
VÄSTRA GÖTALANDSREGIONEN
THE SNEEZE BOX
SE ÖPPETTIDER FÖR VACCINATION
INFLUENSAVACCINERING
PRIMÄRVÅRDENS IPHONEAPPLIKATION

NÄSTA GÅNG KAN DET VARA PÅ RIKTIGT

VÅGAR DU
TA CHANSEN?
Pröva lyckan här!

Agencies Anorak, Oslo
Haaland, Eidsvåg & Strøm, Oslo
Creative Directors Jens-Petter Aarhus
Simen Eidsvåg
Art Directors Anders Gudmundstuen
Jørgen Krogsveen
Eirik Johansen
Media Starcom, Oslo:
Tone Helene Angsund
Record Company Petroleum Records
Advertiser Kaizers Orchestra, "Heartbreaker"

Norway's Kaizers Orchestra were getting ready to release a new single. This time, though, they wouldn't give anybody a chance to pirate a leaked copy. The song would be released on paper before being recorded. On posters and online, the sheet music was released first. The band then challenged fans and musicians to make their own version. Thousands were uploaded. The number of fans on the band's Facebook page doubled. And when the real single was released, it got massive airplay – along with the three best cover versions.

Agency SCP, Gothenburg
Creative Director Tommy Östberg
Copywriter Hanna Samara
Art Directors Tommi Lindholm
Birgitta Grönlund
Producer Dominique Gullic
Digital Producers Russel Clark
Simon Schlüter
John Beijar
Advertiser Primärvården, "Sneeze Box"

The goal of this outdoor event was to encourage people to take a flu vaccination. But it also surprised, entertained and educated the citizens of Gothenburg. In a booth set up in shopping centres, a sickly looking actor on a touch screen encouraged users to click a button. When they did, the actor sneezed and a hidden hydraulic pump doused them with a fine spray. The message: "Next time it could be real – get your flu vaccination". Startled reactions were recorded and uploaded to a campaign site. The result: 2500 flu jabs.

SNEAKER ENGINEER
+
PHOTOGRAPHER
=
ARCHITECTURE?
SEE WHAT THEY HAVE MADE IN MADE
WWW.MADE-BLOG.COM

SNEAKER ENGINEER
+
PHOTOGRAPHER
=
CIRCUS?
SEE WHAT THEY HAVE MADE IN MADE
WWW.MADE-BLOG.COM

VALSE AUTO-MATIQUE

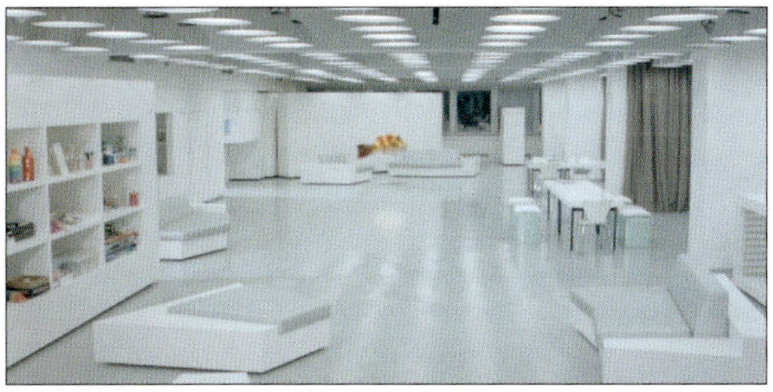

Agencies TBWA\Berlin, Che*Che, Berlin
Executive CDs Nico Zeh, Tatjana Stein, Kurt Georg Dieckert, Stefan Schmidt
Creative Directors Dirk Henkelmann, Philip Borchardt
Copywriters Felicitas Olschewski, Philip Loeffel
Photography Niels Krueger, Robert Wunsch, Ricardo Mueller

Art Director Philipp Migeod
Exec. Producers Luise Biesalski, Philip Gaedicke, Alexis Dornier
Graphic Design Veit Moeller, Andrew Morgan, Ricardo Mueller, Chehad Abdallah, Benedikt Gansczyk, Thomas Kohl
Production Soup Film, Berlin
Director/Editor Johannes von Liebenstein

Producers Katrin Dettmann, Ada Roggendorf, Jana Bloemer
Post Production Das Werk, Berlin
Sound Design Studio Funk, Berlin
Cameraman Christian Datum
IT Erik Scholz, Benjamin Stuerkat
Interface/Nav. Wolf Deiss
Planning Christina Keller, Sonia Lago
Art Buying Katrin Hermuth
Advertiser Absolut Vodka, "MADE"

Absolut wanted to foster "creative collaborations", so it founded the MADE art space in Berlin. Then it brought creatives together for art projects called "Creative Clashes". For instance, a product designer and a composer created a robot that makes art when it hears music. A poster campaign played on the idea of creative clashes. The space was promoted through screens in hip bars and restaurants. These showed live feeds from the space. Slowly, the image was invaded by seemingly real bizarre events: a fish swimming through the air, an out of control hairdo... Meanwhile, the MADE blog inspires creative people all over the world.

5
minutes
...how long she has to live?
or
how long to stop this happening?
Heritage

Ariel Fashion Shoot
facebook.com/arielsverige

Agency Blacksheep, Chester
Creative Director Rob Smith
Copywriter Rob Smith
Art Director Phil Elliott
Photography Andreas Vogt
Advertiser Cheshire Fire & Rescue, "5 Minutes"

Every year in the UK domestic fires account for over 500 deaths and more than 11,000 injuries. Many of these could be prevented if people had early warning and were able to get out of their homes in time. This "smoking telephone box" was designed to raise awareness of the danger of suffocation by smoke – and encourage people to install smoke alarms. A website address at the bottom of the installation linked to a 5-minute Safety Assessment check offered by the Cheshire Fire & Rescue Service.

Agency Saatchi & Saatchi, Stockholm
Creative Director Adam Kerj
Copywriter Petter Dixelius
Art Directors Gustav Egerstedt, Lisa Engardt
Creative Erik Hiort af Ornäs
Film Production B-Reel, Stockholm
Designer Maria Wester
Planning Per Jaldeborg
Account Team Maria Lindskog Klasén, Charlotta Tibbelin
Advertiser Ariel Actilift

Ariel Fashion Shoot was a live digital event staged in a glass cube at Stockholm Central Station. An industrial robot was connected to Ariel's Facebook page, where users could see a virtual shooting gallery featuring... clean clothing. The user got 30 seconds to stain the rapidly passing clothes, which ranged from basic to designer garments, with ketchup, jam and drinking chocolate. The rules were simple: aim, stain and win! If the player was lucky to hit and stain a garment, it was washed live with Ariel Actilift and sent to their home.

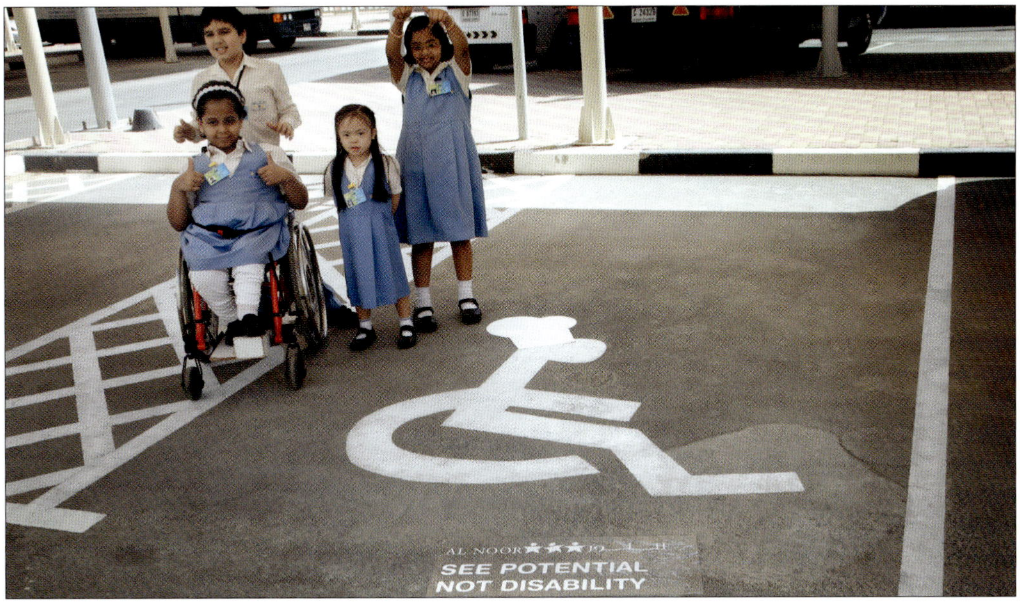
SEE POTENTIAL
NOT DISABILITY

MIGRAINE?
Stopache

MIGRAINE?
Stopache

Agency Young & Rubicam, Dubai
Creative Directors Shahir Zag, Husen Baba, Wilbur D'Costa
Copywriter Wilbur D'Costa
Art Director Husen Baba
Producer Amin Soltani
Account Director Uday Desai
Planner Nadine Ghossoub
Advertiser Al Noor School, "See Potential"

The goal of the Al Noor centre was not just to raise awareness of people with special needs, but to show their contribution to society. The solution was to take a universally recognised symbol – the disabled sign – and adapt it by giving the figure various creative tools, including a chef's hat, a football, a video camera and a microphone. Disabled signs all over the city were "customised" with stickers and the words "see potential, not disability".

Agency Young & Rubicam, Dubai
Creative Directors Shahir Zag, Kalpesh Patankar
Copywriter Parixit Bhattacharya
Art Directors Kalpesh Patankar, Umran Shaikh, Daniel Botezatu
Photography Umran Shaikh, Daniel Botezatu
Account Director Matthew Collier
Planner Nadine Ghossoub
Advertiser Stopache, "Splitting Headaches"

BIG ENOUGH TO TACKLE
BOTH TEAMS AT ONCE.
LG

BIG ENOUGH TO TACKLE
BOTH TEAMS AT ONCE
LG

BIG ENOUGH TO TACKLE
BOTH TEAMS AT ONCE
LG

A pirate copy of Office.
Congrats, you know, it's a very nice idea!
Gifts can never be refused!

MICROSOFT OFFICE 2010
GRATIS!
COPIA PIRATA DI MICROSOFT OFFICE 2010
SCOPRI COME VINCERE UN FANTASTICO SOGGIORNO

OFFERTA STRAORDINARIA
GRATIS!
2010 Office
PIE PIRATA
OMAGGIO
SCOPRI
COME VINCERE
UN FANTASTICO
SOGGIORNO
PIRATA INSIDE

Agency	Young & Rubicam, Johannesburg
Creative Director	Ian Franks
Copywriters	Eric Wittstock Katerine Glover
Art Directors	Bruce Murphy Steve Dirnberger
Advertiser	LG Washing Machine, "Washing Tunnel"

To launch LG's 11 kilo washing machine and demonstrate its effectiveness, posters featuring the machine's giant "mouth" were placed over the players' tunnels at South African Rugby pitches. At the beginning of the games, fans saw players run out of the machine clean. At half time, players ran in dirty, changed into clean kits and ran out for the second half – clean again! Millions saw the effect on TV, online and in the press.

Agency	Y&R Brands/ Wunderman, Milan
Executive CD	Vicky Gitto
Creative Directors	Enrico Spinetta Danilo Puricelli
Copywriters	Valentina Leovino Ileana Infantino Stefano Consiglio Filippo Rizzo
Art Directors	Coenen Toon Silvia Candeago Alberto Massazza
Advertiser	Microsoft

Software piracy is a big problem in Italy. To draw attention to the issue, Microsoft and its agency forced people to recognise their "pirate inside". At the Smau IT exhibition in Milan, covert operatives handed out free copies of Office 2010, making it clear that the software had been pirated. But when the unwitting recipients loaded the CD and entered their personal details to win a vacation abroad, they discovered where their vacation might really take place: prison. To free themselves, they had to visit the Microsoft website.

Dear dog owner,
You can now get a fitted dog box
when you rent a car from Hertz.
Book at hertz.se/dog or call us at 0771-211 212.
Hertz

Agency Pool, Stockholm
Copywriter Jenny Åberg Hüttner
Art Director Philip Arvidson
Producers Hanna Steiner, Carina Claesson Larsson
Prod. Mgr. Patricia Wiegle
Final Artwork Emma Sandler
Advertiser Hertz Dog Cages, "Give the Dog a Bone"

The aim was to inform dog owners that Hertz rental cars now came fitted with compartments for their four-legged friends. But how to reach such a diverse group? The solution was to use the one medium the audience had in common – their dogs. Hertz created branded dog bones, each bearing a tag with information about the service, a link to the website and a phone number for easy rental. The bones were hidden under bushes and behind lamp posts where only a canine nose could sniff them out. The message was delivered to its target – all thanks to their dogs.

Agency kempertrautmann, Hamburg
CDs Simon Jasper Philipp, Christoph Gähwiler, Stefan Walz
Art Directors Simon Jasper Philipp, Stefan Walz, Florian Schimmer
Graphic Design David Scherer, Tobias Lehment
Programming Demodern Digital Design Studio, Cologne
Advertiser Edding, "Wall of Fame"

The Wall of Fame, created to celebrate marker pen brand Edding's 50th anniversary, is an interactive drawing board featuring ten virtual pens with which you can show off your illustrating and graphic skills. As the wall is online, it can be constantly enlarged, turning it into an infinite whiteboard. A collaborative artwork consisting of more than 150,000 drawings was created in the first six months. Now a cult destination with artistic types, the wall is still growing at www.wall-of-fame.com.

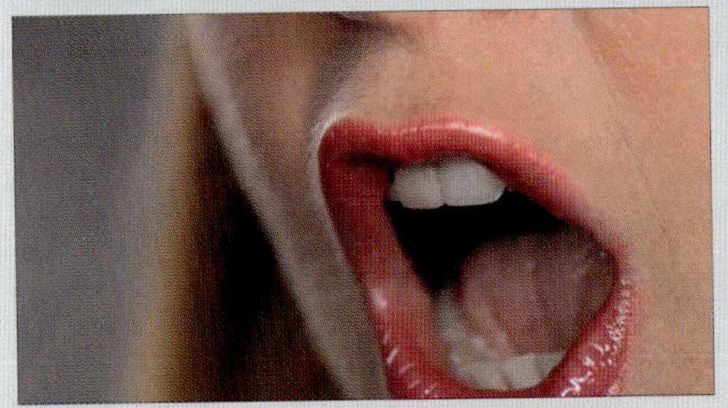

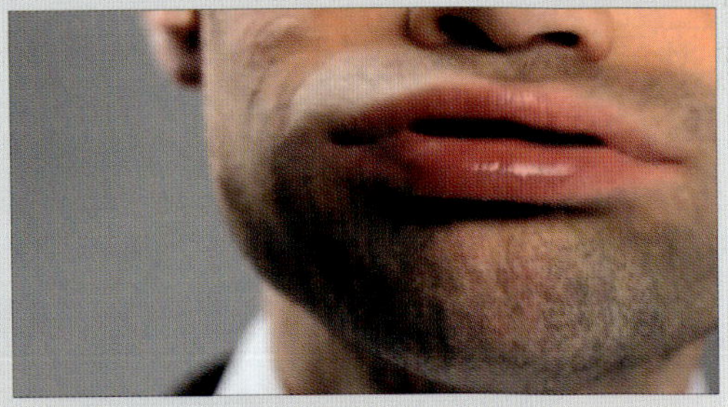

Come on, that wasn't a hard foul.

Damn! Missed...

Bayern attacks.

 Public Relations

Agency	Serviceplan, Munich
CCO	Alex Schill
Creative Directors	Christoph Everke Matthias Mittermüller Tim Strathus
Copywriters	Tim Strathus Juliana Hirsing Tobias Blineder
Art Directors	Matthias Mittermüller Monika Steiner Basma Attalla
Photography	Christoph Mittermüller
Advertiser	Sky, "Football Opera"

TV channel Sky staged the world's first football opera, doing justice to its claim "See something special". The broadcaster selected a much anticipated football match – Schalke 04 against Bayern Munich – and recruited a renowned opera ensemble to improvise a 90 minute operatic version of the match, live, on its sports channel. Watching the match on a screen, the singers interpreted the players, the referee and even the ball. An audience of more than a million viewers tuned in to watch the "parallel" match. Social networks and the media went crazy for the soccer opera, even if it baffled some fans.

HARDCORE REBELLEN
NATIONAL
FREI
WAS DEIN T-SHIRT KANN, KANNST DU AUCH
After just one wash!

Agency Grabarz & Partner, Hamburg
Executive CDs Ralf Heuel, Philipp Schwartz, Sebastian Kuehn, Alexander Milde
Copywriters Anna Wilhelmi, Christian Moehler
Art Director Sebastian Kuehn
Producer Karlotta Ahrens
Concept Nils Ruesenberg
Acct. Supervisor Ina Bach
Advertiser Exit, "Trojan Shirt"

Exit Deutschland is an organisation that helps members of the extreme Right escape the scene. Under an assumed identity, the charity snuck in to the extreme right's most popular rock festival and distributed T-shirts bearing the slogan, "Hardcore Rebels. National and Free." But a surprise awaited the recipients back home. After just one wash, the slogan disappeared to reveal a new message: "If your T-shirt can do it, so can you. We can help you get free of right-wing extremism. Exit Deutschland."

Agency Ogilvy France, Paris
Creative Director Chris Garbutt
Copywriter Benjamin Dessagne
Art Director Emmanuel Bougneres
Production Moonwalk Films, Paris
Director Gustav Johansson
Producer Antoine Bagot
Head of Digital Frederic Levron
Account Team Nathalie Heckel, Delphine Watenberg
Client Laurent Tonnelier
Advertiser Europcar/Autoliberté, "Crush Hour"

Car rental company Europcar has a new scheme offering the flexibility of using a car on demand without the hassle of car ownership. To get the message across, it planned a huge practical joke. Innocent motorists returned to their parked cars to find them "crushed". Their hysterical reactions were filmed by a hidden camera and turned into viral videos. They were also shown on TV news. The videos generated more than 3 million hits on YouTube and widespread coverage. Subscriptions to the new service rose by 83%.

KIA
KIA MOTORS
De 7 jaar garantie van Kia is niet te mooi om waar te zijn.
7 YEAR KIA WARRANTY
Beperkt tot 150.000 km
We begrijpen dat 7 jaar garantie moeilijk te geloven is.
Stel daarom hier tot 15u al je vragen live aan de Algemeen Directeur van Kia, Benoît Morenne.
Vraag niet beantwoord? Stuur u vraag naar info@kia.be
Volledige onderzoek
Chatbox
Deze chatbox is gemodereerd. Je vraag zal niet direct verschijnen.
14:28 - is de kwaliteit van de carosserie uitstekend of zit daar het prijsverschil in tussen andere merken?
14:29 - "Zonder kilometerbeperking de eerste drie jaar": wat als ik reeds 150.000 km bereik voor de drie jaar?
14:29 - hoe komt het dat de kia venga 1600cc in belgie 115pk is en in spanje dezelfde model 128pk
welke kia heeft volgens jou de beste

CAFE ENDLAGER

Verschwendung
ist die größte Energiequelle

 Public Relations

Agency	LDV United, Antwerp
Creative Director	Kristof Snels
Copywriter	Pieter Staes
Art Director	Manuel Ostyn
Photography	Geert de Taeye
Production	Make, Antwerp: Bregt Rogiers
Strategy	Henk Ghesquière Kristof Janssens
Producer	Maarten Debulpaep
CSD	Ann Hostens
Acct. Executive	Tim Janssens
Advertiser	Kia, "Lie Detector"

When people are told that Kia gives a 7-year warranty on all its cars, a lot of them think it's too good to be true and that there must be a catch. To prove the warranty is 100% real, the CEO of Kia Motors Belgium, Benoit Morrenne, was hooked up to a lie detector. Consumers could then grill him about the 7-year warranty during a live Q&A session. The answers and the test results were streamed live to the brand's website. Print ads and online banners reinforced the message that the 7 year warranty is 100% genuine. Honest.

Agency	DDB Tribal Group, Berlin
CCO	Eric Schoeffler
ECDs	Stefan Schulte Bastian Meneses von Arnim
CDs	Ludwig Berndl Kristoffer Heilemann
Copywriters	Mona Sibai Nina Faulhaber
Art Directors	Lars Buri Cathrin Ciuraj Marian Grabmayer
Advertiser	Entega, "Think About It"

Entega is a small German provider of sustainable energy solutions. To attract attention with only a small budget, it used PR initiatives. For example, it encouraged the public to build snowmen demonstrating against climate change. Meanwhile, a café was converted into a repository for nuclear waste, with exhibits and lectures about the problem. Finally, to provoke debate on energy wastage, it built an igloo out of old but still running fridges. A counter monitored the wasted electricity. An Entega magazine complemented the operation.

PANORÁMICA
DE INTERÉS
PITUFANTE

Agency	Bungalow25, Madrid
Executive CDs	Pablo Perez-Solero Julio Galvez
Photography	Ana Alfaro
Producer	Almudena Serrano
Account Team	Cristina Montero Sara Telechea
Coordinator	Fernando Fernandez
Advertiser	Sony Pictures, "Smurf Village"

Something special was needed to launch of the Smurf 3D movie in Spain. There are 1,500 "white towns" scattered throughout the country, and one of these proved the perfect location for the agency's PR initiative: a village called Juzcar in Andalucia. Every house in the village was painted "Smurf blue", even the church. As a result, the new "Smurf village" became one of the country's biggest tourist attractions and a worldwide media sensation. The GDP of region grew by 7%.

THE MOON CHAMELEON
An evil, blood thirsty, world emperor-needy chameleon who can turn into anything. Can easily be spotted by his poor spelling. Or his bad breath.

THE ICELANDIC BANKBIRD
A greedy vulture always on the hunt for money or tradeable securities all over Europe. Brings back it's treasures to Iceland.

THE SOOTSTAINED NAMIBIAN RHINO
During his long stays at the bottom of Namibian lakes, he has a constantly cold. And when this snotty creature sneezes, the earth trembles, far up the Richter scale – making the Namibian desert a dangerous place to stay for both man and animals.

THE NEPALESE DOGBIRD
Looks innocent until he licks your face off. Luckily they mostly live in the Himalaya mountains. And that's why some mountaineers comes home from Nepal with nasty facial wounds.

Agencies	Try, Oslo Apt, Oslo
Copywriter	Lars Joachim Grimstad
Art Director	Egil Pay
Producer	Cathrine Wennersten
Acct. Director	Morten Polmar
Designers	M. Arnesen Eskeland Markus Lind Ole Jakob Skattum Kenneth Svaeren
Clients	Jo Nesbø Trygve Aaslund
Advertiser	Aschehoug, "Dr Proctor"

Jo Nesbø's book for kids, "Dr Proctor and the End of the World, Maybe," is about a cruel monster called the Moon Chameleon. In order to launch the book, the agency commissioned a full-size sculpture of the Moon Chameleon and 23 other dangerous characters. These "animals you wish did not exist" were exhibited at the Natural History Museum in Oslo. Soon, one in two children in Oslo had seen the exhibition and the book had soared to number one on the bestseller list.

Agency	DDB Warsaw
CDs	Zuzanna Duchniewska Maciej Waligóra
Copywriter	Mateusz Książek
Art Director	Magdalena Drozdowska
Project Mgrs.	Kasia Seyfried Natalia Wolska Marta Macke
Client	Barbara Szymańska
Partner	Marta Kołakowska
Advertiser	Audio Description Foundation, "Art Never Seen"

"Audio description" is a technique that allows the blind to participate in art. Only a few museums in Poland provide this service – and few people know what it is. So leading Polish artists donated their work to the exhibition "Art Never Seen" in the Leto Gallery. People were invited via radio and Facebook, but in the gallery visitors found only empty walls and headphones. They "saw" the art using just their ears and imaginations. They could bid for the works at an auction – but saw them only after they had made their purchases.

Search
Georges Matar
What's on your mind?
Search
Georges Ratar
Wall
Georges Ratar
"The closest thing

inclusive
البلد
يومية سياسية شاملة
صدى
غير مخصص للبيع
البلد
يومية سياسية شاملة
صدى
غير مخصص للبيع

Before
Cities got
Smart
Exhibition
ibm.com/smartercities/exhibit
IBM

Before
Cities got
Smart
Exhibition
ibm.com/smartercities/exhibit
IBM

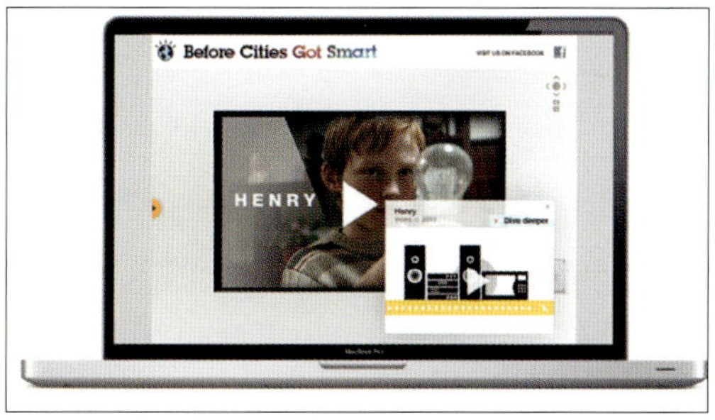
Before Cities Got Smart
HENRY

Agency	Leo Burnett, Beirut
CCO	Bechara Mouzannar
Creative Director	Areej Mahmoud
Digital CD	Patrick Honein
Associate CD	Tania Saleh
Copywriter	Grace Kassab
Art Director	Nayla Baaklini
Deputy MD	Nada Abi Saleh
Strategy	Dima Kfoury
Digital Planner	Michael Chaftari
Account Team	Sarah Sakr Misbah Natour
Advertiser	BPG, "Fake it All"

The brief was to raise awareness of the Brand Protection Group, an association fighting counterfeit goods in Lebanon. The campaign's message was that "everything close to you can be fake". Posters pushing fake goods and TV ads showing suspiciously nice husbands – is he fake? – raised awareness. A newspaper "faked" its front page logo, revealing the ruse the next day. Young actors imitated shoppers' gestures in a mall. Imposters replaced celebrities on radio shows, TV, and on their Facebook pages.

Agency	Ogilvy France, Paris
Creative Directors	Chris Garbutt Susan Westre
Copywriter	Fergus O'Hare
Art Directors	Ginevra Capece Bruno Jesus
Designers	Sid Tomkins Tanya Holbrook
Flash Designer	Frederic Granon
Account Team	Ben Messiaen Eléonore Di Perno
Client	Suzanne Assaf
Advertiser	IBM, "Smarter Cities"

By 2050, 70% of the world's population will live in cities. This will increase the urban problems of overcrowding and pollution. IBM drew attention to some of the solutions it is providing with an exhibition called Before Cities Got Smart. Real artworks showed life in cities today, but with explanations suggesting that the scenes were things of the past: muggings, packed underground trains, wasted electricity and so on. IBM described its solutions. The exhibit is travelling the world and can also be seen online.

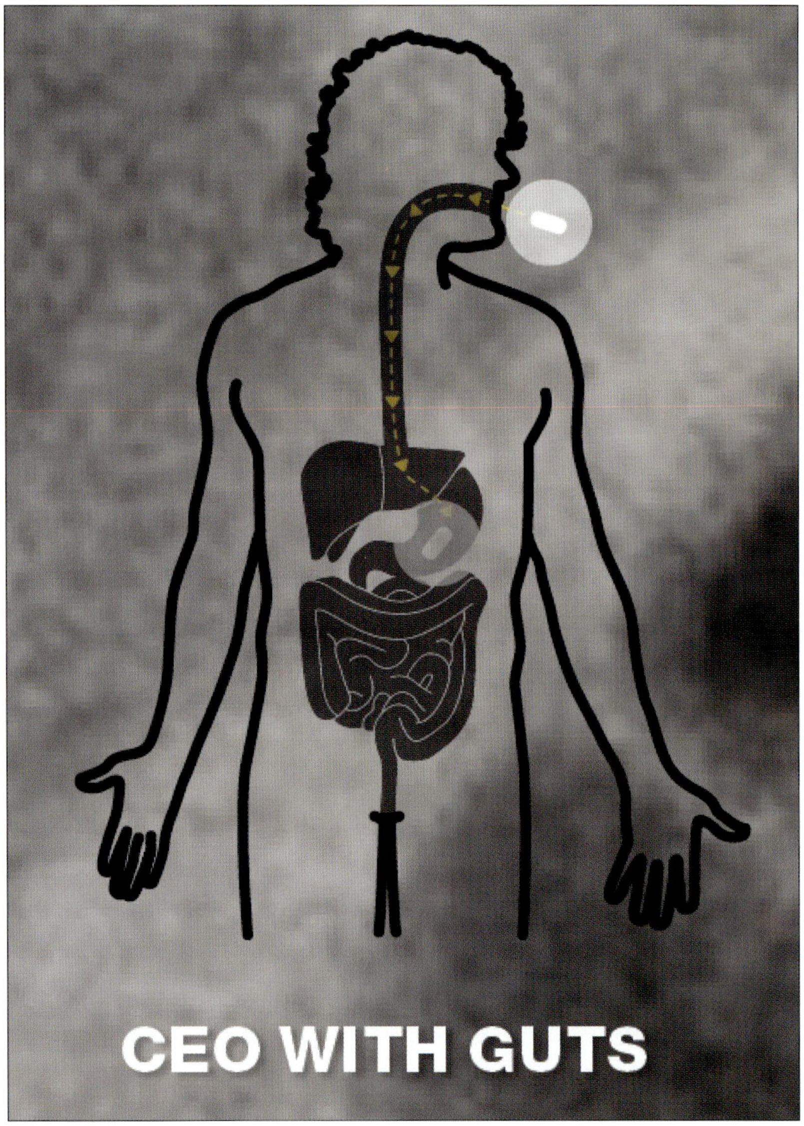
CEO WITH GUTS

THE HUMAN JUKEBOX
SKIP
Hello, my name is Fredrik Hjelmquist
0:04 / 1:23

THE HUMAN JUKEBOX
VIDEOLOG : 25 november
CLOSE X
SONANCE RK63
3.490:-
0:54 / 1:51

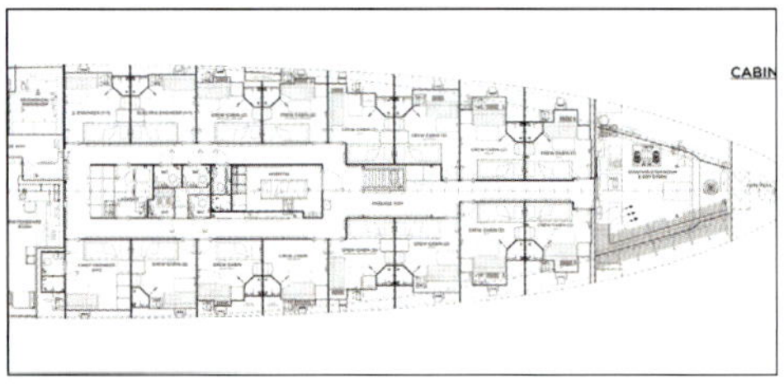
CABIN

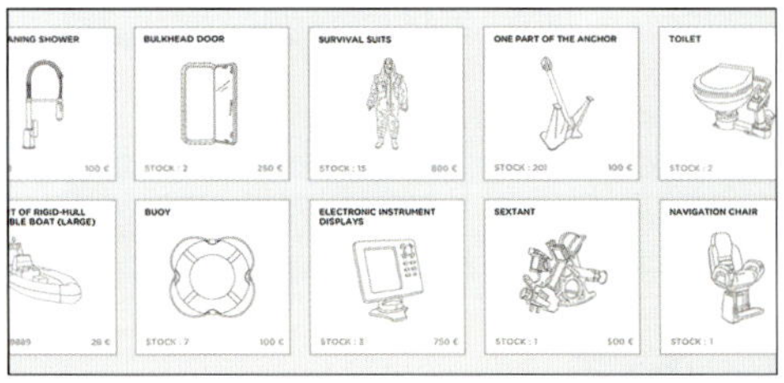
BULKHEAD DOOR
SURVIVAL SUITS
ONE PART OF THE ANCHOR
TOILET
BUOY
ELECTRONIC INSTRUMENT DISPLAYS
SEXTANT
NAVIGATION CHAIR

Rainbow Warrior
PERCENTAGE OF CONSTRUCTION
34,5%
RAINBOW WARRIOR
3D VIEW
ABOUT
LIVE CONSTRUCTION
THE CONTRIBUTORS

Agency Åkestam Holst, Stockholm
CD Andreas Ullenius
Copywriter Joakim Labraaten
Art Director Petra Albrektson
Photography Philip Karlberg
Production From Stockholm With Love, Stockholm
Graphic Design Oscar Gardo
Motion Design Nisse Axman
PR Claes Delin
Acct. Director Henrik Adenskog
Advertiser Pause

Pause is a Stockholm store specialising in bespoke hi-fi systems. To stand out from its rivals, it created "the human juke box". The store's experts invented a tiny wireless receiver contained in an easy-to-swallow capsule. Once the store's boss, Fredrik Hjelmqvist, had swallowed the device, he could pick up any music track sent to it via an online music service. Journalists were invited to a demonstration – and the news spread worldwide. On a website, the public were invited to "send" songs to the CEO's internal music machine.

Agency DDB Paris
Executive CD Alexandre Hervé
Copywriter Olivier Lefebvre
Art Director Benjamin Marchal
Production Les 84, Paris
Account Team Paul Ducré, Xavier Mendiola
Sound Production Panarama
3D Model Virtek
Advertiser Greenpeace, "A New Warrior"

Greenpeace's "Rainbow Warrior" is one of the most famous ships of all time. She's been rammed, boarded and bombed, while protesting against everything from nuclear testing to over-fishing. But Greenpeace needed to raise funds to build a new Warrior. The solution? Invite people to own a piece of the new ship via an e-commerce site. More than 400,000 parts of the vessel were put on sale, from €1 to €7,000. Those who received "Certificates of Ownership" delightedly showed them on social networks, spreading the message.

Bordellen i
Almedalen

The back side
of prostitution
One in every thirteen Swedish men buy sex.
Are you one of them?
Then you are also one of those men helping to finance organised crime.
You are one of those reinforcing the perception of women as objects.
You are one of those causing both psychological and physical harm.
You are one of those who seem to think that prostitution takes place voluntarily, when in fact many of the prostitutes in Sweden start selling sex at the age of 14.
You are one of those who violate individual integrity and human rights.
You are one of those for whom a prostitute is forced to serve with her body.
You are one of those men who break the law.
We don't believe that anyone should be bought or sold for money, or for any other kind of compensation, confirmation or comfort for that matter. No one should have to resort to prostitution because of loneliness, destructiveness, emptiness or vulnerability.
The downside of prostitution is that there is no upside. So stop paying for it. Enjoy voluntary, consensual sex.
Read more at www.bordellenialmedalen.se
(brothelinalmedal)

Bordellen i Almedalen

total!
VERMISST
DEUTSCHLAND-FINDET-EUCH.D

DEUTSCHLAND
FINDET
euch
INITIATIVE
VERMISSTE
KINDER
GERMANY'S BIGGEST SEARCH
FOR MISSING CHILDREN.

Agency	Gyro Communications, Stockholm
Copywriter	Mats Gardmo
Art Director	Mats Wallin
Digital AD	Lina Mehlqvist
Art Design	Tomas Kindberg
Digital Director	Emanuel Lantz
Planner	Olle Svensson
Flash	Jonas Hanström
Account Team	Christina Gillberg Henrik Nordgren
Advertiser	Järfälla Tjejjour, "The Brothel in Almedalen"

In Sweden, it's illegal to visit a prostitute, but still one in 13 men do so. Few are aware of the consequences of prostitution. The brief from an anti-prostitution group was to educate them using only a small media budget. The location was Almedalen, scene of an annual gathering of politicians, journalists and opinion formers. A fake brothel was built on site and those in favour of prostitution were invited via press ads to come along and "practise what they preached". Controversy and media attention were assured.

Agencies	kempertrautmann, Hamburg fischerAppelt, Hamburg
CDs	Marcell Francke Patrick Matthiensen
Copywriter	Sebastian Merget
Art Directors	Bruno Luglio Leif Johannsen
Graphic Design	Patrick Schroer
Programming	BlueMars, Frankfurt
Production	nhb video, Hamburg
Advertiser	Vermisste Kinder, "Germany will Find you"

Every year in Germany more than 100,000 children are reported missing. To recruit a public search party, the "Germany will Find you" campaign was launched using a range of media. Tools included maps giving the children's last whereabouts, pictures of them to download and QR codes linked to their profiles on Facebook. The Bayern Munich football team drew national attention to the campaign on TV when they all entered their stadium accompanied by a child – all except one, who carried a picture of a missing child.

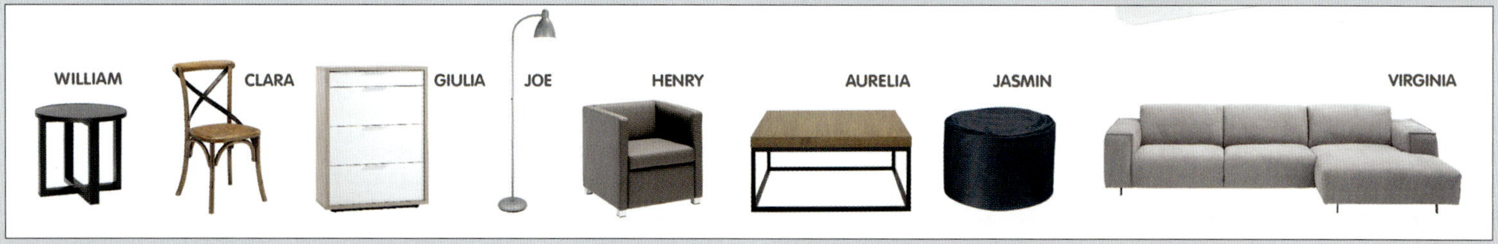
WILLIAM
CLARA
GIULIA
JOE
HENRY
AURELIA
JASMIN
VIRGINIA

50% auf den Artikel im neuen Katalog, der so heisst wie Sie.
Beistelltisch
WILLIAM
74.50
Jetzt bei Micasa im MParc Dreispitz Basel.
micasa
MIGROS
Fürs Leben gemacht.

50% auf den Artikel im neuen Katalog, der so heisst wie Sie.
Stuhl
CLARA
69.50
Jetzt bei Micasa im MParc Ebikon.
micasa
Fürs Leben gemacht.

50% auf den Artikel im neuen Katalog, der so heisst wie Sie.
Decke
DOMINIQUE
39.95
Jetzt bei Micasa in St. Gallen.
micasa
MIGROS
Fürs Leben gemacht.

Agency	Spillmann/Felser/ Leo Burnett, Zurich
Creative Directors	Martin Spillmann Peter Brönnimann
Copywriter	Johannes Raggio
Art Directors	Pablo Schencke Christian Bobst
Production	Pumpkin Film, Zurich
Producers	Suzana Kovacevic
Advertiser	Micasa, "Names" Promotion

It's not easy for a furniture brand to stand out from the competition, but Micasa came up with a witty promotion. Many of its products are named after people – such as Marlene, Clara and Joe. So the idea was simple: if you find an article with your name on it, you can have it for half price. That is, as long as you can prove your identity. This thought led to a popular campaign supported by TV and outdoor ads, while some buyers actively searched for people with the name of the product they wanted.

How far on a single tank of fuel?

Place your bet.

Agencies Try, Oslo
Apt, Oslo
Copywriters Petter Bryde
Anders Holm
Sebastian Prestø
Eva Sannum
Art Directors Thorbjørn Ruud
Markus Lind
Production Gimpville, Oslo
Producers Cathrine Wennersten
Cecilie Fasbender
Advertiser Volkswagen Golf,
"BlueMotion Roulette"

The main benefit of the new Golf BlueMotion is its low fuel-consumption, a mere 0.38 litres of diesel per Norwegian "mil" (10 kms). But that's difficult to communicate in an ad. So an online game turned Norway's E6 highway into a roulette wheel. A real Golf drove north from Oslo. Its route was divided into car-length roulette slots and players were invited to calculate exactly where it would run out of fuel. The person who guessed right would win the car. 27 hours later, the Golf finally came to a halt 1,570 kilometres north of Oslo.

Agency Ogilvy, Frankfurt
CCO Stephan Vogel
CDs Peter Roemmelt
Simon Oppmann
Copywriter Taner Ercan
Art Director Julia Schaefer
Account Team Carola Romanus
Daniela Loesch
Clients Wolfgang Kroul
Peter Baumann
Advertiser DKV (German Health Insurance),
"Shocking Little Beasts"

Some backpackers think it's not cool to get travel insurance – even though they might come across all sorts of snakes and poisonous insects on their travels. The solution? DKV Travel Insurance targeted a store where rugged travellers buy their gear. And then it scared the life out of them, by planting rubber snakes, spiders and scorpions in sleeping bags, backpacks, shoes and other accessories. After the initial shock, the travellers saw the message attached to the creepy crawlies – maybe travel insurance might be a good idea?

facebook
Startseite
Profil
Konto
Deutsche Bahn
Pinnwand
Info
Der Film
Chef-Ticket
Chef-Spiel
Vergleich B...
Exklusiv auf Facebook
Das Chef-Ticket 25,–
Zu den Favoriten meiner Seite hinzufügen
Freunden vorschlagen
54.225 Personen gefällt das
Werbeanzeige erstellen
Tritt mit weiteren Freunden in Verbindung
Weitere Werbeanzeigen
Zum Chef-Spiel
Werde Fan
Hier geht's zum Ticket!
Film abspielen
The BOSS is coming!
Teilen

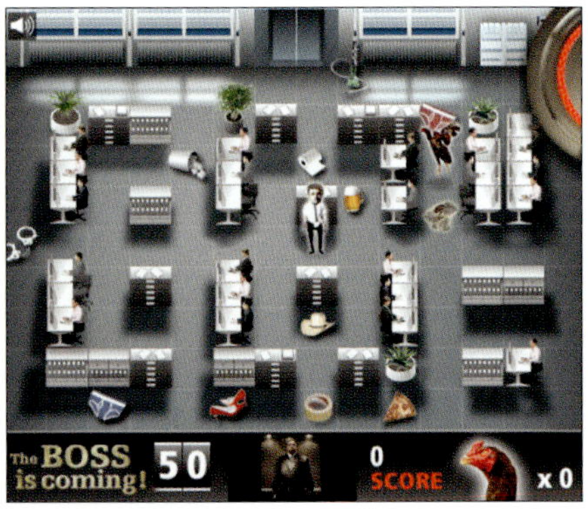
The BOSS is coming!
50
0
SCORE
x 0

Das Chef-Ticket 25,–
Einfache Fahrt, 2. Klasse
Vom 25.10. – 7.11. buchen. Vom 1.11. – 15.12. reisen.
Jetzt buchen!
Zum Chef-Spiel
Zum Film

CAFE LOUNGE
CAFE LOUNGE

COPY & MORE

Briefmarken
COPY & MORE
Briefmarken

COPY & MORE

Agency Ogilvy, Frankfurt
CCO Stephan Vogel
Copywriters Bent Kroggel, Daniel de Leuw
Art Directors Bent Kroggel, Catrin Farrenschon
Production Doity Produktion, Berlin
Director Martin Schmid
Producers Sascha Pollack, Michael Heinemeyer, Julia Staerkel
Advertiser Deutsche Bahn, "The Boss is Coming"

A viral video – featuring a boss who interrupts an wild office party by arriving early thanks to Deutsche Bahn – led to the German rail service's Facebook page. Here they could play a game or comment on the wall. As the "likes" racked up, it was time to get into business: selling rail tickets via Facebook. You want to be like the boss? Buy our special "Boss" ticket. 145,000 of them were sold, along with 17,000 other products. Conclusion? It is possible to do business on Facebook.

Agency Scholz & Friends, Berlin
CCO Martin Pross
Executive CO Matthias Spaetgens
CDs Robert Krause, David Fischer, Philipp Woehler
Copywriters Tobias Deitert, Folke Renken
Art Directors Lisa Baur, Carlo Joest
Graphic Design Dominik Tetzlaff
Advertiser Copy & More

There's a copy-shop on almost every corner in Berlin. It's a huge job attracting attention, specially when there's no money available for conventional advertising. The agency's solution was "The Copied City": they literally copied different parts of the city in the neighbourhood of the store. The message: Copy & More can reproduce everything at an affordable price – from notepaper to frontage.

TIGER OF SWEDEN
/JEANS
DRESSING
ROOM
SESSIONS
.COM

ET FATØL BRYGGET FOR KJENNERE
CENSORED
TROMSØ · NORWAY
NORDLIGSTE BRYGGERI

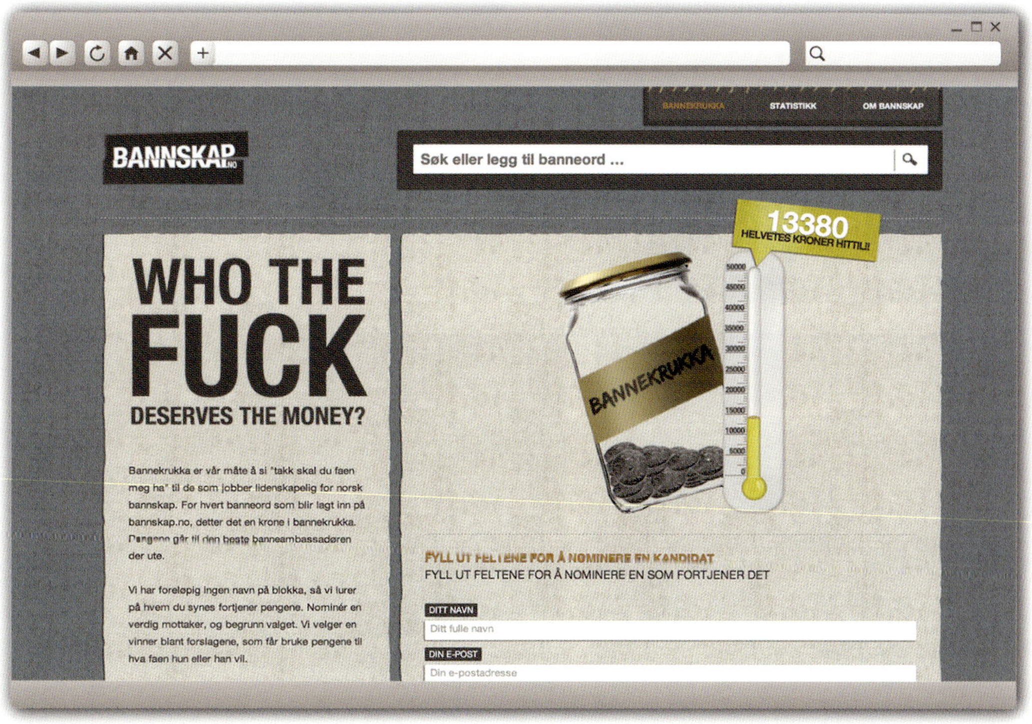
STATISTIKK
OM BANNSKAP
BANNSKAP.NO
Søk eller legg til banneord ...
13380
HELVETES KRONER HITTIL!!
WHO THE FUCK DESERVES THE MONEY?
Bannekrukka er vår måte å si "takk skal du faen meg ha" til de som jobber lidenskapelig for norsk bannskap. For hvert banneord som blir lagt inn på bannskap.no, detter det en krone i bannekrukka. Pengene går til den beste banneambassadøren der ute.
Vi har foreløpig ingen navn på blokka, så vi lurer på hvem du synes fortjener pengene. Nominér en verdig mottaker, og begrunn valget. Vi velger en vinner blant forslagene, som får bruke pengene til hva faen hun eller han vil.
BANNEKRUKKA
FYLL UT FELTENE FOR Å NOMINERE EN SOM FORTJENER DET
DITT NAVN
Ditt fulle navn
DIN E-POST
Din e-postadresse

Agency Lowe Brindfors, Stockholm
Creative Directors Rickard Villard, Martin Bartholf
Art Directors Noel Pretorius, Kristian Luoma
Photography Carl-August Savgård, Marcus Hård
Designers Noel Pretorius, Kristian Luoma
Web Developer Adrian Tomic
Advertiser Tiger of Sweden Jeans

Tiger of Sweden staged "The Dressing Room Sessions" to promote nine new jeans. Nine well-known rock bands, wearing the new jeans, performed nine different songs in a dressing room within stores. The live sessions intrigued shoppers and were transformed into nine music videos, which became part of an in-store campaign throughout Sweden. Shoppers could watch their favourite videos and lyrics were reproduced on display signs. And of course there was a website where users could watch the videos.

Agencies Try, Oslo; Apt, Oslo
Copywriters Sebastian Prestø, Anders Holm
Art Director Sebastian Rasch
Producers Magne Hage, Ole Bolsønes, Erik Huse
Project Manager Lisa Canneaux
Developers Erland Wiencke, Alexander Pope
Advertiser Mack Brewery, "Curses"

Mack is the world's northernmost brewery. But foreign brands are slurping up its market share. And Norway's strict alcohol laws mean Mack can't even show its own products on its website. This makes Mack angry as hell! So since it couldn't talk about its beer, it focused on its language instead. It created an interactive swear jar. The mission: collect as many curses as possible. Write them, categorise them, explain them. The campaign got Mack a lot of attention. Christian conservatives hated it. But they don't drink much anyway.

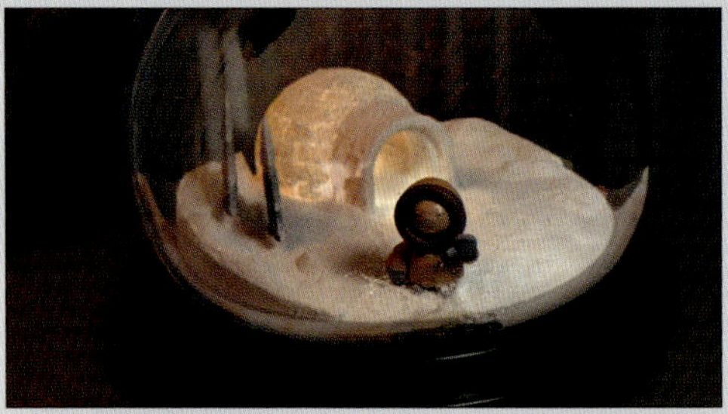

TalkTalk
A brighter home for everyone
talktalk.co.uk

Film Craft

Agency	CHI & Partners, London
Executive CD	Jonathan Burley
Creative Director	Warren Moore
Copywriters	Matt Collier Wayne Robinson
Art Directors	Matt Collier Wayne Robinson
Production	Stink, London
Director	Adam Berg
Producers	Ben Croker David Jones
Advertiser	TalkTalk, "Homes Within Homes"

In her home, a woman chats via her computer. Onlookers watch enviously: a doll in a doll's house; an action figure peering over a cardboard box; an Eskimo in a snow dome; a cuckoo in a cuckoo clock; a signalman on a model railway – even the occupant of a lighthouse in a painting. They can watch one another, but they can't talk. Or can they? Suddenly, the doll's computer chimes – it's a message! In fact, all the animated characters are soon chatting and telephoning. Just like the woman, they are Talk Talk telecom subscribers.

SOLIDARITÉS
INTERNATIONAL
www.solidarites.org

Health insurance for you and your family.
DKV

Agency	BDDP Unlimited, Paris
CD	Guillaume-Ulrich Chifflot
Copywriter	Fabien Duval
Art Director	Fabien Nunez
Production	Hush, Paris
Director	Clement Beauvais
Producers	Nicolas Lhermitte Arthur De Kersauson Christophe Guyot
Acct. Team	Marco de la Fuente Irache Martinez
Advertiser	Solidarités International, "Water & Ink"

A few drops of water on a page, but when ink is added to them, they tell a powerful story. This beautiful yet troubling spot reminds us that polluted water kills eight million people every year all around the world. It was directed by Clement Beauvais, who also provided the magical illustrations.

Agency	Ogilvy, Frankfurt
CCO	Stephan Vogel
Creative Directors	Peter Roemmelt Simon Oppmann
Copywriters	Lukas Liske
Art Director	Julia Schaefer
Production	JO!Schmid, Berlin
Director	Martin Schmid
Producers	Michael Schmid Michael Heinemeyer
Acct. Supervisor	Carola Romanus
Advertiser	DKV, "Very Angry Neighbour"

An immaculate garden on a sunny day. Birds sing, bees hum. The fanatical gardener trims an unruly rose bush and flicks off a ladybird, crushing it underfoot. Suddenly, another invader appears. A model helicopter runs amok through the plants, its blades slashing them to pieces. The massacre is filmed in excruciating slow motion. The chopper crashes and the neighbours – a small boy and his dad with a remote control – look embarrassed. The gardener's dog growls, but he looks like he's about to have a coronary.

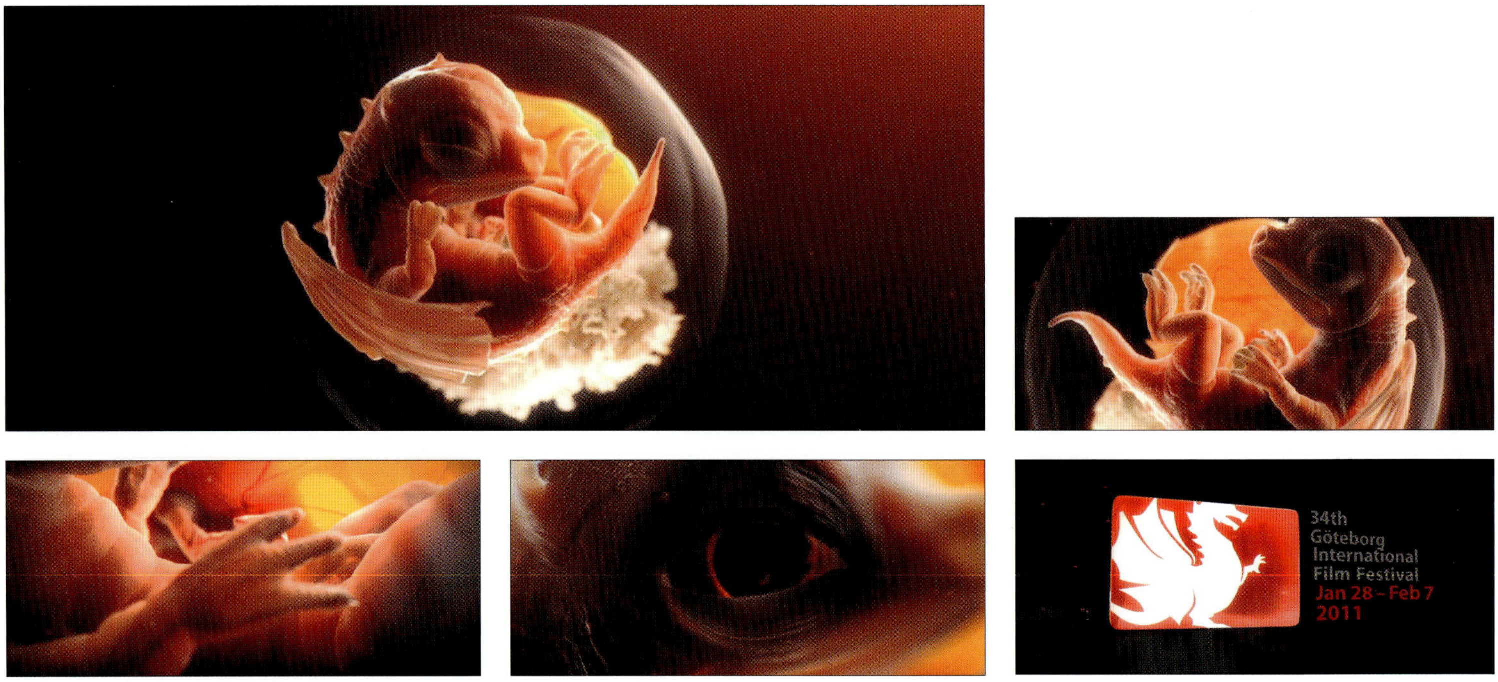
34th
Göteborg
International
Film Festival
Jan 28 – Feb 7
2011

Agency	SCP, Gothenburg
Creative Director	Tommy Östberg
Copywriter	Staffan Dempe
Art Director	Birgitta Grönlund
Production	Bobby Works, Gothenburg
Digital Artist	Thomas Feiner
Advertiser	Göteborg International Film Festival

A baby, still in the womb. But a baby with a difference – a dragon. We watch, fascinated, as the tiny dragon blinks, flexes its wings. We see its heart pounding. In the distance, we can hear disturbing sounds: explosions, conflict. Then, in extreme close up, we see the dragon's eye opening. And when it fixes us with that implacable gaze, suddenly the dragon doesn't look so cute after all. The dragon is the emblem of the Göteborg International Film Festival. Expect drama.

Agency	Herezie, Paris
Creative Director	Andrea Stillacci
Copywriter	Jean-Laurent Py
Art Director	Sebastien Boutebel
Production	Stink, Paris
Director	Nacho Gayan
Producer	Robert Leisewitz
Cinematographer	Linus Sandgren
Post Production	Nightshift, Paris
Sound Design	Tranquille Le Chat
Advertiser	Chevrolet, "The Warehouse"

A foreman with a clipboard leads a man through a strange warehouse. They pass a clown and a girl on horseback. "Life is full of opportunities," says the foreman. "But do you know what happens to those that are missed? They end up here." A woman with a baby, an elephant, a dancer – each missed opportunity is preserved. The foreman warns him that missed opportunities don't come back. The man agrees – and steps outside to choose his new Chevrolet from the range. Chevrolet – make it happen.

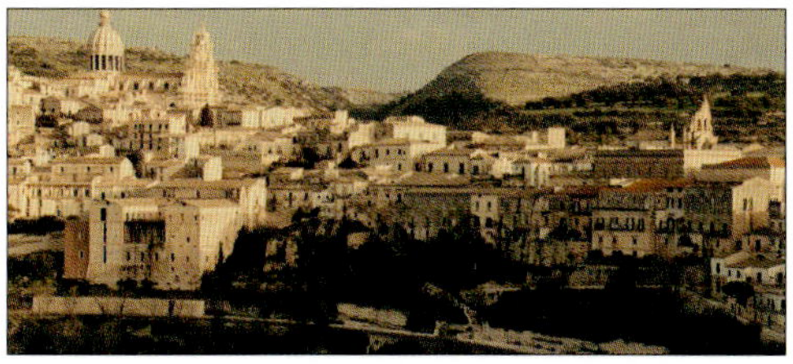

FINE

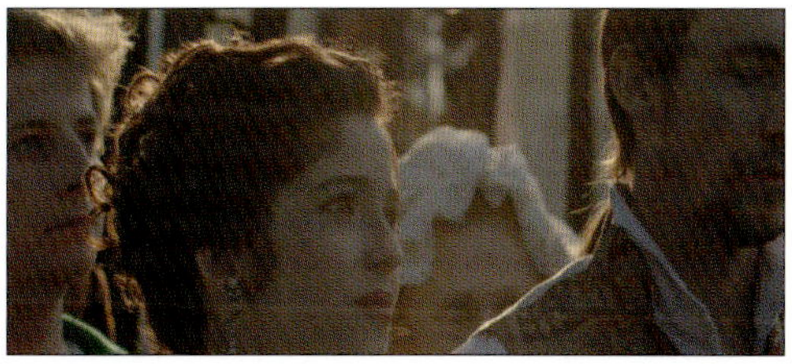

I'll search for him in hell!

... who's that man always behind you?

Orange
Cineday
BUY ONE TICKET
GET ONE FREE

Agency Jack Rouse Associates, Cincinnati
CD Randy Smith
Art Director Juan Jimenez
Production Group.IE, Frankfurt
Stink, London
Director Ivan Zacharias
Producers Nick Landon
Mark Gläser
Anita Daugherty
Advertisers Aldar Properties & Ferrari SPA, "Coppa di Sicilia"

Sicily, 1925. We see a sun-bleached town in a scene tinted with sepia. The crowds take their seats. Glorious racing cars are refuelled and polished. Then they're off! We can almost taste the grit and feel the heat as the drivers race through the magnificent landscape, whizzing around hairpin bends, duelling like charioteers. The film, made for Ferrari World in Dubai, celebrates the Coppa di Sicilia road race. One of the drivers is "Enzo" – Enzo Ferrari, that is, piloting an Alfa Romeo in the days before he started building his own cars.

Agency Publicis Conseil, Paris
CDs Olivier Altmann
Fabrice Delacourt
Olivier Desmettre
Copywriter Patrice Lucet
Art Director Philippe Boucheron
Production Partizan, Paris
Director Antoine Bardou Jacquet
Producers Georges Bermann
Frederic Genest
Pierre Marcus
Muriel Allegrini
Advertiser Orange Cineday, "Hussars"

Can you make a spoof trailer so convincing that the audience wants to see the film? That's the achievement of the agency and its film director, Antoine Bardou Jacquet. The joke behind the fake trailer for a Napoleonic war drama is that a normal bloke in 21st century clothing follows the main character around – because Orange clients can invite a friend to the movies for free on Tuesdays. But the parody is spot on and "Hussars" looks better than most Hollywood offerings.

SCRABBLE

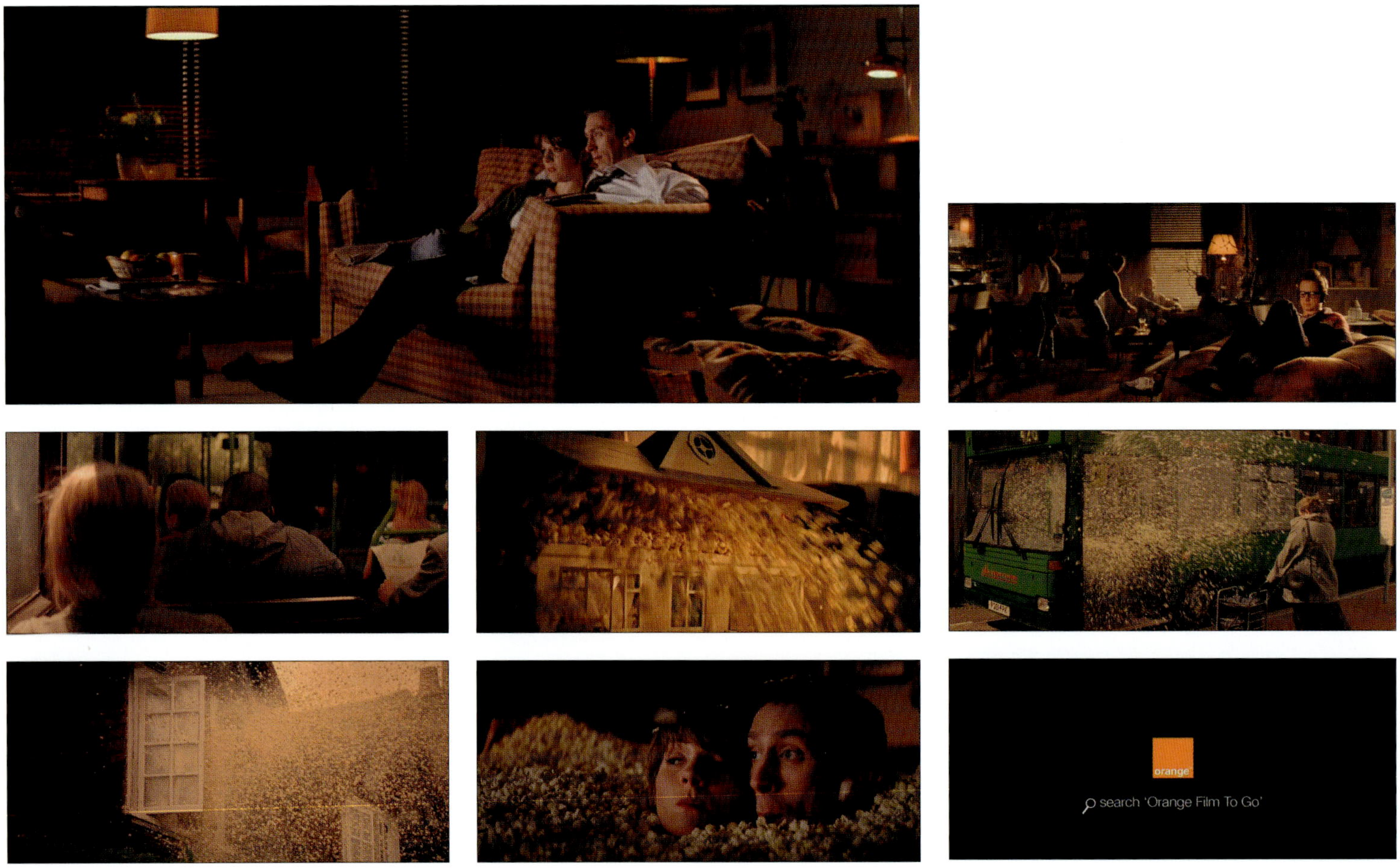
orange
search 'Orange Film To Go'

Agency	Ogilvy France, Paris
CDs	Chris Garbutt Christian Reuilly
Copywriters	Baptiste Clinet Nicolas Lautier Florian Bodet
Art Directors	Baptiste Clinet Nicolas Lautier Florian Bodet
Production	Paranoid, Paris
Directors	Les Vikings Laure Bayle
Advertiser	Scrabble, "Block Project"

Scrabble Trickster is a new, crazier version of the beloved word game. To bring it to life, a cast of bizarre characters portrayed weird words in an apartment block that had been turned into a giant Scrabble board for the occasion. A staged audience watched the live "game" in progress, witnessing a gorilla, Gulliver, a dragon and an unidentified "creature", among others.

Agency	Fallon, London
CD	Gui Borchert
Copywriter	Laura Visco
Art Director	Mariano Cassisi
Production	Gorgeous Enterprises, London
Director	Chris Palmer
Producers	Alicia Bernard Tracy Stokes
D.O.P.	Jess Hall
Editor	One of Us: Scot Crane
Advertiser	Orange, "Popcorn"

A couple are watching TV when their sofa begins to inflate. So does a kid's beanbag. In fact, beds, seats and even clothing all over the country expand and explode – in a shower of popcorn! It's a clever way of explaining that thanks to Orange and iTunes, viewers can download movies and watch them wherever they like, via a service called Film To Go.

Dior
j'adore
Dior

Rethink Possible
att.com/blackberrytorch 866.MOBILITY

Agency TBWA\Paris
CDs Eric Holden, Rémi Noël, Sophie Guyon
Art Directors Sophie Guyon, Stephanie Ragot
Production Wanda Productions, Paris
Director Jean-Jacques Annaud
Producers Francois Lamotte, Maxime Boiron, Herve Dommange, Patrick Barbier
Advertiser Dior, "J'Adore"

A fabulous setting, a beautiful celebrity, the breathy murmur of "J'adore Dior" – this is perfume advertising as we know it. But not entirely, because thanks to special effects wizardry, contemporary star Charlize Theron comes face to face with past screen goddesses Grace Kelly, Marlene Dietrich and Marilyn Monroe. Marilyn exclaims that she loves the Dior fragrance too, a nice touch as in real life she famously stated that she wore nothing in bed apart from Chanel No. 5.

Agency BBDO, New York
CDs Ralph Watson, Greg Hahn
Copywriter Mike Sweeney
Art Director Molly Adler
Production Gorgeous Enterprises, London
Director Peter Thwaites
Producers Anna Hashmi, Grant Gill
D.O.P. Joost van Gelder
Post Prod. The Mill, New York
Advertiser AT&T, "Entertainment"

A man runs across a dusty street in a classic Western shoot-out. He plunges through a doorway – and finds himself in a modern bank heist. One of the robbers dashes up the stairs – and emerges in the midst of a werewolf tale, complete with pitchfork-brandishing peasants. The werewolf falls through a rotten coffin into a sci-fi adventure. And the heroine of that tale shoots her way out of a spacecraft and into an explosive action movie. The fast and furious editing demonstrates the variety of entertainment available on our smart phones, thanks to AT&T.

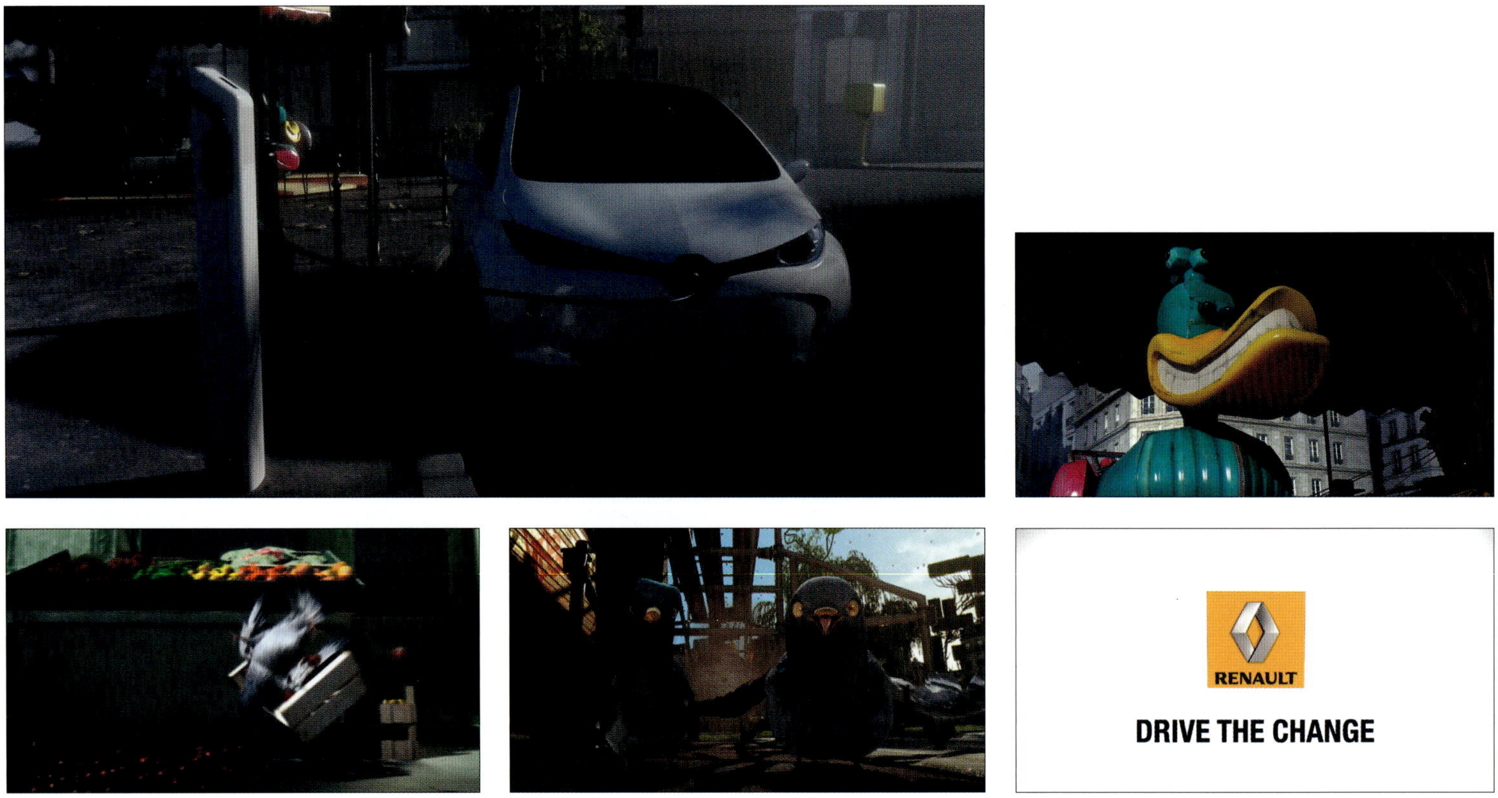
RENAULT
DRIVE THE CHANGE

Raving Rabbids
TRAVEL IN TIME

Agency Blue, Paris
CDs Bruno Delhomme, Guilhem Arnal
Art Directors Gilles Rivollier, Joann Ameline, Guillaume Quéré
Production Digital District
Director Edouard Salier
Advertiser Renault, "A Whirlwind of Change"

Animation is the star of this delightful tale, which introduces us to Renault's electric car, the Zoe. The car is literally a breath of fresh air, but the whirlwind of change it provokes sweeps along a hapless bumble bee, who accidentally wakes two sleepy pigeons. The ensuing chase shows us how an unpolluted Paris could be transformed by colour, brightness, flowers and green trees. All it would take is a few more sales of the Renault Zoe.

Production Wanda Productions, Paris
Director Akama
Producer Claude Fayolle
Post Production Akama Studio, Paris
Advertiser Ubisoft, "Raving Rabbids"

The Raving Rabbids are stars of a hit computer game. This fast-paced animated film launches their new game, in which they travel through time – in a converted washing machine. We see the mischievous rodents "inventing" fire, knocking the nose off the Sphinx and ensuring that Arthur does not pull the sword from the stone. History is in peril when the Rabbids are around – but entertainment is guaranteed.

SEQUOIA
Organic & Natural Market

SEQUOIA
Organic & Natural Market

Agency Marcel, Paris
Production Quad, Paris
Director Rémi Devouassoud
Producer François Brun
Advertiser Sequoia Organic & Natural Market, "Mantis" & "Skunk"

"Nature has nothing to hide", according to natural foods store Sequoia. So naturally, the animals "interviewed" in these ultra-realistic films are upfront about their nasty little habits. In this one, a chatty mantis reveals that she's a very passionate person, but that once she's fallen in love, she's overwhelmed by a compulsive urge to murder and devour her partner. "Maybe it's trauma from childhood," she muses. "My mum killed my dad, my grandmother killed my granddad…" At least she's honest.

An ultra-realistic skunk reflects on his image problem. Or rather, his odour problem. "Last time I took a bath in the lake, the frogs got sick. And each time the wind blows, everybody thinks it's a chemical warfare attack." He admits that he stinks, but it's hard being the joke of the forest. Sometimes, he wonders if he can go on. But at least he's honest. Nature has nothing to hide.

NISSAN JUKE
URBAN-PROOF ENERGISED

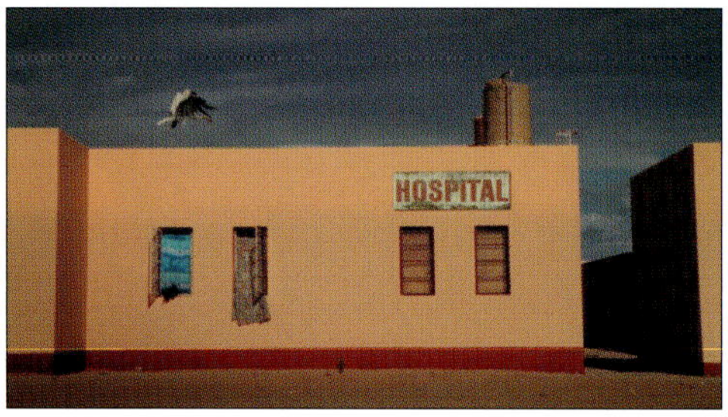
HOSPITAL

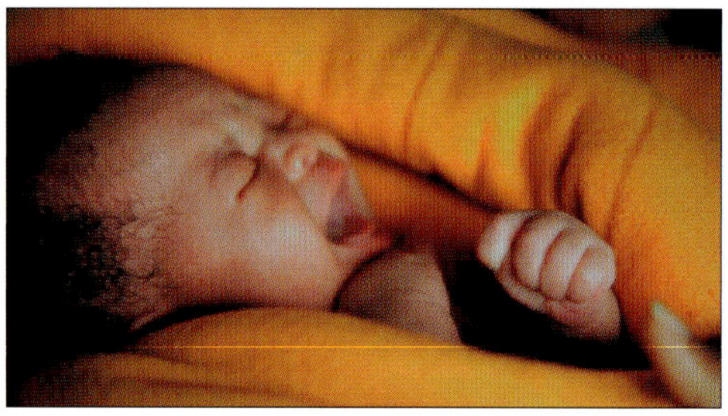

Orange Babies.

Agencies	TBWA\G1, Paris TBWA\Paris
CDs	Eric Holden Alasdhair MacGregor Rémi Noël
Art Directors	Adam Kennedy Brandon Rochon
Production	Wanda Productions, Paris
Director	Philippe Andre
Producers	Patrick Barbier Guillaume Faurel
Advertiser	Nissan Juke, "Stay Awake"

The Nissan Juke is a little car with infectious energy. Here we see it passing through the city, sparking reactions wherever it goes: tunnel lights flicker, office blocks light up, toys spring to life and hair stands on end. In a launderette, washing machines erupt, while a TV health coach goes crazy on his exercise bike. Down the street, a burglar finds himself in the middle of a brightly lit jewellery store. Street cleaning machines waltz unmanned. A metro train takes off with only a rat for a passenger. Finally, neon explodes, showering the Juke with sparks.

Agency	Ogilvy, Amsterdam
Executive CD	Darre van Dijk
Copywriter	Piebe Piebenga
Production	In Case of Fire
Director	Job van As
Producers	Paul Brand Brenda Bentz van de Berg
D.O.P.	Eric Halberstadt
Post Production	Condor Amsterdam
Acct. Supervisor	Tom IJzer
Advertiser	Orange Babies, "The Fight"

Orange Babies supports mothers who are infected with HIV and helps them to deliver healthy babies. The film plays on the legend that storks deliver babies to their mothers. Here the stork is attacked by a vulture, symbolizing death. After a fierce and realistic battle, the stork wins and the vulture flies away. The stork continues its mission and lands on the roof of an African hospital. The moment it lands, we hear the crying of a newborn baby.

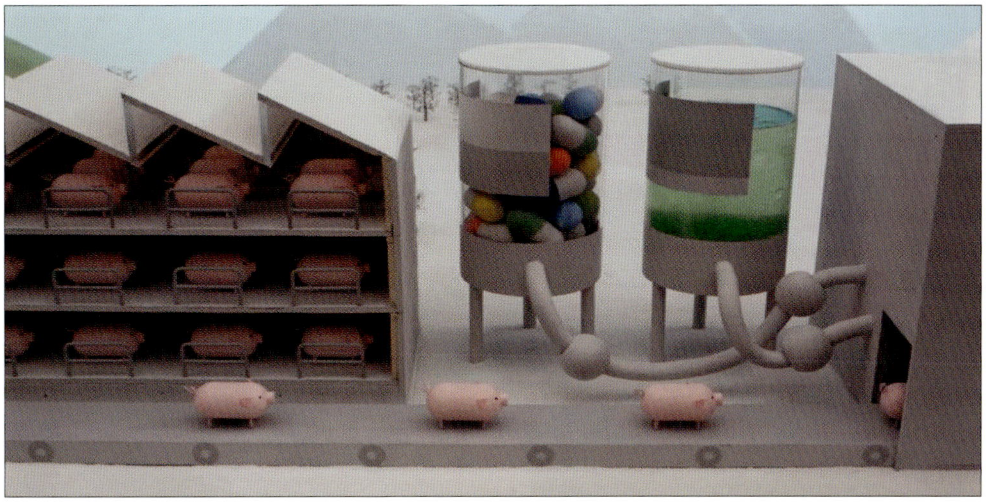

FOOD
WITH
INTEGRITY
chipotle.com

MINI
THE NEW MINI COUPÉ.

Agency	CAA Marketing, Los Angeles
Production	Nexus Productions, London
Director	Johnny Kelly
Producer	Liz Chan
Advertiser	Chipotle Mexican Grill, "Back to the Start"

This film highlights the issues of ethical and sustainable farming. Stop-frame animation captures the life of a pig farmer who adopts industrial production techniques, suffers from depression and then reverts to traditional free-range methods. The animation is underscored by the voice of country singer Willie Nelson, who covers Coldplay's evocative track "The Scientist". The track was released on iTunes with 60 cents from every sale going to the Chipotle Cultivate Foundation.

Agency	BSUR, Amsterdam
CDs	Jason Schragger Karl Dunn Paulo Martins
Copywriter	Gian Carlo Lanfranco
Art Director	Rolando Cordova
Production	Thomas Thomas Films, London
Director	Kevin Thomas
Producers	Philippa Thomas Jeremy Barnes Oscar Thomas
Advertiser	Mini Coupé, "Carnival"

Every day is an adventure with the new Mini Coupé. It's Sunday in Rio, where our hero gets caught up in a race against time when he picks up a hitchhiking performer and agrees to drop him off at the parade. This involves slaloming through the Rio carnival avoiding floats, samba dancers, security guards – and a small dog dressed as an angel. It's fast-moving and glamorous, just like the new Mini.

Batelco
DIRECTORY

Batelco
DIRECTORY

 Print Craft

Agency	FP7/DXB, Dubai
Creative Director	Fadi Yaish
Art Director	Supparat Thepparat
Photography	Illusion, Bangkok: Surachai Puthikulangkura
Illustrators	Illusion, Bangkok: Surachai Puthikulangkura, Supachai U-Rairat
Web Producer	Clarisse Mar Wai May
Advertiser	Batelco, "Batelco Directory"

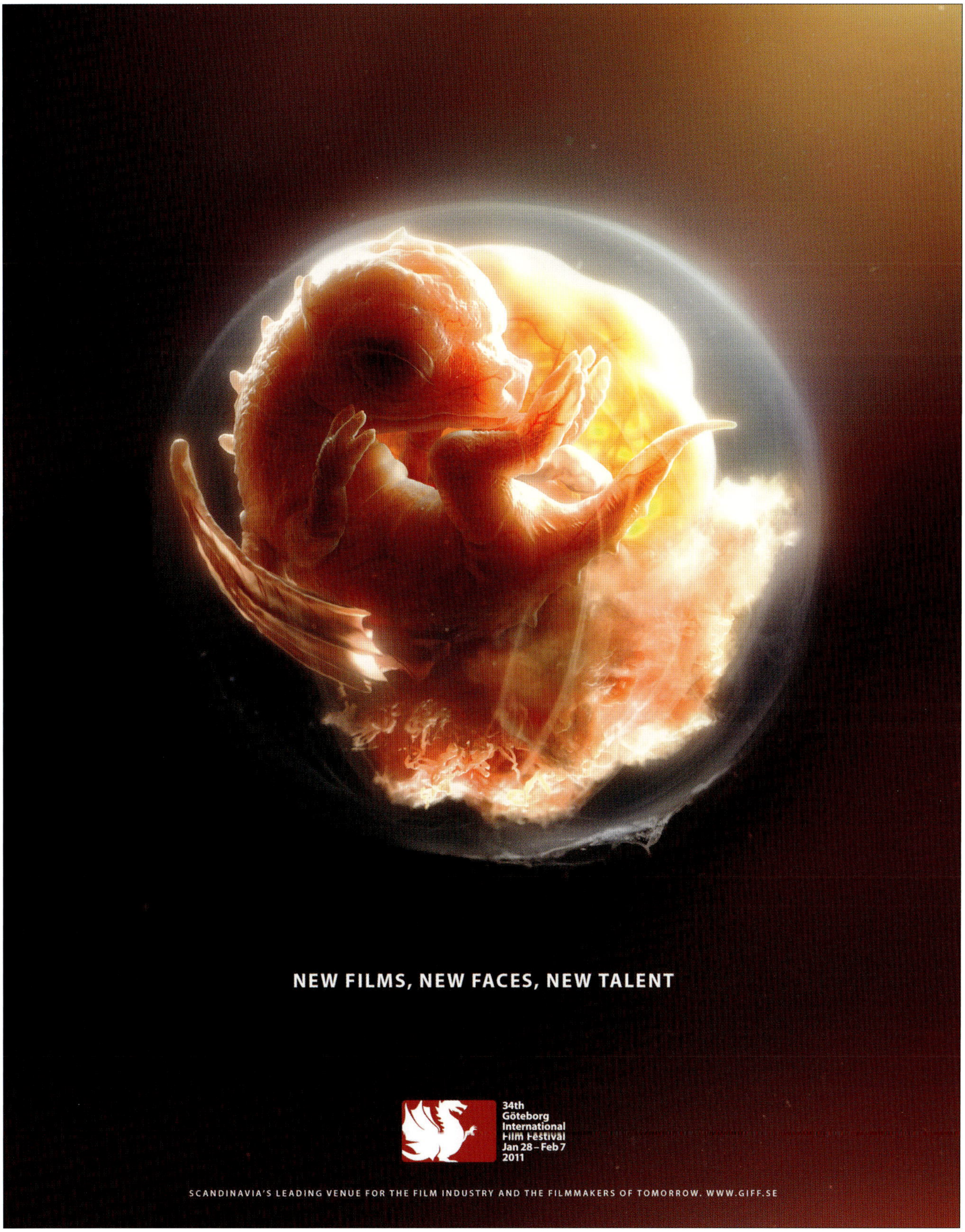
NEW FILMS, NEW FACES, NEW TALENT
34th
Göteborg
International
Film Festival
Jan 28 – Feb 7
2011
SCANDINAVIA'S LEADING VENUE FOR THE FILM INDUSTRY AND THE FILMMAKERS OF TOMORROW. WWW.GIFF.SE

Agency	SCP, Gothenburg
Creative Director	Tommy Östberg
Copywriters	Staffan Dempe Bob Gilbert
Art Director	Birgitta Grönlund
Illustration	Feiner Arts: Thomas Feiner
Advertiser	Göteborg International Film Festival

NO GUTS NO GLORY
SOÖRUZ
Snowboard - Winter 2011 collection

DEFENDER
LAND-ROVER
GO BEYOND

Print Craft

Agency	Publicis Conseil, Paris
Creative Directors	Olivier Altmann Frederic Royer
Copywriter	Didier Aerts
Art Director	Alexandra Offe
Illustrator	Jean-Marie Vives
Art Buying	Jean-Luc Chirio
Account Team	Jean-Patrick Chiquiar Laetitia Vitalis Sophie Gustinelli
Clients	Yann Dalibot Matthieu Barat
Advertiser	Sooruz, “Jump”

Agency	Rainey Kelly Campbell Roalfe/Y&R, London
Creative Directors	Mark Roalfe Graham Lang
Copywriter	Phil Forster
Art Director	Tim Brookes
Photography	Carl Warner
Typographer	Lee Aldridge
Advertiser	Land Rover Defender, “Passport Stamps”

Let the twitter of birds
be music to your ears.
Hearing Aids

Let the chuckle of child's laughter
be music to your ears.
Hearing Aids

Agency	Wunderman, Zurich
CCO	Markus Gut
Creative Director	Roger Rüegger
Copywriters	Florian Tillmann Samuel Textor
Art Directors	Michael Gallmann Silke Heinzelmann
Photography	Ted Sabarese
Typographers	Nora Angstmann Christoph Krummenacher
Strategy	Benedikt Bitzi
Account Mgr.	Renato Di Rubbo
Advertiser	Phonak, "Spice"

Agency	Leo Burnett, Moscow
Creative Director	Mikhail Kudashkin
Copywriter	Rodrigo Linhares
Art Director	Arina Avdeeva
Illustration	Ninjafilms Studio, Moscow
Graphic Design	Dmitry Jakovlev Asya Boukhnina Victoria Prokopavichute
Account Team	Oxana Shevchenko Evgenia Karpenkova
Advertiser	Lego, "Make It"

FOR ZOOLOGISTS:
The Bosavi Giant Woolly Rat was discovered in an extinct volcano. Considered to be the largest in the widespread Muridae family. An active nocturnal forager.
FOR LAND ROVER OWNERS:
Tastes like chicken.
LAND-ROVER
GO BEYOND

Agency	CLM BBDO, Paris
Creative Directors	Jean-Francois Sacco Gilles Fichteberg Fabien Mouillard
Copywriter	Jamie Standen
Art Director	Mark Forgan
3D Production	Mécanique Générale, Paris
3D Designer	Baptiste Masse
Art Buying	Sylvie Etchemaite
Advertiser	Tag Heuer, “Precision”

Agency	Young & Rubicam, Dubai
Creative Directors	Shahir Zag Kalpesh Patankar
Copywriter	Shahir Zag
Art Director	Kalpesh Patankar
Illustrator	Jomy Varghese
Planner	Nadine Ghossoub
Advertiser	Land Rover, “Rare”

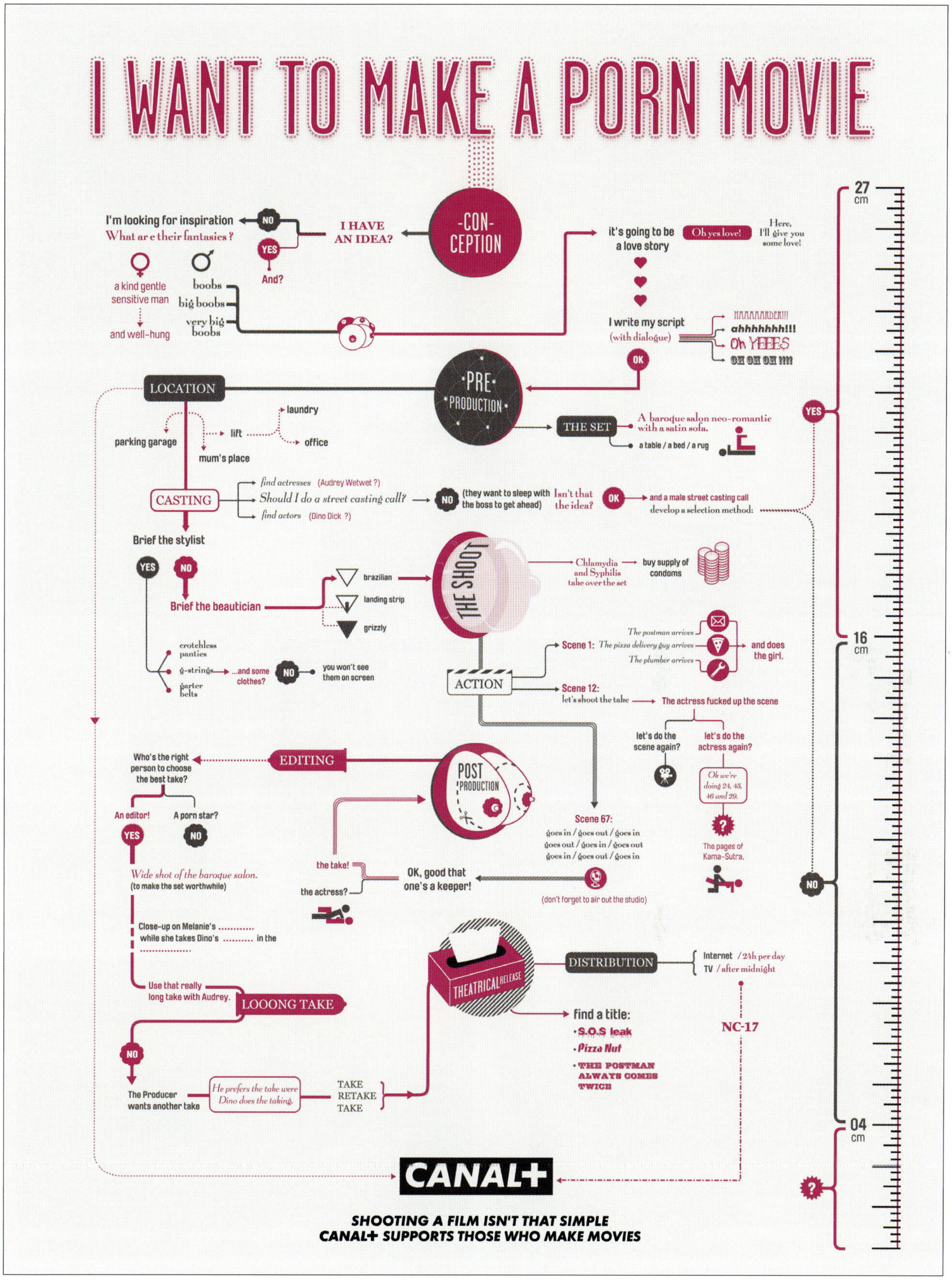

I WANT TO MAKE A PORN MOVIE
-CON- CEPTION
I HAVE AN IDEA?
NO
YES
I'm looking for inspiration
What are their fantasies?
And?
a kind gentle sensitive man
and well-hung
boobs
big boobs
very big boobs
it's going to be a love story
Oh yes love!
Here, I'll give you some love!
I write my script
(with dialogue)
OK
PRE PRODUCTION
LOCATION
laundry
lift
office
parking garage
mum's place
THE SET
A baroque salon neo-romantic with a satin sofa.
a table / a bed / a rug
CASTING
find actresses (Audrey Wetwet ?)
Should I do a street casting call?
find actors (Dino Dick ?)
(they want to sleep with the boss to get ahead)
Isn't that the idea?
and a male street casting call
develop a selection method:
Brief the stylist
Brief the beautician
brazilian
landing strip
grizzly
crotchless panties
g-strings
garter belts
...and some clothes?
you won't see them on screen
THE SHOOT
Chlamydia and Syphilis take over the set
buy supply of condoms
ACTION
Scene 1: The pizza delivery guy arrives
The postman arrives
The plumber arrives
and does the girl.
Scene 12: let's shoot the take
The actress fucked up the scene
let's do the scene again?
let's do the actress again?
Oh we're doing 24, 45, 46 and 29.
The pages of Kama-Sutra.
Scene 67: goes in / goes out / goes in goes out / goes in / goes out goes in / goes out / goes in
POST PRODUCTION
EDITING
Who's the right person to choose the best take?
An editor!
A porn star?
Wide shot of the baroque salon.
(to make the set worthwhile)
Close-up on Melanie's
while she takes Dino's in the
the take!
the actress?
OK, good that one's a keeper!
(don't forget to air out the studio)
Use that really long take with Audrey.
LOOONG TAKE
The Producer wants another take
He prefers the take were Dino does the taking.
TAKE RETAKE TAKE
THEATRICAL RELEASE
DISTRIBUTION
Internet / 24h per day
TV / after midnight
NC-17
find a title:
S.O.S leak
Pizza Nut
THE POSTMAN ALWAYS COMES TWICE
27 cm
16 cm
04 cm
CANAL+
SHOOTING A FILM ISN'T THAT SIMPLE
CANAL+ SUPPORTS THOSE WHO MAKE MOVIES

Agency	BETC Euro RSCG, Paris
Creative Directors	Stéphane Xiberras Olivier Apers
Copywriters	David Troquier Gregory Ferembach
Art Directors	David Troquier Gregory Ferembach
Illustration	Les Graphiquants, Paris
Advertiser	Canal+, “Movie Flowcharts”

Wrangler
WE ARE ANIMALS

Wrangler

Wrangler

Wrangler

Advertising Photography

Agency Fred & Farid, Paris
CDs & Copywriters Fred Raillard
Farid Mokart
Art Directors Fred Raillard
Farid Mokart
Juliette Lavoix
Céline Moeur
Photography Cass Bird
Account Team Emmanuel Ferry
Nathalie Chopra
Advertiser Wrangler, "Stunt" Campaign

////////////// TEXT WHILE YOU'RE DRIVING
////////////// AND YOU'RE 23 TIMES MORE LIKELY
////////////// TO HAVE AN ACCIDENT

TASTE THE GOOD OLD DAYS
MENIER

Agency Abbott Mead Vickers BBDO, London
Executive CD Paul Brazier
Creative Directors Ant Nelson, Mike Sutherland
Photography Trevor Ray Hart
Producer Simon Pedersen
Final Artwork Mark Deamer
Advertiser London Borough of Tower Hamlets, “Girls”

Agency Publicis Conseil, Paris
Creative Directors Olivier Altmann, Fabrice Delacourt, Olivier Desmettre
Copywriter Patrice Lucet
Art Directors Philippe Boucheron, Antoine Dezes-Richard
Photography Herve Plumet
Art Buying Soone Riboud
Acct. Supervisor Celine Colin
Clients Bernd Homann, Florence Audoyer
Advertiser Menier Chocolate, “Old Days”

Nº27
XCTRAVELS.COM

Nº35
XCTRAVELS.COM

Nº42
XCTRAVELS.COM

Advertising Photography

Agency	Forsman & Bodenfors, Gothenburg
Copywriter	Fredrik Jansson
Art Directors	Staffan Lamm Andreas Malm
Art Designer	Mikko Timonen
Account Team	Anders Bothén Anna Levegård
Client	Bengt Junemo
Advertiser	Volvo XC, “XC Travels”

Schweppes
Fruits...well kind of.

TAXI
Schweppes
Lemon
Schweppes
Fruits...well kind of.

Agency	Fred & Farid, Paris
Creative Directors	Fred Raillard Farid Mokart
Copywriters & ADs	Fred Raillard Farid Mokart Feng Huang
Photography	David LaChapelle
Art Buying	Carmela Guiragossian
Account Team	Nathalie Chopra
Clients	Hugues Pietrini Stanislas de Parcevaux
Advertiser	Schweppes, "Uma"

CHARGE. PART SALE.
bloomingdale's

BRAUN
Silk-épil

BRAUN
Silk-épil
precision trimmer

Agency Lowe Mena, Dubai
Creative Director Komal Bedi Sohal
Copywriters Komal Bedi Sohal, Mansoor Bhatti, Umer Razzak
Art Directors Komal Bedi Sohal, Mansoor Bhatti
Photography Tejal Patni
Advertiser Bloomingdale's Dubai, "Charge"

Agency Impact BBDO, Dubai
Executive CD Fouad Abdel Malak
Copywriter Darren McCall
Art Directors Mohammed Diaa, Mark Held, Andrej Arsenijevic
Photography Andreas Franke
Illustrator Mladen Penev
Art Buying Mariam Moin
Account Team Talal Sheikh Elard, Noura Al Nazer
Client Omar Saheb
Advertiser Braun, "Monkey" & "Squirrel"

THOUSANDS OF PEOPLE
OWE THEIR LIVES TO ORGAN DONORS
Sign up for your donor's card at france-adot.org
FRANCE
ADOT

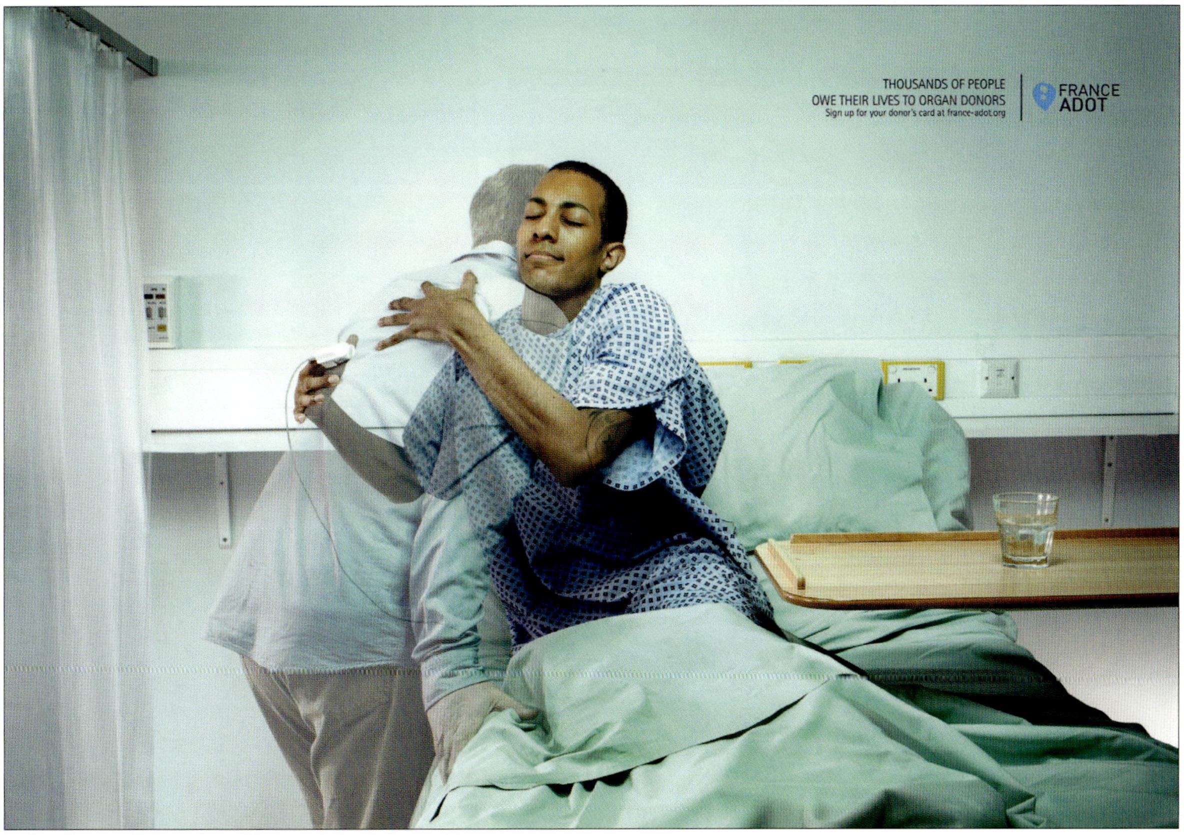
THOUSANDS OF PEOPLE
OWE THEIR LIVES TO ORGAN DONORS
Sign up for your donor's card at france-adot.org
FRANCE
ADOT

Agency CLM BBDO, Paris
Creative Directors Jean-Francois Sacco
Gilles Fichteberg
Copywriter Julien Perrard
Art Director Lucie Vallotton
Photography Deirdre O'Callaghan
Advertiser France Adot Organ Donation,
"The Ghost"

the art of preserving vitamins
With peelers by WMF
WMF

the art of saving time
With peelers by WMF
WMF

 Illustration

Agency	KNSK, Hamburg
Creative Directors	Tim Krink Ulrike Wegert
Copywriter	Dieter Kolaja
Art Directors	Julian Heidt Thomas Thiele Oliver Fermer
Photography	Peter Backens
Graphic Design	Julian Heidt Sara Stowasser
Account Director	Kirsten Kohls
Advertiser	WMF, "Peelers"

EVERY 60 SECONDS A SPECIES DIES OUT.
EACH MINUTE COUNTS. EACH DONATION HELPS: BUND.NET
BUND
FRIENDS OF THE EARTH
10
11
12
1

STIHL® MS 880
EXTREMELY STRONG POWER
THE STRONGEST CHAINSAWS IN THE WORLD. STIHL.com

Agency	Scholz & Friends, Berlin
CCO	Martin Pross
Executive CO	Matthias Spaetgens
Creative Directors	Florian Schwalme Mathias Rebmann
Art Directors	René Gebhardt Bjoern Kernspeckt Ksenia Slavcheva Sebastian Frese
Illustration	Peppermill, Berlin
Account Mgr.	Christine Scharney
Advertiser	BUND, "Time Up, Life Over"

Agency	Scholz & Friends, Berlin
CCO	Martin Pross
Executive CO	Matthias Spaetgens
Creative Director	Michael Winterhagen
Copywriter	Felix John
Art Director	Philipp Weber
Illustration	Recom, Berlin
Post Production	Recom, Berlin
Account Team	Benjamin Baader Sven Weiche Albert Petzold
Advertiser	Stihl Chainsaws, "Warriors"

Coca-Cola
1886
2011
125 years of sharing happiness

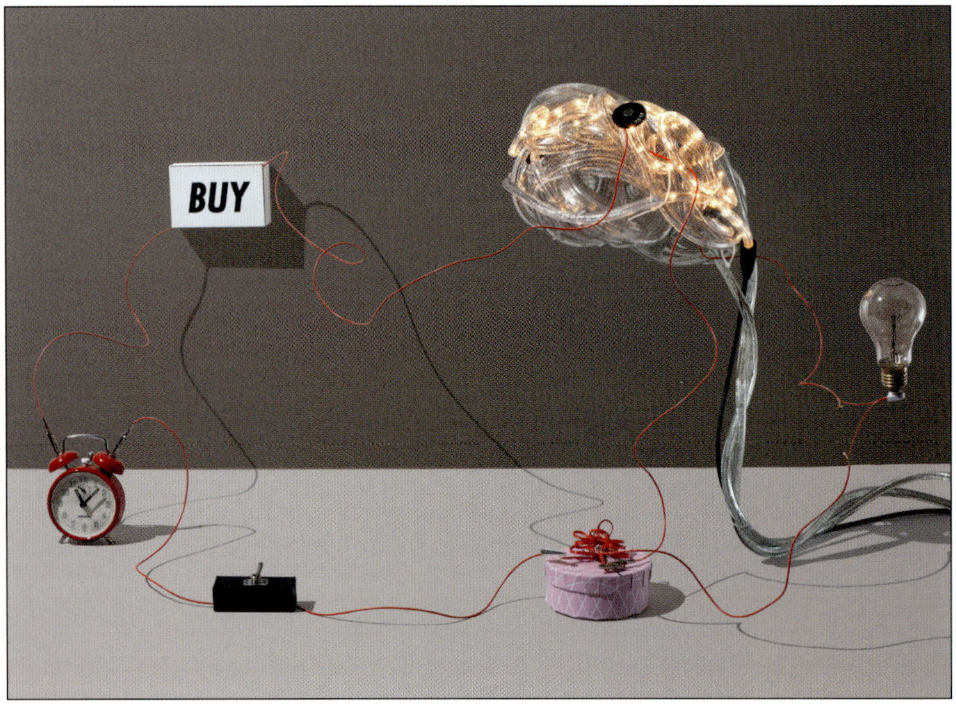
BUY

 Illustration

Agency	Bcube, Milan
Creative Director	Francesco Bozza
Copywriter	Bruno Vohwinkel
Art Director	Daniele Pancetti
Illustrator	Lorenzo Petrantoni
Graphic Design	Lorenzo Petrantoni
Typographer	Lorenzo Petrantoni
Advertiser	Coca-Cola, "Bubbles"

Agency	Ogilvy, Frankfurt
Creative Directors	Helmut Meyer Delle Krause
Art Director	Catrin Farrenschon
Illustrator	Sarah Illenberger
Producer	Bianca Elbert
Photography	Alexander Pfaff Johanna Woetzel
Art Buying	Nathalie Schulz
Artwork	Joachim Becker Peter Belz
Advertiser	Ogilvy Germany, "HowTo Magazine"

THE FAMILY HOT FAN
A FEMALE SYMBOL SHAPED FAN
BY KIRSI NISONEN
& JANI LEINONEN
TASTEBUDDIES BY HEINEKEN

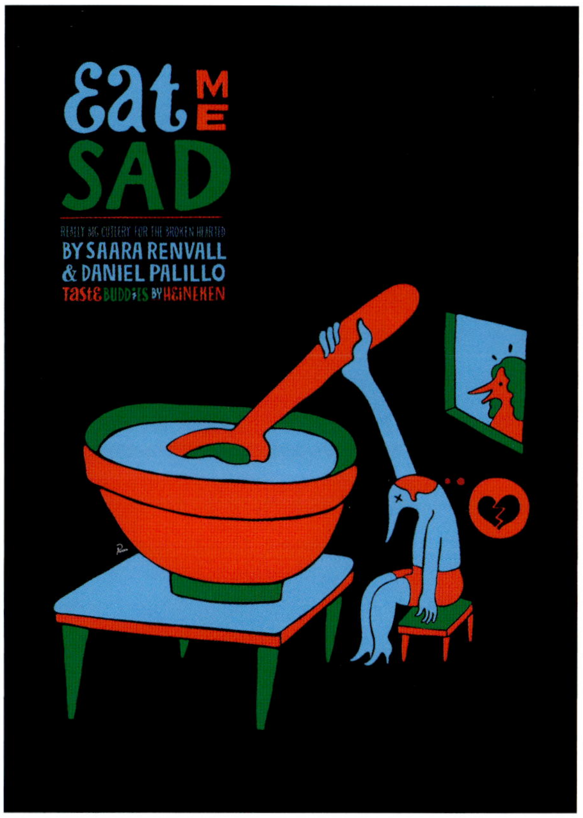
Eat ME SAD
REALLY BIG CUTLERY FOR THE BROKEN HEARTED
BY SAARA RENVALL
& DANIEL PALILLO
TASTEBUDDIES BY HEINEKEN

THE MIKROGRAPH. PRECISE TO 1/100TH OF A SECOND
TAGHeuer

Agency	358 Helsinki
Creative Directors	Erkki Izarra Antero Jokinen
Copywriters	Valtteri Väkevä Jonathan Mander
Art Director	Maria Fridman
Illustrator	Parra
Graphic Design	Ville Kovanen
Typographer	Parra
Producers	Peggy Petrell Petra Yli-Hemminki
Strategy	Panu Nordlund
Advertiser	Heineken, "Tastebuddies"

Agency	CLM BBDO, Paris
Creative Directors	Jean-Francois Sacco Gilles Fichteberg Fabien Mouillard
Copywriter	Jamie Standen
Art Director	Mark Forgan
3D Production	Mécanique Générale, Paris
3D Designer	Baptiste Masse
Art Buying	Sylvie Etchemaite
Advertiser	Tag Heuer, "Precision"

NO GUTS NO GLORY
SOÖRUZ
Snowboard - Winter 2011 collection

NO GUTS NO GLORY
SOÖRUZ
Wakeboard - Summer 2011 collection

Agency	Ogilvy, Frankfurt
CCO	Stephan Vogel
Copywriter	Peter Strauss
Art Director	Christian Leithner
Account Manager	Michael Fucks
Clients	Monika Zilleken Peter Gerdemann
Advertiser	IBM, "Unknown Artists"

With the right tools, data can be depicted in an artistic way. Indeed, as this intriguing calendar from IBM demonstrates, data visualization can become art. The various pictures are created by transforming different forms of data into imagery: from the fluctuating price of gold on the stock market, to the number of births around the world and even the path of lost luggage.

Agency	Publicis Conseil, Paris
Creative Directors	Olivier Altmann Frederic Royer
Copywriter	Didier Aerts
Art Director	Alexandra Offe
Illustrator	Jean-Marie Vives
Art Buying	Jean-Luc Chirio
Account Team	Jean-Patrick Chiquiar Laetitia Vitalis Sophie Gustinelli
Clients	Yann Dalibot Matthieu Barat
Advertiser	Sooruz, "Jump"

Museum of Childhood
Bethnal Green
museumofchildhood.org.uk
V&A
kids soon discover fingers aren't just for sticking up nostrils.

Museum of Childhood
Bethnal Green
museumofchildhood.org.uk
V&A
CHILDREN.
PLASTICINE.
WHO'S
STRETCHING
WHO?

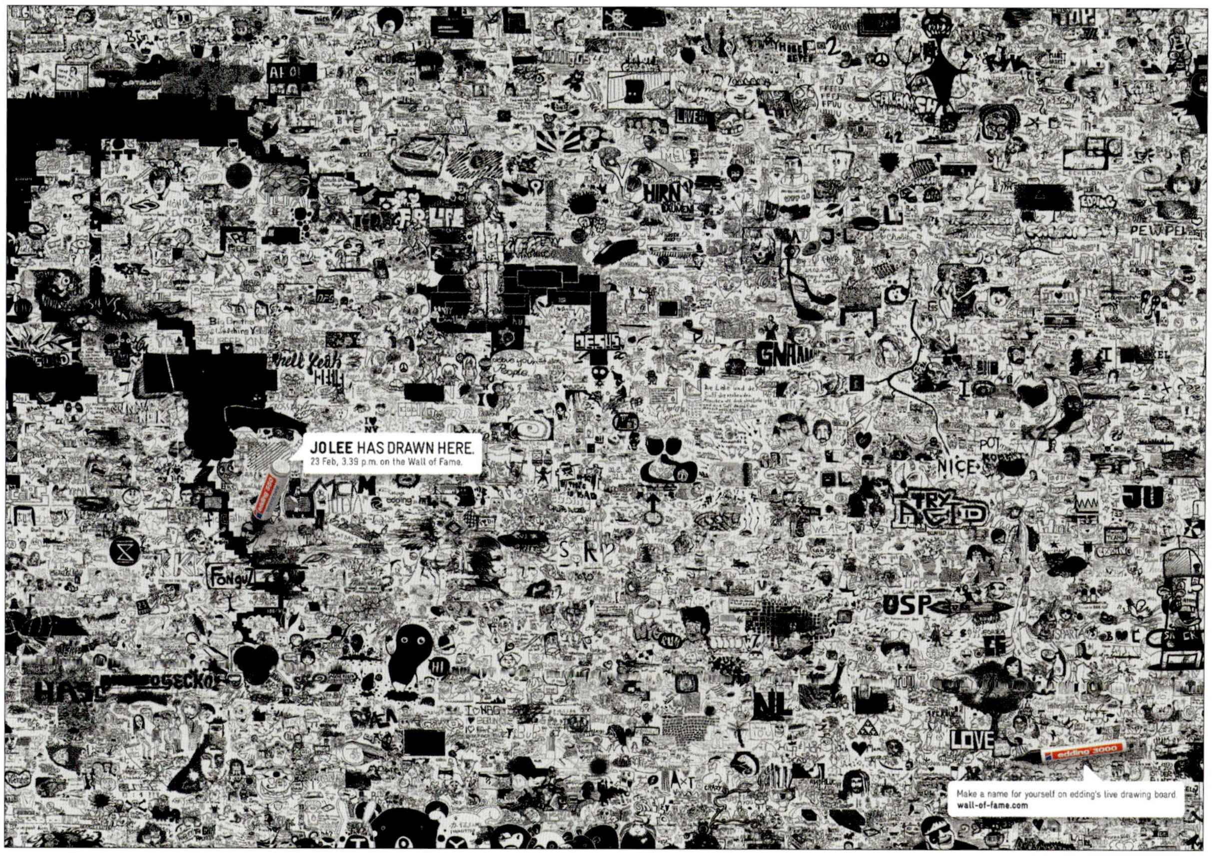
JOLEE HAS DRAWN HERE.
23 Feb, 3.39 p.m. on the Wall of Fame.
Make a name for yourself on edding's live drawing board
wall-of-fame.com

Agency	Abbott Mead Vickers BBDO, London
Executive CD	Paul Brazier
Creative Director	Mark Fairbanks
Illustrator	Mick Marston
Art Producer	Kirstie Johnstone
Advertiser	V&A Museum of Childhood, "Nostrils" & "Plasticine"

Agency	kempertrautmann, Hamburg
Creative Directors	Simon Jasper Philipp Christoph Gähwiler Stefan Walz
Art Directors	Simon Jasper Philipp Stefan Walz Florian Schimmer
Graphic Design	David Scherer Tobias Lehment
Programming	Demodern Digital Design Studio, Cologne
Advertiser	Edding, "Wall of Fame"

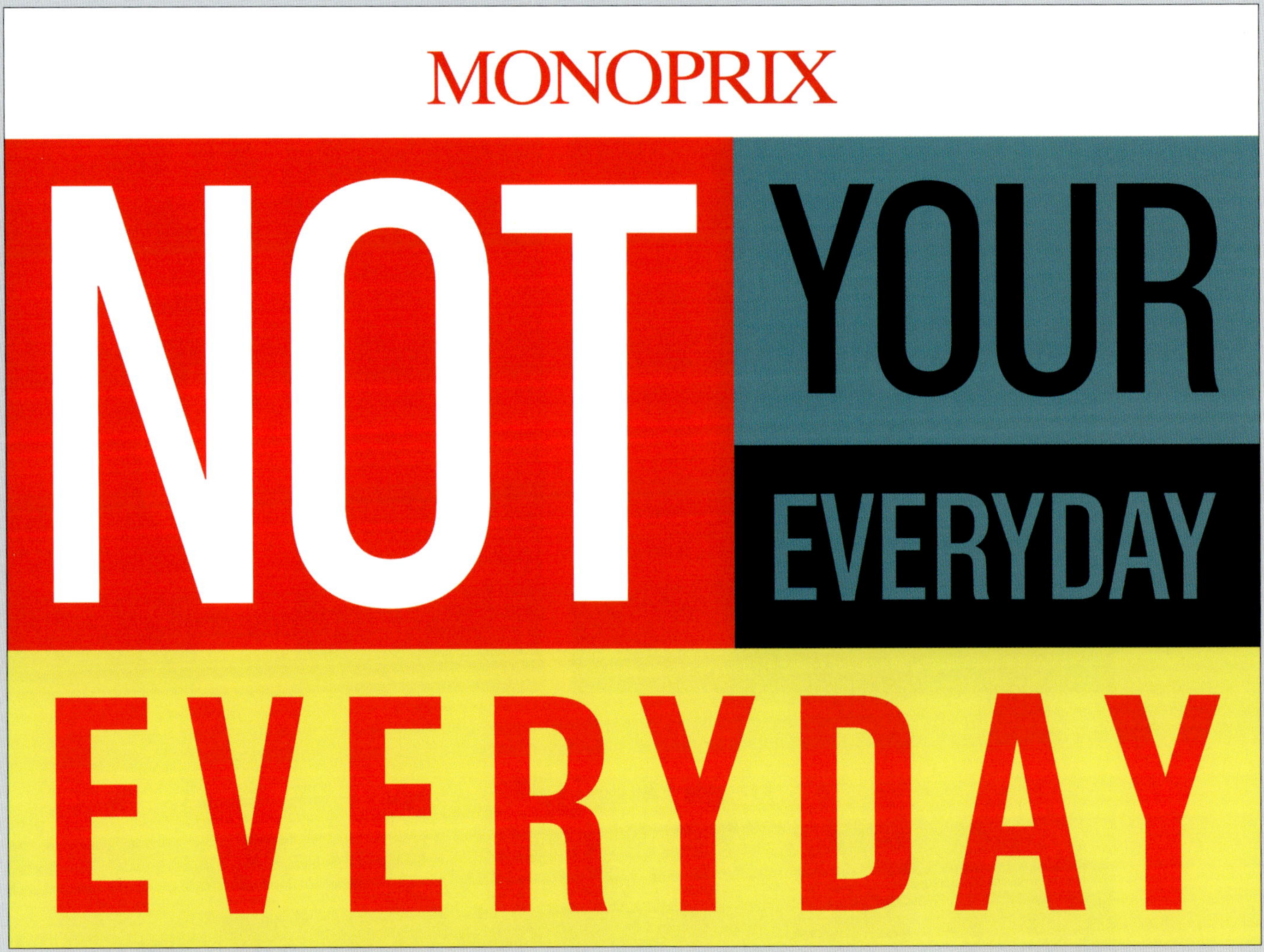
MONOPRIX
NOT
YOUR
EVERYDAY
EVERYDAY

MONOPRIX
12 ROLLS
BE KIND TO YOUR BOTTOM
MONOPRIX
ALMOST
TOO GOOD
TO FLUSH

2 CHEESEBURGERS
EAT LIKE HOLLYWOOD'S ELITE
MONOPRIX
NO TO JUNK
DESIGN

MONOPRIX
TEA
ENGLISH
MONOPRIX
OPEN THOSE
MORNING EYES
TO SOMETHING NICE

SPRING WATER FROM
THE ALPS
STILL MOUNTAIN WATER
MONOPRIX
STILL
BUT STILL
SPARKLING

Agency	Havas City, Paris
Creative Director	Florence Bellisson
Copywriter	Dominique Marchand
Art Directors	Jean-Michel Alirol Pierre Boutin
Illustrator	Baptiste Massé
Design Concept	Cleo Charuet
Designer	Arnaud Deroudilhe
Account Team	Charlotte David Anne-Cécile Galloy Aurélie Fossoux
Art Buying	Chloé Bartoletti Virginie Moitessier
Advertiser	Monoprix, "Not Your Everyday Everyday"

Monoprix, France's leading city-centre supermarket chain, created new packaging to give more visibility and impact to its own-label products. The actual contents are not shown, just named in big capital letters accompanied by an amusing comment or word-play. 2,000 products received this treatment. The graphic look also translated to advertising in shop windows and on billboards across France, with the slogan, "Not your everyday everyday". Clearly inspired by Pop Art, the design is bold yet optimistic and underlines Monoprix's message: daily life should be beautiful and fun.

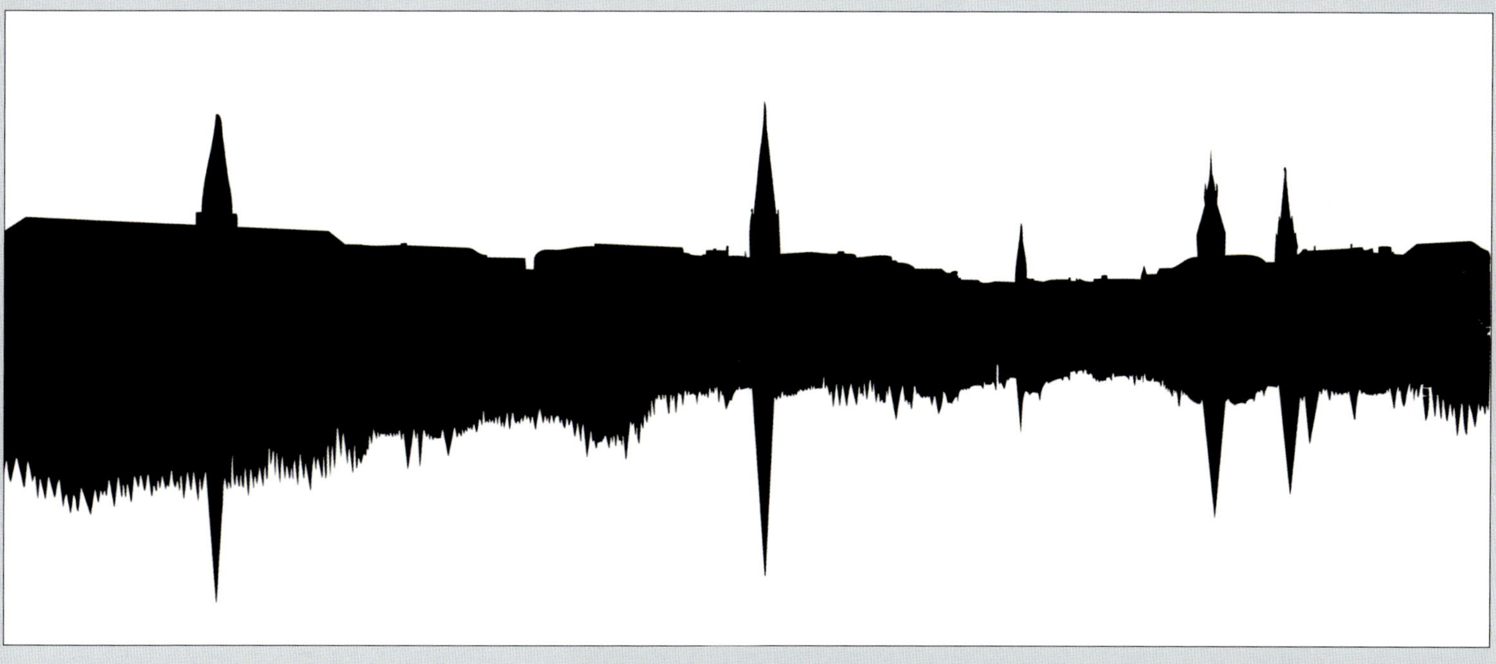

Agency kempertrautmann, Hamburg
Creative Directors Marcell Francke, Patrick Matthiensen
Copywriter Sebastian Merget
Art Directors Leif Johannsen, Bruno Luglio
Production Audioforce, Berlin
Cinematographer Eric Bosaller
Account Team Constanze Frink, Caterina Leisinger
Advertiser Philharmoniker Hamburg, "A Sound Logo - Inspired by Hamburg"

The brief was to create a "sound logo" that echoed the Philharmoniker Hamburg orchestra's deep relationship with the city and its culture. The idea: Hamburg's beautiful skyline is reflected in the Alster lake. In fact, the reflection resembles a sound wave. A composer transformed this wave into a unique sound logo, directly inspired by Hamburg.

THE
PENCIL
RANKINGS

100 BESTE PLAKATE 10
DEUTSCHLAND ÖSTERREICH SCHWEIZ
neuesmuseum
30. JULI BIS 2. OKTOBER 2011

Agencies Turner Duckworth Design, London & San Francisco
CDs David Turner, Bruce Duckworth
Designer Jamie McCathie
Typographers Jamie McCathie, David Bateman
Advertisers The One Club and D&AD, "Pencil Rankings Logo"

The One Club and D&AD joined forces to provide a creative ranking system for the advertising, design, interactive and communications industries. Turner Duckworth created a logo for these rankings that stripped back and combined the iconic shapes and colours of the two organisations to create a distinctive new brand identity.

Agency Phocus Brand Contact, Nürnberg
Creative Director Darius Gondor
Production Hopf Design, Schwanstetten
Producer Robert Brzuske
Project Manager Sabrina Weyh
Advertiser 100 Beste Plakate

This die-cut poster was designed to promote an exhibition of the 100 best posters from Germany, Austria and Switzerland. The poster can be used flexibly; it could be glued over classic outdoor billboards to reveal new content each time, used on mirrors and as press ads, with its high-impact yellow colour ensuring recognition each time.

„HOUSTON,
WE HAVE
A PROBLEM."
LOEWE Individual 3D – a new reality.
LOEWE.

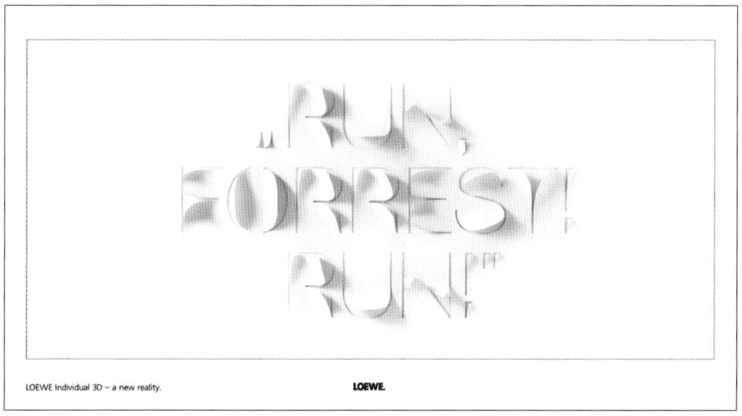
„RUN,
FORREST!
RUN!"
LOEWE Individual 3D – a new reality.
LOEWE.

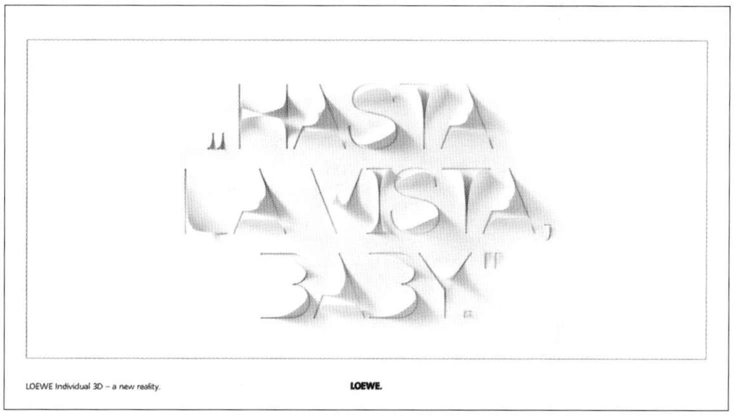
„HASTA
LA VISTA,
BABY."
LOEWE Individual 3D – a new reality.
LOEWE.

„HASTA
LA VISTA,
BABY."

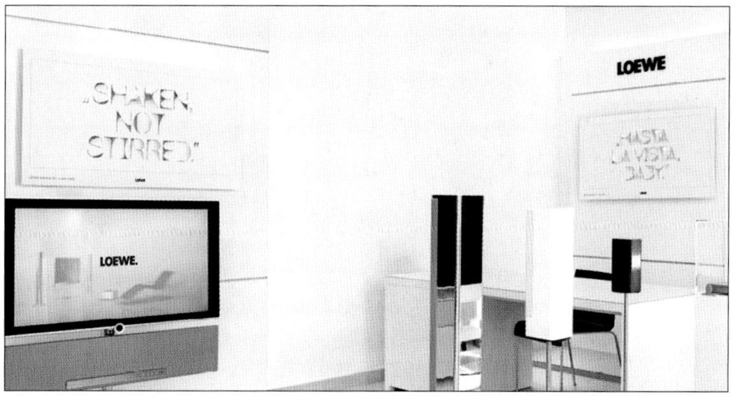
„SHAKEN,
NOT
STIRRED."
LOEWE
„HASTA
LA VISTA,
BABY."
LOEWE.

Agency	Scholz & Friends, Berlin
CCO	Martin Pross
Executive COs	Matthias Spaetgens Wolf Schneider
Copywriter	Gito Lima
Art Directors	Gito Lima Juergen Krugsperger Desiree Denner
Typographer	Gito Lima
Acct. Team	Stefanie Wurst Joris Jonker
Advertiser	Loewe 3D TVs, "3D Posters"

Thanks to 3D technology, viewers will be able to watch older movies in a whole new way. To communicate this, Loewe took unforgettable movie quotes and expressed them on in-store posters that were specially cut to create a 3D effect.

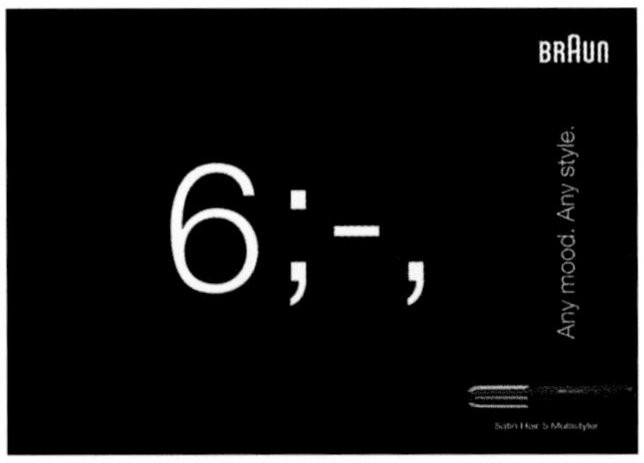
BRAUN
6;-,
Any mood. Any style.

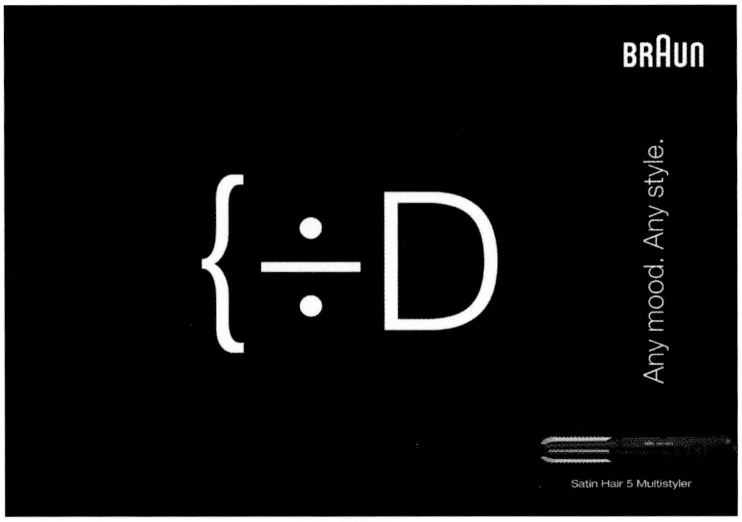
BRAUN
{÷D
Any mood. Any style.
Satin Hair 5 Multistyler

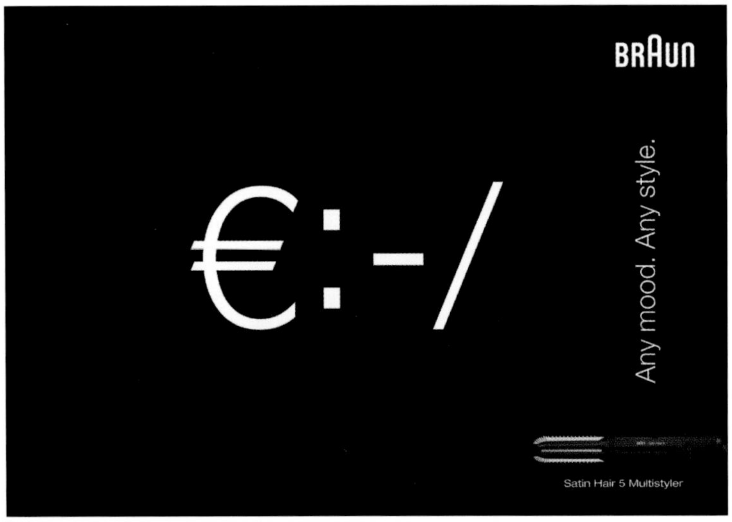
BRAUN
€:-/
Any mood. Any style.
Satin Hair 5 Multistyler

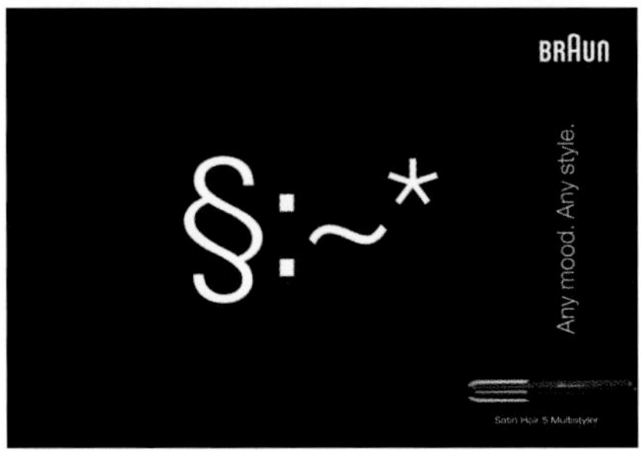
BRAUN
§:~*
Any mood. Any style.

Agency Studio International, Zagreb
Creative Director Boris Ljubicic
Advertiser Clavis (Music Teachers Association), "Chopin 200"

The poster for music teachers at the Clavis piano school celebrated the 200th anniversary of Chopin's birth in an unusual way. It drew a comparison between the piano keyboard and Venetian blinds: by moving your fingers on the blind, you can let more or less light in – allowing for a visual representation of playing a Chopin sonata. Students and teachers loved the poster for the way it turned sound into vision. And the windows of their building are shaded with exactly this sort of slatted blind.

Agency BBDO Proximity, Düsseldorf
CCOs Christian Mommertz, Wolfgang Schneider
Creative Director Olaf Reys
Copywriter Christopher Fink
Art Directors Stephan Eichler, Thomas Satori, Sebastian Steinhoff
Account Director Phoebe Moll
Advertiser Braun Multistyler, "Hairmoticons"

Emoticons are no longer bald! With the "Hair Emoticons" one can express one's mood with an individual hair style, just like in real life.

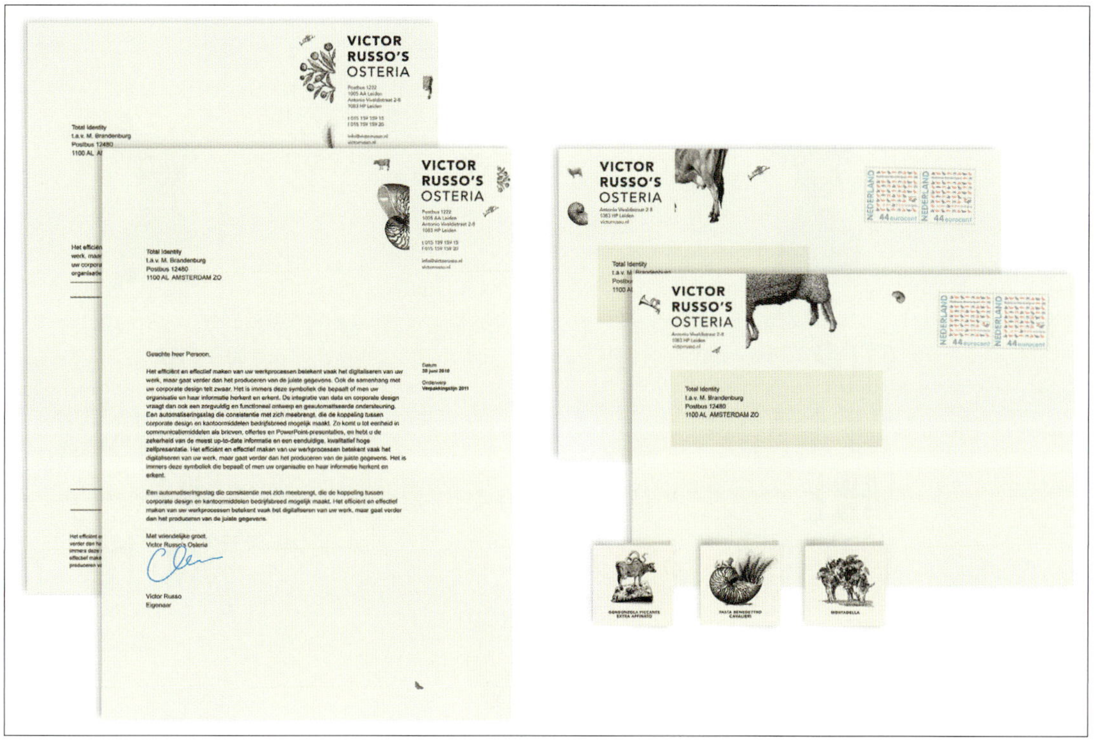
VICTOR
RUSSO'S
OSTERIA

FRIENDS

Agency Total Identity, Amsterdam
Creative Director Felix Janssens
Art Directors Maarten Brandenburg, Felix Janssens
Illustrator Maarten Brandenburg
Advertiser Victor Russo's Osteria, Corporate Design

Victor Russo is an enthusiastic young Italian entrepreneur with a passion for his national cuisine. The graphic identity programme is based on 18th century engravings to demonstrate the authenticity of his traditional offerings.

Agency & Co., Copenhagen
Art Director Sanne Frank
Advertiser Friends Film Company, Corporate Identity

Friends is a Danish film production company that defines its mission as a friendly cooperation between client, agency and crew. So all elements of its corporate identity are designed to reflect the idea of friendship; the merging letters in its logo, the green/black yin/yang graphics and the photos of friends on the roll of adhesive tape that resembles a reel of film.

STOP
THE WATER
WHILE
USING ME!
ALL NATURAL
ORANGE WILD HERBS
SHOWER GEL

STOP
THE WATER
WHILE
USING ME!
ALL NATURAL
LEMON HONEY
SOAP

PINO

PINO

PINO

Agency Kolle Rebbe/KOREFE, Hamburg
Creative Director Katrin Oeding
Copywriters Thomas Voelker, Till Felber
Art Directors Christine Knies, Christian Doering
Photography Robin Kranz, Ulrike Kirmse
Graphic Design Saara Jaervinen, Derya Sevim
Advertiser Stop the Water While Using Me!

The minimalistic design and absence of colours reinforce the ideas of conservation and environmental protection that are at the heart of this new skin-care range's promise. "Stop the Water While Using Me!" aims to set new ethical production standards in an ecologically aware society.

Agency Bond, Helsinki
Creative Directors Jesper Bange, Aleksi Hautamäki
Photography Paavo Lehtonen
Advertiser Pino Corporate Identity

Pino is a shop that sells functional and innovative design objects. The store's new graphic identity is inspired by its name; Pino, which means "pile" or "stack" in Finnish. This idea is extended from the logo to the interior design of the stores themselves.

dizao organics
100% NATURAL
95% ORGANIC

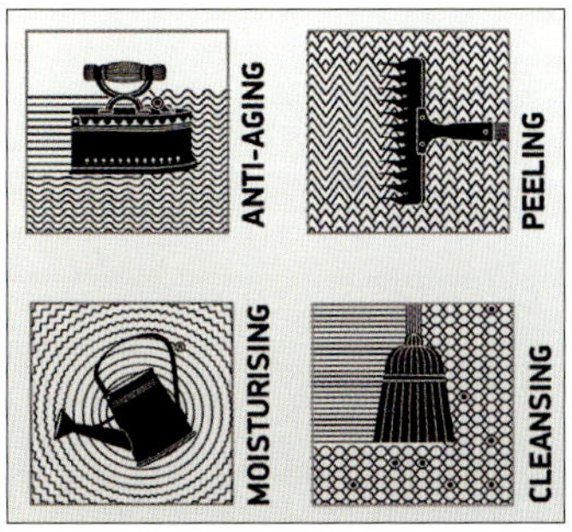
ANTI-AGING
PEELING
MOISTURISING
CLEANSING

TRIAL

MOTHER

Agency Depot WPF, Moscow
CD Alexey Fadeev
Art Director Lyudmila Galchenko
Pre-Press Kurban Kurbanmagomedov
Advertiser Dizao Organic Skin Care Products

Black and white graphics convey the essence of each product in this new skin-care range and are the basis of the brand's identity. A system of symbols showing the functionality of each product replace written descriptions that are relegated to the back panel of the packaging.

Agency Ogilvy, Frankfurt
CCO Stephan Vogel
Creative Director Peter Strauss
Art Director Christian Leithner
Artist Julius Popp
Exhibitor Victoria & Albert Museum, London
Account Manager Veronika Sikvoelgyi
Client Barbara Windisch
Art Buying Christina Hufgard
Advertiser SAP, "Bit.Code by Julius Popp"

What if software could create art? SAP teamed up with artist Julius Popp during an exhibition of digital art at the Victoria & Albert Museum in London. Popp built a giant black and white puzzle whose sliding "pixels" formed words filtered from the web in real time by SAP software. A website and documentary described the "Bit Code" project, which attracted coverage from the art and computer press, as well as mainstream media.

NUR
NICHT DEN
FADEN
VERLIEREN

HALT
MAL DIE
LUFT
AN.

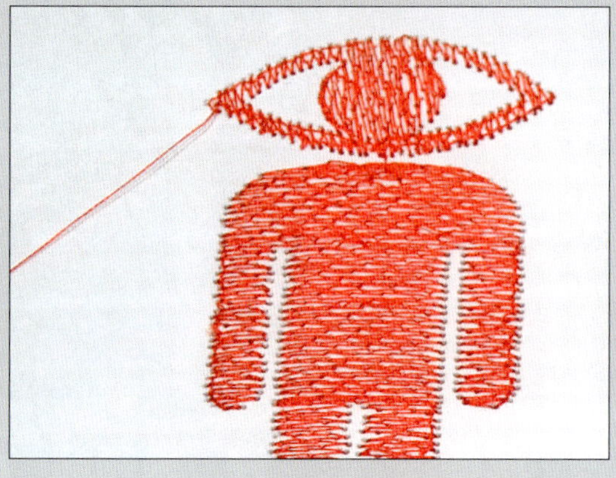

DAS
KANNST DU
LAUT
SAGEN.
SPRICH KLAR
UND DEUTLICH.

ALLES
BEHALTEN?
FÜR GEDÄCHTNIS
UND KONZENTRATION:
GINKGO PLUS

Agency	Ogilvy & Mather, Düsseldorf
Creative Directors	Rainer Maass Rob Bruenig
Copywriters	Katharina Kiklas Markus Bredenbals
Art Director	Sandra Prescher
Producers	Carol Redfield Markus Jaeger
Embroidery	Eleonore Bappert
Bindery	Buchbinderei Mergemeier
Advertiser	Abtei Ginkgo Plus, "The Red-Thread-Book"

Abtei Gingko Plus is a dietary supplement that aids memory and concentration. Ever lost the thread of a subject during a talk or a presentation? That may be a thing of the past. The book contains ten tips for university students who are under pressure to perform at exam times and its entire contents are stitched onto the pages with a single red cotton thread.

JANUAR
Ein Jahr ohne Zigarette. Und Ihre Lunge atmet auf. www.aok.de/ich-werde-nichtraucher
AOK

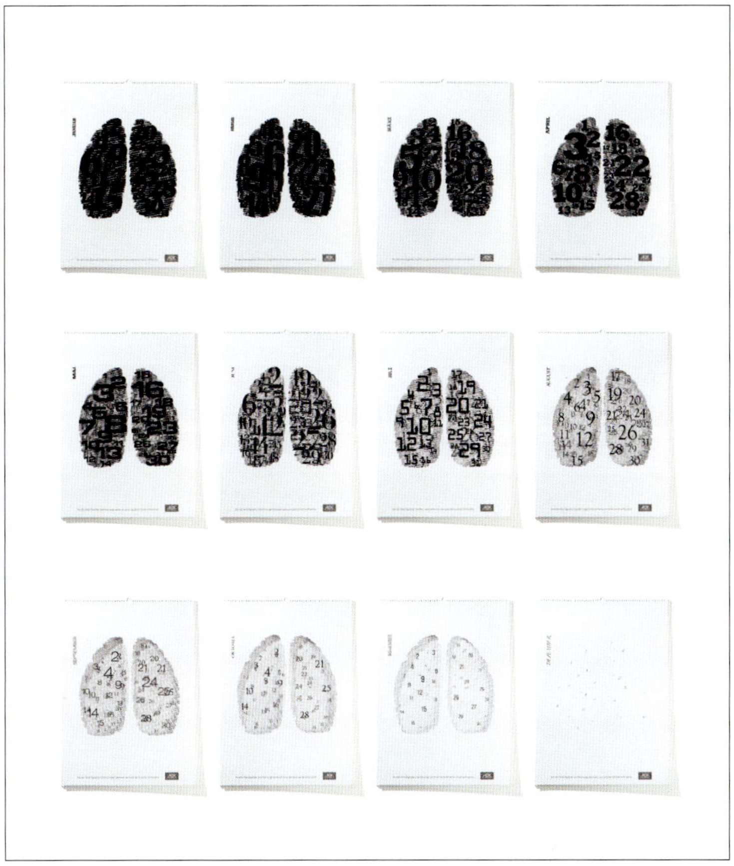

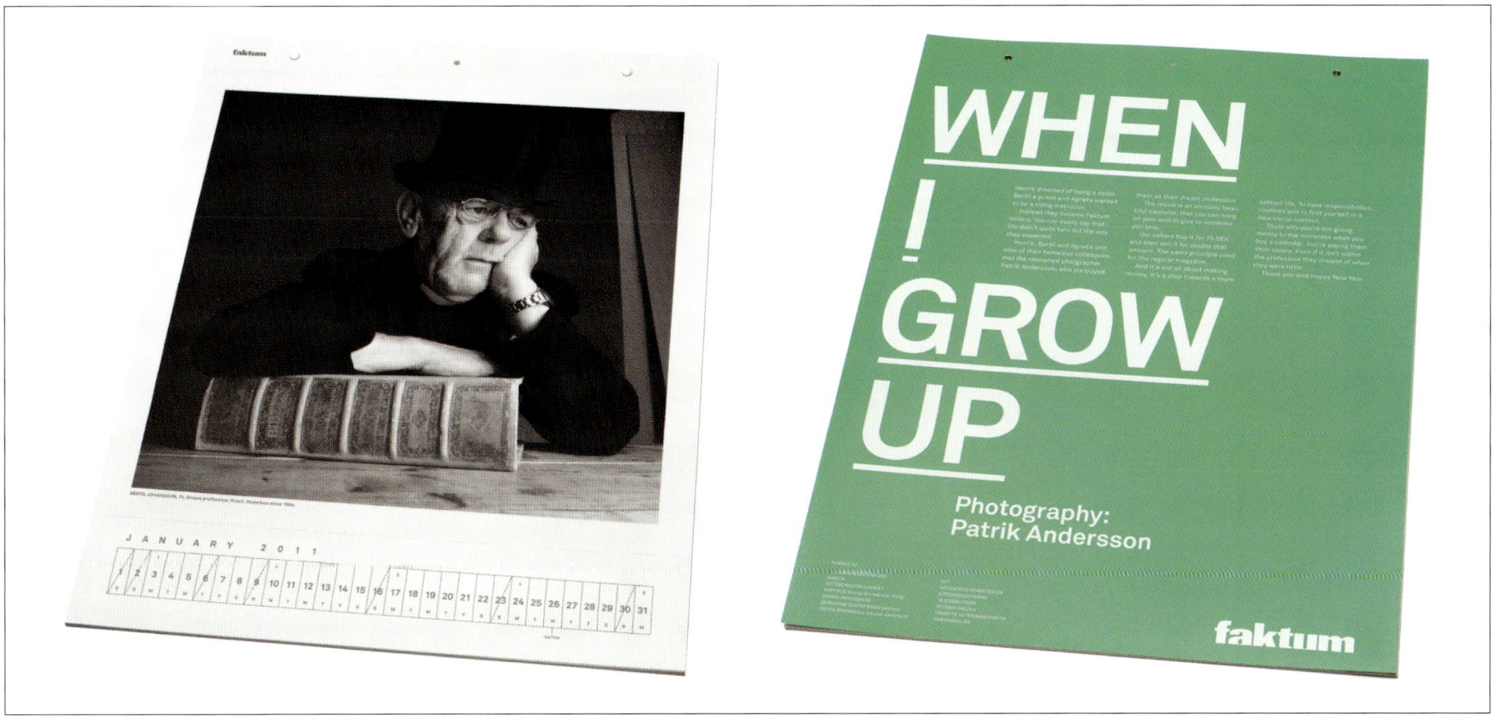
JANUARY 2011
WHEN
I
GROW
UP
Photography:
Patrik Andersson
faktum

Agency Serviceplan, Munich
CDs Mike Rogers, Wolfgang Nagel
Copywriter Christoph Bohlender
Art Director Wolfgang Nagel
Producers Gabi Grötzbach-Fischer, Johannes Keppler
Advertiser AOK Health Insurance, "The Non-Smokers Art Calendar"

This typographic calendar promotes a "quit smoking" programme run by insurance company AOK. As you can see, the blackened lungs of January grow gradually less murky as the year goes by, until after a year of non-smoking they are clean again.

Agency Forsman & Bodenfors, Gothenburg
Copywriter Martin Ringqvist
Art Director Staffan Forsman
Photography Patrik Andersson
Designers Staffan Håkansson, Christoffer Persson
Account Team Susanna Fagring, Linda Tiderman
Client Max Markusson
Advertiser Faktum, "When I Grow Up"

Faktum is Gothenburg's monthly street magazine, sold by the homeless. Of course, homeless people start out with other dreams and ambitions. The magazine's 2011 calendar gave some of them a chance to live those dreams, at least for a month, in collaboration with photographer Patrik Andersson. Henrik dreamed of being a sailor. Bertil wanted to be a priest. Agneta a riding instructor. Life didn't quite work out as they planned, but proceeds from the calendar sales helped give them a more settled existence.

HOW
TO
2
Die
schwarze
Ausgabe
HOW
TO
.2

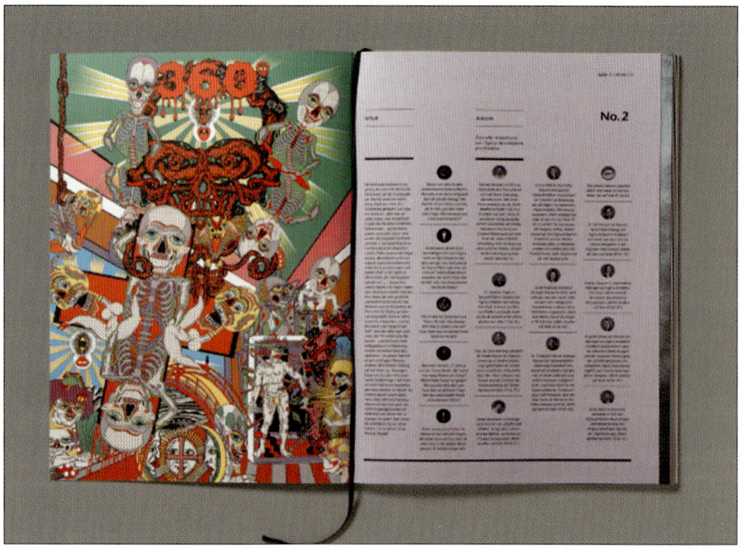
360
No.2

360

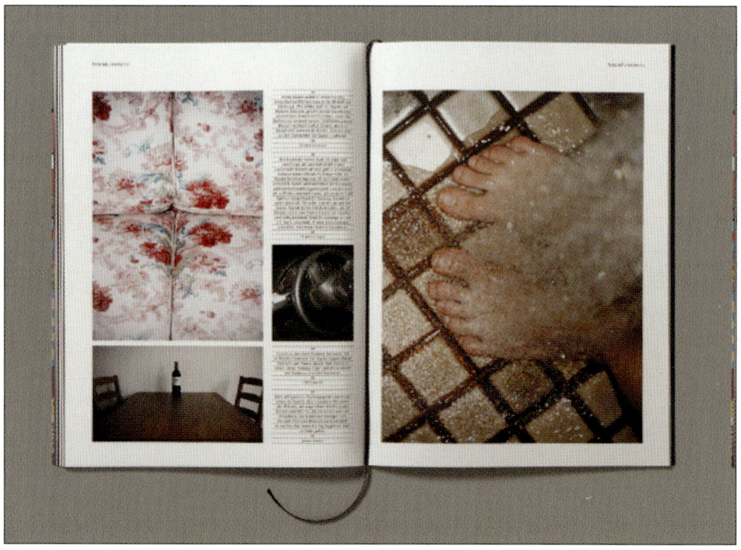

Publication Design

Agency	Ogilvy, Frankfurt
Creative Directors	Helmut Meyer Delle Krause
Art Directors	Helmut Meyer Catrin Farrenschon
Photography	Joachim Bacherl Oliver Blohm
Producer	Bianca Elbert
Final Artwork	Joachim Becker Peter Belz
Designer	Helmut Meyer
Editors	Thomas Strerath Jonas Baily Alexander Pfaff Johanna Woetzel
Art Buying	Nathalie Schulz
Advertiser	Ogilvy Germany, “HowTo Magazine” (The Black Issue)

This corporate magazine by the German outpost of Ogilvy provides inspiring ideas about how to negotiate the digital age. Due to the success of the first HowTo magazine, a second edition was produced for a discerning target audience of marketing opinion leaders. Renowned illustrators such as Hampus Erickstam, Markus Färber, Nora Fehr, Sarah Illenberger, Keeichi Tanaami and Nick White contributed their work. Guest authors include leading academics, advertising experts and retail professionals.

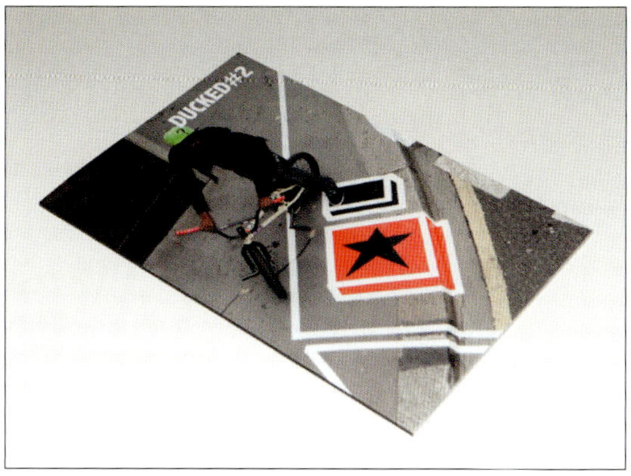
DUCKED#2

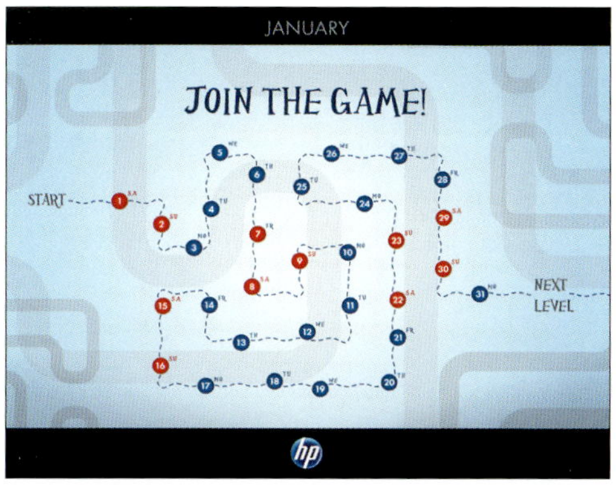
JANUARY
JOIN THE GAME!
START
NEXT LEVEL

FEBRUARY
COMMUNICATE!

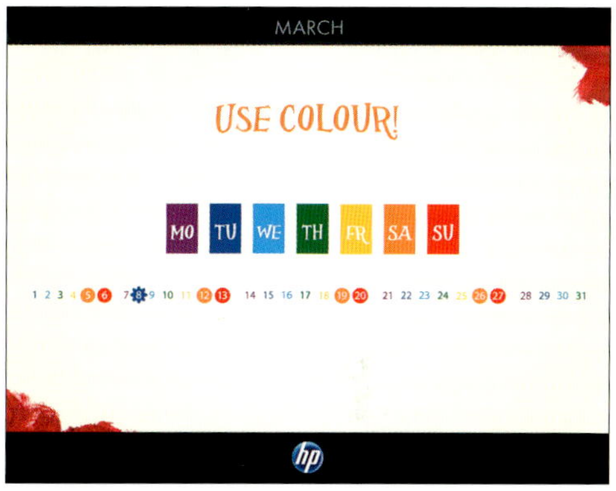
MARCH
USE COLOUR!
MO TU WE TH FR SA SU

APRIL
MAKE A CALCULATION!

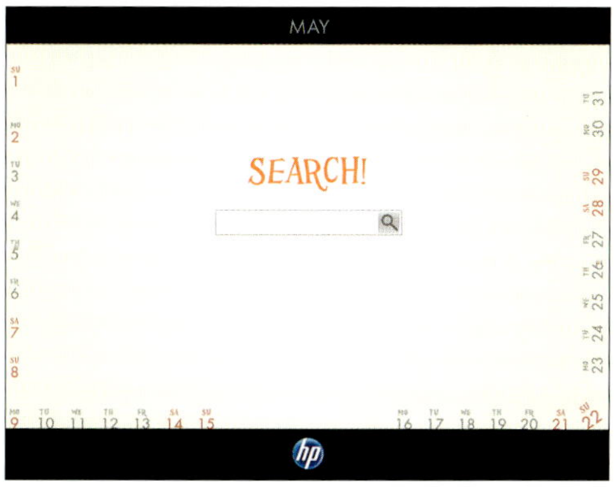
MAY
SEARCH!

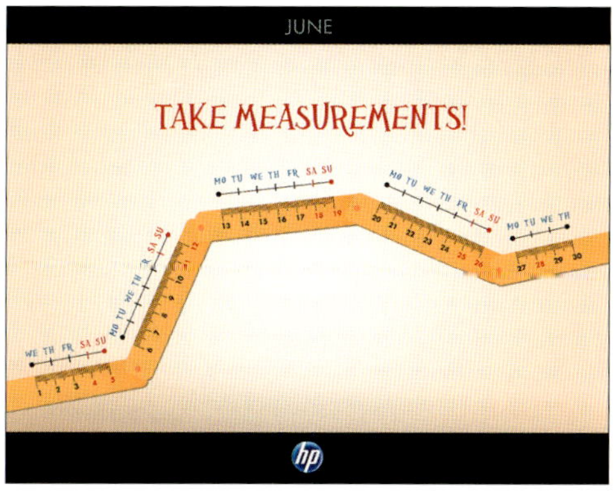
JUNE
TAKE MEASUREMENTS!

Agency SapientNitro, London
European CCO Malcolm Poynton
CDs Justin Barnes, Ben Callis
Copywriter Justin Barnes
Art Director Ben Callis
Photography Alexander Basile
Producer Dan Eagles
CSD James Graham
Account Mgr. Tempe Hughes
Advertiser Foot Locker, In-Store Magazine "Ducked"

The "Ducked" magazine series was produced as part of a mixed media campaign to launch the new Converse Padded Collar range of sneakers. Issues were given as a gift-with-purchase in branches of Foot Locker across Europe. The title refers to the use of duct tape by graffiti artists to create a new form of street art. By encouraging the artists to wear Converse sneakers, the brand became associated with the "tape art" phenomenon.

Agency Publicis Visage, Kiev
Creative Director Julia Rukavitsina
Copywriter Viktoriya Bodnarchuk
Art Director Ruslan Palamarchuk
Illustrator Ruslan Palamarchuk
Producer Olga Tolkunova
Designer Ruslan Palamarchuk
Advertiser Hewlett-Packard, Corporate Calendar

A month is not just a page in a calendar – it's part of your life that you can spend doing all sorts of interesting and creative things. To reflect this idea, a calendar for HP offered 12 entirely different calendar formats, giving people the opportunity to play games, make calculations, prioritize tasks and so on. At the same time, it revealed the equivalent HP product features.

2011
HEUTE.
AUF DER TITELSEITE
VON GESTERN.
Frankfurter Allgemeine
ZEITUNG FÜR DEUTSCHLAND
Frankfurter Allgemeine
ZEITUNG FÜR DEUTSCHLAND
Frankfurter Allgemeine
THE NEWSPAPER FOR GERMANY
2011
TODAY.
ON YESTERDAY'S
FRONT PAGE.
365 Front Pages from over 50 Years
of Frankfurter Allgemeine Zeitung.

Agency Scholz & Friends, Berlin
CCO Martin Pross
Executive CD Matthias Spaetgens
Creative Directors Mathias Rebmann, Florian Schwalme
Copywriter Nils Tscharnke
Art Director Johannes Stoll
Producer Franziska Ibe
Account Team Marie Toya Gaillard, Eva Verena Schmidt
Advertiser Frankfurter Allgemeine Zeitung, "The Front Page Calendar"

The task was to develop a premium giveaway to promote the high-quality coverage the Frankfurter Allgemeine Zeitung (FAZ) has been delivering since 1949. The answer was to use the daily newspaper's archive to create a tear-off calendar comprising 365 full-size front pages. The pages spanned six decades of contemporary history; they were carefully selected to match the date and weekday combinations of 2011.

2011
КВІТЕНЬ
ТРАВЕНЬ
ЧЕРВЕНЬ

03
П'ЯТНИЦЯ
02
ЧЕРВНЯ

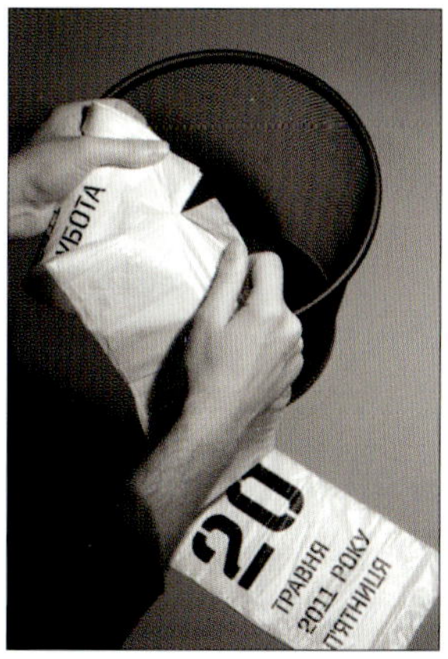
20
ТРАВНЯ
2011 РОКУ
П'ЯТНИЦЯ

01
КВІТНЯ
2011 РОКУ
П'ЯТНИЦЯ

2011
Januar
Februar
März
April
Mai
Juni
Juli
August
September
Oktober
Dezember
FIT
Lieferung zum Wunschtermin.
PAKETVERSAND & SPEDITION

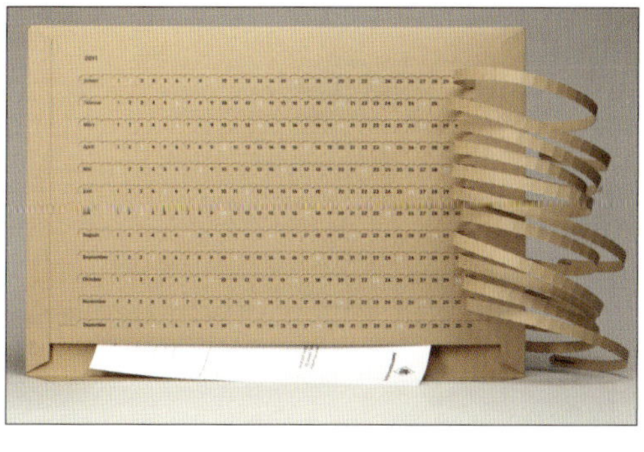

Agency Yurko Gutsulyak Graphic Design Studio, Kiev
Creative Director Yurko Gutsulyak
Art Director Yurko Gutsulyak
Producer Zoryana Gutsulyak
Advertiser Yurko Gutsulyak Graphic Design Studio, "Trash Calendar"

This calendar from a graphic design studio takes the fatalistic view that every piece of design ultimately ends up in the trash. Thus, every day is a new trash bag, with one roll of bags for every month. The date is printed on each bag so that you can see it when the bag is placed in the trash bin. The text on the calendar suggests that only useful designs are really successful.

Agency Heye & Partner, Munich
Creative Directors Fabian Hinzer, Zeljko Pezely, Jan Okusluk
Copywriter Christina Meister
Art Director Marcus Feil
Producers Alex Birner, Silvia Balog
Advertiser FIT Logistics, "The Prefered Date Calendar"

At first glance, the FIT logistics calendar looks like a normal craft envelope, but on the back it features not one, but 12 opening strips, one for each month. Underneath each strip there's a calendar that reveals itself day-by-day, until the end of December when the envelope is finally opened. Inside there's an order form for the following year's calendar with the message, "Delivered by your desired deadline."

THE DELI GARAGE
ESSLACKIEREREI
VIER LEBENSMITTELSPRÜHFARBEN
THE DELI GARAGE
ESS LACK GOLD
ESS LACK SILBER
ESS LACK BLAU
ESS LACK ROT

ESS LACK GOLD
ESS LACK ROT

THE DELI GARAGE
SCHOKO
BACK STEINE
400g | 6 BACKSTEINFÖRMCHEN
100% GLUTENFREI
THE DELI GARAGE
STRACCIATELLA
BACK STEINE
300g | 6 BACKSTEINFÖRMCHEN
REINES DINKELMEHL

SCHOKO
BACK STEINE

Agency Kolle Rebbe/KOREFE, Hamburg
CD Katrin Oeding
Copywriters Till Felber, Gereon Klug, Thomas Voelker
Art Director Reginald Wagner
Photography Ulrike Kirmse
Production Romey von Malottky, Hamburg
Account Mgr. Kristina Wulf
Advertiser The Deli Garage, "Food Paint Shop"

The Deli Garage was founded in a disused factory and this is the inspiration of all its packaging. The brand's core idea is to combine high-quality design with the functionality of garage tools. The Paint Shop is food-finish confectionery made specially for your own spray colouring ideas. Use the perforated stencils to liven up any type of delicacy in gold, silver, blue or red.

Agency Kolle Rebbe/KOREFE, Hamburg
CD Katrin Oeding
Copywriters Till Felber, Thomas Voelker
Art Director Reginald Wagner
Photography Ulrike Kirmse
Production Romey von Malottky
Graphic Design Derya Sevim, Marko Grewe
Account Mgr. Marie Steinhoff
Final Artwork Maik Spreen
Advertiser The Deli Garage

Brickstones; the world's first cake mix packed in miniature cement bags. Instead of muffins, cupcakes or do-nuts, bricks are now served on the table. The six cake moulds serve as an inspiration for creative cake constructions. Used in conjunction with the Deli Garages Paint Shop products, the results become even more spectacular.

Portion 1
PESTO
TRÜFFEL
20
30
40

TRÜFFEL
PESTO
THE DELI GARAGE
KÄSE STIFTE
CHILI . PESTO . TRÜFFEL
INKL. ANSPITZER
Markieren Sie Ihre Pasta, Ihre Pizza oder Ihren Salat mit einer fein gespitzten Käsespirale.
PORTIONIERUNGS-VORSCHLÄGE
Von Käsestiften kann man nie genug bekommen. Aber es reicht, wenn Sie sich an diese Portionierungsvorschläge halten.
Bitte trennen Sie das Schutzpapier vor dem Anspitzen an der perforierten Stelle ab.

THE DELI GARAGE
LUTSCH WERK ZEUG
GESCHMACKS ANLEITUNG
Rot = Himbeere
Gelb = Zitrone
Orange = Bitterorange
18 g Genuss

Agency Kolle Rebbe KOREFE, Hamburg
Creative Director Katrin Oeding
Copywriter Thomas Voelker
Art Director Reginald Wagner
Photography Ulrike Kirmse
Producer Franziska Ziegler
Account Mgr. Marie Steinhoff
Advertiser The Deli Garage, "Parmesan Pencils"

Take the Parmesan Pencil, sharpen it using the enclosed pencil sharpener and you have delicious, fresh Parmesan cheese on your meal. There couldn't be an easier way to decorate your pasta and salads. And the packaging also plays a central role: using a scale on the pens and on the back of the packaging, it's not only easy to tell how much grated Parmesan Pencil you need for each dish, you can even see how many calories each serving contains.

Agency Kolle Rebbe KOREFE, Hamburg
Creative Director Katrin Oeding
Copywriter Gereon Klug
Art Directors Reginald Wagner, Christine Knies
Photography Ulrike Kirmse
Producers Franziska Ziegler, Arne Trost
Advertiser The Deli Garage, "Lolly Tools"

The Deli Garage's Lolly Tools are lollipops in six different flavours, shaped like screwdrivers and packaged in the same kind of blister packs used for drill bits and other workshop tools. The authentic screwdriver-look extends to the stick itself that's also made from sugar confectionery.

Bandelė
Bun
I won't get angry
if you eat me secretly.

Dark
Although I was born dark,
my roots are in Lithuania.
Tamsi

1944

Batonas
Long Loaf

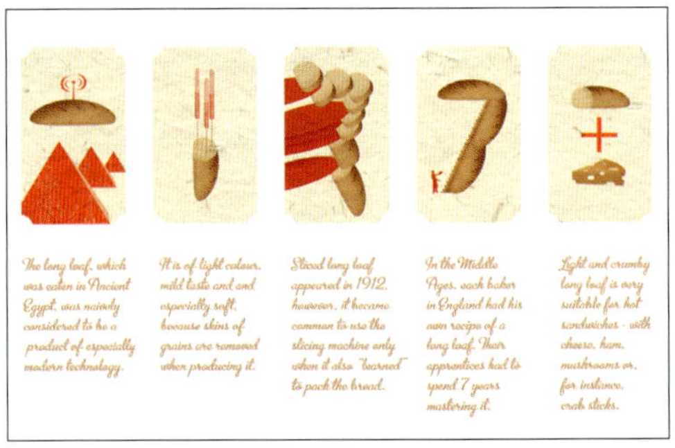

Duona be E
Bread
with no E additives

Na
K
Mg
Ca
P

Agency Love, Vilnius
Creative Director Tomas Ramanauskas
Copywriter Aiste Jure
Art Director Migle Rudaityte
Illustrator Darius Uzpalis
Advertiser Made in IKI, "When People Dream of Tasty Bread"

Lithuanian retail chain IKI wanted updated packaging for its in-house bakery products. But instead of simply providing beautiful graphics, the designers invented…talking patisserie items. Each one was given a character and a voice via the packaging ("I won't mind if you eat me secretly," says a tempting croissant); fun historical facts about the products were also added (the Egyptians considered long loaves to be the product of new technology). The new designs not only increased sales, they also strengthened IKI's image as the tastiest food store in the market.

ECO
BAG
nature-friendly
garbage

ECO
BAG
nature-friendly
garbage
Camomile
Iris

PRET
MALDON
SEA SALT
HAND COOKED CRISPS
PRET
SEA SALT
&CIDER
VINEGAR
HAND COOKED CRISPS
PRET
MATURE
CHEDDAR
& RED ONION
HAND COOKED CRISPS
PRET
CURRY
LIME PICKLE
HAND COOKED CRISPS

Agency	Depot WPF, Moscow
CD	Alexey Fadeev
Copywriter	Ekaterina Lavrova
Designers	Vera Zvereva Yulia Zhdanova Maria Mordvintseva
Strategy	Olga Chernokova
Pre-Press	Kurban Kurbanmagomedov
Advertiser	EcoBag

The average person throws away about 300 bags per year. Most plastic bags will end up in a landfill decomposing for centuries (a thousand years on average). What if this troublesome product was turned into an ecologically-friendly one? The EcoBag's paper contains the seeds of various plants. Wherever users throw it away, it will disintegrate after rain and turn into a small lawn of grass, camomile or clover.

Agencies	Balloon Dog, Norwich & London
Creative Director	Cordell Burke
Art Director	Martyn Skillings
Photography	Richard Pullar Jorgen Ahlstrom
Production	Balloon Dog, Norwich
Account Team	Ella A'Court Will Cole
Advertiser	Pret Crisps

This new range of hand-cooked crisps from Pret aimed to clearly differentiate the flavours while maintaining the brand's obsession with good ingredients and its progressive approach to flavours. The packs are instantly recognisable as coming from Pret - clear, confident and with a touch of humour.

Diet Coke
12 CANS
Diet Coke
12 CANS
Diet Coke
12 CANS

STOP THE WATER WHILE USING ME!
ALL NATURAL ORANGE WILD HERBS SHOWER GEL
STOP THE WATER WHILE USING ME!
ALL NATURAL SESAME SAGE BODY LOTION
STOP THE WATER WHILE USING ME!
ALL NATURAL LEMON HONEY SOAP
STOP THE WATER WHILE USING ME!
ALL NATURAL ROSEMARY GRAPEFRUIT SHAMPOO

Agencies	Turner Duckworth Design, London & San Francisco
Creative Directors	David Turner Bruce Duckworth Sarah Moffat
Art Directors	Rebecca Williams Josh Michels
Client	Pio Schunker Hazel Van Buren
Advertiser	Coca-Cola, Diet Coke

As it's the number two sparkling beverage brand in the US, consumers were already familiar with Diet Coke. The Coca-Cola Company North America challenged Turner Duckworth to extend that confidence to Diet Coke's packaging. The resulting design provided a bold new perspective on the brand by focusing on the D and K as the most recognizable elements of the logo. The graphically cropped name is at the centre of a visual identity that appears in point of sale and advertising for Diet Coke.

Agency	Kolle Rebbe/KOREFE, Hamburg
Creative Director	Katrin Oeding
Copywriters	Thomas Voelker Till Felber
Art Directors	Christine Knies Christian Doering
Photography	Robin Kranz Ulrike Kirmse
Graphic Design	Saara Jaervinen Derya Sevim
Advertiser	Stop the Water While Using Me!

The "Stop the Water While Using Me!" skin care range is totally committed to environmental protection, even to the point of encouraging users to save water while applying the products. This positioning is reinforced by a minimalistic design without the use of colour, refillable biodegradable bottles with certified organic ingredients, no synthetic perfumes, colouring or preservatives and an ethical production process that eschews any form of animal testing. What more can a manufacturer do to demonstrate its social responsibility?

ИРИС С НАЧИНКОЙ
С ШОКОЛАДНЫМ ВКУСОМ
I will
THE FURTHER I LOOK
THE BETTER I NOTTICE
ИРИС С НАЧИНКОЙ
С ШОКОЛАДНЫМ ВКУСОМ
I will
ACHILLES HEEL
ИРИС С НАЧИНКОЙ
С ШОКОЛАДНЫМ ВКУСОМ
I will
TOFFEE IS NOT WHAT YOU EAT

PEAR
PEAR
PLUM
PLUM
APPLE
APPLE

Agency Depot WPF, Moscow
CD Alexey Fadeev
Illustrators Vera Zvereva, Vadim Briksin
Pre-Press Kurban Kurbanmagomedov
Advertiser I Will Toffees

"I Will" toffees are designed for young people. The graphic design takes its inspiration from photos and stories posted on social networks. The illustrations are non-judgemental and simply reflect the flow of life, as reflected on Facebook. Brand character is further reinforced by various amusing phrases under the logo, like "Toffee is not what you eat with a square face", and the absence of product images on the packaging.

Agency New Moment New Ideas Company Y&R, Skopje
Creative Director Dusan Drakalski
Art Director Nikola Vojnov
Designer Hari Dudeski
Advertiser Viva Juices, "Fruit Invaders"

The design brief for these special edition cartons of fruit juice was to come up with packaging that's "cool, modern and attention-getting". Inspiration came from the design team's nostalgia for their high-school days; they combined the fact that Viva only uses freshly squeezed fruits with the well-loved video game "Space Invaders". Vivid colours brought the iconic game into the modern era and ensured maximum in-store impact.

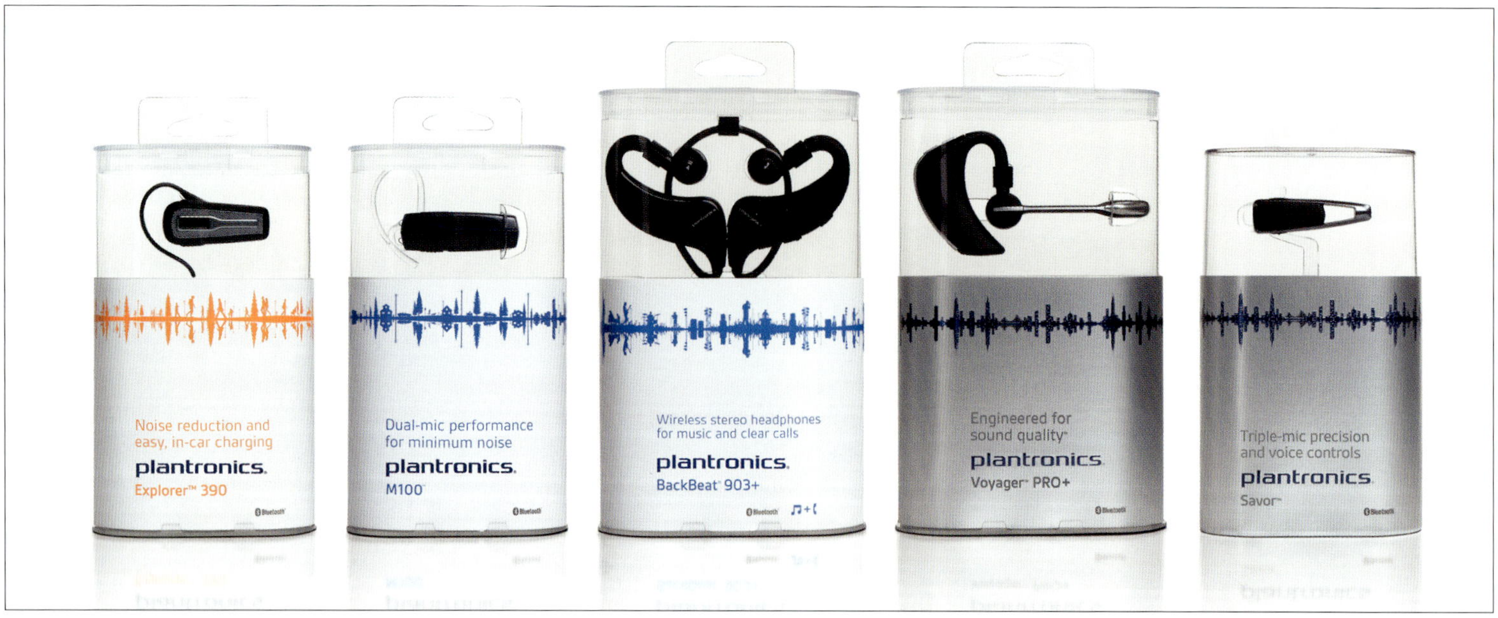
Noise reduction and
easy, in-car charging
plantronics.
Explorer™ 390
Dual-mic performance
for minimum noise
plantronics.
M100
Wireless stereo headphones
for music and clear calls
plantronics.
BackBeat 903+
Engineered for
sound quality
plantronics.
Voyager PRO+
Triple-mic precision
and voice controls
plantronics.
Savor

TRATA on ice

 Packaging Design

Agencies Turner Duckworth Design, London & San Francisco
Creative Directors David Turner, Bruce Duckworth, Sarah Moffat
Art Director Brian Steele
Advertiser Plantronics, "SoundWorld"

New packaging for Plantronics audio accessories feature a system of Sound-World icons adapted to each product. At first glance these resemble normal sound waves, but closer examination reveals details of the world around us; a park scene, a suburban commute, a cosmopolitan cityscape or a music venue. Each SoundWorld relates to the target consumer for the product in question with details of colour and finish further differentiating products across the range.

Agency Beetroot Design, Thessaloniki
CDs Yiannis Haralambopoulos, Alexis Nikou
Art Director Vangelis Liakos
Illustrator Alexis Nikou
Advertiser Trata on Ice, "Konva"

A black background, subtle typography and mono-coloured illustrations underline the quality of these frozen seafood products and give them a delicatessen feel. The cut-out illustrations show what part of the seafood is inside the package and allow it to be seen. The brand's V-shaped fishtail logo is reflected in the structure of the packages that are recognisable from any viewing angle.

Peeze
Peeze
Peeze
Peeze

MAKEDONSKO BELO
WHITE
SMEDEREVKA
WHITE
VILAROV
ROSE
VRANEC
RED
MAKEDONSKO CRVENO
RED
ALLEGRO
ROSE
AMINTA
RED
VRANEC VERITAS
RED

Agency Sogood, Haarlem
Creative Director Rob Verhaart
Photography Oscar Seijkens
Advertiser Peeze Coffee

Peeze has been producing premium quality coffee for 130 years. Sustainability across the Peeze range is illustrated by showing proud coffee growers from each country of origin enjoying the final product. With one strong image on each pack the brand does justice to the human side of the production process.

Agency New Moment New Ideas Company Y&R, Skopje
Creative Director Dusan Drakalski
Art Director Nikola Vojnov
Photography Dragoljub Nikolovski
Designer Jana Miseva
Advertiser Stobi Wines, "Wine is Music"

Every Stobi wine has a different taste, tone, aroma and alcohol content; like music, each wine is a different composition. For this reason, each wine is associated with a different musical instrument; for example, a drum for the strong local Vranec grape and a violin for the more sophisticated red Barrique. Eight different musical instruments were used to differentiate wine varieties across the range.

THE JUMPER
400 $

SAMURAI

BUY YOUR
SAMURAI
NOW.
Buy Now
450 €
Buy Now
620 $

Consumer Internet Sites - Durables

Agency Ogilvy, Frankfurt
Creative Directors Michael Kutschinski, Uwe Jakob, Jens Steffen, Ulf Schmidt
Copywriter Ulf Schmidt
Art Director Uwe Jakob
Programmer Jens Steffen
Animation Jens Steffen, Ralf Zimmermann
Developers Jens Steffen, Ralf Zimmermann, Frank Schwarzhoff, Isabell Grasshoff
Project Managers Jens Steffen, Uwe Jakob
Music & Sound Sinus AV Studio: Lars Kellner
Advertiser Moto Waganari, “Directing Shadows”

The brief was to create a virtual showroom for the filigree figures of Japanese sculptor Moto Waganari. But how to capture the beauty of these three-dimensional artworks on a screen? Especially since the figures require light and space to be truly appreciated. The solution: Directing Shadows, an interactive light gallery. Take your lighter or your smart phone display, hold it in front of your webcam. The light beam on the website reacts to your movements. Immerse into the play of light and shadow and hear the artist’s comments.

MINI PHOTO BOX

IT'S PERSONAL.
BE MINI.

IT'S PERSONAL.
BE MINI.

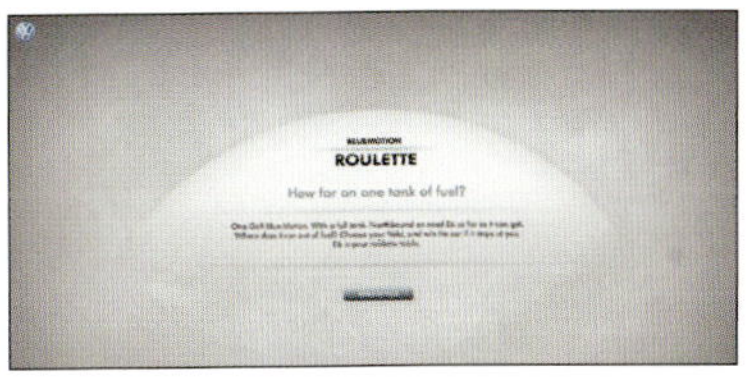
ROULETTE

0,38

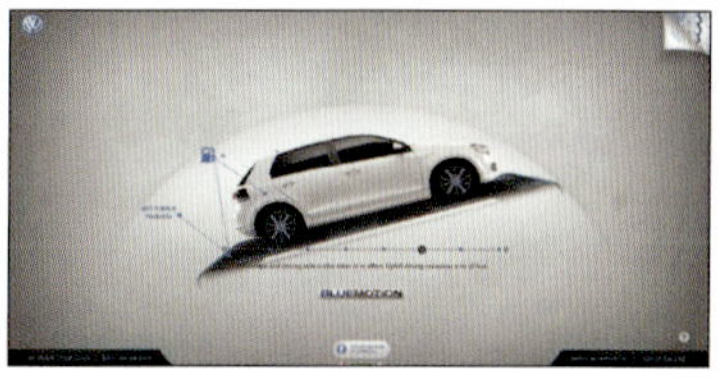

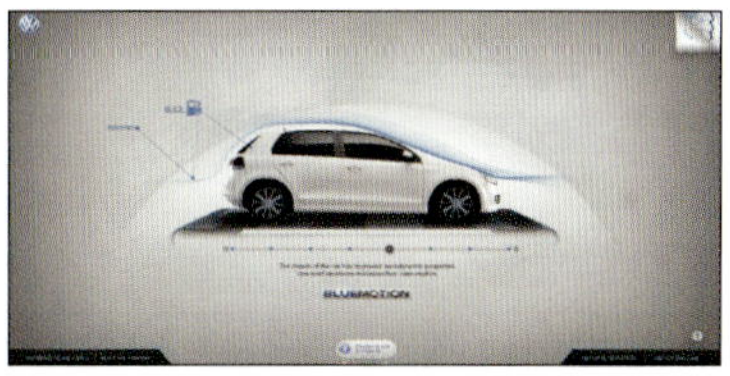

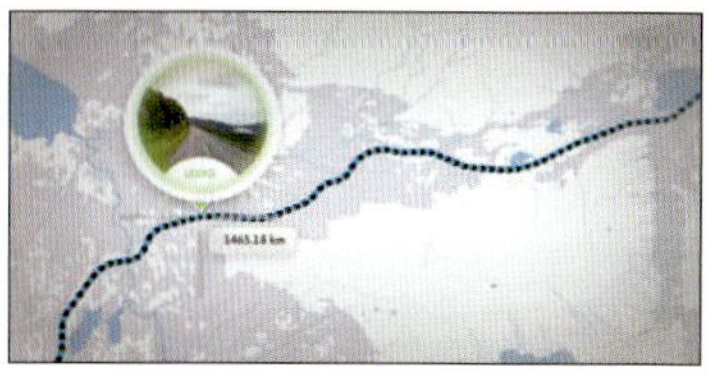

Agencies KKLD, Berlin & New York
Creative Director Alex Diehl
Copywriters Nathan Grigolla, Miho Tanaka
Art Directors Antonio Ferreira, Christian Meinke, Holger Herrmann
Head of Strategy Christoph Riebling
Head of Design Sascha Burk
Digital Concept Miho Tanaka
Project Mgrs. Fabian Blume, Stephan Lämmermann
Advertiser Mini, "Photo Box"

A photo booth was set up in the middle of Berlin. But not just any photo booth: those who entered could choose their preferred colour of Mini headphones and – just after they were snapped wearing them – see their portrait projected on a giant digital billboard across the street. People who couldn't make it to Berlin could join in the fun thanks to a Facebook page. Mini – it's personal.

Agencies Try, Oslo; Apt, Oslo
Copywriters Petter Bryde, Anders Holm, Sebastian Prestø, Eva Sannum
Art Directors Thorbjørn Ruud, Markus Lind
Production Gimpville, Oslo
Producers Cecilie Fasbender, Cathrine Wennersten
Advertiser Volkswagen Golf, "BlueMotion Roulette"

To demonstrate the VW Golf BlueMotion's economical fuel consumption, the E6 highway – the Norwegian equivalent of Route 66 – was turned into an interactive roulette wheel. As a Golf set off up the highway, visitors to the site could bet in real time on exactly where the car would run out of petrol. The road was divided into car-length roulette slots and bets were based on its fuel consumption and various other statistics that could be found on the car's website.

ROM
Baton cu
Cremă Rom
ROM
Baton cu
Cremă Rom

ROM
Baton cu
Cremă Rom
TRY THE NEW ROM
PATRIOTISM
WON'T FEED YOU
www.noulrom.ro

ROM
THE AMERICAN DREAM
NOW IN THE ROMANIAN
CHOCOLATE
TRY THE NEW ROM
www.noulrom.ro

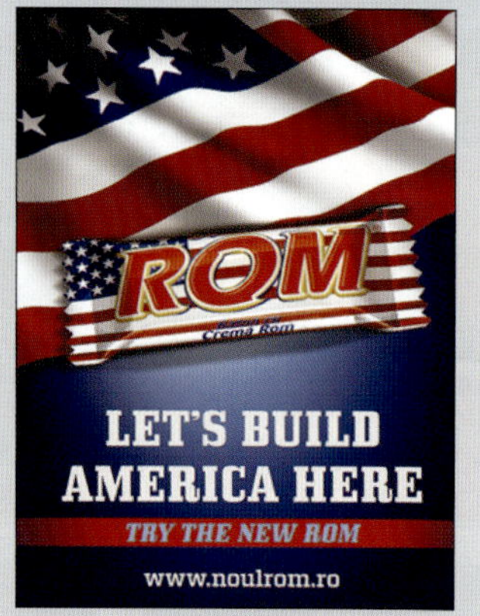
ROM
LET'S BUILD
AMERICA HERE
TRY THE NEW ROM
www.noulrom.ro

ROM

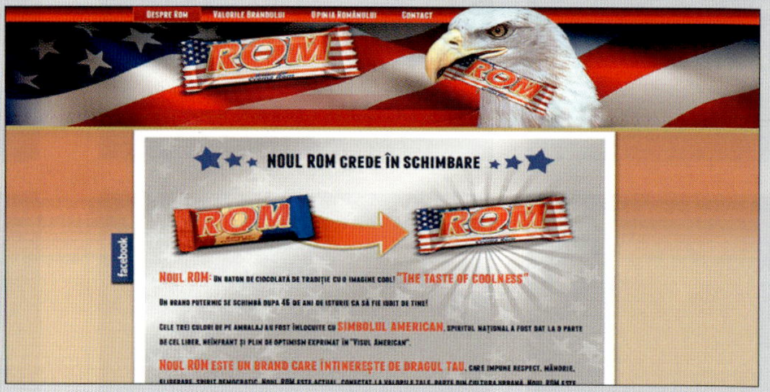
ROM
NOUL ROM CREDE ÎN SCHIMBARE
ROM
ROM
facebook
"THE TASTE OF COOLNESS"
SIMBOLUL AMERICAN

Agency	McCann Erickson, Bucharest	**Director**	Radu Munteanu
Creative Directors	Adrian Botan Catalin Dobre Dinu Panescu	**Strategic Planner**	Ileana Serban Parau
		Account Team	Ruxandra Savulescu Lavinia Vaduva
Copywriter	Florin Florea	**AV Producers**	Ilinca Nanoveanu Tiberiu Munteanu
Art Directors	Ionut Cojocaru Andra Badea	**Media Directors**	Alina Carasol Victor Croitoru Monica Stoica
Production	Multimedia Est, Bucharest	**Advertiser**	Rom, "American Rom"

Rom chocolate bar bears the Romanian flag on its wrapping. But its popularity was waning among the young in the face of overseas competition and disillusionment about life in Romania. In order to reclaim Rom as a national icon, the Romanian flag was replaced with…an American one. A TV ad featuring an annoying American ("now you can be proud to eat Rom") set the scene. Outraged comments came flooding in via a website, Facebook and Twitter. A second TV ad revealed the truth: the American takeover was just a joke. Rom would always be Rom. A patriotic ballad appeared on the site to celebrate this news.

Wrangler
WE ARE ANIMALS

930
Wrangler
WE ARE ANIMALS

Wrangler®
WE ARE ANIMALS
CREDITS
VIDEO

Wrangler

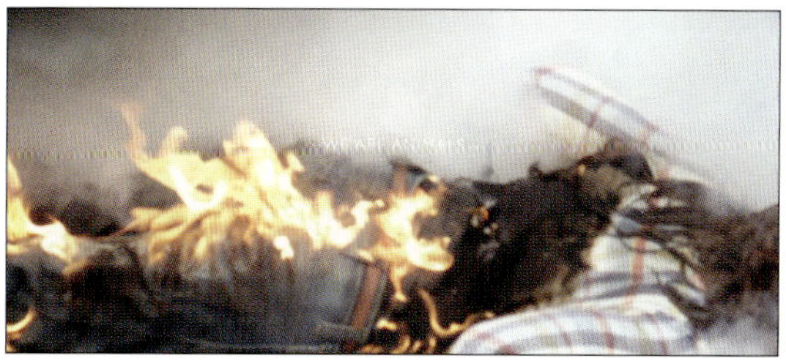

Agency	Fred & Farid, Paris
Creative Directors	Fred Raillard Farid Mokart
Copywriters	Fred Raillard Farid Mokart
Art Directors	Fred Raillard Farid Mokart Juliette Lavoix Céline Moeur
Photography	Cass Bird
Director	Cass Bird
Web Art Director	Assaf Dagan
Account Team	Emmanuel Ferry Nathalie Chopra Johanna Najar
Clients	Adam Kakembo Yasemin Akkaya
Advertiser	Wrangler, “Stunt”

Wrangler's slogan is “we are animals”. This campaign showed people trying to escape modern life in wild and dangerous ways, as enacted by stunt professionals. The visually stunning campaign was launched via an online gallery showing exclusive pictures from the shoot, as well as a teaser film. As the buzz began to build across blogs and social media, the images began to appear in the press, especially trendy magazines such as Dazed & Confused, Wear and i-D. There was also an outdoor element, including giant billboards in Warsaw. The stunts themselves recalled classic cowboy movies and referred obliquely to Wranger's heritage.

מכירת נשים לפי טעם אישי
WOMANTOGO
לילה
₪ 37,700
סופיה
₪ 22,500

WOMANTOGO
Katya
₪ 38,700

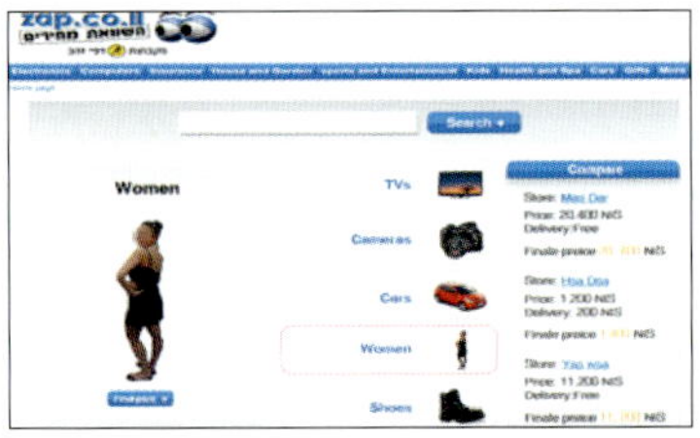
zap.co.il
Search
Compare
Women
TVs
Cameras
Cars
Women
Shoes

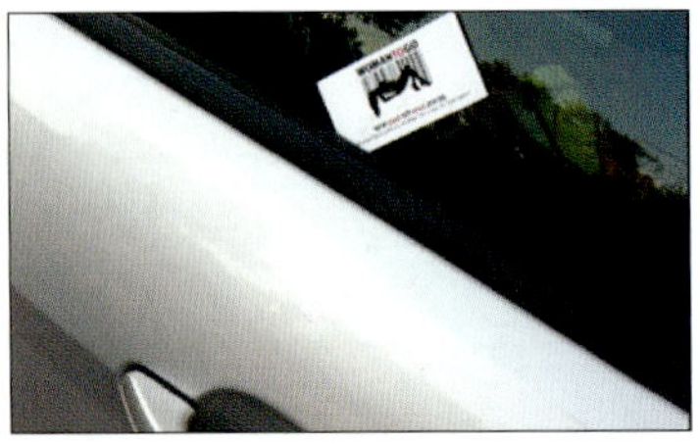

WOMANTOGO
WOMEN ARE NOT FOR SALE

WOMANTOGO

Agency Shalmor Avnon Amichay/Y&R Interactive, Tel Aviv
CCO Gideon Amichay
Executive CDs Tzur Golan, Zeev Ravid
Creative Directors Yariv Twig, Roy Cohen, Sagi Blumberg
Copywriters Oren Meir, Sharon Refael, Liron Ben Yakov
Director Roy Shalem
Art Directors Gil Aviyam, Dan Kashani
Photography Eyal Nevo, Uriel Sinai
Production Eyal Naor EXP, Tel Aviv
Producers Marina Akilov, Shira Robas, Sigal Nugasy
Programmer Roman Rozanov
Designer Gilad Boby
Head of Strategy Yoni Lahav
Advertiser Atzum Task Force On Human Trafficking

Aztum, the task force on human trafficking, wanted to draw attention to the plight of women sold into sexual slavery. In a busy Tel Aviv mall, it created a pop-up store that appeared to "sell" women, including price tags and statistics such as height, weight and country of origin. Task Force volunteers were on hand to explain. Online, a site was created where users could "purchase" women. And the price comparison site zap.co.il created a new category: women. A catalogue was sent to opinion leaders. And a YouTube video encouraged viewers to press the "Dislike" button and protest against human trafficking.

GET BILLBOARDED HERE.
AND WIN YOUR PERSONAL MINI.
THE BILLBOARD LIVE FROM K'DAMM BERLIN.

MINI PHOTO BOX

IT'S PERSONAL.
BE MINI.

IT'S PERSONAL.
BE MINI.

IT'S PERSONAL.
BE MINI.

THE GARDENER DID IT
A. Christie
Mystery. German style.
Banking. German style.
www.forum.ua
BANK FORUM
Commerzbank Group

Dies ist eine Pfeife.
Surrealism. German style.
Banking. German style.
www.forum.ua
BANK FORUM
Commerzbank Group
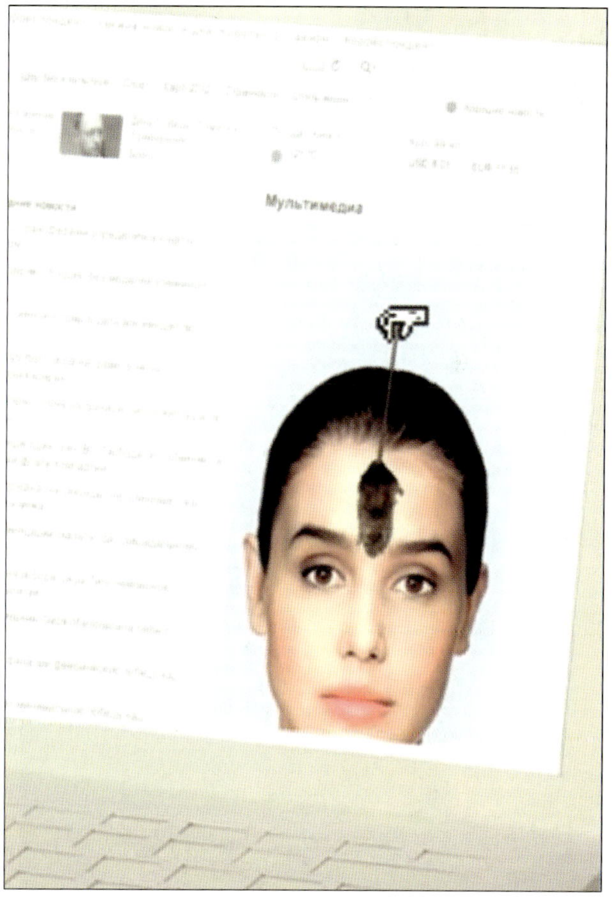
Мультимедиа

Agencies KKLD, Berlin & NY
Creative Director Alex Diehl
Copywriters Nathan Grigolla, Miho Tanaka
Art Directors Antonio Ferreira, Christian Meinke, Holger Herrmann
Head of Design Sascha Burk
Project Leader Stephan Lämmermann
Head of Strategy Christoph Riebling
Digital Concept Miho Tanaka, Imran Sheikh
Advertiser Mini, "Photo Box"

The Mini photo booth gave Mini fans a moment of fame. Stepping into the booth, fans snapped a photo of themselves in the headphone colour of their choice. Then they chose one of four Mini models to be matched up with. As if by magic, their image appeared on a giant digital billboard nearby, giving them the impression of being the face of Mini. Fans who couldn't make it to the booth at Berlin's Kurfürstendamm could still join in thanks to a Facebook app that replicated the physical experience.

Agency Ogilvy & Mather, Kiev
CDs Will Rust, Ferenc Benesch
Copywriters Alexandra Doroguntsova, Karolina Galacz, Balazs Szaday
Art Directors Taras Dzendrovskii, Zoltan Visy
Production Feel Films, London; Sauna International
Director Mikko Lehtinen
Producer Nick Hirschkorn
Advertiser Bank Forum

Bank Forum was virtually unknown in Ukraine until it was acquired by Germany's Commerzbank. This gave it a point of difference. So it played on a familiar German trait: reliability. The concept was expressed in a witty fashion in print, TV spots and an online ad featuring a "hysterical" German bank manager, who raises an eyebrow slightly when you show her a mouse. The "German Style" campaign became a national favourite.

DEUTSCHLAND
FINDET
Euch
INITIATIVE
VERMISSTE
KINDER

TOP 5
APPS
iTunes Store
HINWEISE MELDEN!
ACHTUNG:
DEUTSCHLAND
FINDET
Euch
INITIATIVE
VERMISSTE
KINDER
HILF MIT, DASS GANZ DEUTSCHLAND
KINDER SUCHT UND FINDET!

total!
VERMISST
DEUTSCHLAND-FINDET-EUCH.D

ÜBER
100.000
JETZT
MERKE
DIR

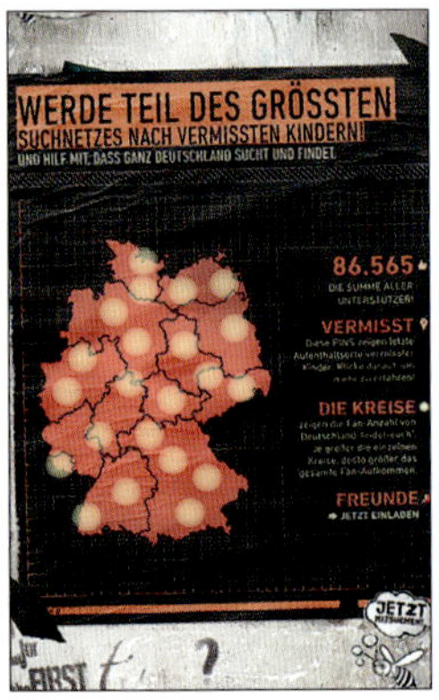
WERDE TEIL DES GRÖSSTEN
SUCHNETZES NACH VERMISSTEN KINDERN!
86.565
VERMISST
DIE KREISE
FREUNDE
JETZT

SPIEGEL ONLINE
SERVER-FEHLER 404
Dokument nicht gefunden
Außerdem nicht auffindbar:

Agencies kempertrautmann, Hamburg
fischerAppelt, Hamburg
CDs Marcell Francke
Patrick Matthiensen
Copywriter Sebastian Merget
Art Directors Bruno Luglio
Leif Johannsen
Graphic Design Patrick Schroer
Account Team Marcell Francke
Patrick Matthiensen
Carolin Panier
Biljana Retzlik
Moritz Fürste
Production nhb video, Hamburg
Programmer BlueMars, Frankfurt
Advertiser Initiative Vermisste Kinder
"Germany will Find you"

Germany's Missing Children Initiative launched a giant search party called "Germany will Find you". The Bayern Munich football team kicked off the campaign by running onto the pitch with children before a big match – all except one, who carried a picture of a missing child. This led to a Facebook page giving everyone an active role. Maps indicated the children's last whereabouts; users could download posters and QR codes leading to profiles.

Other initiatives included a sliding elevator door featuring a "disappearing" child. Pictures of missing kids appeared on photo stock sites when the desired image "could not be found". And an app kept people informed about missing kids and provided an emergency number to call. The campaign was a success: at least one missing child was soon found after police received new information from a participant.

I don't have a car anymore..

Automobile Balance Authority, hello

AutoLiberté
LA GRANDE
COMPRESSION
La Grande Compression
Vidéos ajoutées
WHY BUY A CAR WHEN YOU CAN RENT ONE?
C'est de la folie!
Commentaires sur la chaîne (13)

TURBONEWS
RATATINÉE !

KONZERTMILCH
DORTMUND

Agency	Ogilvy France, Paris
CD	Chris Garbutt
Copywriter	Benjamin Dessagne
Art Director	Emmanuel Bougneres
Director	Gustav Johansson
Production	Moonwalk Films, Paris
Producer	Antoine Bagot
Head of Digital	Frederic Levron
Account Team	Nathalie Heckel Delphine Watenberg
Client	Laurent Tonnelier
Advertiser	Europcar/Autoliberté, "Crush Hour"

AutoLiberté is a monthly subscription that allows drivers to hire a car on demand without all the hassle of ownership. A series of viral videos captured a prank in which car owners were tricked into thinking their cars had been crushed. Radio station NRJ partnered with the project and broadcast calls from distressed car owners live. On air discussion and videos on NRJ's website generated YouTube hits, and soon the campaign had taken a life on its own, with huge blog and media coverage.

Agency	Jung von Matt, Hamburg
CDs	Sascha Hanke Tobias Grimm Jens Pfau Jo Marie Farwick
Copywriters	Robert Henning Jan-Hendrik Scholz
Art Director	Damjan Pita
Production	Markenfilm, Wedel
Director	Silvio Helbig
Producer	Johannes Bittel
Advertiser	Dortmund Concert Hall, "Concert Milk"

The goal was to increase ticket sales for the Dortmund Concert Hall. The solution? Allow people to "taste" the music. Research has shown that cows give better milk when they hear music. So the orchestra visited a herd of lucky cows and played music from the latest season – in the cow stalls. When the milk was packaged, it was labeled "Dortmund Concert Milk", with extra information about the artists. Thanks to bloggers, the cows became something of a tourist attraction; and the media lapped up the story.

edding
Übertragung von der Wall of Fame! LIVE
Graffiti Artist DAIM
Donnerstag, 17.2. ab 21h hier – und unter:
WALL-OF-FAME.COM

facebook
Sök
Edding | Wall of Fame
Gilla
App
logg
Edding | Wall of Fame · Alla (topphändelser)
Dela: Inlägg Foto Länk Filmklipp
Skriv något...
Edding | Wall of Fame har lagt till 16 nya foton i albumet edding | Wall of Fame | Highlights
Gilla · Kommentera · Dela · den 19 mars kl. 16:32
41 personer gillar detta.
1 delning
Kommentera...
logg
Information
Vänners aktivitet
Foton
5 233
gillar detta
31
pratar om detta

Agency kempertrautmann, Hamburg
Creative Directors Simon Jasper Philipp, Christoph Gähwiler, Stefan Walz
Copywriters Christoph Gähwiler, Samuel Weiß, Michael Götz
Art Directors Simon Jasper Philipp, Stefan Walz, Florian Schimmer
Graphic Design David Scherer, Tobias Lehment
Account Team Niklas Kruchten, Elisabeth Einhaus, Andrea Bison, Dorothea Feurer
Production Demodern Digital Design Studio, Cologne, Appel Grafik
Art Buying Susi Kastner-Linke, Lina Eggers
Advertiser Edding, "Wall of Fame"

This integrated campaign marked Edding's 50th anniversary. Its centrepiece was the Wall of Fame interactive live drawing board, featuring eight pens you can use to draw and illustrate in real time. Outstanding illustrations are posted on a Facebook page, which is also a forum for users. Guest appearances by international artists turned the Wall into a stage, while Edding's outdoor projections meant their work could be followed live, not just online but also in the real world. Static print ads showcased the work on the wall and proved that Edding pens are creative tools.

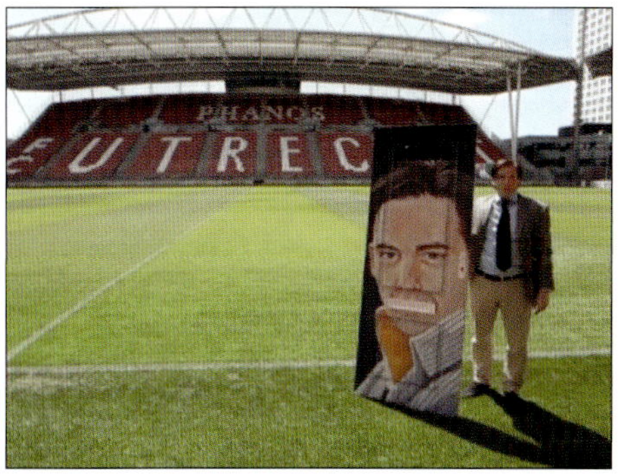

Ariel Fashion Shoot
Fashion shoot
ARIEL

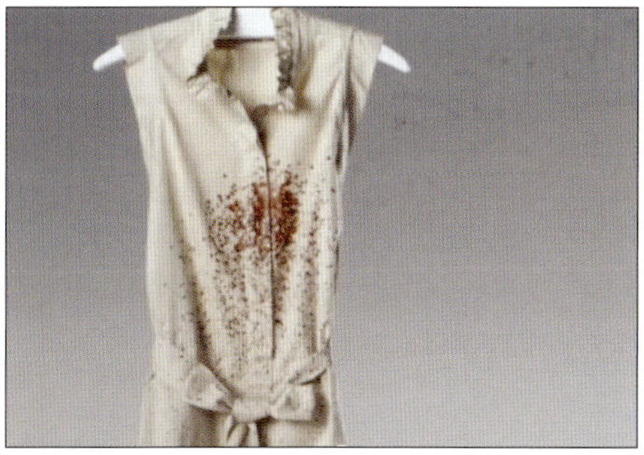

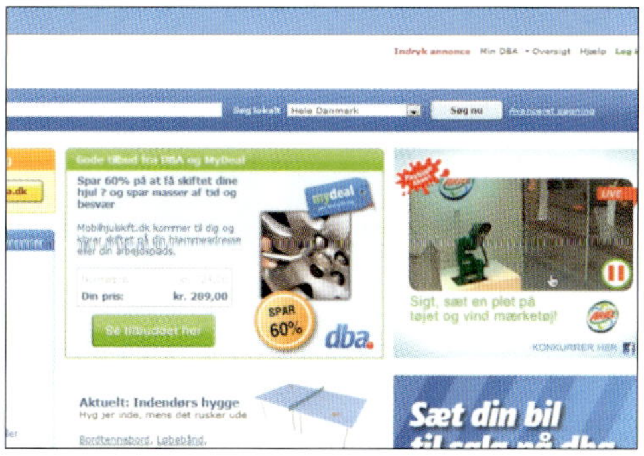
dba
Sæt din bil

facebook
Fashion shoot
LIVE

Agency Ogilvy, Amsterdam
Executive CD Darre van Dijk
CD Piebe Piebenga
Photography Arno Bosma
Illustrators Andrea Reis, Sylvan Steenbrink, Josefien Kooiman, Arne van der Ree, Symen Enkeling
Account Mgr. Nigel Hassall
Planner Hans Veldhorst
Art Buying Jan Willem de Jong
Advertiser TNT Logistics

Delivery service TNT wanted to remind advertisers of the power of direct mail. So it focused on the personal. Behind every front door, after all, lies a real person. To capture this idea, TNT asked artists to depict the personalities behind real front doors, placing the letterbox where their mouth should be – symbolising the dialogue between advertiser and audience. The doors featured in press ads. TNT also delivered real personalised front doors to its clients. All of them responded to requests for a meeting, underlining the power of direct marketing.

Agency Saatchi & Saatchi, Stockholm
Creative Director Adam Kerj
Creative Erik Hiort af Ornäs
Copywriter Petter Dixelius
Art Directors Gustav Egerstedt, Lisa Engardt
Production B-Reel, Stockholm
Designer Maria Wester
Planning Director Per Jaldeborg
Account Team Charlotta Tibbelin, Jenny Larsson
Advertiser Ariel Actilift

Ariel Fashion Shoot was a live Nordic digital event that took place for one week in a glass cube at Stockholm Central Station. An industrial robot was repurposed and connected to Ariel's Facebook page, where participants got 30 second slots to try and stain clothes with ketchup, jam or drinking chocolate. The rules were simple – aim, stain and win! If the player was lucky to hit and stain a garment it was washed live with Ariel Actilift and sent to the player's home.

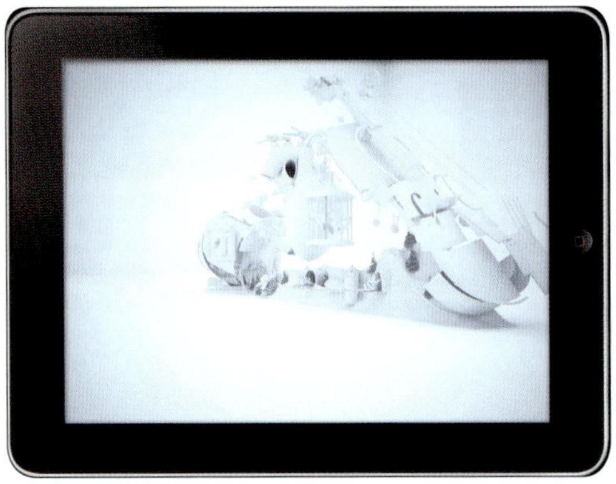

MADE
TURN OBJECT

MADE
BUREAU OF PUBLIC WEIGHTLESSNESS
ALL
MADE NEWS
MADE PROJECTS
VISIONS OF VISIONARIES
MORE MADE
Search
VALSE AUTOMATIQUE OPENING SHOW, THURSDAY 09.12
ABOUT MADE
VISIONARIES GALLERY
PRESS
IMPRESSUM
GET OUR FEEDS
RSS
FACEBOOK
NEWSLETTER
05.01.11
VALSE AUTOMATIQUE VERNISSAGE
29.12.10
ALASTAIR WIPER
24.12.10
WE WISH ALL OF YOU
HAPPY HOLIDAYS

Agencies TBWA\Berlin, Che*Che, Berlin
Executive CDs Nico Zeh, Tatjana Stein, Kurt Georg Dieckert, Stefan Schmidt
CDs Dirk Henkelmann, Philip Borchardt
Copywriters Felicitas Olschewski, Philip Loeffel
Photography Niels Krueger, Robert Wunsch, Ricardo Mueller
Art Director Philipp Migeod
Exec. Producers Luise Biesalski, Philip Gaedicke, Alexis Dornier
Graphic Design Veit Moeller, Andrew Morgan, Ricardo Mueller, Chehad Abdallah, Benedikt Gansczyk, Thomas Kohl
Director/Editor Johannes von Liebenstein
Production Soup Film, Berlin
Producers Katrin Dettmann, Ada Roggendorf, Jana Bloemer
Post Production Das Werk, Berlin
Sound Design Studio Funk, Berlin
Cameraman Christian Datum
IT Erik Scholz, Benjamin Stuerkat
Interface/Nav. Wolf Deiss
Strategy Planning Christina Keller, Sonia Lago
Art Buying Katrin Hermuth
Advertiser Absolut Vodka, "MADE"

Absolut wanted to create a space to inspire artistic collaborations. So it founded MADE, a logo-free space in Berlin designed by 12 creative minds. Soon, artists arrived to collaborate on projects: for instance, a journalist, a rapper and two musicians created a ballet with typography as its theme. A poster campaign promoted "creative clashes", while MADE screens placed in cafés and bars beamed live streams from the gallery, films of the art clashes or news of upcoming events. A blog and a Facebook page were also launched. MADE was embraced by the media and has become an unmissable place to visit in Berlin.

Stockholm
MINI
Gamla stan
Skeppsholmen

MINI
YOU
TAKE THE MINI NOW!

SORRY, BUT YOU HAVE NO CHOICE. YOU ARE PLAYING THE REALITY GAME
GETAWAY STOCKHOLM 2010 »
NEXT WEEK.
WIN THE NEW MINI COUNTRYMAN.
» DOWNLOAD THE APP AT MINIGETAWAYSTOCKHOLM.COM
MINI

DO THE IMPOSSIBLE IN STOCKHOLM NEXT WEEK.
KEEP 50 METRES AWAY FROM ALL STOCKHOLMERS.
GETAWAY STOCKHOLM 2010 »
WIN THE NEW MINI COUNTRYMAN.
» READ MORE OR DOWNLOAD THE APP AT MINIGETAWAYSTOCKHOLM.COM
MINI

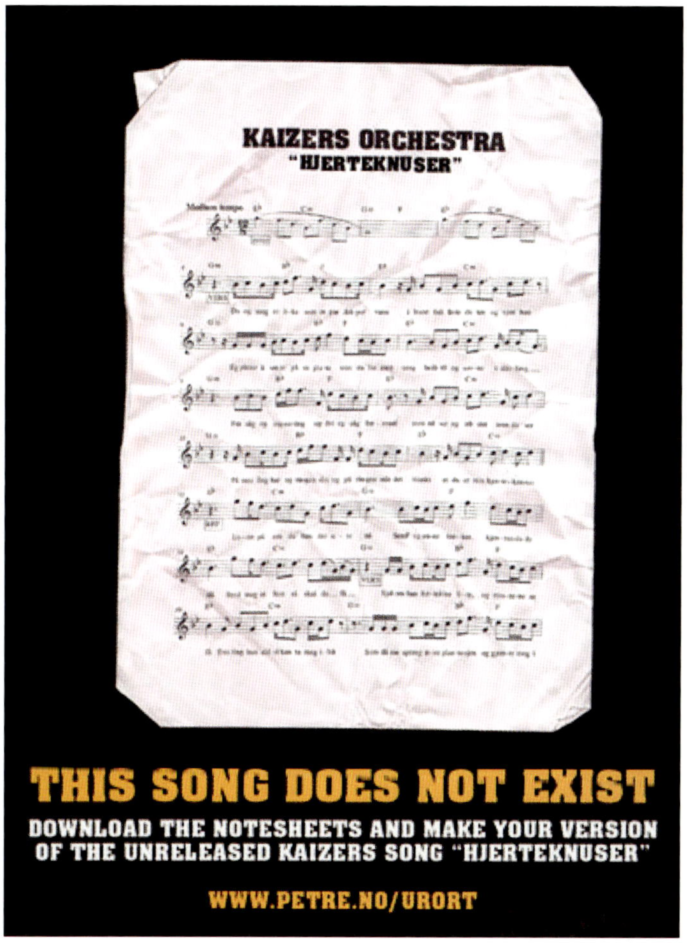
KAIZERS ORCHESTRA
"HJERTEKNUSER"
THIS SONG DOES NOT EXIST
DOWNLOAD THE NOTESHEETS AND MAKE YOUR VERSION OF THE UNRELEASED KAIZERS SONG "HJERTEKNUSER"
WWW.PETRE.NO/URORT

YouTube
Me Playing Kaizers Orchestra - Hjerteknuser (Unreleased single!)

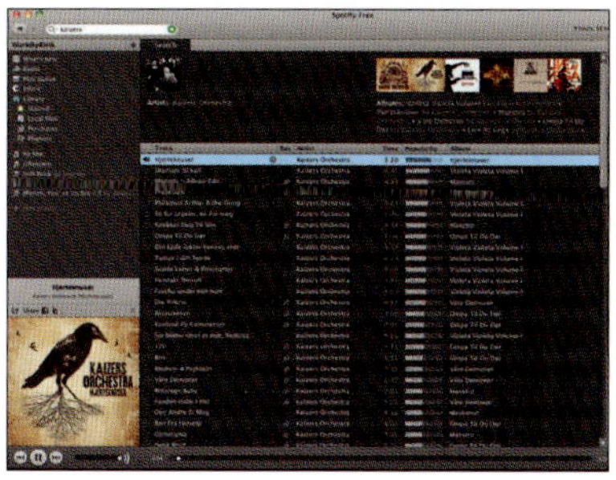

Agency Jung von Matt, Stockholm
CD Johan Jäger
Copywriter Magnus Andersson
Art Director Daniel Wahlgren
Illustrator Daniel Forero
App Monterosa, Stockholm
Web Suddenly
Media Carat
Planner Leon Phang
Final Artwork Jon Palmqvist
Account Mgr. Jan Casserlöv
Project Mgr. Ida Modin
Advertiser Mini, "Mini Getaway"

Posters and a witty radio ad led the way to a website that had some amazing news: for seven days, everyone with an iPhone could hunt a virtual Mini in Stockholm. If they got closer than 50 metres to the virtual car, they could "take" it with their phone. But then they had to get away, because the person with the car in their iPhone when the game finished would win a real Mini Countryman. As the competition heated up, he buzz quickly grew online and in the media. People from 90 countries followed the game on minigetawaystockholm.com.

Agencies Anorak, Oslo; Haaland, Eidsvåg & Strøm, Oslo
CDs Jens Petter Aarhus; Simen Eidsvåg
Art Directors Anders Gudmundstuen; Jørgen Krogsveen; Eirik Johansen
Media Starcom, Oslo: Tone Helene Angsund
Record Company Petroleum Records
Advertiser Kaizers Orchestra, "Heartbreaker"

Top Norwegian band Kaizers Orchestra decided they'd rather win fans for their live shows in the long term than sell a record in the short term. Their new song would be released not as a CD, on mp3, or on vinyl – but on paper. In fact, it was released as sheet music, online and on posters. The band then challenged fans to "record" their own version of the song. Thousands of versions were uploaded. The band doubled the number of their Facebook fans. And when the song was released, it got huge airplay – along with the three best cover versions.

INDEX

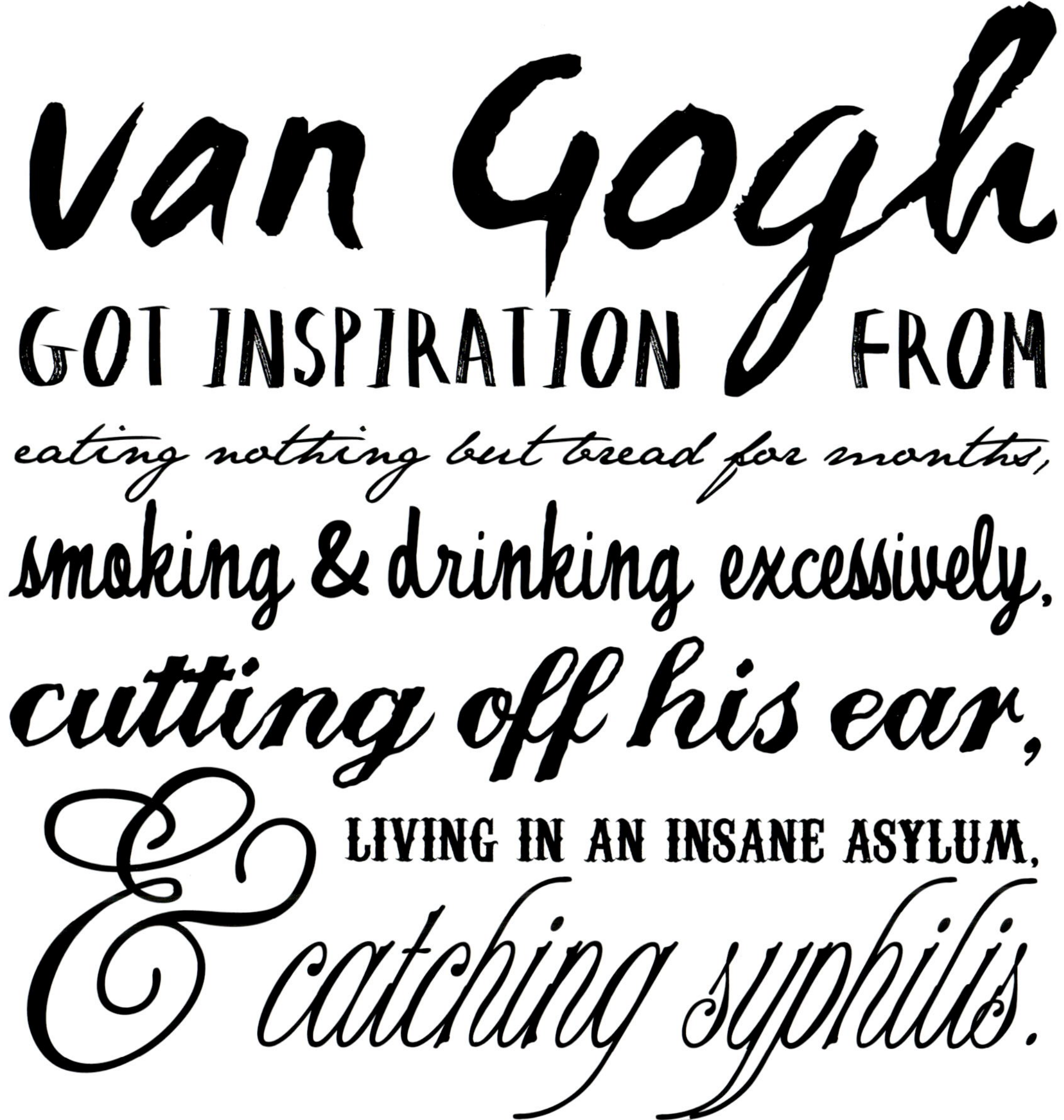

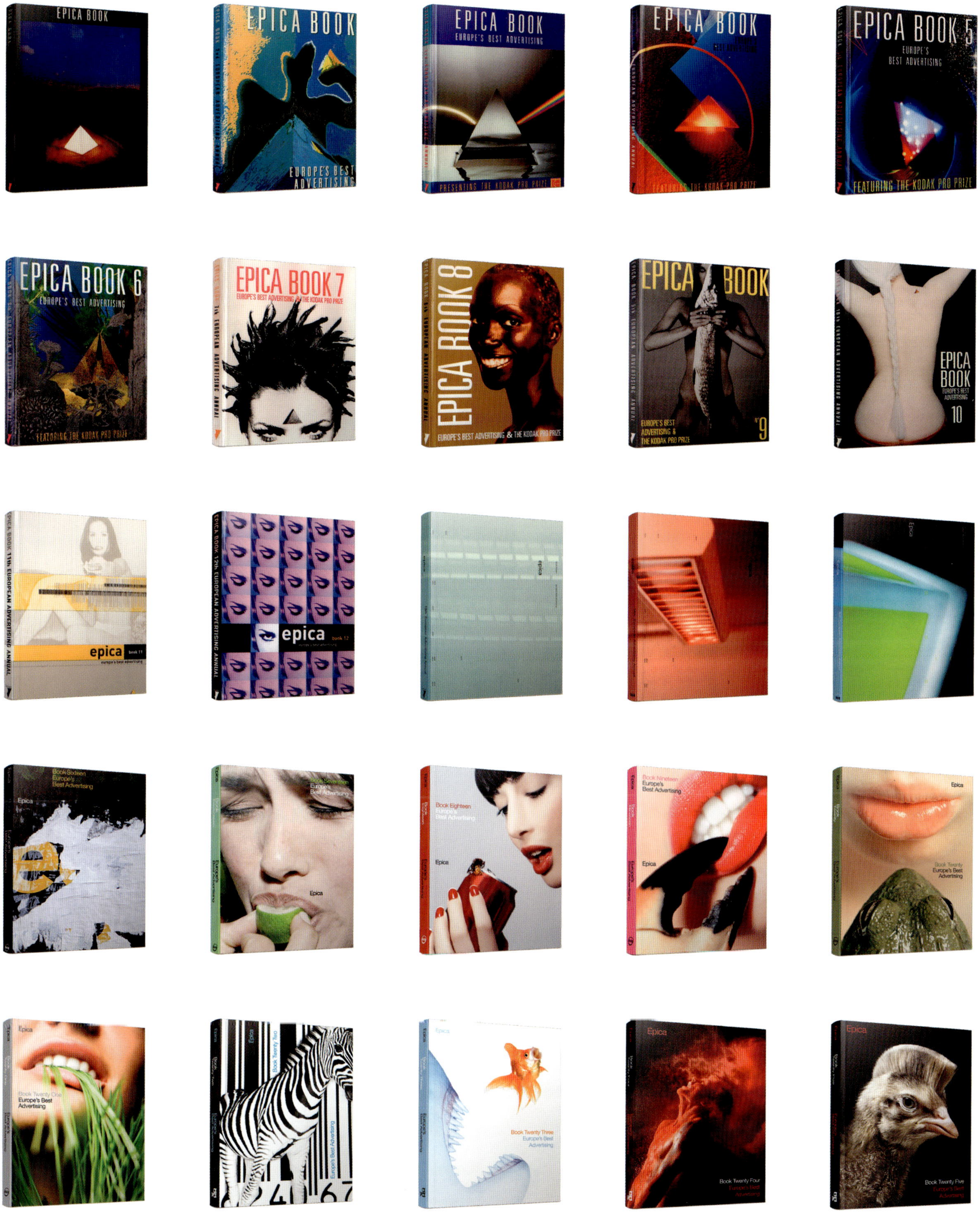
EPICA BOOK
EPICA BOOK
EUROPE'S BEST ADVERTISING
EPICA BOOK
EUROPE'S BEST ADVERTISING
PRESENTING THE KODAK PRO PRIZE
EPICA BOOK
FEATURING THE KODAK PRO PRIZE
EPICA BOOK 5
EUROPE'S BEST ADVERTISING
FEATURING THE KODAK PRO PRIZE
EPICA BOOK 6
EUROPE'S BEST ADVERTISING
FEATURING THE KODAK PRO PRIZE
EPICA BOOK 7
EUROPE'S BEST ADVERTISING & THE KODAK PRO PRIZE
EPICA BOOK 8
EUROPE'S BEST ADVERTISING & THE KODAK PRO PRIZE
EPICA BOOK
EUROPE'S BEST ADVERTISING & THE KODAK PRO PRIZE
N°9
EPICA BOOK
EUROPE'S BEST ADVERTISING
10
EPICA BOOK 11th EUROPEAN ADVERTISING ANNUAL
epica book 11
EPICA BOOK 12th EUROPEAN ADVERTISING ANNUAL
epica book 12
Book Sixteen
Europe's
Best Advertising
Epica
Book Eighteen
Europe's
Best Advertising
Epica
Book Nineteen
Europe's
Best Advertising
Epica
Epica
Book Twenty
Europe's Best
Advertising
Epica
Book Twenty One
Europe's Best
Advertising
Book Twenty Three
Europe's Best
Advertising
Epica
Book Twenty Four
Europe's Best
Advertising
Epica
Book Twenty Five
Europe's Best
Advertising

Epica Book Volumes 1-25

More than 9.300 pages celebrating Europe's best advertising since 1987